COLLECTI
FIRST D

15th Edition 1996

A Complete guide for all issues of
Great Britain First Day Covers

by

N. C. PORTER

Designed & Edited by

A. G. BRADBURY

PUBLISHED BY A. G. BRADBURY
3 Link Road, Stoneygate, Leicester LE2 3RA

ISBN 0 9517463 4 0

Phototypeset by Studio Photoset

Printed by A. T. Shelley (Printers) Ltd., Leicester.

PREFACE

The history of collecting first day covers, like other aspects of philately, has witnessed many major milestones in its development; the early years saw plain covers with ordinary operational postmarks form the basis of our hobby. Over time, specially designed covers were produced followed by special postmarks. During the 1960's and 1970's cds and slogan postmarks grew in popularity and with the widespread introduction of 'official' or privately sponsored covers, the main components of the modern hobby were now in place.

Taking account of this history of the hobby, it is hardly surprising that further developments and variations have evolved in more recent times. 'Double-postmarked' covers, and more recently, 'meter mark' covers, are evidence that the hobby retains its dynamism. Although this catalogue attempts to be a source of comprehensive information on first day covers, it is not possible or practical to produce one catalogue with all possible variations. This approach is not meant to discourage the collecting of particular types of first day cover or stifle the development of new trends in collecting. To this end, we would always encourage the publication of catalogue information in these more specialised areas of collecting and are pleased to note that Peter Withers of Stoke-on-Trent has produced a catalogue listing over 300 'meter mark' covers; for further details, his advertisement can be found on page 180.

We are also pleased to record that a GB First Day Cover Association has been formed by a group of keen collectors. For a modest annual fee, collectors are able to receive information on many aspects of the hobby and can contribute information and articles to the regular newsletter; details of the Association can be found on page 194.

This year the General Notes, at the beginning of the catalogue, have been expanded to include lots of useful tips on collecting first day covers with more pictures. Please spend a little time reading these as they often provide the answers to many of the enquiries received. Particular attention should be given to Section (D) on page 8 which relates to prices and condition.

ACKNOWLEDGEMENTS

As always, we thank all those who have contributed with the compilation of this work. In particular: Alan Finch and Colin Peachey of the British Postmark Society; Ghazi Choudhury (Sajal), Brian Reeve, Peter Middleton, Mark Grimsley and Steven Scott for help with prices; Mr. Wellman, Geoff Todd, Colin Young and all those collectors who take the time and trouble to write in with their new discoveries; Peter Withers for all his help with the slogan listings; and John G. Rice, John Swanborough and other dealers who supply their postmark listings for each issue. All of this assistance is greatly appreciated. Special thanks to Geoff Todd for the many hours he spent proof-reading.

A final note to all collectors: Please mention this book when replying to advertisements – thank you.

N. C. PORTER

A partner in Greenberg & Porter – a cover producing partnership formed in 1981 – Norman is responsible for the text and compilation of the prices in the catalogue.

A. G. BRADBURY

Specialist in covers, trading under his own name since 1974 and producing 'official' covers since 1980. Besides being the editor and publisher, Adrian is also responsible for design and layout – and searching out all those postmark illustrations!

September 1995

GENERAL NOTES

The General Notes set out at the beginning of this catalogue should answer most of the questions concerning the hobby – 'Collecting British First Day Covers'. After studying these notes and the body of the catalogue, it will become apparent that this fascinating subject can prove to be a very worthwhile and absorbing hobby with the added bonus of being educational.

It is beyond the means of most collectors to purchase every available cover for each stamp issue. However the number and range of covers produced should be viewed as an advantage since this provides the collector with a wide variety of choice – with the possibility of creating either a specialised or general interest collection.

(A) WHAT ARE FIRST DAY COVERS?

First day covers (FDCs) are essentially envelopes with newly issued postage stamps affixed and postmarked on the first day that those stamps are placed on sale by Royal Mail. Early first day covers, in the main, are usually available only on plain envelopes – specially designed envelopes only began appearing regularly in the 1950s. Further details of the variety of covers and postmarks available are provided in these notes.

Shown above are two modern examples of first day covers. The Nature Conservation cover bears the set of stamps postmarked on 20th May 1986, the day the stamps were issued by the Royal Mail. The Cats stamps were issued on 17th January 1995 and the above cover bears a special postmark of that date.

All first day of issue dates are listed alongside each stamp issue in the catalogue. Values should be treated as a guide and are for covers with the full set of stamps affixed unless otherwise stated - please read the section PRICES AND CONDITION.

First day covers should not be confused with souvenir or commemorative covers which are usually produced to celebrate or commemorate a particular event or anniversary. Souvenir covers are normally issued on the actual day of the anniversary or event being commemorated and their value is more related to the collectors own connection with the event. First day covers, on the other hand, are issued on the day of a particular stamp issue and command a more universal appeal.

Shown below are three more **first day covers**.

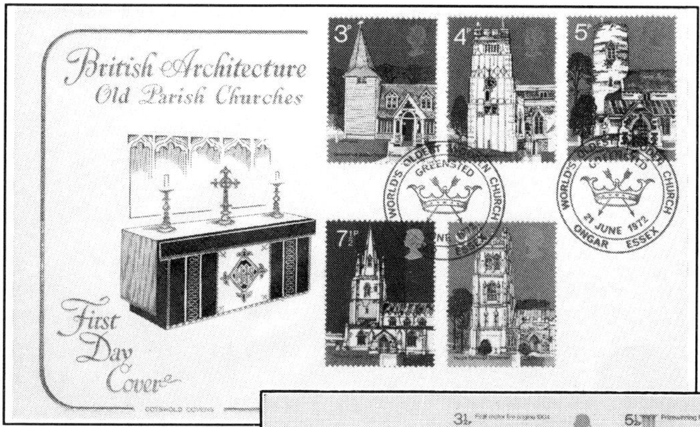

Village Churches
21st June 1972
This fdc envelope was produced by Cotswold and bears a Greensted, Ongar, Essex Churches special postmark.

Please read the General Notes for details of the different types of postmarks available.

Fire Service
24th April 1974
This Post Office fdc envelope has a special Binns Philatelic & Fire Exhition postmark.

Please read the General Notes for details of the different types of covers available.

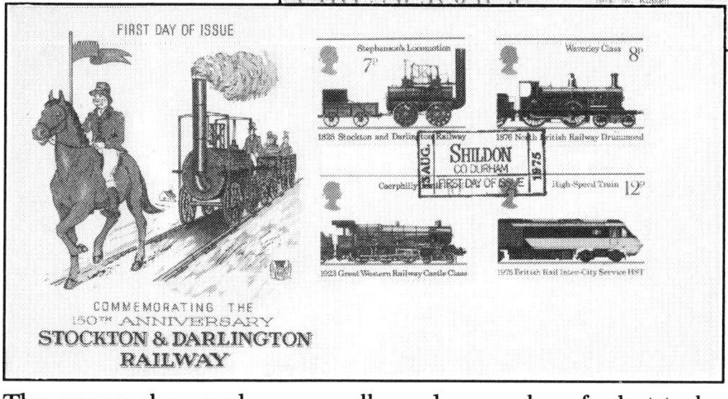

Railways
13th August 1975
This fdc envelope was produced by Stuart and has a special Shildon Railway postmark.

Please read the General Notes for a full understanding of prices and condition.

The covers shown above are all good examples of what to look for when buying fdc's, viz: (1) clean covers with the stamps positioned in a neat manner; (2) the postmarks are clearly legible and relevant to the issue, and (3) the covers are either unaddressed or have a small printed label.

(B) SCOPE OF THE CATALOGUE

All standard first day covers for both British commemorative and definitive stamp issues are listed in this catalogue. The number of different combinations and variations available for each envelope and stamp issue is so large that it would not be possible to list every variation; it is doubtful whether there are many collectors who would wish to purchase an expensive volume nearer the size of an encyclopaedia.

The author and publisher make no judgement as to the suitability of the various types of cover envelopes and postmarks for their 'collectability' – this is a decision solely in the hands of collectors. It should be remembered, that like many things in life, a first day cover may come into fashion and increase in value. Likewise, first day covers which are collectable now may not be sought after in ten years time.

(C) FORMAT

The layout of this catalogue has been established to reflect the changing nature of British first day covers over the years. On compiling the catalogue it was found that **commemorative issues** could be divided into three distinct periods, viz:

(1) **1924 Wembley – 1961 Parliament issues**
Prices for this period have been set out in two columns – the first is for illustrated covers and the second for plain covers (i.e. non-illustrated covers).

(2) **1962 National Productivity Year – 1967 Wild Flowers**
During this period commemorative stamps were issued both with and without phosphor bands. The two column price structure reflects values for both of these types of first day covers. All prices from this date are for illustrated covers. Plain covers are often available for this period but not generally collected. They are usually only worth a small fraction of their illustrated equivalent.

(3) **1967 British Paintings – present day**
With effect from this issue, all commemorative stamps were phosphor coated. It was also around the late 1960s that more 'official' or sponsored covers were produced. Consequently the two columns now reflect prices for 'ordinary' covers and 'official' covers (see para (F) 'Types of Covers').

Definitives, regionals, booklet panes etc. on first day covers are all listed together in an easy to follow section at the end of the catalogue.

British Empire Exhibition
23rd April 1924
The first British commemorative stamps. The above first day cover, produced by Harmers, is known as a DISPLAY cover, i.e. with text but no illustrations.

It is interesting to note that between 1924 and 1964 there were only 32 commemorative stamp issues - on average, less than one per year. Shown below are a few examples.

Silver Jubilee
7th May 1935
A good example is this first day cover produced by the Westminster Stamp Co.

Coronation
13th May 1937
Covers from this period are acceptable with neat hand written addresses especially with relevant postmarks, as in this case - Windsor.

Stamp Centenary
6th May 1940
Issued to celebrate the centenary of the first adhesive postage stamp, the Penny Black.

Parliament
12th September 1957
Notice the neatly typed address and clear postmark. A good example for this issue.

Freedom from Hunger
21st March 1963
Another good example. The address, although hand-written, is neat and perfectly acceptable for a cover from this period.

(D) PRICES AND CONDITION

This catalogue has been compiled as a work of reference and is not the publisher's or author's own price list.

The prices quoted are intended as a GUIDE ONLY and are for clean, undamaged covers and unless otherwise stated, serviced with a full set of stamps. Many factors may affect the price of first day covers, for example:

(1) Condition The following are important factors in determining the price of cover:

(a) the proper siting of stamps;
(b) the neatness of the address, and
(c) the quality and legibility of the postmarks.

It should be remembered that invariably older covers will be of inferior quality when compared to their modern counterparts. However shortages of available older covers should be taken into account by the collector when buying such covers. As a general guide the prices quoted in the catalogue are for clean covers with a small address label, or a printed, typed or rubber stamped address. Earlier covers, primarily before 1964, are acceptable with neat hand-written addresses, whilst later covers from, say 1970, usually command a premium if unaddressed.

Very scarce covers may well retail at full catalogue value even if they do not conform to the above guidelines. **Condition is everything – a scruffy cover in poor condition will be worth only a fraction of its pristine counterpart.**

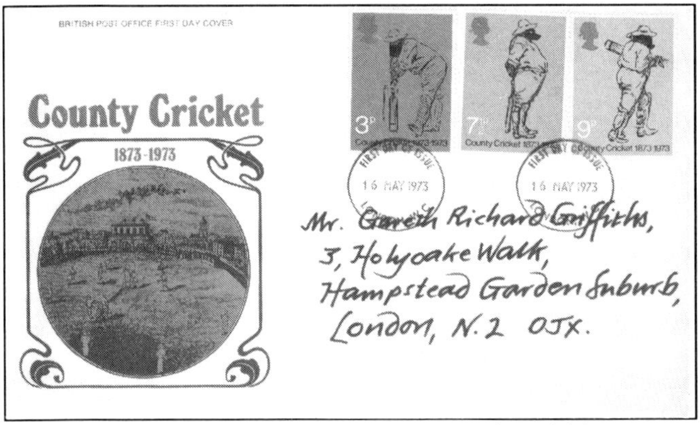

Study for a moment the cover illustrated alongside – it has almost everything wrong with it, viz:

(i) hand written address;

(ii) a postmark which bears no relevance to the stamp issue; and

(iii) the stamps are not aligned.

Compare this to the covers illustrated opposite which are more attractive propositions.

(2) Supply and Demand The market in first day covers is no different from the market in any commodity and is subject to the same economic forces. For example, if 600 collectors wish to purchase a cover of which only 500 were produced, then that cover will inevitably rise in price. Conversely, if only 100 of a particular cover exists but a mere 50 collectors wish to buy that cover, then the price will remain static or even fall until demand exceeds supply. The early 1980s is a good example of a period when several covers were over-produced and are now only beginning to recover to price levels above their new issue price.

In addition there may be significant variations in the stock position of individual dealers at any particular time. A dealer holding a stock of say 50 covers may well be prepared to sell that cover for much less than a dealer holding a stock of only one or two .

(3) Locality In the same way that house prices vary according to the locality, to a lesser degree this can also affect first day cover prices.

In the final analysis, the value of a cover is determined at a price at which both the dealer and collector feel is acceptable to them. The prices quoted in the catalogue are based on the **AVERAGE** of several dealers' lists, and, for the scarcer covers on auction realisations.

PLEASE NOTE: Prices quoted with an **(s)** appended or where this appears after the official cover description, indicates that the covers are only known with a single value or incomplete set of stamps. The initials **'n.k.'** in the price columns indicate that as far as the author is aware the covers do not exist. **Values include VAT.**

Illustrated below are a few more fine examples of first day covers.

British Army
6 July 1983
TA Official cover.

Find out more about Official covers in Section (F) of these General Notes.

Railways
22 Jan 1985
Southall Railway Centre Official cover

Christmas
14 Nov 1989
Ely Cathedral Official cover

Produced by Benham in their BLCS series. Please refer to Section (F) for full details.

(E) TYPES OF POSTMARKS

Each commemorative stamp issue has been classified according to the type of postmarks found. They can be divided into four distinct categories: special handstamps, ordinary first day of issue postmarks, counter date stamps (CDS) and slogan postmarks.

(1) SPECIAL HANDSTAMPS

These are specially designed postmarks which are by far the most popular with the general collector. Unitl the 1990s special handstamps were applied with hand held stamping machines. However, today's covers are serviced with the more advanced 'pad canceller' machines which give much better impressions, and allow for more detailed designs.

Any member of the public is permitted to sponsor a special handstamp – at a current cost of £195 (plus VAT) – providing that they adhere to certain Royal Mail rules governing their use. The special handstamp remains the property of the Royal Mail and is applied to philatelic items by trained Royal Mail staff. All special handstamps to be used are advertised in advance in the "Postmark Bulletin" – a fortnightly newsletter issued by the Royal Mail (currently £10 per annum available from the Philatelic Bureau in Edinburgh). Anyone can subscribe to the Bulletin and thereby know which handstamps have been sponsored before the stamp issue date. Collectors can then send their first day covers to the Special Handstamp Centres for franking with the special handstamps. This is known as the *re-posting facility*.

Forth Road Bridge
4th September 1964
This GPO cover has a North Queensferry Special Handstamp.
During the early 1960s there were very few special handstamps sponsored for each stamp issue. Although still moderately priced, a good example like this is quite difficult to find.

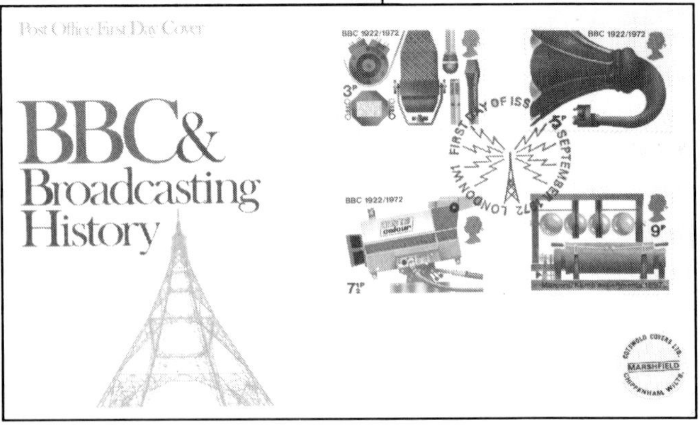

BBC & Marconi
13th September 1972
This Post Office cover has a London W1 Special Handstamp.
By the end of the 1970s collectors and dealers were much more aware that these postmarks enhanced a covers appearance and value! This cover is still quite cheap, but you do not see many nice clean copies in unaddressed condition.

Historic Buildings
1st March 1978
This Philart cover has a Stampex Special Handstamp.
The late 1970s and early 1980s saw vast quantities of first day covers being produced - even today covers of this period can be bought at very reasonable prices.

To improve the quality of service offered to collectors Royal Mail operates six Special Handstamp Centres providing an efficient service for customers. These Centres employ staff working full-time on philatelic items. All special handstamps are now applied at these Centres, each of which covers a specific area of the country viz:

Royal Mail London – for London postal area
Royal Mail Slough – for the rest of SE England and most of East Anglia
Royal Mail Cardiff – for Wales and SW England
Royal Mail Birmingham – for the Midlands and East to The Wash
Royal Mail Newcastle – for Northern England
Royal Mail Glasgow – for Scotland and Northern Ireland

All special handstamps in use on the first day of an issue of a set of commemorative stamps are included in the catalogue whether they are relevant to the stamp issue or not. Some covers serviced with handstamps which are not relevant may be priced higher than others with more relevant postmarks. This is because past issues are often more difficult to obtain, as fewer were serviced – especially with a full set of stamps.

There are permanent pictorial special handstamps which are available on every first day of issue but, except where relevant to an issue, these have been omitted. These postmarks, currently in use are illustrated and listed in Section (G).

D Day, 6th June 1994
This PPS cover has an Imperial War Museum Special Handstamp.

Some issues attract the sponsorship of more special handstamps than others, e.g. the 1994 'D' Day issue attracted 35 different handstamps, whilst only 12 were sponsored for the Postcard Centenary issue of the same year.

(2) ORDINARY FIRST DAY ISSUE (F.D.I.) HANDSTAMPS

These are circular postmarks specially made and paid for by Royal Mail and used in many towns and cities throughout the U.K. They are in use for all commemorative stamp issues and many definitive stamp issues. F.D.I. handstamps – like special handstamps – are applied by Royal Mail staff usually by hand. These are also made available to collectors under the *re-posting facility*. It was not until the 1960s that the then G.P.O. recognised a need for proper philatelic handstamping. The F.D.I. handstamps are listed from their introduction (1964 Shakespeare issue) up to the Christmas issue of 1970. The start of the decimal period saw a much wider use of special handstamps. However there are numerous examples where no special handstamps were available at places with an obvious connection with the stamp issues. In such cases, where a F.D.I. postmark was available, these have been listed.

Sir Winston Churchill
8th July 1965
Churchill is buried at Bladon - this is a good example of an early FDI handstamp.
During the 1960s most FDI handstamps were quite large in design.

Churchill Centenary
9th October 1974
Tunbridge Wells FDI with Posted at Chartwell special cachet.
The larger designed FDI handstamps were soon replaced with the more attractive smaller versions.

(3) COUNTER DATE STAMP (C.D.S.) POSTMARKS

Sometimes known as circular date stamps, these are ordinary everyday cancellations available at all Post Office counters. In most cases, the only way to obtain these operational postmarks is to use the PRIORITY SERVICES (Guaranteed Special or Registered Delivery), although some Post Offices still cancel ordinary mail. It is sometimes difficult to obtain these cancellations on first day covers because the Royal Mail insist that covers for Priority Services are handed over in person at the Post Office counter concerned; no re-posting facility being permitted.

During the early years, first day covers were generally only available with circular date stamp (C.D.S.) postmarks. Whether such postmarks had any connection with an issue was, in most cases, fortuitous. Relevant C.D.S. postmarks were clearly the exception rather than the rule.

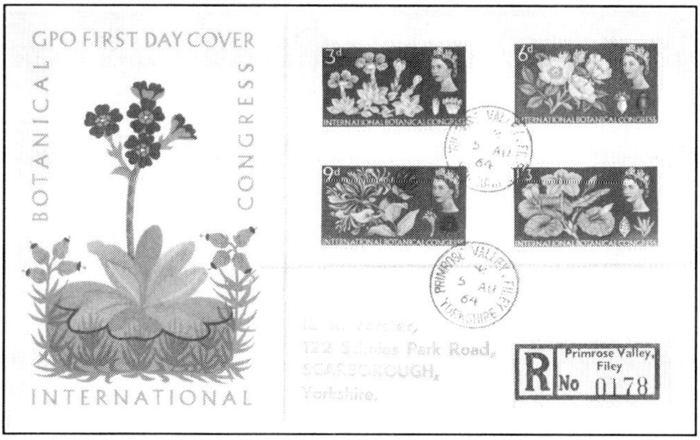

Botanical Congress
5th August 1964
This is a lovely early example of what to look for when buying CDS covers.
The name of the Post Office, Primrose Valley, is very relevant to the stamp issue. The postmarks can be read easily - the date and name are very clear.
Many early CDS covers also have the name of the Post Office incorporated in the Registered label.

During the 1960s and up to the present day the collecting of relevant C.D.S. postmarks has become a special interest. The criterion used for the inclusion of these C.D.S. postmarks is that they should have a bearing on the theme of the stamp issue. Items which are 'one-off' or have a dubious connection with the issue are not listed. The items included were available in commercial quantities - i.e. twenty or more covers. The C.D.S. postmarks are included even if there is a special handstamp or ordinary F.D.I. postmark available for the same area because often the C.D.S. are more valid. For example, for the 1992 Civil War issue the Naseby Special Handstamp was applied at the Midlands Special Handstamp Centre in Birmingham; therefore the only authentic Naseby cancellations are the C.D.S. postmarks applied at the Naseby sub Post Office.

RSPCA
23rd January 1990.
The very appropriate 'Bunny' CDS for an issue which includes a Rabbit stamp!

Royal Wedding
22nd July 1986
Ascot CDS where the Royal romance started.
Many CDS covers have printed or rubber stamp cachets to explain the significance of the postmark.

The proliferation of C.D.S. postmarks (from the 1979 Christmas issue) has necessitated the classification of C.D.S. postmarks into main and ancillary listings. Those postmarks which, in the opinion of the Author, have a close or direct connection with an issue, are given a full listing with a descriptive note where necessary. Other C.D.S. postmarks are recorded in italics below the main listing.

N.B. The covers illustrated are all very fine examples. However it should be noted that it is not always possible to get such good postmark impressions. Post Office Counter staff who agree to frank covers in this way do so at little or no reward. Quite often the metal counter date stamps can be old or worn or the ink pad being used might be under-inked or over-inked giving feint or smudged postmarks. The general rule is that at least one of the postmarks should provide a legible place name and date.

Greetings Stamps 31st January 1989.
With Cupid on one of the stamps Gretna Green CDS is very appropriate.

Parliamentary Conference 3rd September 1975.
House of Commons and House of Lords CDS are always popular on Parliament issues.

Sea Birds 17th January 1989.
Fair Isle, famous for its bird-migration observatory, is a popular choice for this stamp issue.

Broadly speaking, the criteria used for determining whether a particular postmark is included in the main listing are as follows:

(a) Name association
Where the name of a Post Office has a strong link with the issue concerned. For example, with the 1976 and 1991 Roses stamp issues, first day covers were postmarked at the village of 'Rose' in Cornwall.

(b) Place association

Where a Post Office is located in, or is the nearest to, an area which is being commemorated by the stamp issue, or otherwise has geographical connections with the subject matter of the issue. For example, with the 1991 stamps featuring Maps, first day covers were franked at 'Maybush', Southampton – the headquarters of the Ordnance Survey.

(c) House of Commons & House of Lords

These C.D.S. postmarks are not ordinarily available to members of the general public, the cancellation of mail being primarily on correspondence sent by members of both Houses of Parliament. These postmarks are only listed where they are relevant, for example:

(i) Where an issue commemorates the passing of legislation (e.g. the 1974 issue commemorating the 200th anniversary of the first fire service legislation); or reform (e.g. the 1976 issue commemorating Social Pioneers and Reformers); or

(ii) Where an event commemorated is connected with Parliament (e.g. the 1973 issue commemorating the 19th Commonwealth Parliamentary Conference); or

(iii) Where a featured individual has a connection with Parliament (e.g. the 1974 issue commemorating the centenary of the birth of Sir Winston Churchill); or

(iv) Royalty issues.

(d) Balmoral Castle, Buckingham Palace, Sandringham House and Windsor Castle

Postal facilities in Balmoral Castle, Buckingham Palace, Sandringham House and Windsor Castle are only available to members of the Royal Family or staff of the Royal Household. Whilst these types of covers are extremely scarce and therefore valuable, they are only relevant where an issue of stamps involves a 'Royal' theme. Prices in the catalogue reflect their rarity. Sandringham House and Balmoral Castle postmarks are more rare than those of Buckingham Palace and Windsor Castle.

(e) Other associations

This final criterion embraces any of those associations which do not readily fit into the four categories mentioned above, but nevertheless merit inclusion. For example, 'Paquebots' used on the 1973 European Communities issue or the 1970 Direct Elections issue; Travelling Post Office (T.P.O.) cancellations on railway related issues; etc.

Commonwealth 9th March 1983
Gleneagles Hotel CDS with cachet: The Gleneagles Agreement on Apartheid in Sport was issued from here in 1977.
Recent years have seen a proliferation of CDS covers for each stamp issue. The most sought after and valuable are those with a strong connection to the stamp issue.

(4) SLOGAN POSTMARKS

These are machine cancellations applied to the vast majority of British mail. A slogan postmark consists of two parts viz: a circular element which incorporates the sorting location, time and date; and more often than not, an advertising 'slogan'. These postmarks can be sponsored for a specified period of time at a cost of £300 or more depending on the number of 'dies' (postmark cancellation) and length of time these are in operation. The dates the slogans are to be used are advertised in advance in the "Postmark Bulletin" and are available to collectors under the *re-posting facility*.

Three types of slogan postmarks are available to the collector,viz:

(a) First Day of Issue Slogans

These were first introduced with the 1963 Paris Postal issue. They were used on covers posted in special posting boxes at selected Post Offices. From 1964 slogans were mostly replaced by ordinary F.D.I. handstamps (see Section (2) above. However slogans continued in use mainly for bulk mailings. Where F.D.I. slogans are used at a place connected with an issue they have been listed. For the 1963 Compac issue the Philatelic Bureau used this type of slogan postmark.

(b) 'Wavy line' machine cancels

These have only been listed if the location at which they were used was connected with the stamp issue.

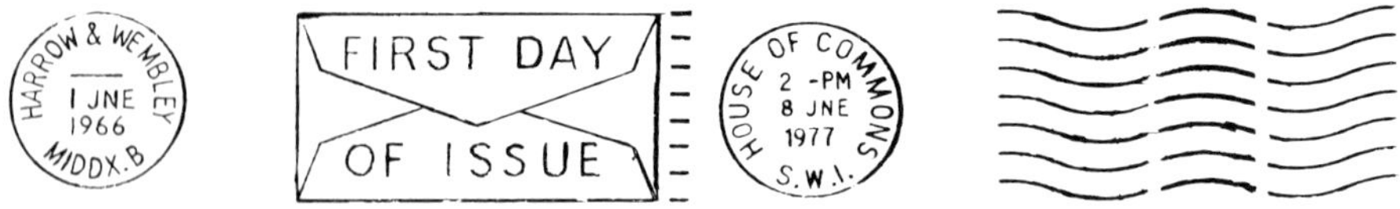

(c) Commemorative or Campaign slogans

The criterion used to determine whether a particular slogan should be included depends on its relevance to the stamp issue concerned. Unlike C.D.S. postmarks, the location of a Post Office at which a slogan is used is not as important as the wording or illustration of the slogan, which should have a good connection with the stamp issue. The proliferation of slogan postmarks (from 1979 Christmas issue) has necessitated their classification to main and ancillary listings. Those which, in the opinion of the Author, have a close or direct connection with an issue, are given a full listing. Other, less relevant slogans are recorded in italics.

Late use of slogans: Slogan postmark campaigns are booked to run for a specified period and are advertised as such in the Postmark Bulletin. However, sometimes slogans run over their allotted time because there is no available alternative. In recent years there have been a number of instances where this has happened. This sometimes results in a slogan being in use on the first day of issue of a new set of stamps where the subject of the stamps and the slogan are closely linked. This situation can produce some very collectable covers.

Butterflies
13th May 1981
This is a good example of the National Butterfly Museum Slogan pmk. ***The stamps have been positioned so that both parts of the slogan can be read clearly. Notice also the addition of the Special Handstamps on this cover .***

Year of the Child 11th July 1979
This slogan reads 'Give a Child a Home, Leeds Social Services' and as such is very appropriate to the stamp issue.
When collecting slogan postmarks it is very important to make sure that all the stamps are franked. Sometimes the remaining stamps will be franked, as here with a CDS postmark, or often, as below with a FDI postmark - very rarely as above with a Special Handstamp.

Earlier covers are usually only available with a slogan which obliterates the stamps - often making the slogan difficult to read. However, with effect from 1974 most covers are available with the stamps positioned in such a way as to make the slogan clearly legible. To achieve this the stamps have to be sited in such a way that the slogan will only cancel one stamp, the remaining stamps being franked with a C.D.S. or ordinary F.D.I. postmark. Once again it has to be stressed that it is not always possible to get good clean impressions. To obtain these postmarks the covers are fed through automatic franking machines which handle thousands of items each day. Quality can depend upon the co-operation of the staff.

Kew Gardens
5th June 1990
This is a lovely example of a 'late use'.
The slogan was scheduled to be withdrawn a few days before the Kew Gardens stamp issue.

(F) TYPES OF COVER

First day cover envelopes fall into two categories: ordinary (or commercial) covers and 'official' (or sponsored) covers.

(1) ORDINARY (OR COMMERCIAL) COVERS

These are produced primarily for the general FDC collector and are usually sold as 'blanks' (i.e. with no stamps affixed). They are available from most good stamp shops before the day of issue of the postage stamps. Collectors purchase the 'blanks' and then affix stamps to the covers themselves. They then have to make their own arrangements concerning franking. The Royal Mail produce their own FDC envelope which is available from most Post Offices prior to the issue date. The number of privately produced covers has diminished in recent years, with only three makes now available for each issue, viz: Cotswold, Sotheby's 'silk' (PPS), and Stuart. The list below summarises the different covers which have been available since first day cover collecting became an active hobby.

Abbey: These covers were produced from 1969 until 1982. They were not sold as blanks but fully serviced – usually with appropriate special handstamps. They were all numbered limited editions and recognisable by their 'Abbey' logo.

Artcraft: This company was based in America – their first cover was for the 1948 Olympic Games issue with several more up to and including the Battle of Hastings issue of 1966.

Benham 'silks': These are only available fully serviced – usually sets of single stamp covers. They have been produced from the 1980 Bird issue to date. See also entries in 'official' covers section.

Benham 'woodcut': The only Benham covers which were available as blanks were first produced for the 1968 Bridges issue. The series ended with the 1978 Historic Buildings issue.

Cameo: The Cameo Stamp Centre produced a few covers in 1970 and 1971 and these bear a 'Cameo' logo.

Colorano 'silk': These were first produced for the 1974 Horse Chestnut issue and appeared for most issues up to the early 1980s.

Connoisseur: These were produced for all issues from the 1963 Freedom from Hunger issue until 1970. Recognisable by an Old English 'C' logo they were produced by R.F. Grover of Fareham, Hants.

Cotswold: Cotswold die-stamped covers were first introduced with the 1970 Christmas issue and have appeared ever since. They are easily recognisable by their large 'C' border which is common to all their designs.

Heyden: At least three designs for each issue. Published by Jeffrey Booth (Stamp Searchers) since 1990. Not available as blanks.

Mercury: These were first introduced in 1972 and appeared for all stamp issues until 1993. Produced by Harry Allen of Rickmansworth they all have a 'Mercury' logo. These were also die-stamped. The Westminster Stamp Co. produce fully serviced Mercury covers for some of the current issues.

Philart: First produced in 1964 for the Geographical issue, they ceased production in 1990. Philart 'Luxury' die-stamped covers were sold from the 1969 Ships issue until the early 1980s.

PPS: Presentation Philatelic Services (PPS) produced their first blank for the 1981 Butterflies issue. Christmas 1981 saw their first 'silk' – these continued until Christmas 1983. With effect from the 1984 Heraldry issue the SOTHEBY'S 'silk' range was introduced. The Sotheby's series is now produced by Benham. The Cigarette Card 'silk' series commenced with the 1988 Linnean issue through to the 1994 Christmas issue.

PTS/BPA: The Philatelic Traders Society and the British Philatelic Association produced a number of covers jointly. These commenced with 1948 Olympic Games issue and continued through to the early 1960s.

Peter Scot: Peter Scot covers were introduced with the 1978 Energy issue and ceased in 1988.

Royal Mail: The first Post Office first day covers appeared for the 1964 Shakespeare issue. They have been produced for all subsequent issues with the following exceptions: 1965 Salvation Army, Joseph Lister, Commonwealth Arts, U.N., I.T.U., and 1966 England Winners.

Save the Children Fund: These were produced for the earlier decimal issues, commencing with 1973 Royal Wedding.

Stuart: The first Stuart cover was for the 1965 Churchill issue. They are still available for all the current issues and are now produced by Cotswold Covers. The envelopes are die-stamped and have a 'thistle' logo.

Thames: These were first issued for the 1968 Bridges issue and continued until the 1974 Christmas issue. The covers have a similar appearance to die-stamping. The earlier covers had a 'Thames estuary' logo printed on their flaps.

Trident: These were produced for some of the 1969/70 issues and bear a 'Trident' logo.

Wessex: These have a 'Wyvern' logo and were first produced for the 1967 EFTA issue and regularly until 1973. A few have been produced since, most notably for the 1977 Queen's Silver Jubilee. Covers are still produced by Rembrandt Philatelics but are now souvenir covers – no first day covers are produced.

Silver Wedding Anniversary
20th November 1972
This Philart cover is typical of the high standard the company achieved in the early 1970s. The company also produced ***Luxury die-stamped*** *covers - these were considered by many as the 'Rolls-Royce' in first day covers.* ***Once again, a good clean cover, with small address label and relevant postmark - all points to look for when buying covers. It is not advisable to buy hand-written covers for this period.***

(2) 'OFFICIAL' (OR SPONSORED) COVERS

In the context of this catalogue, 'official' covers are defined as covers produced by private organisations or cover producers, who at the same time sponsor a special handstamp to accompany their cover. Such covers, bearing the full set of stamps, are often more rare than the 'ordinary' covers with the same handstamp, because in most cases fewer official covers exist. Some are particularly rare, e.g. the 'Jeol' cover on the 1989 Microscopes issue where probably fewer than 60 official covers exist with full sets of stamps.

Sometimes an organisation will not affix the full set of stamps, because only one or two of the values are relevant to them. The only way to get such covers cancelled with the full set of stamps is to try to obtain blank covers from the sponsors and affix the stamps yourself. However this is often not possible because the sponsor may not wish to sell blank covers. In instances where official covers only exist with a single or incomplete set, the official cover description is suffixed with **(s)**.

Since the mid 1980s Royal Mail relaxed the rules governing the sponsoring of special handstamps. As a result the concept of an 'official' cover has changed. It is now possible for anyone to sponsor postmarks mentioning such places as Clarence House, Glamis Castle, Windsor Castle etc. which were used on the 1990 Queen Mother issue. The covers produced to accompany these handstamps are only official in the sense that the sponsor of the handstamp has also produced his/her own envelope. No special sanction is necessarily conferred upon a cover by a particular place or organisation. This will help explain why there were four Westminster Abbey, and two Dummer special handstamps for the 1986 Royal Wedding stamp issue.

For simplicity all these covers are classed as 'official' in the catalogue. However, it would perhaps be more correct to refer to those described in the previous paragraph as 'sponsored covers'.

The numerous official covers have been categorised below together with the abbreviations used in the text of this catalogue.

(a) Covers marketed by First Day Cover Producers

(i) those forming a F.D.C. series (numbered or otherwise)

*BL**	– British Library (1976-1982)
BLS	– Benham large 'silk' (1982-1984)
BLCS	– Benham luxury cover series (1985 to date)
Benham L	– Benham limited edition (1981 to date)
B'ham 500	– Benham 500 series (1985 to date)
BOCS	– Benham official covers series (1978-1984)
Benham SG	– Benham Special Gold (1986 to date)
FDP Co	– First Day Publishing Co. (1994 Xmas to date)
Fine Art	– Fine Art covers of Brentwood (1985-1986)
LFDC	– Leicester First Day Covers (1980 to date)
Brad. V.P.	– Bradbury's Victorian Prints (1991 to date)
RFDC	– Forces first day covers (1981-1992)
RAF FDC	– Forces Charities (1992 to date)
Havering	– Havering covers of Romford (1980-1984)
Hawkwood	– Hawkwood covers of Chingford (1980-1986)
S. Petty	– Stewart Petty covers of Weybridge (1981-1984)
B. Reeve	– Brian Reeve/B. Alan (1992 Only)
(f)	– denotes forerunner to the series

Official covers forming a numbered series are listed with the appropriate number after the abbreviation, e.g. *BOCS (2) 3* indicates the third cover in the second series of the Benham official cover series. Sometimes the sequence of numbers will be broken, because no handstamp was sponsored.
*BL covers – values quoted are for British Library covers with British Library handstamps. Many B.L. covers exist with other handstamps.

Benham of Folkestone were the first cover producer to promote the concept of 'official' covers. The idea of being able to purchase fully serviced first day covers for each stamp issue quickly caught on with collectors as a trouble free way of collecting covers. Furthermore most of the covers were linked to organisations connected with the stamp issue. Benham has developed the idea by incorporating gold borders surrounding the main designs which are printed on silk like material. These are usually referred to as 'silks'. Whilst official or sponsored covers have grown in popularity, the 'blank' cover market has contracted - whether the two events are connected is difficult to ascertain. Illustrated below are a few recent examples of Benham covers.

Roman Britain
15th June 1993
This cover is No. 21 in Benham's Special Gold Series.
Sometimes the same number is allocated to more than one cover. This appears in the catalogue as
Benham SG21

Autumn
14th Sept. 1993
Cover No. 38 in Benham's 'L' (Limited Edition) series.
This appears in the catalogue as
Benham L38

Picture Postcards
12th April 1994
This cover is No. 93 in Benham's Luxury Cover Series.
Sometimes the same number is allocated to more than one cover. This appears in the catalogue as
BLCS 93

The only other on-going official cover series are published by the editor of this catalogue, A. G. Bradbury. These are the LFDC series which by the end of 1994 reached LFDC No 128 and the Victorian Prints series which started in 1985.

Picture Postcards
12th April 1994
Cover No. 122
in A. G. Bradbury's
LFDC series.
Note the different design approach to the Benham cover illustrated over for the same issue.

(ii) those not forming a F.D.C. series

Cotswold } *Philart* }	– These should not be confused with the 'ordinary' covers which were available for the same issues.
Cotswold (g)	– Where Cotswold sponsored a handstamp and utilised their ordinary cover, not producing a separate cover.
A.C.C.	– Action for the Crippled Child (Philart)
Arlington	– J.& M. Arlington of London
Benham	– Benham of Folkestone (other than series above)
Bradbury	– A.G.Bradbury (other than LFDC or VP series)
Cameo	– Cameo Stamps of London
Cam.S.C.	– Cambridge Stamp Centre
CoverCraft	– CoverCraft (R. de Swarte), Beckenham
Dawn	– Dawn Covers of Stockport
D.F.	– David Fletcher of Coventry
Des. Enc.	– Design Encounter (R. de Swarte), Beckenham
F.A.A.	– Fleet Air Arm Museum
G. & P.	– Greenberg & Porter of Horsham
H.R.	– Historic Relics
K. & D.	– K. & D. Covers of London
Markton	– Markton Stamps of Norwich
S.Muscroft	– Stan Muscroft of Guisborough
Pilgrim	– Pilgrim Philatelics of Canterbury
P.P.S.	– Presentation Philatelic Services, Leicester
R. Skinner	– R. Skinner of Epsom
S.P.	– Stamp Publicity of Worthing
Sumner	– The Sumner Collection
D.G.T.	– D.G. Taylor formerly of Harrow
B. Travers	– Travers Publications of Cleveland
W & W	– Warwick & Warwick
Westminster	– Westminster Stamp Co.
P. Withers	– P.Withers of Stoke-on-Trent
BFPS	– British Forces Postal Services
Royal Eng.	– Royal Engineers
B Legion	– British Legion
RH/RHDR	– Railway History/Romney Hythe & Dymchurch Rly.

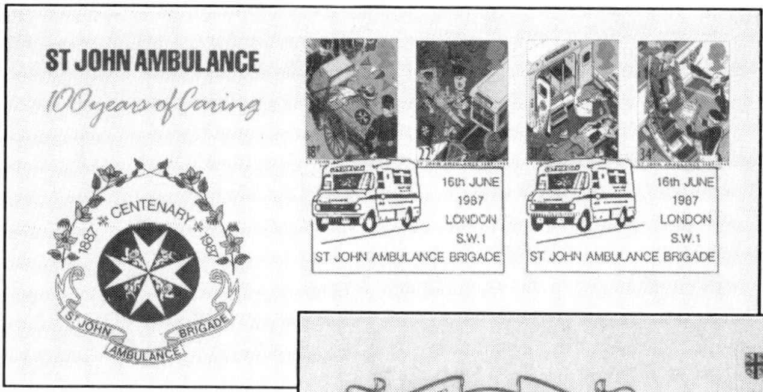

St. John Ambulance
16th June 1987
This cover was produced by Arlington.
Most of the covers produced by Arlington are sponsored by the organisation. Usually, therefore, only small numbers find their way on to the first day cover market.

Heraldry
17th January 1984
This cover, produced by Cotswold, is the official cover for the College of Arms.
Cotswold still produce 'blanks' for each issue, but the last official cover was for the 1989 Microscopes issue.

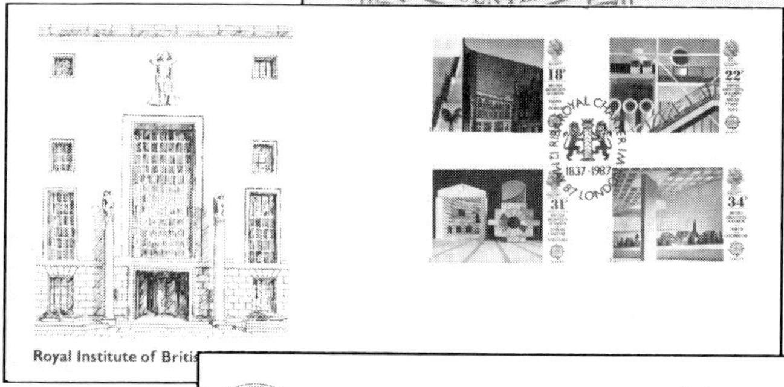

British Architects
12 May 1987
This cover was produced by CoverCraft for the Royal Institue of British Architects.
Several CoverCraft covers have become quite scare.

Linnean Society
19th Jan. 1988
This cover, produced by A. G. Bradbury, is the official cover for the Linnean Society.
LFDC 65

N.B. The covers illustrated in these General Notes should give the reader a good idea of what to look for when buying covers. Remember scruffy or 'dog-eared' covers are worth very little - always insist on the best and buy from reputable dealers.

Other abbreviations used in the official covers column:

n.o.c. – indicates that no official cover exists, or is known, but NOT with the commemorative stamps of the issue concerned.

Post Office / *Royal Mail* } – indicates a special handstamp sponsored by the Post Office, no special cover being produced.

(b) Covers produced by Private Organisations

Many organisations have produced their own special covers to raise funds or to foster public relations – usually where their work/activity is related to the theme of the stamp issue. The abbreviations used in the official covers column should be easy to interpret once you view the cover. The value of a cover can differ dramatically depending whether it is the official cover or not. If in doubt, then seek advice from an expert - ***Caveat emptor*** (let the buyer beware)!

(c) Other Categories

There are many so called 'official' covers produced which use special handstamps sponsored by other organisations or by the Royal Mail, e.g. 1971 Christmas issue with Canterbury Post Office handstamp used on a special Canterbury Stained Glass Window cover; 1975 Jane Austen issue with Stevenson Post Office handstamp used on a special cover produced by Jane Austen Bicentenary Committee.

Neither Canterbury Cathedral nor the Jane Austen Bicentenary Committee sponsored these handstamps, but made use of the handstamp provided free of charge of the Royal Mail. It would be almost impossible to list all such privately sponsored covers which have been produced, so we have made no attempt to do so.

(d) C.D.S. and slogan postmarks used on official covers

It has been the practice in recent years for official cover producers, amongst others, to offer their covers with alternative postmarks – C.D.S., slogans, etc. It would be impossible to list all these variations. Such covers usually command a premium over, say the same C.D.S. on an ordinary cover. This is especially so where there is a direct link between the cover and postmark.

Sherlock Holmes
12th October 1993
The official cover produced for the Sherlock Holmes Museum in Baker Street with
Baker Street C. D. S.

(G) PERMANENT PICTORIAL HANDSTAMPS

As mentioned earlier (see section E (1)), there are now numerous philatelic handstamps available to the collector which are in use on each first day of issue to new stamps. These have been omitted from the text except where relevant to particular stamp issues, e.g. the Shakespeare handstamp is listed under the 1982 British Theatre issue; London S.W. (Buckingham Palace) and the Windsor Philatelic Counter are listed under the royalty issues, and so on. These handstamps are available under the "re-posting facility" and are shown below:

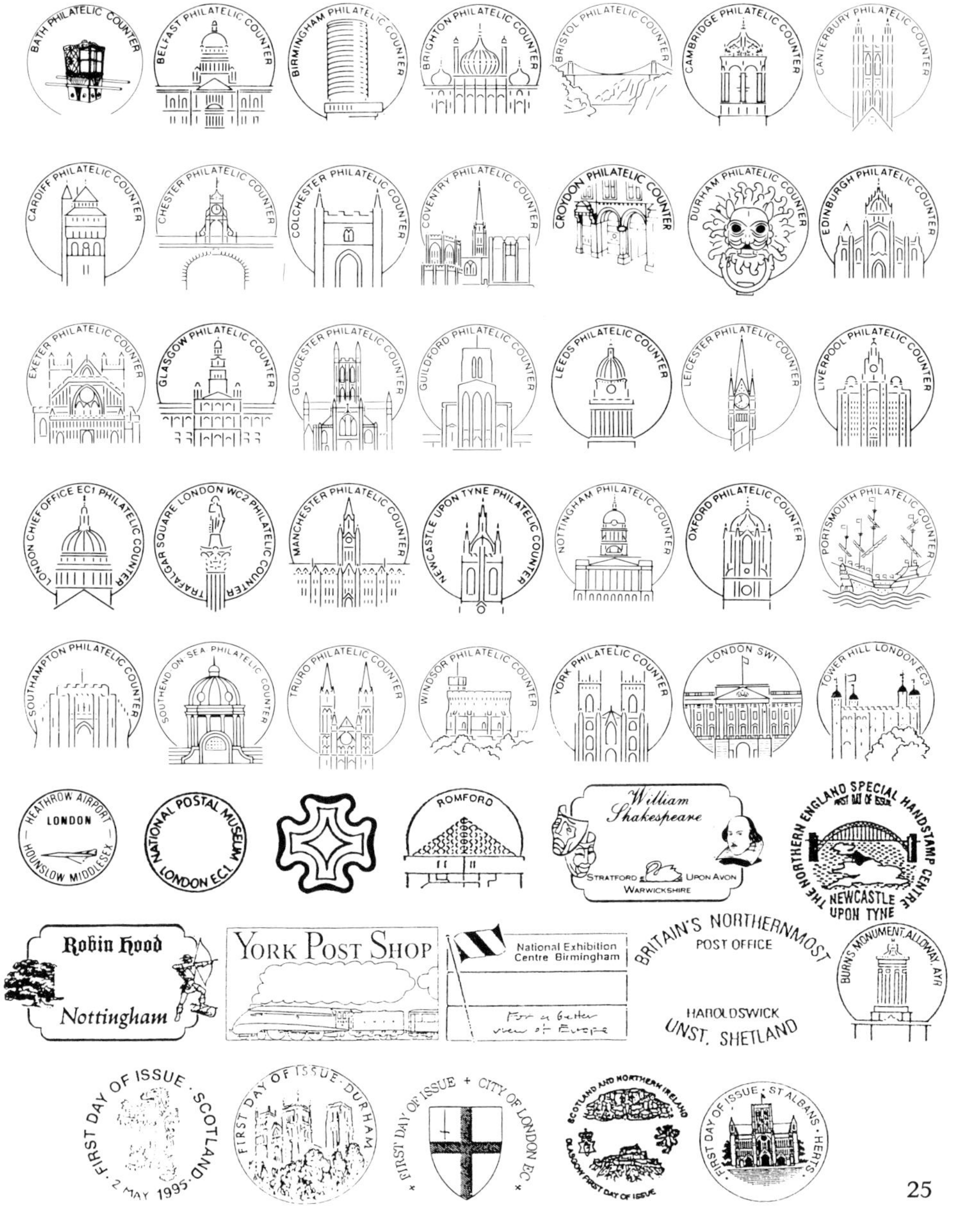

HOW TO USE THIS CATALOGUE

The commemorative issues follows the format below:

(1) Official date of issue of stamps

(2) Title of stamp issue

(3) Brief description of stamp designs and values. Reference to these will often explain the significance of many of the postmarks

6th Feb. 1990 - GREETINGS STAMPS

10 x 20p Famous 'Smiles':
Teddy Bear; Dennis the Menace, Mr. Punch, Cheshire Cat, Man in the Moon, Laughing Policeman, Clown, MonaLisa, Queen of Hearts, Stan Laurel

	ordinary covers £	official covers £		(4)
SPECIAL HANDSTAMPS				
(1) First Day of Issue - Philatelic Bureau	6	-	*Post Office*	
(2) First Day of Issue - Giggleswick	8	-	*Post Office*	
(3) Greetings, Clowne, Chesterfield	8	10	*Benham D135*	
(4) Greetings, Puncheston, Haverfordwest	8	3	*Benham(s)*	(5)
(5) Greetings, The Teddy Bear Shop, Ironbridge	8	18	*B'ham (500)50*	
(6) Greetings, Hartford, Cheshire	8	18	*BLCS 50*	
(7) No.604 Squadron, BF 2217 PS	8	12	*RFDC 80*	
C.D.S. POSTMARKS				(6)
(8) Bearpark, Catsfield, or Pudsey *each*	12			
(9) Bow St., Constable Rd., Constable Burton, or Law	12			
(10) Fleet Street, EC4 - where 'Beano' is published	12			
(11) Giggleswick	12			(7)
(12) Greet, Birmingham	12			
(13) Oxford - Lewis Carrol wrote 'Alice in Wonderland'	12			
(14) Ulverston - birthplace of Stan Laurel	15			

Also: Colemore Circus, Greets Green, Big Top, Merry Hill, Laurel Lane, Puncheston, London E.C. Prices from £9.

SLOGAN POSTMARKS		(8)
(15) Take a Bite Out of Crime, Newcastle	20	
(16) Collect British Stamps, Lincoln ('Lincoln Imp')	20	

Also: Darlington Open Day; Stampex; Collect British Stamps. Prices from £15.

(4) Two column price structure: *1924-1961 illustrated covers/plain covers*
1962-1967 non-phosphor/phosphor
1967- date ordinary covers/official covers
See Section (C) of General Notes (page 6)

(5) Brief description of official cover/series number
See Section (F - 2) of General Notes (page 20)

(6) Abbreviated wording of postmarks.

(7) Price guide.
See Section (D) of General Notes (page 8)

(8) Type of postmark.
See Section (E) of General Notes (page 10)

The purpose of this catalogue is to give the reader a guide to the variety of covers and postmarks available for each stamp issue. It is not the publisher's or author's own price list. Prices are a guide - see General Notes.

Whilst every care has been taken to ensure complete accuracy in the compilation of this catalogue, the publisher and author cannot accept responsibility for any errors or omissions.

COMMEMORATIVE ISSUES

23rd April 1924 – BRITISH EMPIRE EXHIBITION, WEMBLEY

1d, 1½d Wembley Lion

	illustrated covers	plain covers
SPECIAL HANDSTAMPS	£	£
(1) Empire Exhibition, Wembley Park, 1924	–	250
(2) Palace of Engineering or Palace of Industry *each*	–	525
SLOGAN POSTMARKS		
(3) Wembley Park (Lion) 1924	–	225
(4) -do- on H. R. Harmer *display cover*	300	–
POSTAL STATIONERY		
(5) 1d Postcard – Wembley special h/s or slogan	–	100
(6) 1½d Postcard (foreign) – Wembley h/s or slogan	–	125
(7) 1½d Printed envelope – Wembley h/s or slogan	–	150

(2) (1)

(3)

9th May 1925 – BRITISH EMPIRE EXHIBITION, WEMBLEY

1d, 1½d Wembley Lion

	illustrated covers	plain covers
SPECIAL HANDSTAMPS		
(1) British Empire Exhibition, Wembley or Wembley Park..	–	1,000
(2) Empire Exhibition Wembley, Palace of Industry	–	1,250
SLOGAN POSTMARKS		
(3) Wembley Park (Lion) 1925	–	1,000
POSTAL STATIONERY		
(4) 1d Postcard – Wembley special h/s or slogan	–	175
(5) 1½d Postcard (foreign) – Wembley h/s or slogan	–	200
(6) 1½d Printed envelope – Wembley h/s or slogan	–	225

(3)

(1) (2)

10th May 1929 – 9th UNIVERSAL POSTAL UNION CONGRESS

½d, 1d, 1½d, 2½d King George V; £1 St. George and the Dragon

	illustrated covers	plain covers
C.D.S. POSTMARKS		
(1) Postal Union Congress, London – £1 value	–	5,500
(2) Postal Union Congress, London – 4 low values	–	800
(3) -do- on P.U.C. stationery or envelope (crest on flap)	–	800
(4) -do- on P.U.C. stationery – all 5 values	–	4,000
(5) Registered P.U.C., London (oval) – 4 low values	–	1,000
(6) Any other postmark – £1 value	–	3,500
(7) Any other postmark – 4 low values	–	350
(8) Any other postmark – all five values	–	4,000
SLOGAN POSTMARKS		
(9) Any postmark – 4 low values	–	250

(1)

(5)

7th May 1935 – KING GEORGE V SILVER JUBILEE

½d, 1d, 1½d, 2½d King George V

	illustrated covers	plain covers
C.D.S. POSTMARKS		
(1) Windsor, Berks	600	200
(2) London. SW1	525	150
(2a) -do- on Westminster Stamp Co. cover	550	–
(3) Any other postmark	500	75
SLOGAN POSTMARKS		
(4) London SW1 or Windsor – wavy line pmks *each*	12(s)	6(s)
(5) Any other postmark	400	75

13th May 1937 – CORONATION OF KING GEORGE VI

1½d King George VI and Queen Elizabeth

	illustrated covers	plain covers
C.D.S. POSTMARKS		
(1) Windsor, Berks.	150	25
(2) Hampton Court Camp, Kingston-on-Thames	150	n.k.
(3) Pirbright Camp – used for troops for Coronation	100	n.k.
(4) Any London SW postmark	35	8
(5) London & New York (Anglo/American Air Mail cvr)..	–	35
(6) Any other postmark	25	2
SLOGAN POSTMARKS		
(7) Windsor – wavy line	150	30
(8) London SW1 – wavy line	35	7
(9) Any other postmark	20	2

6th May 1940 – CENTENARY OF FIRST ADHESIVE POSTAGE STAMPS

½d, 1d, 1½d, 2d, 2½d, 3d Victoria & George VI

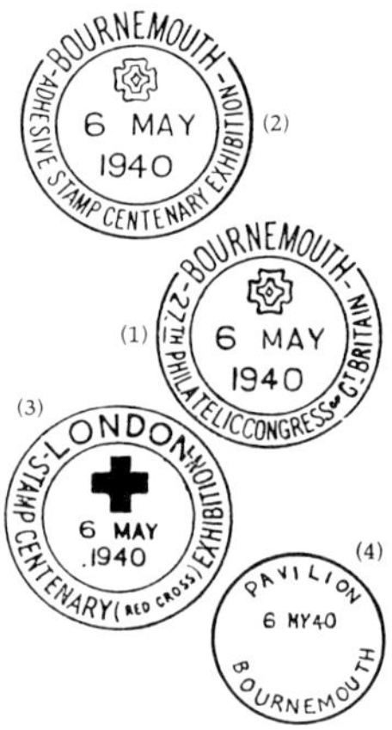

	illustrated covers	plain covers
SPECIAL HANDSTAMPS	£	£
(1) 27th Philatelic Congress, Bournemouth	65	20
(2) Adhesive Stamp Centenary Exhib., Bournemouth	40	7
(3) Stamp Centenary (Red Cross) Exhib., London	40	7
(3a) -do- on Perkins Bacon cover	75	–
(4) Pavilion, Bournemouth	35(s)	20(s)
C.D.S. POSTMARKS		
(5) Dundee – James Chalmers, first adhesive stamps	150	–
(6) Kidderminster - birthplace of Rowland Hill	–	15
(7) Any other postmark	30	5
SLOGAN POSTMARKS		
(8) Post Early in the Day	–	50
(9) Any other postmark	25	4

11th June 1946 – VICTORY COMMEMORATION

2½d, 3d Symbols of Peace and Reconstruction

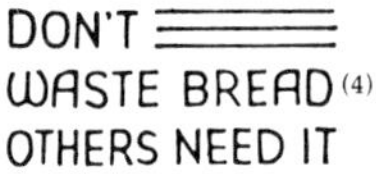

C.D.S. POSTMARKS		
(1) Any central London postmark	60	5
(2) Jersey or Guernsey – German occupation *each*	60	10
(3) Any other postmark	45	4
SLOGAN POSTMARKS		
(4) Don't Waste Bread–Others Need It	35	10
(5) Any other postmark	40	3

26th April 1948 – SILVER WEDDING OF KING GEORGE VI & QUEEN ELIZABETH

2½d, £1 Photographic portraits of the King and Queen.

C.D.S. POSTMARKS		
(1) Georgetown, Jersey	500	250
(2) Any central London postmark	350	75
(3) Any other postmark	300	70
SLOGAN POSTMARKS		
(4) London SW1 - wavy line postmark	20(s)	5(s)
(5) Any other postmark	275	60

10th May 1948 – 3rd ANNIVERSARY OF THE LIBERATION OF THE CHANNEL ISLANDS

1d, 2½d Gathering Vraic (seaweed)

C.D.S. POSTMARKS		
(1) Guernsey or Jersey *each*	20	4
(2) Sark or Alderney *each*	50	10
(3) British Industries Fair, Birmingham (registered)	50	25
(4) Any other postmark	20	4
SLOGAN POSTMARKS		
(5) Guernsey or Jersey–wavy line pmks *each*	20	4
(6) A Distinguished Career–Nursing	60	20
(7) British Industries Fair, Birmingham	100	35
(8) Any other postmark	15	3

29th July 1948 – OLYMPIC GAMES, WEMBLEY

2½d, 3d, 6d, 1s Olympic Symbols

C.D.S. POSTMARKS		
(1) Wembley, Middx. (single ring or double ring)	70	12
(1a) ditto–used at Games (bearing nos.11 to 16 in pmk.)	70	30
(2) Any other postmark	25	4
SLOGAN POSTMARKS		
(3) Olympic Games, Wembley	45	15
(4) Any other postmark	20	3

PRICES & CONDITION – PLEASE READ GENERAL NOTES
n.k. indicates covers not known
(s) after value indicates covers only known with single stamp

10th October 1949 - 75th ANNIVERSARY OF UNIVERSAL POSTAL UNION

2½d Two Hemispheres; 3d UPU Monument, Berne; 6d Goddess Concordia; 1s Posthorn and Globe	illustrated covers	plain covers
C.D.S. POSTMARKS	£	£
(1) London Chief Office–postal headquarters	75	30
(2) Any other postmarks	50	8
SLOGAN POSTMARKS		
(3) Any postmark	50	8

3rd May 1951 - FESTIVAL OF BRITAIN

2½d Commerce and Prosperity; 4d Festival Symbol

C.D.S. POSTMARKS		
(1) British Industries Fair, Birmingham	n.k.	10(s)
(2) Registered B.I.F. Birmingham (oval)	n.k.	40
(3) Battersea SW11 - Festival Gardens	40	12
(4) Buckingham Palace, SW1 or Windsor	250	50
(5) London SE1 - Festival site was on the South Bank	40	15
(6) Any other postmark	25	3
SLOGAN POSTMARKS		
(7) Battersea, SW11–wavy line	50	15
(8) Festival of Britain May 3-Sept 30 (used at Cardiff)	300	175
(9) Any other postmark	25	3

*N.B. A Festival handstamp and slogan were in use on the opening day of the Festival, 4th May. These are commemorative covers **NOT** first day covers.*

(8)

(1)

(2)

3rd June 1953 - CORONATION OF QUEEN ELIZABETH II

2½d, 4d, 1s 3d, 1s 6d

C.D.S. POSTMARKS		
(1) Arundel - Earl Marshal/Coronation arrangements	100	–
(2) Buckingham Palace SW1	675	–
(3) Windsor Castle or Sandringham	675	–
(4) Windsor, Berks.	250	50
(5) Queen's Head, Queensborough, Queen Camel, Queensferry or Queensbury *each*	12(s)	
(6) Any central London postmark	45	15
(7) Any other postmark	30	10
SLOGAN POSTMARKS		
(8) Long Live the Queen, Windsor	200	40
(9) Long Live the Queen, London SW1	60	20
(10) Long Live the Queen, any other location	45	15
(11) Any other postmark	30	7

(8) (9) (10)

1st August 1957 - WORLD SCOUT JUBILEE JAMBOREE

2½d, 4d, 1s 3d Scouting Symbols

C.D.S. POSTMARKS		
(1) Sutton Coldfield	60	20
(2) Any other postmark	15	4
SLOGAN POSTMARKS		
(3) World Scout Jubilee Jamboree, Sutton Coldfield	25	5
(4) -do- different design (see illustration)	100	15
(5) Wavy line cancellation–Sutton Coldfield	20	5
(6) Any other postmark	15	3

(3)

(4)

12th September 1957 - 46th PARLIAMENTARY CONFERENCE

4d Overprinted definitive

SPECIAL HANDSTAMPS		
(1) 46th Parliamentary Conference, London SW1	90	20

The special handstamp is known both with and without a time recorded in its design (found above the date). The version without the time recorded was used on registered mail and is more scarce, thus commanding a premium. Collectors are advised that a forged London W1 h/s is known to exist.

C.D.S. POSTMARKS		
(2) Northern Parliament, Belfast	225	80
(3) Any London SW postmark	75	20
(4) Any other postmark	65	15
SLOGAN POSTMARKS		
(5) Any postmark	65	7

(1)

18th July 1958 - 6th BRITISH EMPIRE & COMMONWEALTH GAMES, CARDIFF

3d, 6d, 1s 3d Welsh Dragon and Games Emblem

	illustrated covers	plain covers
C.D.S. POSTMARKS	£	£
(1) Empire Games Village, Barry (double ring pmk)	225	75
(2) Empire Games Village, Barry or Barry (single ring)	275	90
(3) Empire Games Village, Barry ('hooded' pmk)	350	75
(3a) -do- on R.A.F.A. Philatelic Society cover	375	–
(4) Games Mobile Post Office	–	200
(4a) Any other postmark	35	7
(5) Empire Games Village, Barry Parcel Post	n.k.	25(s)
SLOGAN POSTMARKS		
(6) British Empire & Commonwealth Games–Barry	60	25
(7) British Empire & Commonwealth Games–Llanberis	75	30
(8) British Empire & Commonwealth Games–Cardiff	75	30
(9) Any other postmark	30	5

(1)  (3)

 (6) (7) (8)

 (2)

7th July 1960 - THE GENERAL LETTER OFFICE

3d, 1s 3d Post boy and Post horn of 1660

C.D.S. POSTMARKS		
(1) Lombard Street, EC3 – General Letter Office	60	20
(2) London Chief Office, EC – postal headquarters	60	20
(3) Any other postmark	35	5
SLOGAN POSTMARKS		
(4) International Postal Conference, Eastbourne	175	50
(5) Any other postmark	30	5

 (4)

19th Sept. 1960 - 1st ANNIV. EUROPEAN POSTAL & TELECOMMUNICATIONS CONFERENCE (CEPT) - 'EUROPA'

6d, 1s 6d Conference Emblem

C.D.S. POSTMARKS		
(1) Lombard Street, EC3 – General Letter Office	50	n.k.
(2) London Chief Office, EC – postal headquarters	45	20
(3) Norwich – first use of post codes in 1960	40	17
(4) London F.S. (Foreign Section)	50	25
(5) Any other postmark	30	7
SLOGAN POSTMARKS		
(6) Express Good Wishes by Greeting's Telegram	100	n.k.
(7) London EC - wavy line	40	n.k.
(8) Any other postmark	30	5

28th August 1961 - CENTENARY OF THE POST OFFICE SAVINGS BANK

2½d, 3d, 1s 6d Thrift Plant and Growth of Savings

C.D.S. POSTMARKS		
(1) Blythe Rd., W14 – HQ of the P.O.S.B.	275	75
(2) London Chief Office, EC – postal headquarters	75	25
(3) Any London postmark	50	20
(4) Any other postmark	45	7
SLOGAN POSTMARKS		
(5) Express Good Wishes by Greeting's Telegrams	75	15
(6) Any other postmark	40	6

(5) 

18th Sept. 1961 - EUROPEAN POST & TELECOMMUNICATIONS CONFERENCE (CEPT)

2d, 4d, 10d Doves and CEPT Emblem

C.D.S. POSTMARKS		
(1) London Chief Office, EC – postal headquarters	30	n.k.
(2) Any other postmark	3	1
(3) Torquay – Conference venue	30	n.k.
SLOGAN POSTMARKS		
(4) CEPT European Conference, Torquay	6	2
(5) Post Office Savings Bank 1861-1961	175	25(s)
(6) Express Good Wishes by Greeting's Telegram	–	15
(7) Any other postmark	3	1

 (5)

 (4)

25th September 1961 - 7th COMMONWEALTH PARLIAMENTARY CONFERENCE

6d Hammer Beam Roof, Westminster Hall; 1s 3d Palace of Westminster

	illustrated covers	plain covers
C.D.S. POSTMARKS	£	£
(1) House of Commons, SW1	175	45
(2) House of Lords, SW1	200	60
(3) London SW1 or Westminster Bridge Road	40	20
(4) Any other postmark	25	5
SLOGAN POSTMARKS		
(5) Commonwealth Parliamentary Conference	35	8
(6) Any other postmark	25	4

(5)

With effect from the National Productivity Year issue, all commemorative stamps were produced with and without phosphor bands. Prices listed from this issue are for illustrated covers only. Plain covers are generally available for subsequent issues but are worth considerably less than illustrated covers.

14th November 1962 - NATIONAL PRODUCTIVITY YEAR

2½d, 3d, 1s 3d Productivity Emblems

	non-phos. covers	phosphor covers
C.D.S. POSTMARKS	£	£
(1) Any postmark	40	80
SLOGAN POSTMARKS		
(2) National Productivity Year, November 1962-63	40	130
(3) Export & Prosper, NW1 *plain covers*	50	50
(4) Southampton T – wavy line cancellation	n.k.	110
(5) Any other postmark	35	80

(2)

(3)

21st March 1963 - FREEDOM FROM HUNGER CAMPAIGN

2½d, 1s 3d Campaign Emblems

SPECIAL HANDSTAMPS		
(1) Tenth Anniversary Stampex 1963, SW1	60	60
C.D.S. POSTMARKS		
(2) Any postmark	25	30
SLOGAN POSTMARKS		
(3) Freedom From Hunger Week 17-24 March 1963	35	40
(4) Southampton T – wavy line cancellation	n.k.	35
(5) Any other postmark	20	30

(1)

(3)

With effect from the next issue 'Any other postmark' in the SLOGAN POSTMARKS section is not listed. Special 'First Day of Issue' (envelope design) slogan postmarks were introduced and are listed for the remaining issues of 1963 (and some later issues where relevant).

7th May 1963 - PARIS POSTAL CONFERENCE CENTENARY

6d 'Paris Conference'

SPECIAL HANDSTAMPS		
(1) Post Office Tercentenary, Dover Packet Service	20	400
(1a) - ditto - Dover Philatelic Society official cover	25	n.k.
C.D.S. POSTMARKS		
(2) Any postmark	10	20
SLOGAN POSTMARKS		
(3) First Day of Issue–any office	10	20
(4) Southampton T–wavy line cancellation	n.k.	20

(1)

(3)

16th May 1963 - NATIONAL NATURE WEEK

3d Posy of Flowers; 4½d Woodland Life

SPECIAL HANDSTAMPS		
(1) Brownsea Island Opening Week, Poole, Dorset	80	80
(2) Esperanto Kongresso, Stoke on Trent	n.k.	50
C.D.S. POSTMARKS		
(3) Botanic Gardens, Belfast	–	100
(4) Selborne – 'Natural History of Selborne'	75	75
(5) Forest Row, Colliers Wood or similar	100	100
(6) Any other postmark	20	25
SLOGAN POSTMARKS		
(7) First Day of Issue–any office	20	25
(8) Southampton T–wavy line cancellation	n.k.	25

(1)

(2)

31st May 1963 - 9th INT. LIFEBOAT CONFERENCE

2½d Rescue at Sea; 4d Lifeboat; 1s 6d Lifeboatmen

	non-phos. covers	phosphor covers
C.D.S. POSTMARKS	**£**	**£**
(1) Edinburgh	50	n.k.
(2) Sites of Lifeboat Stations, e.g. Cromer	60	60
(3) Any other postmark	25	30
SLOGAN POSTMARKS		
(4) International Lifeboat Conf. –Edinburgh	50	65
(5) International Lifeboat Conf. –any other office	40	55
(6) Southampton T–wavy line cancellation	n.k.	45
(7) First Day of Issue–Edinburgh	40	55
(8) First Day of Issue–any other office	25	40

(4) (5)

15th August 1963 - RED CROSS CENTENARY CONGRESS

3d, 1s 3d, 1s 6d Red Cross

C.D.S. POSTMARKS		
(1) West Wellow, Romsey – Florence Nightingale	90	100
(2) Any hospital Post Office	175	175
(3) Any other postmark	30	45
SLOGAN POSTMARKS		
(4) Red Cross Centenary – A Century of Service	65	100
(5) Southampton T–wavy line cancellation	n.k.	70
(6) First Day of Issue–any office	35	50

(4)

(1)

3rd December 1963 - COMMONWEALTH PACIFIC CABLE

1s 6d Commonwealth Cable (COMPAC)

C.D.S. POSTMARKS		
(1) Any postmark	20	25
SLOGAN POSTMARKS		
(2) First Day of Issue – Philatelic Bureau GPO, EC1	25	35
(3) Southampton T – wavy line cancellation	30	30
(4) First Day of Issue – any other office	20	25

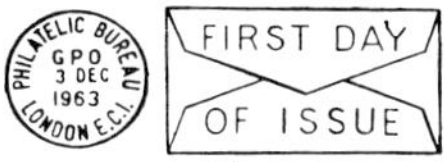

(2)

The 'Ordinary F.D.I. postmarks' were introduced with effect from the 1964 Shakespeare issue. In general, these were collected in preference to the F.D.I slogan (envelope design). The latter are now only listed if used with the full set of stamps at an office relevant to the issue. The Post Office also issued their own first day covers commencing with this issue.

23rd April 1964 - SHAKESPEARE FESTIVAL

3d, 6d, 1s 3d, 1s 6d + 2s 6d (non-phos. only) scenes from plays

SPECIAL HANDSTAMPS		
(1) Shakespeare 400th Anniversary, Stratford	30	22
ORDINARY F.D.I. POSTMARKS		
(2) Stratford-upon-Avon, Wks	13	13
(3) Any other office	7	10
C.D.S. POSTMARKS		
(4) Any postmark	5	7
SLOGAN POSTMARKS		
(5) Shakespeare Anniversary Year, Stratford	500	650
(6) First Day of Issue, Stratford	15(s)	15(s)

(1) (2)

(5)

1st July 1964 - 20th INT. GEOGRAPHICAL CONGRESS

2½d Flats; 4d Shipbuilding; 8d Forestry; 1s 6d Nuclear Power.

SPECIAL HANDSTAMPS		
(1) Lawn Tennis Championships AELTC, Wimbledon	200	n.k.
ORDINARY F.D.I. POSTMARKS		
(2) GPO Philatelic Bureau, London EC1	25	35
(3) London	25	35
(4) Any other office	20	30
C.D.S. POSTMARKS		
(5) South Kensington – Royal Geographical Society	150	150
(6) Forest Row, or similar	50	50
(7) Any other postmark	20	30
SLOGAN POSTMARKS		
(8) F.D.I. - Greenwich (Geographical expeditions)	300	300
(9) F.D.I. - SE10 (Greenwich) with triangle..	300	300
(10) Ralph Allen of Bath, Postal Pioneer	300	n.k.
(11) The Country Code–Leave no litter	200	n.k.

(2)

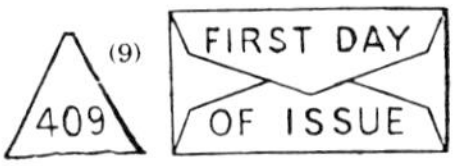

(9)

(10)

5th August 1964 - 10th INT. BOTANICAL CONGRESS

3d Spring Gentian; 6d Dog Rose; 9d Honeysuckle; 1s 3d Water Lily

	non-phos. covers	phoshor covers
SPECIAL HANDSTAMPS	**£**	**£**
(1) Tenth International Botanical Congress, Edinburgh	200	225
ORDINARY F.D.I. POSTMARKS		
(2) GPO Philatelic Bureau, London EC1	25	30
(3) Edinburgh	30	50
(4) Any other office	20	30
C.D.S. POSTMARKS		
(5) Kew Gardens, Richmond	200	200
(6) Primrose Valley, Filey, N. Yorks	150	150
(7) Forest Row, Wood Green or similar	150	150
(8) Any other postmark	20	30
SLOGAN POSTMARKS		
(9) First Day of Issue–Richmond & Twickenham (Kew)	200	200

(1)

(6)

4th September 1964 - OPENING OF THE FORTH ROAD BRIDGE

3d, 6d

SPECIAL HANDSTAMPS		
(1) Forth Road Bridge, North Queensferry	25	90
(2) Forth Road Bridge, South Queensferry	20	70
(3) Apostolatus Maris – Int. Congress, Liverpool	n.k.	150
ORDINARY F.D.I. POSTMARKS		
(4) GPO Philatelic Bureau, London EC1	10	15
(5) Edinburgh (local F.D.I. for Forth Road Bridge)	10	15
(6) Any other office	7	10
C.D.S. POSTMARKS		
(7) Balmoral Castle – The Queen proceeded to Balmoral after opening the Forth Road Bridge	225	225
(8) South Queensferry, West Lothian	90	90
(9) North Queensferry, Fife	125	125
(10) Any other postmark	6	9
SLOGAN POSTMARKS		
(11) F.D.I. – Edinburgh (local F.D.I.slogan for Bridge)	40	50
(12) Midlothian for Industrial Sites	50	n.k.
(13) Edinburgh – wavy line cancellation	30	n.k.

(2)

(1)

(12)

8th July 1965 - SIR WINSTON CHURCHILL

4d, 1s 3d

ORDINARY F.D.I. POSTMARKS		
(1) Bladon, Oxford – Churchill buried at Bladon	15	20
(2) London SW1	10	15
(3) GPO Philatelic Bureau, London EC1	9	12
(4) Any other office	5	7
C.D.S. POSTMARKS		
(5) Churchill, Bristol or Oxford *each*	75	75
(6) House of Commons, SW1	75	75
(7) House of Lords, SW1	125	125
(8) Marlborough – the Churchill ancestral home	200	n.k.
(9) Woodford Green – MP for Woodford	125	n.k.
(10) Any other postmark	4	6
SLOGAN POSTMARKS		
(11) First Day of Issue–Westminster, London SW1	95	95
(12) London SW1–wavy line cancellation	50	n.k.

(11)

(1)

19th July 1965 - 700th ANNIVERSARY OF SIMON DE MONTFORT'S PARLIAMENT

6d De Montfort's Seal; 2s 6d (non-phos. only) Parliament

ORDINARY F.D.I. POSTMARKS		
(1) Dover or Lincoln – first boroughs to be represented at the Parliament by commoners *each*	40	40
(2) Evesham – Simon De Montfort killed at Evesham	30	30
(3) London SW	20	20
(4) Leicester – De Montfort was Earl of Leicester	25	25
(5) Oxford – Parliament sometimes met at Oxford	25	25
(6) GPO Philatelic Bureau, London EC1	10	15
(7) Any other office	9	12

Simon De Montfort's Parliament (contd.)

C.D.S. POSTMARKS	non-phos. covers £	phosphor covers £
(8) Buckingham Palace, SW1	150	150
(9) Dover or Lincoln (see note in F.D.I. section) *each*	60	60
(10) Evesham – Simon De Montfort killed at Evesham	100	100
(11) House of Commons, SW1	100	100
(12) House of Lords, SW1	125	125
(13) North Warnborough – De Montfort's home was Odiham Castle, North Warnborough	200	200
(14) Parliament Street, SW1	100	100
(15) Any other postmark	8	10

9th August 1965 – CENTENARY OF THE SALVATION ARMY

3d. ls6d

(1)

SPECIAL HANDSTAMPS		
(1) Portsmouth & District Philatelic Society	90	100
(1a) -ditto- on Philatelic Society official cover	80	90
ORDINARY F.D.I. POSTMARKS		
(2) London EC – International HQ of Salvation Army	35	40
(3) Nottingham – Birthplace of William Booth	45	45
(4) Any other office	20	25
C.D.S. POSTMARKS		
(5) Any postmark	18	23

1st September 1965 – CENTENARY OF THE DISCOVERY OF ANTISEPTIC SURGERY BY JOSEPH LISTER

4d Carbolic Spray; 1s Lister

(1)

SPECIAL HANDSTAMPS		
(1) Eyam Plague Tercentenary Commemoration	150	n.k.
ORDINARY F.D.I. POSTMARKS		
(2) Edinburgh – Professor of Clinical Surgery	40	40
(2a) - ditto - (Royal Infirmary Edinburgh special cover)	60	60
(3) Glasgow – Lister was Professor of Surgery here	40	40
(4) Any other office	10	12
C.D.S. POSTMARKS		
(5) Royal Infirmary Edinburgh (Royal Infirmary cover)	225	225
(6) Glasgow – Lister was Professor of Surgery here	125	150
(7) Any other postmark	9	11
SLOGAN POSTMARKS		
(8) First Day of Issue – Edinburgh	125	125

1st September 1965 – COMMONWEALTH ARTS FESTIVAL

6d Trinidad Carnival Dancers; 1s 6d Canadian Folk Dancers

(10)

(7)

(8)

(9)

SPECIAL HANDSTAMPS		
(1) Eyam Plague Tercentenary Commemoration	150	n.k.
ORDINARY F.D.I. POSTMARKS		
(2) Cardiff, Glasgow, Liverpool or London – major events	30	30
(3) Any other office	15	20
C.D.S. POSTMARKS		
(4) Balmoral Castle – Duke of Edinburgh travelled from Balmoral Castle to open the Festival	150	150
(5) Stratford-upon-Avon (on Arts Centre cover)	80	n.k.
(6) Any other postmark	14	18
SLOGAN POSTMARKS		
(7) Commonwealth Arts Festival, Glasgow	500	550
(8) Commonwealth Arts Festival, Liverpool	450	500
(9) Commonwealth Arts Festival – any other office	400	450
(10) 4th Bach Festival Bath, October 1965, Bath	500	n.k.

PRICES & CONDITION – PLEASE READ GENERAL NOTES
n.k. indicates covers not known
(s) after value indicates covers only known with single stamp

13th Sept. 1965 – 25th ANNIVERSARY OF THE BATTLE OF BRITAIN

6d x 4d; 9d, 1s 3d Battle scenes

	non-phos. covers £	phoshor covers £
ORDINARY F.D.I. POSTMARKS		
(1) Biggin Hill, Westerham, Kent	70	70
(2) GPO Philatelic Bureau, London EC1	12	15
(3) Any other office	18	20
C.D.S. POSTMARKS		
(4) Biggin Hill, Westerham or Cranwell, Sleaford *each*	70	80
(5) Churchill, Bristol	75	n.k.
(6) Dover, Kent	30	30
(7) Any RAF Post Office postmark	70	80
(8) Any other postmark	16	18

8th October 1965 – OPENING OF THE POST OFFICE TOWER

3d Georgian Buildings and Tower; 1s 3d Nash Terrace and Tower

SPECIAL HANDSTAMPS		
(1) Leicester Philatelic Society Diamond Jubilee	30	25
(1a) ditto – on Leicester Philatelic Society official cover	50	60
ORDINARY F.D.I. POSTMARKS		
(2) London W1 – Site of P.O. Tower	20	20
(3) GPO Philatelic Bureau, London EC1	7	9
(4) Any other office	6	8
C.D.S. POSTMARKS		
(5) Gt. Portland St. – nearest P.O. to the Tower	90	90
(6) Any other postmark	5	7
SLOGAN POSTMARKS		
(7) Have you taken out your licence for Radio-TV?	50	50
(8) London W1 (wavy line) – site of P.O. Tower	20	n.k.

25th October 1965 – 20th ANNIVERSARY OF THE U.N. & INTERNATIONAL CO-OPERATION YEAR

3d U.N. Emblem; 1s 6d I.C.Y. Emblem

SPECIAL HANDSTAMPS		
(1) Leicester Philatelic Society Diamond Jubilee	50	50
(1a) ditto – on Leicester Philatelic Society official cover	75	100
ORDINARY F.D.I. POSTMARKS		
(2) London SW – U.N. London HQ	10	12
(3) Any other office	12	15
C.D.S. POSTMARKS		
(4) House of Commons, London SW1	35	35
(5) Any other postmark	10	12
SLOGAN POSTMARKS		
(6) International Co-operation Year, Reading	450	450

(1)

(6)

15th November 1965 – CENTENARY OF THE INTERNATIONAL TELECOMMUNICATIONS UNION (ITU)

9d Telecommunications; 1s 6d Radio Waves

ORDINARY F.D.I. POSTMARKS		
(1) Any office	12	17
C.D.S. POSTMARKS		
(2) Helston – Goonhilly Downs Ground Station	200	200
(3) Any other postmark	12	17
SLOGAN POSTMARKS		
(4) Have you taken out your licence for Radio-TV?	250	n.k.

(4)

25th January 1966 – ROBERT BURNS

4d, 1s 3d Portraits of Burns

SPECIAL HANDSTAMPS		
(1) The friend of man – to vice alone a foe – Dumfries	10	10
(2) That man to man the warld o'er..... – Alloway	10	10
(3) That man to man the warld o'er..... – Ayr	10	10
(4) That man to man the warld o'er..... – Edinburgh	10	10
(5) That man to man the warld o'er..... – Glasgow	10	10
(6) That man to man the warld o'er..... – Greenock	35	40
(7) That man to man the warld o'er..... – Kilmarnock	12	12
(8) That man to man the warld o'er..... – Mauchline	35	40

These special handstamps were sponsored by the Post Office. Although various organisations produced covers using these handstamps, they are not 'official'

(1)

(7)

(6)

Robert Burns (contd.)

	non-phos. covers	phosphor covers
ORDINARY F.D.I. POSTMARKS	**£**	**£**
(9) Any Scottish postmark	7	7
(10) Any other office	4	4
C.D.S. POSTMARKS		
(11) Burns Statue, Ayr	200	200
(12) Any other postmark	3	3

(11)

28th February 1966 - 900th ANNIVERSARY OF WESTMINSTER ABBEY

3d Abbey; 2s 6d (non-phos. only) Henry VII Chapel

	non-phos.	phosphor
ORDINARY F.D.I. POSTMARKS		
(1) London SW	15	15
(2) GPO Philatelic Bureau, London EC1	6	9
(3) Any other office	7	10
C.D.S. POSTMARKS		
(4) Buckingham Palace SW1	150	150
(5) House of Commons } Early Parliaments were often	100	100
(6) House of Lords } held at Westminster Abbey	100	100
(7) Any other postmark	6	9
SLOGAN POSTMARKS		
(8) Westminster Abbey 900th Anniversary Year, SW7	150	120
(9) First Day of Issue - Westminster, London SW1	120	100

(8)

(9)

2nd May 1966 - BRITISH LANDSCAPES

4d Sussex; 6d Antrim; 1s 3d Harlech; ls 6d The Cairngorms

	non-phos.	phosphor
ORDINARY F.D.I. POSTMARKS		
(1) Lewes, Sussex - appropriate for 4d value	50	65
(2) Harlech, Merioneth - appropriate for 1s 3d value	60	70
(3) Coleraine - appropriate for 6d value	60	80
(4) Grantown-on-Spey - appropriate for 1s 6d value	75	100
(5) GPO Philatelic Bureau, London EC1	10	10
(6) Any other office	8	8
C.D.S. POSTMARKS		
(7) Antrim - appropriate for 6d value	125	125
(8) Coleraine - appropriate for 6d value	125	125
(9) Grantown-on-Spey - appropriate for 1s 6d value	125	125
(10) Harlech - appropriate for 1s 3d value	125	125
(11) Forest Row, Heath Common or similar	30	30
(12) Any other postmark	7	7
SET of four single stamp covers with appropriate pmks - usually (1), (2), (3) and (4)	30	40

(8)

1st June 1966 - WORLD CUP FOOTBALL COMPETITION

4d, 6d, 1s3d

	non-phos.	phosphor
ORDINARY F.D.I. POSTMARKS		
(1) Wembley, Middx	25	25
(2) GPO Philatelic Bureau, London EC1	9	9
(3) Birmingham, Liverpool, Manchester, Middlesbrough, Sheffield, Sunderland - World Cup Games *each*	15	15
(4) Any other office	9	9
C.D.S. POSTMARKS		
(5) Any postmark	9	9
SLOGAN POSTMARKS		
(6) First Day of Issue - Harrow & Wembley	60	60
(7) World Cup City, Sheffield, City of Steel	425	n.k.
(8) The Dairy Festival, Time for Sport	275	n.k.

(1)

(7)

(6)

(8)

8th August 1966 - BRITISH BIRDS

4 x 4d Black-headed Gull; Blue Tit; Robin; Blackbird

	non-phos.	phosphor
ORDINARY F.D.I. POSTMARKS		
(1) GPO Philatelic Bureau, London EC1	12	12
(2) Any other office	10	10
C.D.S. POSTMARKS		
(3) Any postmark	10	10

18th August 1966 – WORLD CUP - 'ENGLAND WINNERS'

4d (non-phosphor only)

	non-phos. covers £	phoshor covers £
SPECIAL HANDSTAMPS		
(1) World Methodist Conference, SW1 (*plain covers*)	50	–
(2) Opening of the Tay Road Bridge, Dundee	50	–
(2a) - do - on official cover	70	–
(3) Ballater Highland Games (official cover)	70	–
ORDINARY F.D.I. POSTMARKS		
(4) Harrow & Wembley	6	–
(5) Birmingham, Liverpool, Manchester, Middlesbrough Sheffield, Sunderland - World Cup Games *each*	10	–
(6) Any other office	4	–
C.D.S. POSTMARKS		
(7) Harrow & Wembley, Middx	25	–
(8) Any other postmark	4	–
SLOGAN POSTMARKS		
(9) Harrow & Wembley - wavy line cancellation	20	–

(4)

(1)

(2)

(3)

1st June & 18th Aug 1966 – WORLD CUP & 'ENGLAND WINNERS' DOUBLE DATED COVERS

As no 'England Winners' phosphor stamps were issued, these double dated covers may exist with phosphor and ordinary stamps.

	£
(1) Harrow & Wembley FDI – both dates on one cover	175
(2) Birmingham, Liverpool, Manchester, Middlesbrough Sheffield or Sunderland – both dates on one cover	100
(3) Any other postmark – both dates on one cover	50

19th September 1966 – BRITISH TECHNOLOGY

4d Jodrell Bank; 6d Motor Cars; 1s 3d Hovercraft; 1s 6d Nuclear Power

	non-phos.	phosphor
ORDINARY F.D.I. POSTMARKS		
(1) GPO Philatelic Bureau, Edinburgh 1	6	8
(2) Birmingham, Coventry or Oxford - car industry *each*	9	12
(3) Carlisle, Cumberland - Windscale Reactor	9	17
(4) Manchester - Jodrell Bank	9	12
(5) Newport, Isle of Wight - Hovercraft	9	17
(6) Portsmouth - Hovercraft	9	17
(7) Luton, Beds - car industry	9	17
(8) Any other office	4	4
C.D.S. POSTMARKS		
(9) Macclesfield, Cheshire (with Jodrell Bank cachet)	125	175
(10) Cowes, I.O.W. (on British Hovercraft Corp. cover)	175	150
(11) Calderbridge, Seascale - Windscale reactor	10(s)	–
(12) Lower Withington - Jodrell Bank	10(s)	–
(13) Any other postmark	4	4
SLOGAN POSTMARKS		
(14) Build Your New Factory at Grimsby	60	–
SET of four single stamp covers with appropriate pmks – usually (2), (3), (4) and (5)	30	45

(14)

(2)

14th October 1966 – 900th ANNIVERSARY OF THE BATTLE OF HASTINGS

6 x 4d, 6d, 1s 3d Battle Scenes

	non-phos.	phosphor
SPECIAL HANDSTAMPS		
(1) Battle of Hastings 900th Anniv. Battlefield	7	8
ORDINARY F.D.I. POSTMARKS		
(2) Battle, Sussex or Normandy Guildford *each*	6	7
(3) Hastings, Sussex	5	6
(4) GPO Philatelic Bureau, Edinburgh 1	3	5
(5) Guernsey or Jersey *each*	10	10
(6) Any other office	2	3
C.D.S. POSTMARKS		
(7) Battle, Sussex or Normandy, Guildford	40	40
(8) Any other postmark	2	3
SLOGAN POSTMARKS		
(9) Les Iles Normandes, Guernsey (on 2 covers)	250	250
(10) Les Iles Normandes, Jersey (on 2 covers)	250	250
(11) Hastings Popular with Visitors since 1066	20(s)	20(s)

(1)

(9)
(10)

(11)

1st December 1966 - CHRISTMAS

3d, 1s 6d Children's Paintings

	non-phos. covers	phosphor covers
SPECIAL HANDSTAMPS	£	£
(1) British Stamp Exhibition, BF 1000 PS	30	30
(1a) - ditto - on BFPS official cover	25	25
ORDINARY F.D.I. POSTMARKS		
(2) Bethlehem, Llandeilo, Carms	5	5
(3) GPO Philatelic Bureau, Edinburgh 1	3	3
(4) Any other office	2	2
C.D.S. POSTMARKS		
(5) Bethlehem or Nasareth *each*	250	250
(6) Isle of Whithorn - first seat of Christianity	150	n.k.
(7) St. Nicholas, Guildford	100	n.k.
(8) Any other postmark	2	2
SLOGAN POSTMARKS		
(9) Britain Leads the World in Helping Spastics	40	40
(10) Reedham School Caring for Children	60	n.k.
(11) John Groom's Cares for the Disabled	40	50
(12) Post Early for Christmas	250	n.k.

(1)

(2)

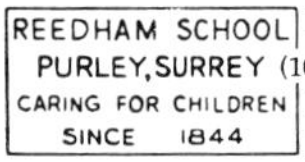

(10)

20th February 1967 - EUROPEAN FREE TRADE AREA (EFTA)

9d Sea Freight; 1s 6d Air Freight

	non-phos. covers	phosphor covers
SPECIAL HANDSTAMPS		
(1) Radiation Biology Conference, NATO, Portmadoc	35	35
ORDINARY F.D.I. POSTMARKS		
(2) GPO Philatelic Bureau, Edinburgh 1	4	4
(3) London SW	6	6
(4) Hull, Grimsby or Newcastle - EFTA Trading Ports	15	15
(5) Any other office	2	2
C.D.S. POSTMARKS		
(6) House of Commons, SW1	25	30
(7) House of Lords, SW1	40	45
(8) Any other postmark	2	2
SLOGAN POSTMARKS		
(9) Ship Early Through the Port of London	175	175
(10) Southend - Business and Industry	50	50
(11) Tees Side Means Business *plain covers*	15	15
(12) New Industry in Sunderland	50	50
(13) Southampton T (port) - wavy line pmk	–	20

(1)

(9)

(10)

24th April 1967 - BRITISH WILD FLOWERS

4d Hawthorn, Rosaceae, Bramble; 4d Larger Bindweed, Echium; 4d Daisy, Coltsfoot, Buttercup; 4d Bluebell, Red Campion, Wood Anemone; 9d Dog Violet; 1s 9d Primroses

	non-phos. covers	phosphor covers
SPECIAL HANDSTAMPS		
(1) RSH Health Congress, Eastbourne	175	200
ORDINARY F.D.I. POSTMARKS		
(2) GPO Philatelic Bureau, Edinburgh 1	7	7
(3) Kingston-upon-Thames (local F.D.I. for Kew)	15	15
(4) Any other office	4	4
C.D.S. POSTMARKS		
(5) Bluebell Hill, Flore, Hawthorn or Primrose St *each*	175	175
(6) Kew Gardens, Richmond	125	125
(7) Hedgend, Weedswood or similar	20	20
(8) Any other postmark	4	4

(1)

With effect from the 1967 Paintings issue all stamps were phosphor coated. It was around this time that more 'official' covers were being produced (see General Notes). C.D.S. pmks are now only catalogued if relevant to an issue.

10th July 1967 - BRITISH PAINTINGS

4d 'Master Lambton' (Lawrence); 9d 'Mares and Foals in a Landscape' (Stubbs); 1s 6d. 'Children Coming Out of School' (Lowry)

	ordinary covers	official covers	
SPECIAL HANDSTAMPS	£	£	
(1) Art on Stamps Exhibition, Stamp Centre, WC2	20	40	*P.R. O'Connell*
ORDINARY F.D.I. POSTMARKS			
(2) GPO Philatelic Bureau, Edinburgh 1	5		
(3) Bishop Auckland -'Master Lambton' at Wilton Castle	25		
(4) Any other office	3		

(1)

24th July 1967 - WORLD VOYAGE OF SIR FRANCIS CHICHESTER

1s 9d Gipsy Moth IV

	ordinary covers	official covers
SPECIAL HANDSTAMPS	£	£
(1) Sir Francis Chichester, Philatelic Bureau	5	- *Post Offfice*
(2) Sir Francis Chichester, Greenwich, SE10	5	- *Post Office*
(3) Sir Francis Chichester, Plymouth	5	- *Post Office*
(4) International Camp, E. Mersea, Colchester	100	- *n.o.c.*
ORDINARY F.D.I. POSTMARKS		
(5) Barnstaple - Birthplace of Sir Francis Chichester	10	
(6) Chichester, Sussex	10	
(7) Gosport, Hants.	15	
(8) Any other office	2	
C.D.S. POSTMARKS		
(9) Barnstaple - Birthplace of Sir Francis Chichester	25	
(10) House of Commons (Outward Bound Trust cover)	20	

19th September 1967 - BRITISH DISCOVERY

4d Radar; 1s Penicillin; 1s 6d Jet Engine; 1s 9d Television

SPECIAL HANDSTAMPS		
(1) Penicillin/Sir Alexander Fleming, W2	15	- *n.o.c.*
(2) Exhibition of F.D.C.s - HMS Discovery, WC	15	- *n.o.c.*
(3) BF 1000 PS (used at RAF Bruggen Stamp Exhib.)	70	60 *Forces*
ORDINARY F.D.I. POSTMARKS		
(4) GPO Philatelic Bureau. Edinburgh 1	3	
(5) Coventry - birthplace of Frank Whittle	15	
(6) Hounslow - associated with jet aircraft	15	
(7) London SW (on British Drug Houses cover)	3(s)	
(8) Paddington W2 - discovery of penicillin	15	
(9) Plymouth, Devon (with Westward TV logo)	20	
(10) Any other office	2	
C.D.S. POSTMARKS		
(11) Benenden Chest Hospital, Cranbrook, Kent	300	
(12) Brechin - birthplace of Sir Robert Watson-Watt	5(s)	
(13) Darvel - birthplace of Sir Alexander Fleming	5(s)	
(14) Helensburgh - birthplace of John Logie Baird	150	
SLOGAN POSTMARKS		
(15) First Day of Issue - Paddington W2	100	
SET of four single stamp covers with appropriate pmks - usually (5), (11), (12) and (13)	40	

18th October 1967 - CHRISTMAS

4d 'Madonna and Child'

ORDINARY F.D.I. POSTMARKS		
(1) Bethlehem, Llandeilo, Carms	3	
(2) GPO Philatelic Bureau, Edinburgh 1	2	
(3) Any other office	1	
C.D.S. POSTMARKS		
(4) Nasareth	150	
(5) St. Nicholas	50	
SLOGAN POSTMARKS		
(6) First Day of Issue - Bethlehem, Llandeilo, Carms	10	
(7) Oxfam - 25th Year	25	
(8) Visit Roman Bath	100	

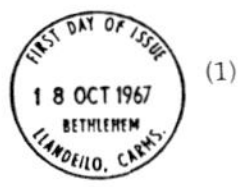

27th November 1967 - CHRISTMAS

3d, 1s 6d 'Adoration of the Shepherds'

SPECIAL HANDSTAMPS		
(1) Dulwich Millennium AD967–AD1967 SE21	100	100
ORDINARY F.D.I. POSTMARKS		
(2) GPO Philatelic Bureau, Edinburgh 1	2	
(3) Bethlehem, Llandeilo, Carms	3	
(4) Any other office	1	
SLOGAN POSTMARKS		
(5) First Day of Issue - Bethlehem, Llandeilo, Carms	75	
(6) See the Christmas Illuminations, Cheltenham	325	
(7) First Ever Christmas Present, Londonderry	325	
(8) Visit Roman Bath (plain cover)	25	

18th Oct & 27th Nov - CHRISTMAS (DOUBLE DATED)

	ordinary covers £	official covers £
(1) Bethlehem, Llandeilo– both dates on one cover	30	
(2) Any other office – both dates on one cover	15	

29th April 1968 - BRITISH BRIDGES

4d Tarr Steps, Dulverton; 9d Aberfeldy Bridge; 1s 6d Menai Bridge; 1s 9d M4 Viaduct, Chiswick

SPECIAL HANDSTAMPS

(1) First Day of Issue, GPO Philatelic Bureau	5	– *Post Office*
(2) First Day of Issue, Bridge, Canterbury	5	– *Post Office*
(2a) RSH Health Congress, Eastbourne	150	200 *R.S.H.*

ORDINARY F.D.I. POSTMARKS

(3) Perth – local office for Aberfeldy	6	
(4) Bath (Severn Bridge/Pulteney Bridge cover)	20	
(5) Any other office	3	

C.D.S. POSTMARKS

(6) Aberfeldy – featured on 9d value	125	
(7) Chiswick – featured on 1s 9d value	175	
(8) Dulverton – featured on 4d value	175	
(9) Menai – featured on 1s 6d value	125	

SLOGAN POSTMARKS

(10) First Day of Issue – Bridge, Canterbury	60	
(11) First Day of Issue – Menai Bridge	60	
(12) First Day of Issue – Aberfeldy	60	
(13) Chiswick – wavy line cancellation	120	

SET of four single stamp covers with appropriate pmks – usually (7), (8), (11) and (12) 40

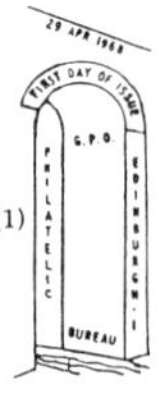
(1)

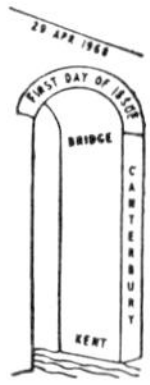
(2)

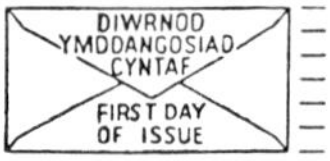

(11)

(2)

29th May 1968 - BRITISH ANNIVERSARIES

4d TUC; 9d Votes for Women; 1s RAF; 1s 9d James Cook

SPECIAL HANDSTAMPS

(1) First Day of Issue, Manchester TUC 100	70	– *Post Office*
(2) First Day of Issue, Women's Suffrage, Aldeburgh	70	– *Post Office*
(3) First Day of Issue, Hendon, NW4	70	– *Post Office*
(4) First Day of Issue, Whitby	70	– *Post Office*
(5) 50th Anniversary RAF Leuchars, Fife	190	10 *Force(s)*
(6) 50th Anniv. RAF Medmenham RAF Post Office	190	– *n.o.c.*
(7) RAF 50th Anniv. Fylingdales RAF Post Office	190	10 *Force(s)*
(8) RAF 50th Anniv. RAF College Cranwell	190	10 *Force(s)*
(9) RAF Escaping Society, BF 1067 PS	190	10 *Force(s)*
(10) BF 1000 PS (used at RAF Laarbrucke)	190	– *n.o.c.*
(11) P.O. Engineering Union 100000, Ealing W5	190	20 *P.O.E.U.(s)*
(12) RNIB Centenary Exhibition, London SW1	190	– *n.o.c.*

ORDINARY F.D.I. POSTMARKS

(13) GPO Philatelic Bureau, Edinburgh 1	5	
(14) Any other office	4	

C.D.S. POSTMARKS

(15) House of Commons, SW1	35	
(16) House of Lords, SW1	45	
(17) Forces Post Office or any Field Post Office	50	
(18) Digby Aerodrome (RAF Digby cover)	50	
(19) Marton-in-Cleveland – birthplace of Captain Cook	10(s)	
(20) Any R.A.F. Post Office e.g. Hawkinge, Syerston	100	
(21) Tolpuddle, Dorset – Tolpuddle Martyrs	15(s)	

SLOGAN POSTMARKS

(22) Bi-centenary Captain Cook 1768-1968, Whitby	25(s)	

SET of four single stamp covers with appropriate pmks – usually (1), (2), (3) and (4) 8

(1)

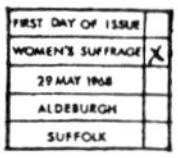

(2)

(3)

(4)

(7)

(8)

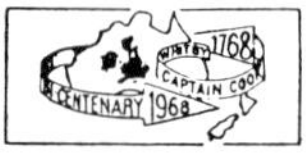

(22)

12th August 1968 - BRITISH PAINTINGS

4d Elizabeth I (artist unknown); 1s Pinkie (Lawrence); 1s 6d Ruins of St. Mary le Port (Piper); 1s 9d Hay Wain (Constable)

SPECIAL HANDSTAMPS

(1) Philatex 68 Woburn, Bletchley	10	20 *Woburn (4cvrs)*
(2) Portsmouth & District Philatelic Society	25	30 *Phil. Soc.*
(3) Parish Church Restoration Kettering	25	30 *Parish Ch.*
(4) SAGA (Scouts and Guides Assoc'n.), Beeley	–	20 *SAGA (s)*

(1)

(2)

(3)

1968 Paintings (contd.)

	ordinary covers £	official covers £
ORDINARY F.D.I. POSTMARKS		
(5) GPO Philatelic Bureau, Edinburgh 1	5	
(6) Bristol – Lawrence born at Bristol	6	
(7) Ipswich – local F.D.I. for 'Constable Country'	8	
(8) Any other office	4	
C.D.S. POSTMARKS		
(9) Blackheath SE3 – Queen Elizabeth's portrait probably commissioned by a member of the Admiralty	160	
(10) East Bergholt, Colchester – Constable's birthplace	450	
(11) Greenwich, SE10 – Birthplace of Elizabeth I	225	
(12) Richmond, Yorks – 'Pinkie' associated with Richmond.	225	
SLOGAN POSTMARKS		
(13) F.D.I. – Hatfield – QEI associated with Hatfield Hse...	40	
(14) F.D.I. – London SE1 – Birthplace of Elizabeth I	40	
(15) F.D.I. – London W1 – London art galleries	40	
SET of 4 single stamp covers with appropriate pmks....*from*	10	

(4)

25th November 1968 - CHRISTMAS

4d, 9d, 1s 6d Childrens Toys

	ordinary covers £	official covers £
SPECIAL HANDSTAMPS		
(1) Selfridges Christmas Toy Fair, London W1	13	10 *Selfridges(s)*
(2) HMS Hermes, BF 1074 PS	100	100 *Forces*
ORDINARY F.D.I. POSTMARKS		
(3) GPO Philatelic Bureau, Edinburgh 1	3	
(4) Bethlehem, Llandeilo, Carms	5	
(5) Any other office	1	
SLOGAN POSTMARKS		
(6) First Day of Issue – Bethlehem, Llandeilo. Carms	40	
(7) See the Christmas Illuminations in Cheltenham	10(s)	

(1)

(2)

(4)

(7)

15th January 1969 - BRITISH SHIPS

5d 'Queen Elizabeth 2'; 9d 'Cutty Sark'; 9d Elizabethan Galleon; 9d East Indiaman; 1s 'SS Great Britain'; 1s RMS 'Mauretania'

	ordinary covers £	official covers £
SPECIAL HANDSTAMPS		
(1) Lloyd's New Coffee House Opened 1769, EC3	80	– *n.o.c.*
(2) Cutty Sark Stamp Day, Greenwich SE10	25	– *n.o.c.*
ORDINARY F.D.I. POSTMARKS		
(3) GPO Philatelic Bureau, Edinburgh 1	8	
(4) Belfast, Glasgow or Newcastle – Shipbuilding........*each*	20	
(5) Bristol, Liverpool, Plymouth or Portsmouth...........*each*	20	
(6) London EC or SE1 ....*each*	10	
(7) Southampton – Home port of the QE2	10	
(8) Any other office	6	
C.D.S. POSTMARKS		
(9) Clydebank – Cutty Sark built here	200	
(10) Maritime Mail, London I.S.	250	
(11) The Quarterdeck, Millwall	150	
(12) Southampton or Plymouth..........*each*	60	
(13) Seaview, Isle of Wight	35	
SLOGAN POSTMARKS		
(14) F.D.I. – Greenwich SE10	100	
(15) F.D.I. – Great Britain W2 (SS Great Britain on 1s)	50	

(1)

(2)

3rd March 1969 - FIRST FLIGHT OF CONCORDE

4d Concorde in flight; 9d Plan and elevation; 1s 6d Nose and tail

	ordinary covers £
ORDINARY F.D.I. POSTMARKS	
(1) Filton, Bristol	5
(1a) - ditto - with 'Conseil de L'Europe' postmark	15
(2) GPO Philatelic Bureau, Edinburgh 1	4
(3) Hounslow Middx. – Heathrow	10
(4) Any other office	2

PLEASE READ THE GENERAL NOTES
AT THE BEGINNING OF THIS CATALOGUE
These often provide the answers to enquiries received.

2nd April 1969 - NOTABLE ANNIVERSARIES

5d Alcock & Brown, 9d Europa;
1s International Labour Organisation;
1s 6d NATO; 1s 9d 1st England/Australia flight

	ordinary covers	official covers	
SPECIAL HANDSTAMPS	£	£	
(1) Alcock & Brown, Vickers Vimy, Manchester	30	12	*Man.Airp.(s)*
(2) 20th Anniversary NATO HQ BF 1080 PS	200	150	*N.A.T.O.*
(3) 20th Anniversary NATO SHAPE BF 1081 PS	200	10	*N.A.T.O.(s)*
(4) Hoverlloyd Inaugural Flight, Pegwell Bay	240	8	*Hoverlloyd(s)*
(5) BF 1000 PS (used at Mill Hill)	190	150	*Forces*
(6) The Grammar School Centenary, Doncaster.	175	100	*Grammar Sch.*
ORDINARY F.D.I. POSTMARKS			
(7) Hounslow - Eng./Aust. flight - Heathrow	15		
(8) London SW - Int. Labour Organisation	10		
(9) Manchester - Alcock & Brown	15		
(10) GPO Philatelic Bureau, Edinburgh 1	6		
(11) Any other office	3		
C.D.S. POSTMARKS			
(12) Farnborough, Hants	125		
SLOGAN POSTMARKS			
(13) Manchester Airport Salutes Alcock & Brown	40(s)		
(14) Fly the Prestwick Way	50		
SET of 5 single stamp covers with appropriate pmks....*from*	8		

(1)

(2)

(3)

(4)

28th May 1969 - BRITISH CATHEDRALS

4 x 5d - Durham, York, Canterbury, Edinburgh; 9d St. Paul's; 1s 6d Liverpool

SPECIAL HANDSTAMPS			
(1) Metropolitan Cathedral, Liverpool	20	-	*n.o.c.*
(2) Philatex St. Pauls, London EC	15	-	*n.o.c.*
(3) York Minster	20	30	*York Mins.*
(4) Lewis's Stamp Exhibition, Manchester 1	75	-	*n.oc.*
(5) Croeso 69 Tywyn Merioneth	20	20	*Tywyn*
(6) German British Culture Week BF 1078 PS	30	20	*Forces*
(7) Ulster Recruiting BF 1085 PS	40	20	*Forces*
ORDINARY F.D.I. POSTMARKS			
(8) GPO Philatelic Bureau, Edinburgh 1	5		
(9) London EC - St. Paul's	6		
(10) Canterbury, Durham, Edinburgh, Liverpool or York	10		
(11) Any other office	3		
C.D.S. POSTMARKS			
(12) Alcester (Alcester Church Restoration cover)	75		
(13) Durham	40		
SET of 6 single stamp covers with appropriate pmks	10		

(10)

(7)

(1)

(2)

(10)

1st July 1969 - THE INVESTITURE OF THE PRINCE OF WALES

3 x 5d Caernarvon Castle; 9d Celtic Cross; 1s Prince Charles

SPECIAL HANDSTAMPS			
(1) Croes Geltaidd, Margam Abbey	100	-	*n.o.c.*
(2) Croeso 69, Investiture Day, Cardiff	100	-	*n.o.c.*
(3) Talyllyn Railway, Tywyn, Merioneth	35	40	*Tywyn*
(4) Nettleham, Lincoln	100	80	*Nettleham*
(5) BF 1000 PS (troop camp involved in Investiture)	150	150	*Forces*
(6) Lawn Tennis Championships	150	-	*n.o.c.*
ORDINARY F.D.I. POSTMARKS			
(7) GPO Philatelic Bureau, Edinburgh 1	5		
(8) London SW	3		
(9) Windsor, Berks.	10		
(10) Day of Investiture, Caernarvon	5		
(11) Any other Welsh postmark	3		
(12) Any other office	2		
C.D.S. POSTMARKS			
(13) Buckingham Palace, SW1	250		
(14) House of Commons or House of Lords....*each*	65		
(15) Windsor Castle, Berks	250		
SLOGAN POSTMARKS			
(16) Dydd yr Arwisgo, Investiture Day, Caernarvon	275		
(17) Wales Tomorrow Exhibition, Cardiff	20(s)		

(3)

(4)

(2)

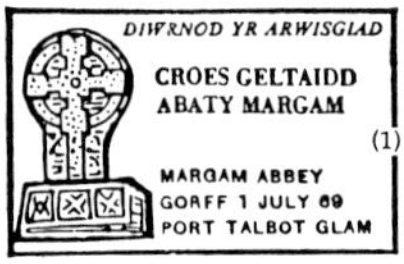

(1)

(16)

(17)
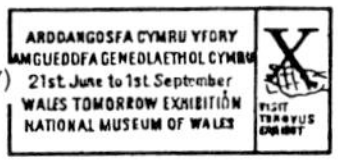

1969

13th August 1969 - GANDHI CENTENARY YEAR

1s 6d Mahatma Gandhi

	ordinary covers	official covers	
SPECIAL HANDSTAMPS	£	£	
(1) Gandhi Centenary Year HCRC, E8	5	30	*Hackney CRC*
(2) Trade Fair & Exhibition Llanelli, Carms	100	-	*n.o.c.*
(3) International Youth Camp, Colchester	100	-	*n.o.c.*
ORDINARY F.D.I. POSTMARKS			
(4) GPO Philatelic Bureau, Edinburgh 1	3		
(5) Any other office	2		

(3)

(2)

1st October 1969 - POST OFFICE TECHNOLOGY

5d Giro; 9d & 1s Telecommunications; 1s 6d Automatic Sorting

	ordinary covers	official covers	
SPECIAL HANDSTAMPS			
(1) Posted in the Post Office Tower, W1	5	-	*n.o.c.*
(2) Post Office Technology University College, WC1	5	-	*n.o.c.*
(3) Philatelic Stand Ideal Homes, Birmingham	175	-	*n.o.c.*
(4) 1st Southampton Boat Show, Mayflower Park	175	20	*Boat Show(s)*
(5) National Postal Museum, EC1	60	-	*Post Office*
ORDINARY F.D.I. POSTMARKS			
(6) GPO Philatelic Bureau. Edinburgh 1	2		
(7) Norwich - first use of postal coding	4		
(8) Any other office	1		
C.D.S. POSTMARKS			
(9) Bootle - National Giro HQ - featured on 5d value	15(s)		
SLOGAN POSTMARKS			
(10) Remember to use the Postcode	400		
SET of 4 single stamp covers with appropriate postmarks - usually (1), (2), (7) and (9)	25		

(1)

(5)

(2)

(3)

26th November 1969 - CHRISTMAS

4d, 5d, 1s 6d The Nativity

	ordinary covers	official covers	
SPECIAL HANDSTAMPS			
(1) Jerusalem, Skellingthorpe, Lincs	40	40	*Temple of Jerusalem*
ORDINARY F.D.I. POSTMARKS			
(2) GPO Philatelic Bureau, Edinburgh 1	3		
(3) Bethlehem, Llandeilo, Carms	3		
(4) Any other office	2		
C.D.S. POSTMARKS			
(5) Bethlehem, Llandeilo, Carms	150		
(6) Nasareth, Gwynedd	150		
SLOGAN POSTMARKS			
(7) First Day of Issue - Bethlehem, Llandeilo, Carms	60		
(8) See the Christmas Illuminations in Cheltenham	40(s)		
(9) Christmas 69 Dick Whittington, Lewisham	100		
(10) National Childrens Home	50		

(1)

(8)

11th February 1970 - BRITISH RURAL ARCHITECTURE

5d Fife harling; 9d Cotswold limestone; 1s Welsh stucco; 1s 6d Ulster thatch

	ordinary covers	
ORDINARY F.D.I. POSTMARKS		
(1) British Philatelic Bureau. Edinburgh 1	3	
(2) Aberaeron - 1s Welsh stucco	5	
(3) Belfast (1s 6d) or Dunfermline (5d) *each*	5	
(4) Edinburgh (5d) or Gloucester (9d) *each*	5	
(5) Any other office	2	
C.D.S. POSTMARKS		
(6) Auchtermuchty, Fife - 5d Fife harling	10(s)	
(7) Bibury, Cirencester - 9d Cotswold limestone	100	
(8) Chipping Campden - 9p Almshouses	100	
(9) Cirencester, or Stroud - 9d Cotswold limestone	75	
(10) Culross, Dunfermline, Fife - 5d Fife harling	80	
(11) Holywood, Co. Down - 1s 6d Ulster thatch	20(s)	
SLOGAN POSTMARKS		
(12) Keep Britain Green - European Conservation Year	150	
(13) Visit the 1970 Furniture Show - (*plain cover*)	20	
SET of 4 single stamp covers with appropriate pmks	6	

(2)

(3)

(3)

(9)

(12)

(13)

1st April 1970 - GENERAL ANNIVERSARIES

5d Declaration of Arbroath; 9d Florence Nightingale; 1s International Co-operative Alliance; 1s 6d Mayflower; 1s 9d Royal Astronomical Society

	ordinary covers	official covers
SPECIAL HANDSTAMPS	£	£
(1) British Anniversary Stamps, Canterbury, Kent	17	- *n.o.c.*
(2) Florence Nightingale Hospital, London NW1	50	- *n.o.c.*
(3) Florence Nightingale Birthday Exhibition, SE1	30	50 *F.N. Cttee*
(4) The Crimean War, BF 1206 PS	275	8 *Forces(s)*
(5) 150th Anniv. Florence Nightingale, BF 1121 PS	175	8 *Forces(s)*
(6) 150th Anniv. Florence Nightingale, BF 1205 PS	200	8 *Forces(s)*
(7) London Co-op Golden Year, London E15	225	8 *Co-op(s)*
(8) International Co-operative Alliance ICA, W1	175	- *n.o.c.*
(9) Mayflower '70, Scrooby, Doncaster	175	8 *Scrooby(s)*
(10) Sir William Herschel, Slough	65	- *n.o.c.*
(11) Air-sea Warfare Dev. Unit, RAF Ballykelly	225	- *n.o.c.*
(12) Air Mountains Base, Gibraltar, BF 1112 PS	225	8 *Forces(s)*
ORDINARY F.D.I. POSTMARKS		
(13) British Philatelic Bureau, Edinburgh 1	4	
(14) Arbroath - 5d value Declaration of Arbroath	25	
(15) Billericay - associated with 'Mayflower'	12	
(16) Boston - associated with 'Mayflower'	12	
(17) London W1 - World HQ of ICA	10	
(18) Plymouth - 1s 6d Pilgrim Fathers	10	
(19) Rochdale - first Co-op	15	
(20) Southampton - Pilgrim Fathers	10	
(21) Any other office	3	
C.D.S. POSTMARKS		
(22) Immingham or Scrooby - Pilgrim Fathers *each*	20(s)	
SLOGAN POSTMARKS		
(23) Plymouth Mayflower 70, 2 May - 30 Sept	35(s)	
(24) Boston Lincs. Mayflower 70, May - Sept	35(s)	
SET of 5 single stamp covers with appropriate pmks....*from*	8	

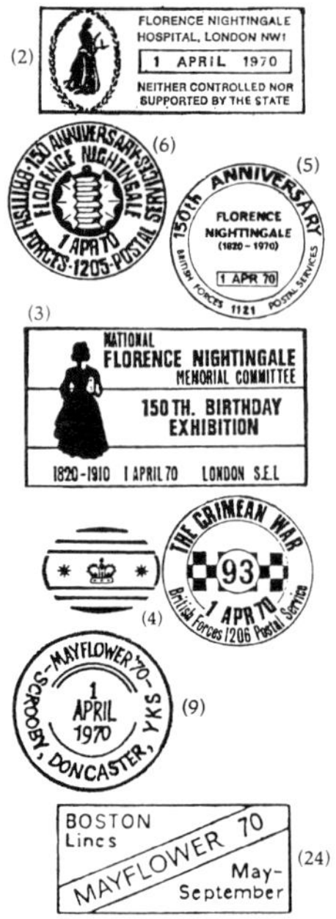

3rd June 1970 - LITERARY ANNIVERSARIES

4 x 5d Dickens characters; 1s 6d Wordsworth

	ordinary covers	official covers
SPECIAL HANDSTAMPS		
(1) E78 Chigwell, Essex	50	60 *Chigwell*
(2) Dickens Fellowship, Broadstairs Branch	30	50 *Broadstairs*
(3) Dickens Centenary Year, Old Curiosity Shop, WC2	20	30 *Cameo (g)*
(4) Dickens Centenary, Pickwick, Corsham	50	80 *Corsham*
(5) David Copperfield, Dickens, Winterbourne	50	80 *Winterbourne*
(6) Living Exhibition '70, Sheffield	n.k.	10 *Exhib.(s)*
ORDINARY F.D.I. POSTMARKS		
(7) British Philatelic Bureau, Edinburgh 1	5	
(8) Broadstairs - 'Bleak House'	10	
(9) Cambridge - Wordsworth educated at St. John's	10	
(10) Cockermouth - birthplace of Wordsworth in 1770	25	
(11) Portsmouth - Dickens born here in 1812	10	
(12) RochesterDickens died here in 1870	10	
(13) Any other office	5	
C.D.S. POSTMARKS		
(14) Ambleside - Wordsworth lived at Rydal Mount	150	
(15) Grasmere - Wordsworth lived at Dove Cottage	150	
(16) Portsmouth - Dickens born here in 1812	80	
SLOGAN POSTMARKS		
(17) First Day of Issue - Broadstairs	90	
(18) International Stamp Exhibition (4 x 5d only)	25	
PAIR of covers (4 x 5d on one; 1s 6d on the other) with appropriate postmarks *from*	3	

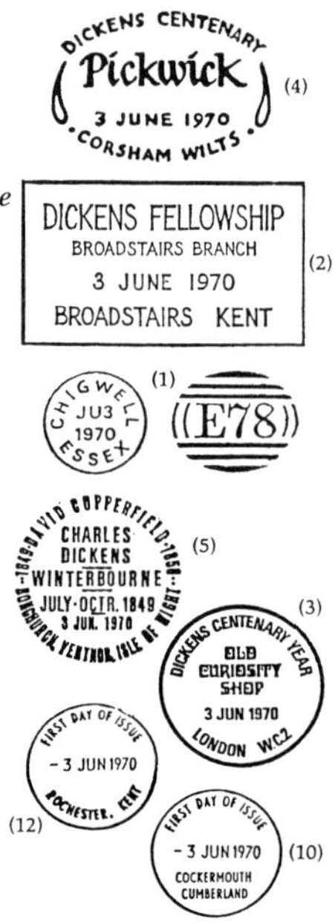

PLEASE READ THE GENERAL NOTESAT THE BEGINNING OF THIS CATALOGUE

These often provide the answers to enquiries received.

Prices should be treated as a general guide.

(s) indicates covers are only known with a single value.

15th July 1970 – IXth BRITISH COMMONWEALTH GAMES EDINBURGH

5d Runners; 1s 6d Swimmers; 1s 9d Cyclists

SPECIAL HANDSTAMPS	ordinary covers £	official covers £	
(1) Centenary RCT, BF 1123 PS	165	5	*Forces(s)*
(2) Enterprise Exhibition Philatelic Stand, Nottingham	165	20	*Nott. Fest.(s)*
(3) Thos. Becket 1170-1970, Canterbury	165	8	*Cant. Cath.(s)*
(4) Cardigan Secondary School	165	100	*Card. Sch.*
(5) IXth Assembly of European Municipalities, SE1	165	–	*n.o.c.*
(6) Great Yorkshire Show, Harrogate	165	10	*G.Y. Show(s)*
(7) Victoria Cross, BF 1210 PS	165	5	*Forces(s)*
(8) Rorke's Drift, BF 1211 PS	165	5	*Forces(s)*
ORDINARY F.D.I. POSTMARKS			
(9) British Philatelic Bureau, Edinburgh 1	3		
(10) Edinburgh 1	4		
(11) Any other office	2		
C.D.S. POSTMARKS			
(12) Edinburgh Mobile Post Office	125		
SLOGAN POSTMARKS			
(13) The National Postal Museum	40		
(14) First Day of Issue – Edinburgh, Great Britain	55		
(15) Edinburgh – wavy line	25		

(2)

(6)

(7)

18th September 1970 – INTERNATIONAL STAMP EXHIBITION 'PHILYMPIA'

5d (Penny Black); 9d (1s Green); 1s 6d (4d Carmine)

SPECIAL HANDSTAMPS			
(1) British Post Office Philatelic Bureau, Edinburgh	2	–	*Post Office*
(2) Philympia Day, London	4	–	*Post Office*
(3) First Flight, Philympia, Calne-IOW., Calne, Wilts	75	15	*B.N.I.*(s)*
(4) First Flight, Philympia, IOW-Calne, Bembridge, IOW	75	15	*B.N.I.*(s)*
(5) 25th Anniv. 23 Base Workshop REME, BF 1136 PS	50	50	*Forces*
(6) National Postal Museum	25	–	*n.o.c.*
**B.N.I. = Britten Norman Islander.*			
ORDINARY F.D.I. POSTMARKS			
(7) London W1 (local F.D.I. for Philympia)	3		
(8) Any other office	1		
C.D.S. POSTMARKS			
(9) House of Commons, SW1 (Postage Act)	40		
(10) Olympia W14	250		
SLOGAN POSTMARKS			
(11) International Stamp Exhibition, Philympia 70	500		
(12) Any Postcode slogans	35		

(1)

(3)

(2)

(11)

25th November 1970 – CHRISTMAS

4d, 5d, 1s 6d The Nativity

SPECIAL HANDSTAMPS			
(1) British Post Office Philatelic Bureau, Edinburgh	2	–	*Post Office*
(2) First Day of Issue – Bethlehem, Llandeilo, Carms	3	–	*Post Office*
(3) Lilleshall Parish Church AD670-1970	100	120	*Lill. P.Ch.*
ORDINARY F.D.I. POSTMARKS			
(4) Any office	1		
SLOGAN POSTMARKS			
(5) First Day of Issue – Bethlehem, Llandeilo, Carms	100		
(6) See the Christmas Illuminations, Cheltenham	40(s)		

(2)

(3)

Ordinary F.D.I. postmarks are now only listed if relevant to a stamp issue.

16th June 1971 – ULSTER '71 PAINTINGS

3p, 7½p, 9p Landscapes

SPECIAL HANDSTAMPS			
(1) First Day of Issue – Philatelic Bureau	3	–	*Post Office*
(2) First Day of Issue – Belfast	5	–	*Post Office*
(3) First Day of Issue – Londonderry	30	–	*Post Office*
(4) First Day of Issue – Coleraine	120	–	*Post Office*
(5) First Day of Issue – Newry	120	–	*Post Office*

(2)

(8)

(3)

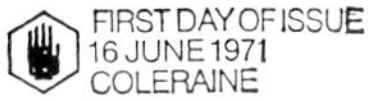

(4)

Ulster Paintings (contd.)

	ordinary covers £	official covers £
(6) First Day of Issue - Ballymena	120	- *Post Office*
(7) First Day of Issue - Armagh	120	- *Post Office*
(8) First Day of Issue - Portadown	120	- *Post Office*
(9) First Day of Issue - Cookstown	120	- *Post Office*
(10) First Day of Issue - Omagh	120	- *Post Office*
(11) First Day of Issue - Enniskillen	120	- *Post Office*
(12) Ulster 71 Exhibition Botanic Gardens, Belfast	60	- *n.o.c.*
(13) Philatelic Cong., Ulster Paintings Day, Norwich	40	50 *Phil Congress*

(1)

(12)

C.D.S. POSTMARKS

(14) Dungiven, Londonderry (3p) } Post Offices situated		
(15) Hilltown, Down (7½p) } close to the scenes		
(16) Newcastle, Down (9p) } depicted on stamps	75(set of three)	
(17) Northern Parliament, Belfast	50	

28th July 1971 - LITERARY ANNIVERSARIES

3p Keats; 5p Gray; 7½p Scott

SPECIAL HANDSTAMPS

(1) First Day of Issue - Philatelic Bureau	4	- *Post Office*
(2) First Day of Issue - London EC	8	- *Post Office*
(3) John Keats, Shanklin 1819, Isle of Wight	80	100 *Shank Library*
(4) Thomas Gray Bicentenary, Stoke Poges	30	125 *Stoke Court*
(4a) Ditto with Carried by Mailcoach cachet	40	125 *Stoke Court*
(5) National Collectors Fair, Royal Horticultural Hall	135	- *n.o.c.*
(6) Ulster 71 Exhibition, Botanic Gardens, Belfast	130	- *n.o.c.*

(5)

(4)

ORDINARY F.D.I. POSTMARKS

(7) Edinburgh - birthplace of Sir Walter Scott	6	

C.D.S. POSTMARKS

(8) Melrose (7½p) - Scott died at Abbotsford, Melrose	5(s)	
SET of 3 single stamp covers with appropriate pmks	6	

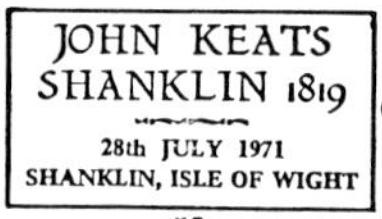

(3)

25th August 1971 - GENERAL ANNIVERSARIES

3p British Legion; 7½p City of York; 9p Rugby Football Union

SPECIAL HANDSTAMPS

(1) First Day of Issue - Philatelic Bureau	3	- *Post Office*
(2) First Day of Issue - Twickenham	15	- *Post Office*
(3) First Day of Issue - Maidstone	15	- *Post Office*
(4) First Day of Issue - York	15	- *Post Office*
(5) Rugby Football Union Centenary, Twickenham	150	225 *R.F.U.*
(6) Rugby Football Union Centenary Year, Rugby	175	200 *Rugby School*
(7) Royal British Legion 50th Anniv., BF 1182 PS	175	10 *Brit. Legion(s)*
(8) 70th Anniversary Royal Aero Club, BF 1170 PS	185	10 *RAF Museum(s)*
(9) Ulster 71 Exhibition, Botanic Gardens, Belfast	160	- *n.o.c.*
(10) Sir Walter Scott Bicentenary, Abbotsford	160	- *n.o.c.*

(8)

(2)

(4)

C.D.S. POSTMARKS

(11) Any Field Post Office	20	
SET of 3 single stamp covers with appropriate pmks - usually (2), (3) and (4)	6	

22nd September 1971 - BRITISH ARCHITECTURE MODERN UNIVERSITY BUILDINGS

3p Aberystwyth; 5p Southampton; 7½p Leicester; 9p Essex

SPECIAL HANDSTAMPS

(1) First Day of Issue - Philatelic Bureau	3	- *Post Office*
(2) First Day of Issue - Aberystwyth	13	- *Post Office*
(3) First Day of Issue - Colchester	13	- *Post Office*
(4) First Day of Issue - Leicester	13	- *Post Office*
(5) First Day of Issue - Southampton	13	- *Post Office*
(6) Opening of the Postal Management College, Rugby	150	200 *P. Man. Coll.*
(7) Sir Walter Scott Bicentenary, Abbotsford	150	- *n.o.c.*
SET of 4 single stamp covers with appropriate postmarks - usually (2), (3), (4) and (5)	6	

(6)

(5)

(4)

(2)

(3)

Note: Welsh bilingual F.D.I. cancellations for the first time were used at the following offices:- Cardiff, Caernarvon, Carmarthen, Colwyn Bay, Haverfordwest, Llandudno, Llanelli, Newport, Monmouthshire, Pontypridd, Rhondda, Rhyl, and Swansea. These will only be included and priced in the catalogue if relevant to an issue.

13th October 1971 - CHRISTMAS

2½p, 3p, 7½p Stained Glass at Canterbury Cathedral

	ordinary covers £	official covers £	
SPECIAL HANDSTAMPS			
(1) First Day of Issue - Philatelic Bureau	4	-	*Post Office*
(2) First Day of Issue - Bethlehem, Llandeilo, Carms	7	-	*Post Office*
(3) First Day of Issue - Canterbury	7	-	*Post Office*
(4) Commonwealth Postal Conference, SW1	135	-	*n.o.c.*
(5) 1900th Anniversary, Emperor Serverus, York	135	160	*Emp. Serv.*

(3)

(5)

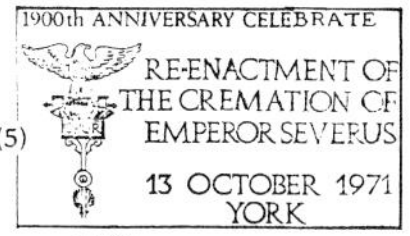

16th February 1972 - BRITISH POLAR EXPLORERS

3p Ross; 5p Frobisher; 7½p Hudson; 9p Scott

SPECIAL HANDSTAMPS			
(1) First Day of Issue - Philatelic Bureau	8	-	*Post Office*
(2) First Day of Issue - London WC	10	-	*Post Office*
ORDINARY F.D.I. POSTMARKS			
(3) Plymouth	15		
C.D.S. POSTMARKS			
(4) Reykjavik, Iceland BFPS (Backstamped) FPO 376	500		
(5) Gravesend, Kent (7½p)	12(s)		
(6) Greenwich B.O. S.E.10	12(s)		
SET of 4 single stamp covers with appropriate pmks - usually (2), (3), (5) and (6)	25		

(1)

(2)

26th April 1972 - GENERAL ANNIVERSARIES

3p Tutankhamun; 7½p HM Coastguard; 9p Ralph Vaughan Williams

SPECIAL HANDSTAMPS			
(1) First Day of Issue - Philatelic Bureau	3	-	*Post Office*
(2) First Day of Issue - London EC	5	-	*Post Office*
(3) Treasures of Tutankhamun Exhibition, WC	30	40	*Tut. Exhib.*
(4) Vaughan Williams Centenary, Down Ampney	30	10	*D. Ampney(s)*
(5) H .M. Coastguard 1822-1972, Hartland Point	30	40	*Philart*
(6) 5th Anniversary Hovercraft Trials BF 1270 PS	125	175	*Hovercraft*
SLOGAN POSTMARKS			
(7) Treasures of Tutankhamun British Museum	25(s)		
SET of 3 single stamp covers with appropriate pmks - usually (3), (4) and (5)	6		

(1)

(2)

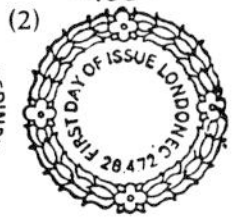

(6)

(7)

21st June 1972 - BRITISH ARCHITECTURE - VILLAGE CHURCHES

3p Greensted; 4p Earls Barton; 5p Letheringsett;
7½p Helpringham; 9p Huish Episcopi.

SPECIAL HANDSTAMPS			
(1) First Day of Issue - Philatelic Bureau	4	-	*Post Office*
(2) First Day of Issue - Canterbury	6	-	*Post Office*
(3) World's Oldest Wooden Church, Greensted	25	70	*St. Andrew's*
(4) Village Churches, AD 970 Earls Barton	17	50	*Earls Barton*
(5) First Day of Issue Exhibition, Huish Episcopi	25	50	*St. Mary's*
(6) Village Churches, Helpringham, Sleaford	25	50	*Helpringham*
(7) Village Churches, Letheringsett, Holt	25	-	*n.o.c.*
(8) Parish Church of St. Mary, Langley	150	170	*Philart*
(9) St. Augustine's Church, Kilburn, NW6	150	200	*St. Augustine's*
(10) Festival of Berkswell, Coventry	170	175	*Berkswell*
(11) Treasures of Tutankhamun Exhibition, WC	100	-	*n.o.c.*
(12) Royal Engineers Military Aeronautics, BF 1312 PS	150	175	*Royal Eng. 3*
C.D.S. POSTMARKS			
(13) Earls Barton, Northampton	100		
(14) New Romney, Kent (St. Nicholas Cover)	75		
SET of 5 single stamp covers with appropriate pmks - usually (3), (4), (5), (6) and (7)	12		

(6)

(2)

(12)

(9)

(7)

> PLEASE READ THE GENERAL NOTES
> AT THE BEGINNING OF THIS CATALOGUE
> These often provide the answers to enquiries received.

13th September 1972 - B.B.C. & BROADCASTING HISTORY

3p, 5p, 7½p BBC; 9p Marconi/Kemp Experiments

	ordinary covers	official covers	
SPECIAL HANDSTAMPS	£	£	
(1) First Day of Issue - Philatelic Bureau	5	-	*Post Office*
(2) First Day of Issue - London W1	10	-	*Post Office*
(3) Marconi-Kemp Wireless Experiments, Chelmsford	35	50	*Mar. Phil Soc*
(4) Royal Engineers, Army Wireless, BF 1326 PS	50	60	*Royal Eng. 4*
(5) Marconi's First Wireless, Flatholm Island	30	125	*Barry College*
(6) BBC Radio Leicester, 5th Anniversary Year	50	75	*Radio Leics*
(7) 21st Anniv T.V. Network Opened, Gloucester	45	100	*British Relay*
(8) Humberside's Own Home Service, Hull	45	100	*Radio Hull*
(9) BBC 50th Anniversary, Pebble Mill, Birmingham	400	*	*Pebble Mill*
(10) John Knox Quatercentenary - Philatelic Bureau	150	-	*n.o.c.*
(11) Manchester City FC Kick-Off in UEFA Cup	160	225	*Dawn*
(12) Treasures of Tutankhamun Exhibition, WC	160	-	*n.o.c.*

**Two types of Pebble Mill official covers exist:*
- covers with BBC logo only @ £150; and fully illustrated covers @ £350.

ORDINARY F.D.I. POSTMARKS		
(13) Brighton (BBC Radio Brighton cover)	20	
(14) Chelmsford (Marconi Philatelic Society cover)	20	
SLOGAN POSTMARKS		
(15) Medium Wave BBC Radio Brighton 202 Metres	350	
PAIR of covers (3p, 5p, 7½p on one; 9p on the other) with appropriate postmarks	*from*	6

(5)

(11)

(1)

(3)

18th October 1972 - CHRISTMAS

2½p, 3p, 7½p Angels

	ordinary covers	official covers	
SPECIAL HANDSTAMPS			
(1) First Day of Issue - Philatelic Bureau	3	-	*Post Office*
(2) First Day of Issue - Bethlehem, Llandeilo, Carms	5	-	*Post Office*
(3) Treasures of Tutankhamun Exhibition, WC	100	-	*n.o.c.*
(4) Rowntree's Philatelic Exhibition, Scarborough	150	-	*n.o.c.*
(5) John Knox Quatercentenary, Philatelic Bureau	125	-	*n.o.c.*
(6) Borough Jubilee 1922-1972, Watford	175	150	*Watford B.C.*

(1)

(6)
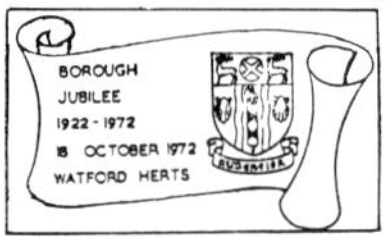

20th November 1972 - SILVER WEDDING ANNIVERSARY

3p, 20p H.M. The Queen and Prince Philip

	ordinary covers	official covers	
SPECIAL HANDSTAMPS			
(1) First Day of Issue - Philatelic Bureau	4	-	*Post Office*
(2) First Day of Issue - Windsor	8	-	*Post Office*
(3) Royal Silver Wedding, Westminster Abbey, SW1	15	15	*Philart ACC 6*
(4) Commemorating Silver Wedding, BF 1307 PS	20	25	*RAF M/Batten*
(5) 16th/5th Queens Royal Lancers, BF 1922 PS	30	50	*R. Lancers*
(6) Royal Regiment of Artillery, BF 1340 PS	40	80	*R.R.A.*
(7) Royal Engineers Military Tanks, BF 1338 PS	40	60	*Royal Eng. 7*
(8) Charlton Athletic, FA Cup Winners	110	120	*Phil. Prom.*
(9) Fiftieth Anniv. of the BBC, W1	125	-	*n.o.c.*
(10) Treasures of Tutankhamun Exhibition, WC	125	-	*n.o.c.*
(11) John Knox Quatercentenary, Philatelic Bureau	125	-	*n.o.c.*
C.D.S. POSTMARKS			
(12) Buckingham Palace, S.W.1	150		
(13) House of Commons, S.W.1	30		
(14) House of Lords, S.W.1	40		
(15) Windsor Castle, Windsor, Berks	150		

(4)

(2)
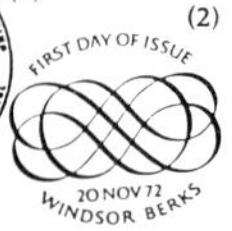

(6)

(8)

3rd January 1973 - EUROPEAN COMMUNITIES

3p, 2 x 5p Maps of Europe (jig-saw design)

	ordinary covers	official covers	
SPECIAL HANDSTAMPS			
(1) First Day of Issue - Philatelic Bureau	4	-	*Post Office*
(2) New Parcel Office, Southampton	35	45	*I.D.C.*
(3) Royal Engineers, Brennan Torpedo, BF 1343 PS	30	35	*Royal Eng. 8*
ORDINARY F.D.I. POSTMARKS			
(4) Dover, Kent	8		
(4a) Dover, Kent with PAQUEBOT markings	35		
(5) Folkestone, Kent	8		
(5a) Folkestone, Kent with PAQUEBOT markings	25		
(6) Harrow & Wembley ('Fanfare for Europe' cover)	35		

(2)

(5)

(3)

1973 European Communities (contd.)

	ordinary covers	official covers
C.D.S. POSTMARKS	£	£
(7) Calais with PAQUEBOT markings	35	
(8) Conseil de l'Europe Strasbourg	8	
(9) Harwich (Harwich Gateway to Europe cover)	30	
(10) House of Commons, S.W.1	50	
(11) House of Lords, S.W.1	60	
(12) Harrow & Wembley (Britain v. EEC Football cachet)	25	

28th February 1973 - BRITISH TREES - THE OAK

9p Oak Tree

SPECIAL HANDSTAMPS			
(1) First Day of Issue - Philatelic Bureau	5	-	*Post Office*
(2) Stampex 73, Royal Horticultural Hall, SW1	7	10	*Stampex*
(3) Hatfield Broad Oak, Plant a Tree Exhibition	10	-	*n.o.c.*
(4) Tree Planting Year, Westonbirt Arboretum,	10	15	*Cotswold (g)*
C.D.S. POSTMARKS			
(5) Oakham, Four Oaks or similar	50		

(2)

(3)

(4)

18th April 1973 - BRITISH EXPLORERS

2 x 3p Livingstone & Stanley; 5p Drake; 7½p Raleigh; 9p Sturt

SPECIAL HANDSTAMPS			
(1) First Day of Issue - Philatelic Bureau	8	-	*Post Office*
(2) Sir Walter Raleigh Exhib., Budleigh Salterton	20	-	*n.o.c.*
(3) Drake's Island Adventure Centre, Plymouth	20	50	*Cotswold*
ORDINARY F.D.I. POSTMARKS			
(4) Plymouth, Devon	10		
(5) Blantyre, Glasgow - birthplace of Livingstone	25		
(6) Denbigh - birthplace of Stanley	20		
(7) Gloucestershire - Sturt buried here	30		
C.D.S. POSTMARKS			
(8) Mildenhall (Scientific Explorers Society cover)	110		
(9) Livingstone, W Lothian	90		
SET of 5 single stamp covers with appropriate pmks	8		

(2)

(3)

16th May 1973 - CENTENARY OF COUNTY CRICKET

3p, 7½p. 9p W.G. Grace - sketches by Harry Furniss

SPECIAL HANDSTAMPS			
(1) First Day of Issue - Philatelic Bureau	4	-	*Post Office*
(2) First Day of Issue - Lord's London NW	6	-	*Post Office*
(3) English County Cricket Exhibition, Lord's, NW8	10	15	*TCCB**
(4) County Cricket Centenary, Chelmsford	25	30	*TCCB**
(5) Headquarters Surrey C.C.C., The Oval, SE11	25	30	*TCCB**
(6) Headquarters Sussex C.C.C., Hove	25	30	*TCCB**
(7) Birthplace of County Cricket, Hambledon	50	100	*Porton Serv*
(8) Downend Cricket Club Exhibition, W.G. Grace	20	25	*Cotswold (g)*
(9) Yorkshire v. Hampshire, Headingley, Leeds	25	30	*TCCB**
(10) IBRA Exhibition Munich, BF 1400 PS	50	90	*BFPS*
ORDINARY F.D.I. POSTMARKS			
(11) Derby - Derbyshire C.C.C.	9		
(12) Cardiff - Glamorgan C.C.C.	9		
(13) Bristol - Gloucestershire C.C.C.	9		
(14) Southampton - Hampshire C.C.C	9		
(15) Canterbury - Kent C.C.C.	9		
(16) Manchester - Lancashire C.C.C.	9		
(17) Leicester - Leicestershire C.C.C.	9		
(18) Northampton - Northamptonshire C.C.C.	9		
(19) Nottingham - Nottinghamshire C.C.C.	9		
(20) Taunton - Somerset C.C.C.	9		
(21) Birmingham - Warwickshire C.C.C.	9		
(22) Worcester - Worcestershire C.C.C.	9		

**Note: Stamp Publicity of Worthing produced a set of 18 covers for the TCCB (Test & County Cricket Board). The set of covers are valued at around £200.*

(5)

(8)

(9)

(6)

(4)

(3)

Prices are for good clean, unaddressed, covers with the full set of stamps.

4th July 1973 - BRITISH PAINTINGS

3p, 7½p Sir Joshua Reynolds; 5p, 9p Sir Henry Raeburn

SPECIAL HANDSTAMPS	ordinary covers £	official covers £	
(1) First Day of Issue - Philatelic Bureau	5	-	*Post Office*
(2) Sir Joshua Reynolds, Royal Academy, W1	10	40	*R. Academy*
(3) Douglas, Isle of Man	30	25	*Post Office*
(4) Whitehaven, Cumberland	30	3	*Post Office(s)*
(5) The Championships 1973 A.E.L.T.C., Wimbledon	110	-	*n.o.c.*
(6) Monarchy 1000, Bath	110	-	*n.o.c.*
(7) Death of General Sikorski Exhibition, SW7	110	-	*n.o.c.*
(8) Llangollen International Musical Eisteddfod	110	5	*Eisteddfod(s)*
(9) APEX 1973, Manchester	85	100	*APEX*
ORDINARY F.D.I. POSTMARKS			
(10) Edinburgh - birthplace of Raeburn	10		
(11) Plymouth - birthplace of Reynolds	10		

(1)

(7)

(9)

15th August 1973 - INIGO JONES - 400th ANNIVERSARY

3p St. Paul's, Covent Garden; 3p Court Masque Costumes;
5p Prince's Lodging, Newmarket; 5p Court Masque Stage Scene

SPECIAL HANDSTAMPS			
(1) First Day of Issue - Philatelic Bureau	5	-	*Post Office*
(2) Inigo Jones Exhibition, Wilton House, Salisbury	10	25	*Cotswold (g)*
(3) 400th Anniversary of Inigo Jones, Newmarket	10	40	*Rotary*
(4) Livestock Market Centenary, Northampton	120	-	*n.o.c.*
(5) Monarchy 1000, Bath	120	-	*n.o.c.*
(6) Third International Orthodontic Congress, SE	120	100	*I.O.C.*
ORDINARY F.D.I. POSTMARKS			
(7) London W.C.	5		
SLOGAN POSTMARKS			
(8) Inigo Jones Banqueting House (on 2 covers)	425		

(8)

(2)

12th September 1973 - PARLIAMENTARY CONFERENCE

8p, 10p Palace of Westminster

SPECIAL HANDSTAMPS			
(1) First Day of Issue - Philatelic Bureau	4	-	*Post Office*
(2) Houses of Parliament, London SW1	6	-	*n.o.c.*
(3) Monarchy 1000, Bath	135	-	*n.o.c.*
(4) British Pharmaceutical Conference 1973, WC	135	-	*n.o.c.*
(5) Surrey's First Sixth Form College, Farnham	135	135	*Farn. Coll.*
C.D.S. POSTMARKS			
(6) Buckingham Palace, S.W.1	125		
(7) House of Commons, S.W.1	75		
(8) House of Lords, S.W.1	85		

(1)

(2)

(5)

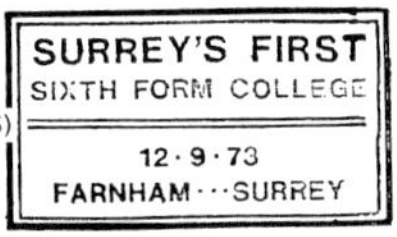

14th November 1973 - ROYAL WEDDING

3½p, 20p Princess Anne and Captain Mark Phillips

SPECIAL HANDSTAMPS			
(1) First Day of Issue - Philatelic Bureau	3	-	*Post Office*
(2) First Day of Issue - Windsor	6	-	*Post Office*
(3) First Day of Issue - Westminster Abbey	6	-	*Post Office*
(4) Royal Wedding, Great Somerford, Chippenham	15	-	*n.o.c.*
(5) Queens Dragoon Guards BF 1434 PS	20	3	*Dragoons(s)*
(6) Royal Engineers, Gibraltar, BF 1387 PS	15	30	*Royal Eng. 17*
(7) The Chinese Exhibition, London W1	20	40	*Ch. Exhib.*
C.D.S. POSTMARKS			
(8) Buckingham Palace, S.W.1	125		
(9) Great Somerford, Chippenham, Wilts	30		
(10) House of Commons or House of Lords *each*	35		
(11) Sandhurst, Camberley	25		
(12) Windsor Castle, Windsor, Berks	150		

(1)

(2)

(6)

(8)

(12)

28th November 1973 - CHRISTMAS

5 x 3p; 3½p 'Good King Wenceslas'

SPECIAL HANDSTAMPS			
(1) First Day of Issue - Philatelic Bureau	4	-	*Post Office*
(2) First Day of Issue - Bethlehem, Llandeilo, Carms	8	-	*Post Office*
(3) The Chinese Exhibition, London W1	50	60	*Ch. Exhib.*
(4) 141st Anniv. Birth of Lewis Carroll, Daresbury	125	125	*Ches. Hist. 3*

(1)

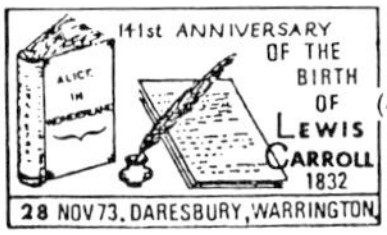

(4)

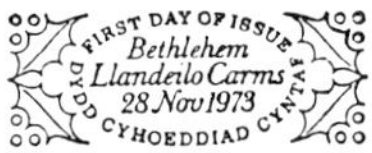

(2)

27th February 1974 - BRITISH TREES - THE HORSE CHESTNUT
10p Horse Chestnut

SPECIAL HANDSTAMPS	ordinary covers £	official covers £	
(1) First Day of Issue - Philatelic Bureau	5	-	*Post Office*
(2) Stampex, Royal Horticultural Hall SW1	8	15	*Stampex*

(2)

24th April 1974 - FIRST FIRE SERVICE LEGISLATION
3½p, 5½p, 8p, 10p Early Fire Engines

SPECIAL HANDSTAMPS			
(1) First Day of Issue - Philatelic Bureau	5	-	**Post Office*
(2) Binns Philatelic & Fire Exhibition, Sunderland	35	-	*n.o.c.*
(3) Open Day, Avon County Fire Brigade, Bristol	20	25	*Cotswold (g)*
(4) Cambridgeshire Fire & Rescue Service	30	80	*Cambs C.C.*
(5) Lansing Bagnall 25 Years at Basingstoke	175	250	*Lan. Bag.*
(6) MCC v Hampshire, NW8	175	200	*S.P.*

**Overprinted: 'Merryweather - the first name in firefighting' or 'Science Museum Souvenir - firefighting collection' prices £7 and £25 respectively.*

ORDINARY F.D.I. POSTMARKS	
(7) London S.E.1 - H.Q. London Fire Brigade	15

C.D.S. POSTMARKS	
(8) Burnt House Lane, Exeter	450
(9) Hose, Melton Mowbray	250
(10) House of Commons, S.W.1	50
(11) House of Lords, S.W.1	40
(12) Tooley St., SE 1 - first fire fought by Ins. Co. brigade	275

SLOGAN POSTMARKS	
(13) The Fire Brigade Needs Men of Courage	575

(1)

(3)

(4)

(13)

12th June 1974 - CENTENARY OF UNIVERSAL POSTAL UNION
3½p P&O Packet Steamer; 5½p First Official Airmail;
8p Air mail Blue Van and Postbox; 10p Imperial Airways Flyingboat

SPECIAL HANDSTAMPS			
(1) First Day of Issue - Philatelic Bureau	5	-	*Post Office*
(1a) Ditto with 'Great Britain Day INTERNABA' cachet	10	-	*Post Office*
(2) Imperial Airways Flying Boat, Southampton	10	75	*Imp. Air.*
(3) Visit of Golden Hind ll, London E.C.	130	-	*n.o.c.*
(4) Churchill Centenary Exhib., Somerset House, WC	130	-	*n.o.c.*
(5) Nat. Postal Museum (reprinted 1890 Jubilee cover)	50	-	*n.o.c.*

ORDINARY F.D.I. POSTMARKS	
(6) Windsor - First Official Airmail Windsor/London	20
(7) Southampton - Flyingboat.	20

C.D.S. POSTMARKS	
(8) Harwich (Amsterdam Paquebot special cover)	25

SLOGAN POSTMARKS	
(9) Any Post Code slogans	*from* 100

(5)

(2)

10th July 1974 - GREAT BRITONS
4½p Robert the Bruce; 5½p Owain Glyndwr;
8p Henry V; 10p Edward of Woodstock

SPECIAL HANDSTAMPS			
(1) First Day of Issue - Philatelic Bureau	6	-	*Post Office*
(2) Robert the Bruce, National Trust, Bannockburn	30	50	*Scot N.T.*
(3) Robert the Bruce, Dunfermline Abbey	30	70	*Dun. Abbey*
(4) Owain Glyndwr's Parliament House, Machynlleth	30	70	*Ow. Glyn.*
(5) Royal Tournament, BF 1974 PS	60	60	*Royal T.*
(6) Visit of Golden Hind II, London EC	140	-	*n.o.c.*
(7) Churchill, Centenary Exhib., Somerset House, WC	140	-	*n.o.c.*
(8) Open Golf Championship, Lytham St. Annes	200	25	*Lytham G.C.(s)*
(9) Trustee Savings Bank, 1824-1974, Sunderland	175	25	*T.S.B. (s)*

ORDINARY F.D.I. POSTMARKS	
(10) Canterbury or Windsor	*each* 15
(11) Dunfermline or Gwent	*each* 15

C.D.S, POSTMARKS	
(12) Calais with PAQUEBOT markings	100
(13) Cardross - where Robert the Bruce died (4½p)	20(s)
(14) Glyndyfrdwy - home of Owain Glyndwr (5½p)	20(s)
(15) House of Commons, S.W.1	25
(16) House of Lords, S.W.1	35
(17) Woodstock - Edward of Woodstock (10p)	20(s)

(2)

(1)

(4)

(5)

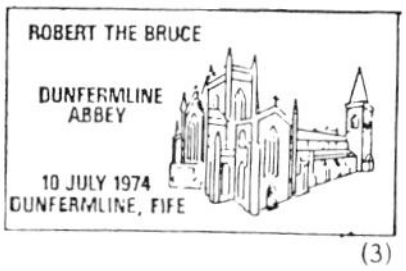

(3)

9th October 1974 - CENTENARY OF THE BIRTH OF WINSTON CHURCHILL

4½p, 5½p, 8p, 10p Portraits of Churchill

SPECIAL HANDSTAMPS	ordinary covers £	official covers £
(1) First Day of Issue - Philatelic Bureau	6	- *Post Office*
(2) First Day of Issue - Blenheim, Woodstock	7	- *Post Office*
(3) First Day of Issue - House of Commons, SW1	7	- *Post Office*
(4) Woodford Green, Action This Day	20	25 *See Note**
(5) Churchill's First Constituency, Oldham	20	20 *Old. Conserv.*
(6) Winston Churchill, RAF Honington, BF 1874 PS	25	5 *RAF 12 Squad(s)*
(7) Churchill Centenary Exhib., Somerset House, WC	30	95 *Som. Hse.*
(8) Universal Postal Union 1874, Clitheroe, Lancs	125	- *n.o.c.*
(9) Oldest Post Office In Britain, 1763, Sanquhar	80	80 *Sanq. PO*
(10) Rotary Club of Paddington, Golden Jubilee, W2	125	150 *Padd. R.C.*
(11) Gold Jubilee of Local Radio, Nottingham	125	30 *BBC(s)*

**Two covers exist: (a) Wanstead & Woodford Synagogue*
(b) Wanstead & Woodford Conservative Association

ORDINARY F.D.I. POSTMARKS	
(12) Tunbridge Wells (with 'Posted at Chartwell' cachet)	30
(13) Medway (HMS Churchill Submarine cover)	30

C.D.S. POSTMARKS	
(14) Bladon, Oxford - Churchill is buried here	135
(15) Churchill, Bristol	125
(16) Churchill, Oxford	125
(17) House of Commons, S.W.1	80
(18) House of Lords, S.W.1	110
(19) Marlborough - Churchill's ancestral home	175
(20) Normandy, Guildford	75
(21) Sandhurst - Churchill went to Sandhurst	75
(22) Winston, Darlington	200

(4) (1) (16) (6)

(10)

(7)

27th November 1974 - CHRISTMAS

3½p York Minster: 4½p St. Helens, Norwich;
8p Ottery St. Mary; 10p Worcester Cathedral

SPECIAL HANDSTAMPS		
(1) First Day of Issue - Philatelic Bureau	4	- *Post Office*
(2) First Day of Issue - Bethlehem, Llandeilo, Carms	7	- *Post Office*
(3) St. Helen's Church, Great Hospital, Norwich	20	35 *Gt. Hosp.*
(4) The Collegiate Church, Ottery St. Mary	20	35 *St. Mary*
(5) Salvation Army Christmas Supermarkets	60	20 *Sal. Army(s)*
(6) Oldest Post Office in Britain, 1763 Sanquhar	60	75 *Sanq. PO*
(7) Churchill County Secondary School, Woking	100	110 *W.C. Sch.*

ORDINARY F.D.I. POSTMARKS	
(8) York - Minster roof boss (3½p)	20
(9) Worcester - Cathedral roof boss (10p)	20

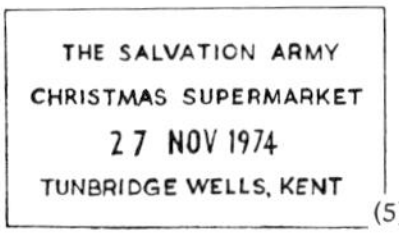

(5)

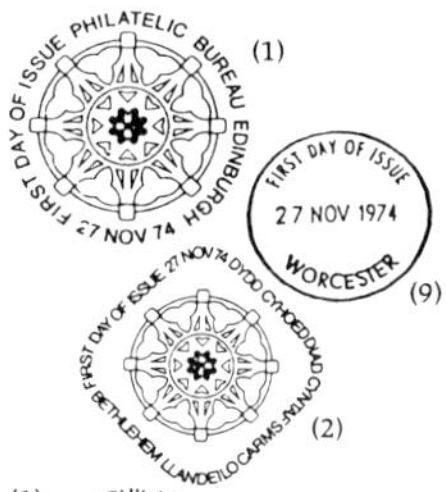

(1) (9) (2)

22nd January 1975 - CHARITY

4½p + 1½p donation to charities

SPECIAL HANDSTAMPS		
(1) First Day of Issue - Philatelic Bureau	3	- *Post Office*
(2) Oldest Post Office in Britain 1763, Sanquhar	20	30 *Sanq. PO*

ORDINARY F.D.I. POSTMARKS	
(3) Kettering (Winged Fellowship Trust cover)	5
(4) Oxford - Oxfam HQ	12

C.D.S. POSTMARKS	
(5) Stoke Charity, Winchester, Hants	200

SLOGAN POSTMARKS	
(6) Menphys Love the Handicapped	80
(7) Tenovus Cares, Cardiff	300
(8) Barnardo's Cares About Children	300

(1) (5)

(6)

(7)

(8)

PLEASE READ THE GENERAL NOTES
AT THE BEGINNING OF THIS CATALOGUE
These often provide the answers to enquiries received.
Prices are for good clean, unaddressed, covers
with the full set of stamps.

19th February 1975 - BRITISH PAINTINGS: J. M. W. TURNER

1975

4½p 'Peace: Burial at Sea';
5½p 'Snowstorm - Steamer off a Harbour's Mouth';
8p 'The Arsenal, Venice'; 10p 'St. Laurent'

	ordinary covers	officials covers
SPECIAL HANDSTAMPS	£	£
(1) First Day of Issue - Philatelic Bureau	5	- *Post Office*
(2) First Day of Issue - London WC	7	- *Post Office*
(3) Oldest Post Office in Britain, 1763, Sanquhar	35	35 *Sanq. PO*
(4) Worksop & District Chamber of Trade 1875-1975	100	- *n.o.c.*
(5) Up Helly - AA Lerwick Shetland	110	- *n.o.c.*
C.D.S. POSTMARKS		
(6) Petworth - Turner did much of his work here	150	
(7) Turner's Hill, Crawley	150	
(8) Harwich - relevant to the 5½p value	20(s)	
SLOGAN POSTMARKS		
(9) Turner: Royal Academy *(plain cover)*	10(s)	

(9)

(6)

(7)

23rd April 1975 - EUROPEAN ARCHITECTURAL HERITAGE YEAR

2 x 7p Charlotte Square, Edinburgh & The Rows Chester;
8p The Royal Observatory, Greenwich; 10p St. George's Chapel, Windsor;
12p The National Theatre, London

SPECIAL HANDSTAMPS		
(1) First Day of Issue - Philatelic Bureau	7	- *Post Office*
(2) 500 Years St. George's Chapel, Windsor, Berks	12	- *see 2(a)*
(2a) Ditto with 'Carried by Coach' cachet	12	20 *St. G. Ch.*
(3) National Trust, 7 Charlotte Sq., Edinburgh	30	50 *Scot N.T.*
(4) Corinium 1900, Heritage, Cirencester	30	50 *Corin. Mus.*
(5) Chester Heritage City	20	40 *Chester EAHY*
(6) Wilton House Open Day, Wilton, Salisbury	30	40 *Cotswold*
(7) Oldest Post Office in Britain, 1763, Sanquhar	40	40 *Sanq. PO*
(8) Meriden Junior School Pool, Watford	125	15 *Meriden Sch.(s)*
ORDINARY F.D.I. POSTMARKS		
(9) Chester or Edinburgh *each*	7	
(10) London S.E. 1 - Observatory & National Theatre	7	
(11) Windsor	7	
C.D.S. POSTMARKS		
(12) Greenwich B.O. (Branch Office), S.E.10	175	
(13) Dartmouth Row, Greenwich S.E.10	200	
(14) Windsor Castle, Windsor, Berks	125	
SLOGAN POSTMARKS		
(15) Chester Heritage City, Chester	275	
(16) European Architectural Heritage Year, Leicester	375	

(1)

(2)

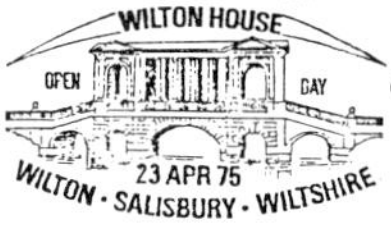

(6)

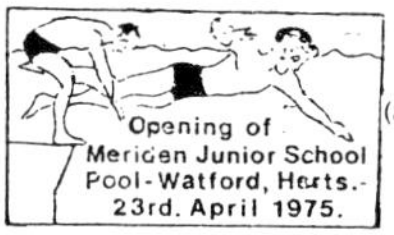

(8)

(16)

(15)

(5)

11th June 1975 - SAILING

7p Dinghies; 8p Keel Boats; 10p Yachts; 12p Multihulls

SPECIAL HANDSTAMPS		
(1) First Day of Issue - Philatelic Bureau	4	- *Post Office*
(1a) Ditto with 'British PO Arphila 75 Paris' cachet	7	- *Post Office*
(2) Royal Dorset Yacht Club centenary, Weymouth	10	25 *R.D.Y. Club*
(3) Royal Thames Yacht Club Bi-centenary, SW	10	25 *R.T.Y. Club*
(4) Oldest Post Office in Britain, 1763, Sanquhar	20	30 *Sanq. PO*
ORDINARY F.D.I. POSTMARKS		
(5) Hastings - Rye Harbour Sailing Club	12	
(6) Newport, I.O.W - famous for yachting	12	
(7) Plymouth, Devon - sailing traditions	12	
(8) Southampton (International Boat Show cover)	20	
(9) Weymouth, Dorset - centre for yachting	12	
(10) Woking - Royal Yachting Association's HQ	12	
C.D.S. POSTMARKS		
(11) Cowes, I.O.W. - yachting centre	95	
(12) Burnham-on-Crouch - yachting centre	60	
(13) House of Commons - Yacht Club - 25th Anniv	35	
(14) Lytham - Ribble Cruising Club - 25th Anniv	75	
(15) Rye Harbour - Sailing Club - 50th Anniv	75	
(16) West Wittering - Sailing Club - 25th Anniv	75	

(1)

(2)

(3)

13th August 1975 – 150th ANNIVERSARY FIRST PUBLIC STEAM RAILWAY

7p Stephenson's Locomotion; 8p Waverley Class; 10p Caerphilly Castle; 12p High Speed Train

SPECIAL HANDSTAMPS	ordinary covers £	official covers £	
(1) First Day of Issue – Philatelic Bureau	6	–	*Post Office*
(2) First Day of Issue – Stockton-on-Tees	10	–	*Post Office*
(3) First Day of Issue – Darlington	10	–	*Post Office*
(4) First Day of Issue – Shildon	10	–	*Post Office*
(5) Wylam, Birthplace of George Stephenson	30	50	*Round Table*
(6) Longmoor Military Railway, BF 1396 PS	20	25	*Royal Eng. 27*
(7) Return of Steam, Buckfastleigh	15	15	*Cotswold*
(8) Torbay Steam Railway, Paignton	20	20	*Cotswold*
(9) Story of a Cathedral Exhibition, Canterbury	125	–	*n.o.c.*
(10) Royal Shakespeare Theatre, Stratford	125	–	*n.o.c.*
ORDINARY F.D.I. POSTMARKS			
(11) Bournemouth (Big Four Railway Museum cover)	20		
(12) Brighton (Bluebell Railway cover)	20		
(13) Crewe – railway centre	15		
(14) Derby – BR Technical/Research Centre	15		
(15) Paddington	15		
(16) York – Railway Museum	15		
(17) Swindon (British Rail Works cover)	20		
C.D.S. POSTMARKS (inc. T.P.O. CANCELS)			
(18) Caerphilly – Caerphilly Castle (10p)	60		
(19) Welshpool (Llanfair Light Railway cover)	40		
(20) Porthmadog (Festiniog Railway Co. cover)	30		
(21) Wylam - birthplace of George Stephenson	75		
(22) N.E. TPO – most appropriate TPO for this issue	30		
(23) Any other TPO (travelling post office)	30		
SLOGAN POSTMARKS			
(24) S & D Rly Jubilee Shildon Co. Durham	325		
(25) 150th S & D Rly Anniversary Darlington	325		
(26) Ravenglass & Eskdale Rly. Centenary Year	25(s)		

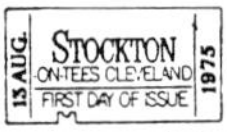

(2)

(3)

(8)

(5)

(24)

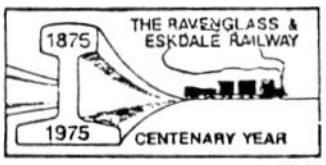

(26)

(1)

3rd September 1975 – INTER-PARLIAMENTARY UNION

12p Palace of Westminster

SPECIAL HANDSTAMPS	ordinary covers £	official covers £	
(1) First Day of Issue – Philatelic Bureau	3	–	*Post Office*
(2) 62nd Inter-Parliamentary Conference, SE1	5	8	*I.P. Conf.*
(3) Story of a Cathedral Exhibition, Canterbury	85	–	*n.o.c.*
(4) Stockton & Darlington Rly, 1825-1975	75	–	*n.o.c.*
C.D.S. POSTMARKS			
(5) Buckingham Palace, SW1	50		
(6) House of Commons, SW1	50		
(7) House of Lords, SW1	60		
(8) Parliament Street, SW1	40		

(2)

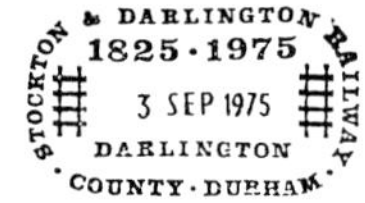

(4)

22nd October 1975 – BICENTENARY OF JANE AUSTEN

8½p Emma and Mr. Woodhouse; 10p Catherine Moorland; 11p Mr. Darcy; 13p Mary and Henry Crawford

SPECIAL HANDSTAMPS	ordinary covers £	official covers £	
(1) First Day of Issue – Philatelic Bureau	4	–	*Post Office*
(2) First Day of Issue – Steventon	5	–	*Post Office*
(2a) Ditto with 'Despatched by Mailcoach' cachet	10	–	*Post Office*
(3) Jane Austen Bi-centenary Exhibition, Bath	10	25	*City of Bath*
(4) Story of a Cathedral Exhibition, Canterbury	70	–	*n.o.c.*
C.D.S. POSTMARKS			
(5) Alton, Hants	125		
(6) Chawton, Alton – Jane Austen lived here	125		
(7) Steventon – Jane Austen's birthplace	125		
SLOGAN POSTMARKS			
(8) Jane Austen Bi-centenary 1775-1975 Hampshire	250		

(2)

(1)

(3)

(8)

PRICES & CONDITION – PLEASE READ GENERAL NOTES

26th November 1975 - CHRISTMAS

6½p, 8½p, 11p, 13p Angels

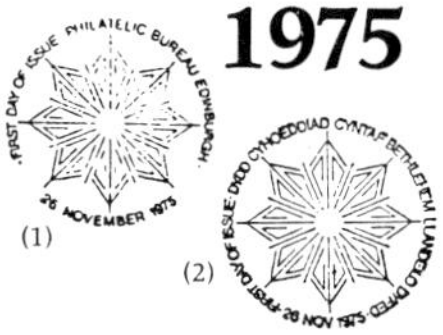

	ordinary covers £	official covers £
SPECIAL HANDSTAMPS		
(1) First Day of Issue - Philatelic Bureau	2	- *Post Office*
(2) First Day of Issue - Bethlehem, Llandeilo, Dyfed	4	- *Post Office*
C.D.S. POSTMARKS		
(3) Angel Hill, Sutton, Surrey	100	

10th March 1976 - CENTENARY OF THE TELEPHONE

8½p, 10p, 11p, 13p The Telephone in the Community

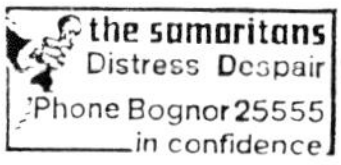

SPECIAL HANDSTAMPS		
(1) First Day of Issue - Philatelic Bureau	2	- *Post Office*
(2) Telecommunications Museum, Taunton	6	- *n.o.c.*
ORDINARY F.D.I. POSTMARKS		
(3) Boston, Lincs - telephone invented in Boston, USA	12	
(4) Edinburgh - birthplace of Alexander Graham Bell	12	
(5) Hull - independent telephone service	12	
(6) Worcester (with Centenary Exhibition overprint)	12	
C.D.S. POSTMARKS		
(7) Hope St., Edinburgh - near to Bell's birthplace	110	
SLOGAN POSTMARKS		
(8) The Samaritans, Phone Bognor 25555	275	

28th April 1976 - SOCIAL PIONEERS & REFORMERS

8½p Thomas Hepburn - miners' union 1831;
10p Robert Owen - improved working conditions;
11p Lord Shaftesbury - child labour reform;
13p Elizabeth Fry - prison reform

SPECIAL HANDSTAMPS		
(1) First Day of Issue - Philatelic Bureau	3	- *Post Office*
(2) World of Islam Festival London SW7	35	60 *Pilgrim*
(3) 1776 Exhibition National Maritime Museum, SE10	60	40 *Pilgrim*
ORDINARY F.D.I. POSTMARKS		
(4) Durham - National Union of Mineworkers	10	
(5) Folkestone - Lord Shaftesbury died here	10	
(6) Norwich - Birthplace of Elizabeth Fry	10	
(7) Rochdale - first Co-op	10	
C.D.S. POSTMARKS		
(8) House of Commons, S.W. 1	30	
(9) House of Lords, S.W. 1	40	
(10) Magdalen St., Norwich - near to Fry's birthplace	60	
(11) Newton, Powys - birthplace of Robert Owen	45	
(12) Parkhurst, I.O.W. - top security prison	70	
(13) New Lanark - Robert Owen	110	
(14) Lanark - Robert Owen	70	
(15) Pelton, Durham - Hepburn's birthplace	120	
(16) Shaftesbury, Dorset	100	
(17) Wimborne St. Giles - Earl of Shaftesbury	80	

2nd June 1976 - BICENTENARY OF U.S.A. INDEPENDENCE

11p Benjamin Franklin

SPECIAL HANDSTAMPS		
(1) First Day of Issue - Philatelic Bureau	2	- *Post Office*
(1a) Ditto with 'Interphil 76 ' cachet	5	- *Post Office*
(2) American Independence, BF 1776 PS	5	8 *BFPS*
(3) USA Independence, Washington, Tyne & Wear	7	15 *Wash. Old Hall*
(4) 1776 Exhibition, National Maritime Museum, SE10	7	15 *Pilgrim*
(5) American Bicentennial, American Museum, Bath	5	5 *Clav. Manor*
(6) 58th Philatelic Congress of G. B., Plymouth	15	20 *Phil. Cong.*
(7) World of Islam Festival, London SW7	15	50 *Pilgrim*

PLEASE READ THE GENERAL NOTES
AT THE BEGINNING OF THIS CATALOGUE
These often provide the answers to enquiries received.

Prices are for unaddressed covers in good condition
with the full set of postage stamps.

U.S.A. (contd.)

	ordinary covers	official covers
ORDINARY F.D.I. POSTMARKS		
(8) Boston, Lincs	5	
(9) Plymouth, Devon – sailing of Pilgrim Fathers	5	
C.D.S. POSTMARKS		
(10) Bunker's Hill, Lincoln	110	
(11) Dallas, Forres, Morayshire	110	
(12) Denver, Downham Market	110	
(13) House of Commons, S.W.1	30	
(14) House of Lords, S.W.1	40	
(15) New York, Lincoln	120	
(16) Northborough – Claypole family, links with U.S.A.	30	
(17) Sulgrave – ancestors of George Washington	50	
(18) Washington, Pulborough, West Sussex	60	

30th June 1976 – CENTENARY OF ROYAL NATIONAL ROSE SOCIETY

8½p Elizabeth of Glamis; 10p Grandpa Dickson; 11p Rosa Mundi; 13p Sweet Briar

	ordinary covers	official covers
SPECIAL HANDSTAMPS		
(1) First Day of Issue – Philatelic Bureau	4	– *Post Office*
(2) Year of the Rose, Northampton	7	20 *N'ton Ph Soc*
(3) Year of the Rose, Bath	7	20 *City of Bath*
(4) Royal National Rose Society, Oxford	6	– *n.o.c.*
(5) Royal National Rose Society, St. Albans	6	– *n.o.c.*
(6) Royal Norfolk Show, Norwich	15	75 *Daniels*
(7) The Mothers' Union Centenary, SW1	45	70 *Mothers Un.*
(8) The Championships A.E.L.T.C., Wimbledon	85	– *n.o.c.*
(9) USA Independence, Washington	85	– *n.o.c.*
(10) Warton Bicentennial Commem., Carnforth	85	– *n.o.c.*
(11) 1776 Exhibition, National Maritime Museum, SE10	85	– *n.o.c.*
(12) First Flight Britain/Australia, BF 1535 PS	85	– *n.o.c.*
ORDINARY F.D.I. POSTMARKS		
(13) Tunbridge Wells (with 'Sissinghurst Castle' cachet)	15	
C.D.S. POSTMARKS		
(14) Glamis, Forfar – 'Elizabeth of Glamis' (8½p)	85	
(15) Kew Gardens, Richmond	125	
(16) Rose, Truro or Rose Cottage, Hull *each*	125	
(17) Rosebush, or Rosebank *each*	75	

4th August 1976 – BRITISH CULTURAL TRADITIONS

8½p & 13p Eiseddfod; 10p Morris Dancing; 11p Highland Gathering

	ordinary covers	official covers
SPECIAL HANDSTAMPS		
(1) First Day of Issue – Philatelic Bureau	3	– *Post Office*
(2) First Day of Issue – Cardigan	4	– *Post Office*
(3) Eisteddfod Genedlaethol Frenhinol Cymru, Cardigan	5	60 *Philart*
(4) Bristol Morris Men, 25th Anniversary	5	50 *Bristol MM*
(5) 1776 Exhibition, National Maritime Museum, SE10	75	– *n.o.c.*
(6) USA Independence, Washington	75	– *n.o.c.*
(7) Story of a Cathedral Exhibition, Canterbury	40	– *n.o.c.*
(8) Colchester Tattoo, BF 1542 PS	95	– *n.o.c.*
(9) Europa 6 Cantat, Leicester	95	75 *Cantat 6*
ORDINARY F.D.I. POSTMARKS		
(10) Exeter (with 'Sidmouth Folk Festival' cachet)	20	
C.D.S, POSTMARKS		
(11) Abbots Bromley – horn dancing	25	
(12) Abingdon – famous morris team	25	
(13) Bampton – famous morris team	25	
(14) Britannia, Bacup – famous morris team	25	
(15) Chipping Campden – famous morris team	20	
(16) Headington Quarry – famous morris team	35	
(17) Padstow – famous for its 'Hobby Horse'	20	
(18) Thaxted – the Morris Ring meet here annually	25	
(19) Caerwys – famous eisteddfod	20	
(20) Carmarthen – famous eisteddfod	20	
(21) Corwen – famous eisteddfod	25	
(22) Llangollen – International Musical Eisteddfod	40	
(23) Braemar – Royal Highland Gathering	40	
(24) Dunoon – Cowal Highland Gathering	20	

29th Sept. 1976 - WILLIAM CAXTON - 500th ANNIVERSARY OF PRINTING IN ENGLAND

8½p 'Canterbury Tales'; 10p Caxton's type-faces; 11p Game of Chess; 13p Printing Press

	ordinary covers	official covers
SPECIAL HANDSTAMPS	£	£
(1) First Day of Issue - Philatelic Bureau	3	- *Post Office*
(2) First Day of Issue - London SW1	4	- *Post Office*
(3) 500 Years of British Printing, Westminster, SW1	6	8 *Br Pr Ind Fed*
(4) Caxton Exhibition, British Library, WC	6	25 *BL 1*
(5) 500th Anniv. Printing, William Caxton, Plymouth	6	35 *Ply. Coll.*
(6) Paper & Printing Study Group, SE1	6	18 *Philart*
(7) NATSOPA, Caxton House, SE1	6	8 *NATSOPA*
(8) Raithby Lawrence, De Montfort Press, Leicester	10	40 *DeM. Press*
(9) British Philatelic Exhibition, London W1	6	10 *B.P.E.*
(10) First School Centenary, Stoke Poges, Bucks	30	40 *S.P. Sch.*
(11) 1776 Exhibition, National Maritime Museum, SE10	30	- *n.o.c.*
(12) Royal Charter Quincentenary, Stow-on-the-Wold	30	45 *S-o-t-W Sch.*
(13) Manchester United v. Ajax, UEFA Cup	85	- *n.o.c.*
ORDINARY F.D.I. POSTMARKS		
(14) Canterbury - Caxton printed 'Canterbury Tales'	6	
C.D.S. POSTMARKS		
(15) Abingdon - first printing was for Abbot of Abingdon	80	
(16) Caxton, Cambridge	70	
(17) Fleet St., E.C.4 - home of British printing today	80	
(18) House of Commons - buried in St Margaret's Chapel	40	
(19) Tenterden - presumed birthplace of Caxton	55	

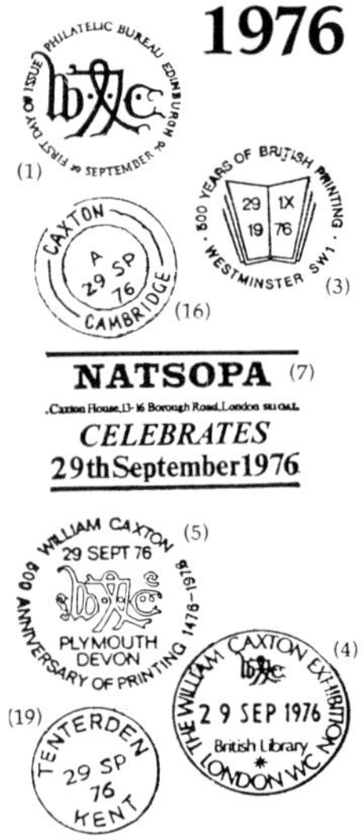

24th November 1976 - CHRISTMAS

6½p, 8½p, 11p, 13p Embroideries

	ordinary covers	official covers
SPECIAL HANDSTAMPS		
(1) First Day of Issue - Philatelic Bureau	3	- *Post Office*
(2) First Day of Issue - Bethlehem, Llandeilo, Dyfed	4	- *Post Office*
(3) Pompeii AD79, Royal Academy of Arts, W1	10	25 *Pomp. Exhib.*
(4) Tonic to the Nation, Victoria & Albert, SW7	10	25 *H.R.*
(5) 1st British Corps, Bielefeld, BF 1923 PS	20	35 *Forces*
(6) 1st British Corps, Aldershot, BF 1901 PS	20	35 *Forces*
(7) Caxton Exhibition, British Library, WC	40	- *n.o.c.*
C.D.S. POSTMARKS		
(8) Angel Hill, Sutton	15	
(9) Pincushion, Boston - embroideries	25	

12th January 1977 - RACQUET SPORTS

8½p Lawn Tennis; 10p Table Tennis; 11p Squash; 13p Badminton

	ordinary covers	official covers
SPECIAL HANDSTAMPS		
(1) First Day of Issue - Philatelic Bureau	3	- *Post Office*
(2) The Badminton Association, Badminton	6	50 *Badm. Assoc.*
(3) Squash Rackets Association, Harrow	6	50 *Philart*
(4) Pompeii AD 79, Royal Academy of Arts, W1	40	- *n.o.c.*
(5) Caxton, Exhibition British Library, WC	40	- *n.o.c.*
ORDINARY F.D.I. POSTMARKS		
(6) Battersea, SW11 - Head P.O. for Wimbledon	8	
(7) Birmingham - World Table Tennis at NEC	8	
(8) Hastings - HQ of English Table Tennis Assoc'n	8	
(9) Warwick & Leamington - first Tennis Club	8	
C.D.S. POSTMARKS		
(10) Wimbledon S.D.O., SW19	125	
(11) Wimbledon Park, Wimbledon SW19	150	
(12) Woodside Parade, Wimbledon SW19	125	

PLEASE READ THE GENERAL NOTES
AT THE BEGINNING OF THIS CATALOGUE
These often provide the answers to enquiries received.

Prices are for unaddressed covers in good condition
with the full set of postage stamps.

2nd March 1977 - BRITISH ACHIEVEMENT IN CHEMISTRY

8½p Steroids (Barton);10p Vitamin C (Haworth); 11p Starch (Martin & Synge); 13p Salt (Bragg)	**ordinary covers**	**official covers**	
SPECIAL HANDSTAMPS	**£**	**£**	
(1) First Day of Issue - Philatelic Bureau	3	-	*Post Office*
(2) Royal Institute of Chemistry, WC 1877-1977	7	20	*RI of Chem.*
(3) Starch Derivatives for Industry, Battersea	7	20	*Garton Ltd*
(4) Royal Silver Jubilee, Stampex, SW1	7	20	*Stampex*
(5) Pompeii AD 79, Royal Academy of Arts, W1	30	35	*Pomp Exh.*
(6) Tonic to the Nation, Victoria & Albert, SW7	35	60	*H.R.*
ORDINARY F.D.I. POSTMARKS			
(7) Liverpool - birthplace of R.L.M. Synge	8		
C.D.S. POSTMARKS			
(8) Barton - Barton on 8½p val	35		
(9) Gravesend - birthplace of D H. R. Barton	35		
(10) Haworth - Haworth on 10p value	35		
(11) Martin - Martin on 11p value	35		
(12) Wigton - birthplace of W. H. Bragg	35		

(1)

(2)
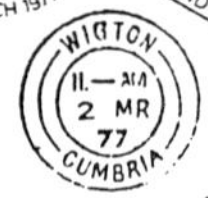
(12)

(3)

(4)

11th May 1977 - THE SILVER JUBILEE OF THE QUEEN'S ACCESSION

8½p, 10p,. 11p, 13p Portrait of H.M. The Queen

SPECIAL HANDSTAMPS			
(1) First Day of Issue - Philatelic Bureau	3	-	*Post Office*
(2) First Day of Issue - Windsor	3	-	*Post Office*
(3) Jubilee Exhibition, Bath, England	15	30	*City of Bath*
(4) A Royal Jubilee Exhibition, British Library	15	25	*BL 2*
(5) Croydon Celebrates Queen's Silver Jubilee	15	30	*Croydon*
(6) Stamp Collecting Promotion Council, SE1	15	-	*n.o.c.*
(7) Queen Elizabeth II, RHDR, Hythe	15	25	*RHDR 1*
(8) St. Martin-in-the-Fields, Silver Jubilee, WC2	15	40	*St. M-i-t-F*
(9) Hayling Island Philatelic Soc., Silver Jubilee	25	35	*HI Phil Soc*
(10) Duke of Edinburgh's Award, SW1	8	10	*DoE A.Scheme*
(11) Stamp of Royalty Exhibition, Glasgow	15	20	*Pal. of Art*
(12) Weymouth & Portland, Philatelic Exhibition	15	40	*W & P Exhib*
(13) Tenth Conference, Dixieme Congress, W1	25	70	*ICTWO*
(14) Exercise Makefast XXV, Chatham, BF 1952 PS	15	20	*Royal Eng.*
(15) Bristol Bordeaux, 30th Anniversary	25	60	*BB Assoc*
(16) Milton Keynes Arts Association	25	60	*MK Festival*
ORDINARY F.D.I. HANDSTAMPS			
(17) Aberdeen ('Posted near Balmoral Castle' cachet)	12		
(18) King's Lynn ('Estate Office, Sandringham' cachet)	25		
(19) Portsmouth - Review of the Fleet	20		
C.D.S. POSTMARKS			
(20) Buckingham Palace, S.W.1	140		
(21) House of Commons, S.W.1	20		
(22) House of Lords, S.W 1	25		
(23) Jubilee Crescent, Coventry	25		
(24) Jubilee Oak; or Jubilee Fields *each*	25		
(25) Queen Elizabeth Avenue, Walsall	25		
(26) Queen's Parade; or Queen's Head *each*	25		
(27) Silver Link, Tamworth	25		
(28) Windsor Castle, Windsor, Berks	150		
SLOGAN POSTMARKS			
(29) Queen's Silver Jubilee Appeal, Belfast	60		
(30) Queen's Silver Jubilee Philatelic Exhib., Cardiff	75		
(31) Queen's Silver Jubilee Philatelic Exhib., Edinburgh	75		
(32) Queen's Silver Jubilee Philatelic Exhib., NPM, EC	75		
(33) Review of Fleet (with Jubilee logo) Portsmouth	80		
(34) St. Neots Jubilee Riverside Festival	100		

(1)

(9)

(8)

(4)

(14)

(3)

(10)

(30)

(34)

(33)

PLEASE READ THE GENERAL NOTES
AT THE BEGINNING OF THIS CATALOGUE
These often provide the answers to enquiries received.

Prices are for unaddressed covers in good condition with the full set of postage stamps.

8th June 1977 – COMMONWEALTH HEADS OF GOVERNMENT MEETING

13p 'Gathering of Nations'

	ordinary covers £	official covers £	
SPECIAL HANDSTAMPS			
(1) First Day of Issue – Philatelic Bureau	2	–	*Post Office*
(2) First Day of Issue – London SW	2	–	*Post Office*
(3) Girl Guides Association, Open Days, SW1	10	20	*Girl Guides*
(4) St. Martin-in-the-Field, Silver Jubilee, WC2	10	20	*St. M-i-t-F*
(5) A Royal Jubilee Exhibition, British Library, WC	10	–	*n.o.c.*
(6) Croydon Celebrates Queens Silver Jubilee	10	20	*Croydon*
(7) British Genius Exhibition, Battersea, SW11	10	–	*n.o.c.*
(8) 6000 King George V, Hereford	10	–	*n.o.c.*
(9) City of Leicester, Silver Jubilee, EIIR	10	–	*n.o.c.*
(10) Jubilee Exhibition, North Devon	10	–	*n.o.c.*
(11) Royal Image Exhibition, Bristol	10	–	*n.o.c.*
(12) The Prince of Wales Division, BF 8677 PS	10	15	*BFPS*
(13) The Queens Silver Jubilee, Windsor	10	–	*n.o.c.*
(14) Silver Jubilee Train, Newcastle	10	–	*n.o.c.*
(15) Queen's Silver Jubilee, Merseyside Police	10	–	*n.o.c.*
(16) Silver Jubilee Festival, Canon Hill Park	10	–	*n.o.c.*
C.D.S. POSTMARKS			
(17) House of Commons, S.W.1	40		
(18) House of Lords, S.W.1	60		
(19) Buckingham Palace, S.W.1	75		
SLOGAN POSTMARKS			
(20) Queen's Silver Jubilee Appeal	20		
(21) House of Commons S.W.1 (wavy line cancel)	15		

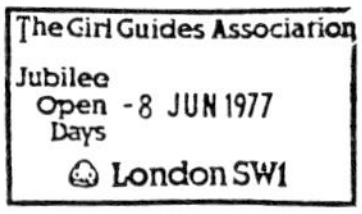

(3)

(16)

(15)

(12)

(14)

15th June 1977 – THE SILVER JUBILEE OF THE QUEEN'S ACCESSION

9p Portrait of H.M. The Queen

	ordinary	official	
SPECIAL HANDSTAMPS			
(1) First Day of Issue – Philatelic Bureau	2	–	*Post Office*
(2) First Day of Issue – Windsor	2	–	*Post Office*
(3) Borough of Blackburn, Silver Jubilee	8	50	*Blackburn BC*
(4) Jubilee Exhibition, North Devon	8	25	*N. Devon*
(5) Silver Jubilee Exhibition, Trafalgar Square, WC2	8	–	*n.o.c.*
(6) Royal Jubilee Exhibition, British Library, WC	8	20	*BL 2*
(7) City of Leicester, Silver Jubilee, EIIR, Leicester	5	8	*City of Leics*
(8) Nuneaton Borough Council, 1952 EIIR 1977	8	15	*Nuneaton BC*
(9) Croydon Celebrates the Queen's Silver Jubilee	8	15	*Croydon*
(10) Royal Image Exhibition, Bristol	12	15	*Royal Image*
(11) British Genius Exhibition Battersea SW11	8	–	*n.o.c.*
ORDINARY F.D.I. POSTMARKS			
(12) Portsmouth – Review of Fleet	5		
C.D.S. POSTMARKS			
(13) Buckingham Palace, S.W.1	75		
(14) House of Commons, S.W.1	8		
(15) House of Lords, S.W.1	10		
(16) Jubilee Oak; Jubilee Cresc.; Jubilee Fields *each*	15		
(17) Silver Link; Queens Head; Queens Parade *each*	15		
(18) Queen Elizabeth Avenue, Walsall	15		
(19) Windsor Castle, Windsor, Berks	75		
SLOGAN POSTMARKS			
(20) The Queen's Silver Jubilee Appeal	15		
(21) Review of the Fleet (Jubilee logo) Portsmouth	20		
(22) Queen's Silver Jubilee Philatelic Exhib., Cardiff	15		
(23) Queen's Silver Jubilee Philatelic Exhib., Edinburgh	15		
(24) Silver Jubilee International Air Tattoo	50		
(25) Portsmouth & Southsea (Jubilee logo)	30		

(3)

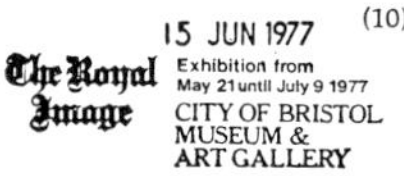

(10)

(7)

(11)

(4)

(25)

(24)

11th May & 15th June 1977 – THE SILVER JUBILEE (DOUBLE DATED COVERS)

Many double-dated covers exist and can be summarised as follows:

(1) special h/s (11 May) + FDI postmark (15 June)	20	30
(2) special h/s (11 May) + special h/s (15 June)	30	30
(3) appropriate CDS (both dates on one cover)	40	

PRICES & CONDITION – PLEASE READ GENERAL NOTES

5th October 1977 - BRITISH WILDLIFE

5 x 9p: Hedgehog, Hare, Red Squirrel, Otter, Badger

SPECIAL HANDSTAMPS	ordinary covers £	official covers £
(1) First Day of Issue - Philatelic Bureau	4	- *Post Office*
(2) Badger Beer, Blandford, 200th Anniversary	8	20 *Hall & Woodhse*
(3) SCT (Shropshire Conservation Trust)	8	20 *SCT*
(4) Norfolk Wildlife in Trust, Norwich	7	7 *Markton (NNT)*
(5) Port Lympne, Wildlife Sanctuary, Hythe	7	7 *RHDR 3*
(6) 11-13 Broad Court, Covent Garden, WC2	7	7 *Garden Studio*
(7) Darley's, 150 Years of Print, Burton	35	45 *Darley's*
(8) Sir Francis Drake, British Library, WC	35	- *n.o.c.*
(9) British Genius Exhibition, London SW11	35	- *n.o.c.*
(10) Army & Navy, Victoria, SW1	35	6 *A. & N.(s)*
(11) Manchester United, FA Cup Winners	50	4 *Dawn(s)*
C.D.S. POSTMARKS		
(12) Badgers Mount, Sevenoaks	20	
(13) Forest Row, East Sussex	15	
(14) Foxton, Leics	20	
(15) Haresfield or Harewood *each*	20	
(16) Hedge End, Southampton	15	
(17) Nettleham - HQ Royal Society Nature Conservation	25	
(18) Otterburn or Otterbourne *each*	20	
(19) Otter Ferry, Tighnabruaich	20	
(20) Squirrels Heath, Romford	25	

23rd November 1977 - CHRISTMAS

5 x 7p; 9p 'The Twelve Days of Christmas'

SPECIAL HANDSTAMPS	ordinary covers £	official covers £
(1) First Day of Issue - Philatelic Bureau	4	- *Post Office*
(2) First Day of Issue - Bethlehem, Llandeilo, Dyfed	5	- *Post Office*
(3) Silver Jubilee, Christmas Greetings, Blackpool	20	10 *Blackpool(s)*
(4) Sir Francis Drake, British Library, WC	20	25 *Br. Lib.*
(5) 40th Anniv. First Mail Flight, Lerwick, Shetland	20	10 *B.A.(s)*
(6) 40th Anniv. First Mail Flight, Dyce, Aberdeen	20	10 *B.A.(s)*
ORDINARY F.D.I. POSTMARKS		
(7) Cambridge - original manuscript (Trinity College)	15	
C.D.S. POSTMARKS		
(8) House of Lords - 'Ten Lords a-leaping'	35	
(9) Partridge Green, Horsham	30	
(10) Pear Tree: Derby, Rugeley or Welwyn *each*	30	
SLOGAN POSTMARK		
(11) Collect through Philatelic Bureau	30	

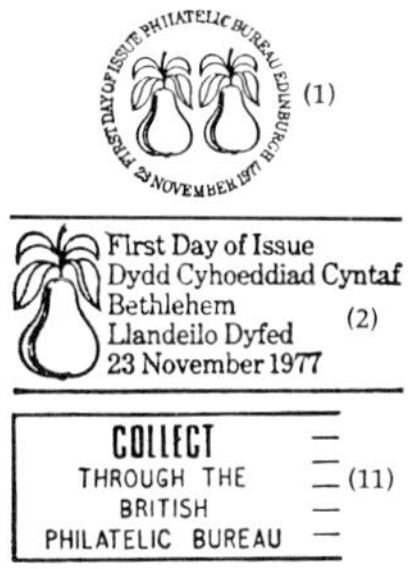

25th January 1978 - ENERGY

9p Oil; 10½p Coal; 11p Gas; 13p Electricity

SPECIAL HANDSTAMPS	ordinary covers £	official covers £
(1) First Day of Issue - Philatelic Bureau	5	- *Post Office*
(2) KW Claymore 'A' Project Team, Peterhead	35	60 *Claymore*
(3) Institute of Fuel, Golden Jubilee Year, W1	8	8 *Cotswold (g)*
(4) Coal is Precious, Ellistown	10	*3 *Green(s)*
(5) Oil is Precious, Melton Mowbray	10	*3 *Green(s)*
(6) British Speedway, Gulf Oil League, W4	10	- *n.o.c.*
(7) SEAGAS, a part of British Gas Croydon	10	- *n.o.c.*
(8) Forties Field, BP, Aberdeen	8	20 *BOCS 1*
(9) West Sole Field, BP, Hull	8	15 *BOCS 1*
(10) 21 Years Nuclear Electricity, Dungerness	8	15 *RHDR 4*

**Note: Greens of Market Harborough sponsored these two handstamps. A set of 4 single value FDCs were produced - the 9p & 10½p values were cancelled with the special handstamps whilst the other two values received the Leicester FDI handstamp. The set is valued @ £12.*

C.D.S. POSTMARKS		
(11) Bacton - North Sea gas pipeline	40	
(12) Coalville, Coal Aston, or Coalpit Heath *each*	40	
(13) Cruden Bay - Forties Field oil pipeline	40	
(14) Seascale - first nuclear power station - Calder Hall	50	
(15) Selby - major U.K. coalfield	40	
SLOGAN POSTMARK		
(16) Collect through Philatelic Bureau	30	

1978

1st March 1978 - BRITISH ARCHITECTURE - HISTORIC BUILDINGS

9p Tower of London; 10½p Holyroodhouse; 11p Caernarvon Castle; 13p Hampton Court

	ordinary covers £	official covers £	
SPECIAL HANDSTAMPS			
(1) First Day of Issue - Philatelic Bureau	3	-	*Post Office*
(2) First Day of Issue - London EC	3	-	*Post Office*
(3) Her Majesty's Tower of London, BF 9000 PS	5	15	*Tower of Lon*
(4) British Architecture, British Library, WC	5	20	*BL 5*
(5) Royal Heritage, Hampton Court Palace	5	12	*BOCS 2*
(6) Hampton Court, England's Oldest Tennis Court	5	40	*S.P.*
(7) Wells Cathedral, 800th Anniversary	10	15	*Cotswold (g)*
(8) 1953-1978 Stampex, Silver Jubilee, SW1	5	10	*Stampex*
(9) Portland 900th, Dorset	10	30	*Portland*
(10) Northwest Genius, Manchester Evening News	60	-	*n.o.c.*
ORDINARY F.D.I. POSTMARKS			
(11) Caernarfon	5		
(12) King's Lynn ('Estate Office Sandringham' cachet)	25		
C.D.S. POSTMARKS			
(13) Holyrood, Edinburgh 8	30		

(2)

(7)

(5)

(10)

1st March 1978 - BRITISH ARCHITECTURE - HISTORIC BUILDINGS

Miniature Sheet

	ordinary covers £	official covers £	
SPECIAL HANDSTAMPS			
(1) First Day of Issue - Philatelic Bureau	5	-	*Post Office*
(2) First Day of Issue - London EC	5	-	*Post Office*
(3) Her Majesty's Tower of London, BF 9000 PS	10	20	*Tower of Lon*
(4) British Architecture, British Library, WC	10	25	*BL 5*
(5) Royal Heritage, Hampton Court Palace	8	50	*BOCS 2d*
(6) Hampton Court, England's Oldest Tennis Court	8	-	*n.o.c.*
(7) Wells Cathedral, 800th Anniversary	15	30	*Cotswold (g)*
(8) 1953-1978 Stampex, Silver Jubilee, SW1	10	20	*Stampex*
(9) Portland 900th, Dorset	15	-	*n.o.c.*
(10) Northwest Genius, Manchester Evening News	75	-	*n.o.c.*
ORDINARY F.D.I. POSTMARKS			
(11) Caernarfon	10		
C.D.S. POSTMARKS			
(12) Earl's Court SW5 - venue of London 1980	30		
(13) Holyrood, Edinburgh 8	35		

(8)

(3)

(9)

(13)

(1)

31st May 1978 - 25th ANNIVERSARY OF THE CORONATION

9p State Coach; 10½p St. Edward's Crown; 11p The Orb; 13p Imperial State Crown

	ordinary covers £	official covers £	
SPECIAL HANDSTAMPS			
(1) First Day of Issue - Philatelic Bureau	3	-	*Post Office*
(2) First Day of Issue - London SW	3	-	*Post Office*
(3) 1953 Coronation 1978, British Library, WC	5	20	*BL 7*
(4) Cameo Stamp Centre, WC2	5	8	*Cameo*
(5) RAF Wattisham, BF 1953 PS	5	10	*RAF Watt.*
(6) Queen Elizabeth II, 25th Anniv Coronation, RHDR	5	5	*RHDR 6*
(7) Caernarfon (depicting castle)	15	-	*n.o.c.*
(8) Official Opening, Prince of Wales, Newcastle	10	30	*Freeman Hosp.*
(9) British Philatelic Fed. Congress, Worthing	10	25	*B.P.F.*
(10) Union of PO Workers, Blackpool	25	35	*U.P.O.W.*
(11) RAF Hospital Wegberg, BF 1612 PS	20	35	*Forces*
(12) Lewis's Celebrate 21 Years in Bristol	20	35	*Lewis's*
(13) Mint, Sutton, Surrey	25	35	*Mint*
(14) The Gatwick Park, Horley	15	40	*G. Park Hotel*
(15) Assoc. Dairies, Benton Royal Opening, Newcastle	15	-	*n.o.c.*
(16) Visit of Prince of Wales, Newton Aycliffe	15	40	*Newton Aycl.*
(17) Temple of Jerusalem, Leicester	15	-	*n.o.c.*
ORDINARY F.D.I. POSTMARKS			
(18) Windsor, Berks	10		
(19) King's Lynn ('Estate Office Sandringham' cachet)	20		

(15)

(9)

(16)

(8)

(12)

PRICES & CONDITION - PLEASE READ GENERAL NOTES

Coronation (contd.)

C.D.S. POSTMARKS	ordinary covers £	official covers £
(20) Buckingham Palace, S.W.1	140	
(21) Coronation Road or Coronation Square ... *each*	20	
(22) House of Commons, S.W.1	20	
(23) House of Lords, S.W.1	25	
(24) Queen Elizabeth Avenue, Walsall	20	
(25) Scone - Stone of Scone part of Coronation Chair	150	
(26) Windsor Castle, Windsor, Berks	150	

5th July 1978 - CENTENARY OF SHIRE HORSE SOCIETY

9p Shire Horse; 10½p Shetland Pony; 11p Welsh Pony; 13p Thoroughbred

SPECIAL HANDSTAMPS		
(1) First Day of Issue - Philatelic Bureau	3	- *Post Office*
(2) First Day of Issue - Peterborough	4	- *Post Office*
(3) Havering Park Riding School	6	20 *Havering (f)*
(4) Tribute to the Horse, Market Weighton School	6	30 *MW School*
(5) Horses of Britain, British Library, WC	6	30 *BL 8*
(6) Courage Shire Horse Centre, Maidenhead	6	50 *BOCS 4*
(7) The Royal Show, 1878-1978, Kenilworth	7	30 *S.P.*
(8) The Sport of Kings, Brighton	8	25 *B.Racecourse*
(9) Shetland Pony Stud Book Society	10	35 *Pilgrim*
(10) Home of the Derby, Epsom	10	- *Post Office*
(11) World Dressage Championships, Goodwood	10	35 *W Dressage*
(12) 700th Anniversary of the Cinque Ports, Hythe	7	10 *RHDR 7*
(13) RNLI Clacton 1878-1978, Clacton	20	30 *Pilgrim*
(14) Ars Gratia Artis, London W1	20	55 *MGM*
(15) Royal Scots Dragoon Guards, BF 1678 PS	20	- *n.o.c.*
(16) Royal Irish Rangers, BF 1621 PS	20	50 *Roy.Ir.Rang.*
(17) Lawn Tennis Championships, Wimbledon	20	- *n.o.c.*
(18) Salvation Army, Wembley	20	15 *S. Army(s)*
(19) Sutton-on-Trent Comprehensive School	20	40 *Sutton Sch*
(20) Big Four Rly Museum, Bournemouth	20	- *n.o.c.*
(21) Llangollen International Musical Eisteddfod	20	15 *L.I.M.E.(s)*
(22) Caernarfon (depicting castle)	15	- *n.o.c.*

ORDINARY F.D.I. POSTMARKS	
(23) Aberystwyth ('Welsh Pony Express' cover).	15
(23a) Aylesbury (Amersham Horse Show cover)	15
(23b) Bournemouth ('Railway Horses' cover).	15
(24) King's Lynn ('Royal Studs Sandringham' cachet)	25

C.D.S. POSTMARKS	
(25) Aintree - famous racecourse	60
(26) Ascot - famous racecourse	75
(27) Blackhorse, Bristol	20
(28) Darley - 'Darley Arabian' one of the three great sires..	40
(29) Godolphin Cross - 'Goldolphin Arabian' - do -	40
(30) Epsom Downs - home of the Derby	60
(31) Gt. Yarmouth (Anna Sewell/Black Beauty cover)	25
(32) Horsefair - Kidderminster or Rugeley ... *each*	20
(33) Lerwick - Shetland pony	35
(34) Riding Mill, Paddock or Shireoaks ... *each*	20
(35) Studlands or Newmarket ... *each*	25

2nd August 1978 - CYCLING CENTENARY

9p Penny Farthing; 10½p Touring Bicycles;
11p Modern Bikes; 13p Road Racers

SPECIAL HANDSTAMPS		
(1) First Day of Issue - Philatelic Bureau	3	- *Post Office*
(2) First Day of Issue - Harrogate	3	- *Post Office*
(3) BCF Centenary Meeting, Leicester	4	15 *City Council*
(4) TI Raleigh, Bicycle Manufacturer, Nottingham	4	20 *BOCS 5*
(5) TI Raleigh, Tour de France, Nottingham	4	12 *BOCS 5*
(6) 1953 Coronation 1978, British Library, WC	12	20 *B. Library*
(7) Colchester Searchlite Tattoo, BF 1606 PS	20	5 *C.S. Tattoo(s)*
(8) Self-righting Lifeboat, Science Museum, SW7	30	- *n.o.c.*
(9) Caernarfon (depicting castle)	12	- *n.o.c.*
(10) 700th Anniversary of the Cinque Ports, Hythe	20	30 *RHDR 7*

(5)

(16)

(8)

(6)

(15)

(10)

(24)

(18)

(25)

(26)

(20)

(21)

(2)

(7)

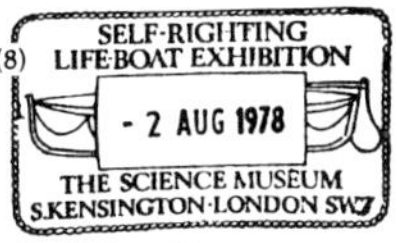

(8)

(5)

PRICES & CONDITION - PLEASE READ GENERAL NOTES

Cycling (contd.)

	ordinary covers £	official covers £
ORDINARY F.D.I. POSTMARKS		
(11) Dumfries - Kirkpatrick MacMillan invented bicycle	25	
C.D.S. POSTMARKS		
(12) Charlbury - Tandem Club was founded here	45	
(13) Godalming - Cylists' Touring Club	45	
(14) Meriden - Cyclists' War Memorial	45	
(15) Raleigh, Torpoint, Cornwall	175	
SLOGAN POSTMARKS		
(16) Driver - Mind that Bike Reading	70	
(17) Driver - Mind that Bike, Sussex Coast	70	

(14)

(16)
(17)

22nd November 1978 - CHRISTMAS

7p, 9p, 11p, 13p Carols

SPECIAL HANDSTAMPS		
(1) First Day of Issue - Philatelic Bureau	2	- *Post Office*
(2) First Day of Issue - Bethlehem, Llandeilo, Dyfed	3	- *Post Office*
(3) Carols for Christmas, British Library, WC	4	20 *BL 9*
(4) Kings College Cambridge	4	9 *BOCS 6*
(5) Parish of Dalgety, Dunfermline	4	5 *Dal Parish*
(6) Music for All, Romford	4	5 *Havering (f)*
(7) History of Philately Exhibition, Warwick	6	20 *W & W*
(8) Meet Your Post Office, Dunfermline	10	- *n.o.c.*
(9) 50 Years of Rotary in Clacton	6	15 *Rotary*
(10) Gold of Eldorado, Royal Academy, W1	6	25 *Pilgrim*
(11) Croeso Cymru I'r Crysau Duon, Cardiff	10	70 *All Blacks*
ORDINARY F.D.I. POSTMARKS		
(12) Oxford - Boars Head Carol, Queens College	5	
C.D.S. POSTMARKS		
(13) Boars Head, Wigan - Boars Head Carol (13p)	40	
(14) Fairy Cross, Bideford	15	
(15) Fir Tree, Crook, Co. Durham	15	
(16) Hollybush, Blackwood	15	
(17) Nasareth, Caernarfon	25	

(4)

(5)

(3)

(9)

(8)

7th February 1979 - DOGS

9p Old English Sheepdog; 10½p Welsh Springer Spaniel; 11p West Highland Terrier; 13p Irish Setter

SPECIAL HANDSTAMPS		
(1) First Day of Issue - Philatelic Bureau	2	- *Post Office*
(2) First Day of Issue - London SW	3	- *Post Office*
(3) Spillers Congratulate Kennel Club, EC4	4	10 *BOCS 7*
(4) New Zealand Exhibition, Warwick	5	20 *W & W*
(5) Gold of Eldorado, Royal Academy, W1	5	25 *Pilgrim*
(6) England v. N. Ireland, Wembley.	12	2 *Dawn(s)*
ORDINARY F.D.I. POSTMARKS		
(7) Battersea - Battersea Dogs Home	8	
(8) Brighton (Coral Brighton & Hove Stadium cover)	25	
(9) Redhill (P.D.S.A. cover)	25	
C.D.S. POSTMARKS		
(10) Barking, Essex	15	
(11) Battersea Park Road - Battersea Dogs Home	40	
(12) Black Dog, Crediton	40	
(13) Dog & Gun, Liverpool	70	
(14) Dog Kennel Lane, Oldbury	75	
(15) Dogsthorpe, Peterborough	30	
(16) Hounds Hill, Blackpool	50	
(17) Isle of Dogs, E14	100	

(5)

(3)

(1)

(6)

21st March 1979 - BRITISH FLOWERS

9p Primrose; 10½p Daffodil; 11p Bluebell; 13p Snowdrop

SPECIAL HANDSTAMPS		
(1) First Day of Issue - Philatelic Bureau	2	- *Post Office*
(2) Royal Botanic Gardens, Kew, Richmond	4	20 *Botanic Gdns*
(3) Bath Floral City Exhibition	4	4 *Cotswold (g)*
(4) Nat. Assoc. Flower Arrangers Soc., St. Marys	3	5 *BOCS 8*
(5) Nat. Assoc. Flower Arrangers Soc., Penzance	3	5 *BOCS 8*

(4)

(6)

(1)

British Flowers (contd.)

	ordinary covers £	official covers £	
(6) Founders Day, Bluebell Railway, Uckfield	4	20	*RHDR 8*
(7) Rural Blisworth Exhibition, Northampton	6	25	*Blisworth*
(8) W.I. Canterbury (Women's Institute)	8	40	*W.I.*
(9) Egypt Postage Stamp Exhibition, Warwick	6	20	*W & W*

C.D.S. POSTMARKS

(10) Blue Bell Hill, Huddersfield	40		
(11) Botanic Gardens, Belfast	30		
(12) Flowery Field, Hyde	30		
(13) Kew Gardens, Richmond	75		
(14) Primrose, Jarrow	50		
(15) Spring Gardens, Lytham St. Annes	30		

SLOGAN POSTMARKS

(16) Bath - Europe's Floral City	55		
(17) 21st Spalding Flower Parade	55		

9th May 1979 - DIRECT ELECTIONS TO EUROPEAN ASSEMBLY

9p, 10½p, 11p, 13p Flags of Member Nations

SPECIAL HANDSTAMPS

(1) First Day of Issue - Philatelic Bureau	3	-	*Post Office*
(2) First Day of Issue - London SW	3	-	*Post Office*
(3) Strasbourg - Leicester's Twin City	4	8	*City Council*
(4) British European Parliamentary Elections, SW1	4	10	*BOCS 10*
(5) Entente Cordiale, Stowmarket	225	100	*Stow. Tw. Com.*
(6) Cameo Stamp Centre, WC2	3	6	*Cameo*
(7) Inst. of Gas Engineers, SW	6	20	*Gas Eng.*
(8) Worth Valley Rly Letter Service, Keighley	6	25	*W V Rly*
(9) Lions Holiday, 79 District, Hayling Island	8	35	*Lions*
(10) Barbados Postage Stamps Exhibition, Warwick	4	15	*W & W*
(11) Nat. Assoc. Flower Arrangers, Blackpool	5	6	*BOCS 8*
(12) Derby 200 Exhibition, Royal Academy, W1	5	6	*BOCS 9*
(13) British Chess Federation, Norwich	7	15	*Chess Fed*

ORDINARY F.D.I. POSTMARKS

(14) Folkestone, Kent - Gateway to Europe	4		

C.D.S. POST.MARKS

(15) Blackrod, Bolton	12		
(16) Dover or Harwich - Gateways to Europe *each*	8		
(17) House of Commons, S.W.1	20		
(18) House of Lords, S.W.1	25		
(19) Newhaven, East Sussex - Gateway to Europe	8		
(19a) Ditto with PAQUEBOT markings	12		
(20) Dieppe with PAQUEBOT markings	12		
(21) Parliament Street or Northern Parliament *each*	12		
(22) Weymouth - Gateway to Europe	8		

SLOGAN POSTMARKS

(23) Are you on the Voters List?, Lincoln	500		
(24) Bath - Europe's Floral City	100		

6th June 1979 - HORSE RACING

9p The Derby; 10½p Aintree; 11p Newmarket; 13p Windsor

SPECIAL HANDSTAMPS

(1) First Day of Issue - Philatelic Bureau	3	-	*Post Office*
(2) First Day of Issue - Epsom, Surrey	3	-	*Post Office*
(3) Jockey Club, Newmarket	4	20	*S.P.*
(4) Derby 200 Exhibition, Royal Academy, W1	4	6	*BOCS 9*
(5) Derby 200, Epsom, Surrey	4	6	*BOCS 11*
(6) England's Oldest Horse Race, Kiplingcotes	4	10	*MW School*
(7) Derbyshire Festival, Matlock	8	30	*Derbys Fest.*
(8) Newbury Show, Berks	5	5	*New. Ag. Soc*
(9) Chigwell School, 1629-1979	8	15	*Chigwell Sch*
(10) Nauru Postal History Exhibition, Warwick	8	20	*W & W*
(11) Norwich Union First Class Insurance	8	30	*Norwich Union*
(12) 35th Anniv. of D-Day, Southampton	8	-	*n.o.c.*
(13) 35th Anniv. Operation Neptune, BF 3544 PS	8	-	*n.o.c.*
(14) First Collection, Edinburgh Eurocrest Hotel	8	50	*Euro Hotel*
(15) First Collection, Glasgow Eurocrest Hotel	8	60	*Euro Hotel*

(8)

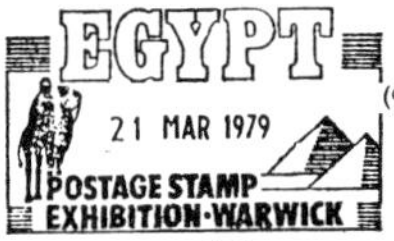

(9)

(13)

(14)

(1)

(13)

(19)

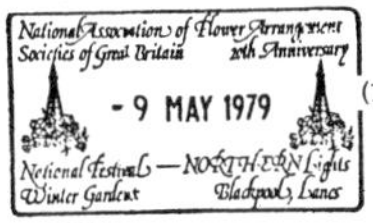

(11)

(6)

(4)

(2)

(1)

(9)

(15)

(5)

(12)

Horse Racing (contd.)

	ordinary covers	official covers
ORDINARY F.D.I. POSTMARKS	**£**	**£**
(16) Derby or Doncaster *each*	6	
(17) King's Lynn ('Royal Studs Sandringham' cachet)	10	
(18) Liverpool - Aintree racecourse	5	
(19) Windsor - Dorsett Ferry, Windsor (13p)	5	
C.D.S. POSTMARKS		
(20) Aintree - famous racecourse	50	
(21) Ascot - famous racecourse	25	
(22) Derby	15	
(23) Epsom Downs - famous racecourse	60	
(24) Horse Fair, Kidderminster	25	
(25) Newmarket	35	
(26) Stud Farm, Polegate	35	
(27) Studlands, Newmarket - horse breeding & training	35	
(28) Tattenham Corner - Epsom racecourse	75	
SLOGAN POSTMARKS		
(29) Come Racing at Great Yarmouth	70	
(30) Derby Fiesta July 3rd-7th, Derby	70	
(31) Derbyshire Festival - Much to Celebrate	125	

(30)

(29)

(31)

11th July 1979 - YEAR OF THE CHILD

9p Peter Rabbit - Beatrix Potter;
10½p Wind in the Willows - Kenneth Grahame;
11p Winnie the Pooh - A. A . Milne; 13p Alice - Lewis Caroll

SPECIAL HANDSTAMPS			
(1) First Day of Issue - Philatelic Bureau	2	-	*Post Office*
(2) Yardley Primary School, Chingford	7	25	*Walth. Forest*
(3) NSPCC, Bethlehem	4	5	*BOCS Sp 1*
(4) Kent & East Sussex Rly, Tenterden	4	4	*RH 9*
(5) Winnie the Pooh, Hartfield	4	15	*BOCS 12*
(6) Beatrix Potter, Near Sawrey, Ambleside	8	-	*Post Office*
(7) Great Ormonde St., WC1	10	-	*n.o.c.*
(8) Palitoy Diamond Jubilee, Leicester	20	200	*Palitoy*
(9) New Parks Boys School, Jubilee, Leicester	8	25	*NPB School*
(10) Lewis Carroll Society, Daresbury	8	20	*L.C. Soc*
(11) Alice in Wonderland, Llandudno	8	35	*Llan Town C*
(12) Year of the Child & Cub Country, Birkenhead	8	15	*Dawn*
(13) Year of the Child, Wokingham	8	10	*Rotary*
(14) IYC, Westminster Cathedral, SW1	8	20	*Cotswold*
(15) Wisbech Grammar School	10	45	*Wisbech GS*
(16) Care for Mother & Baby, Life Care, Leamington	35	20	*LIFE*
(17) Royal Tournament, BF 1979 PS	10	20	*BFPS*
(18) 1979 Anniversaries, British Library, WC	10	20	*BL 10*
(19) Home International Bowls Tournament, Pontypool	15	30	*Pilgrim*
(20) Rhodesia Philatelic Exhibition, NPC, Warwick	15	20	*W & W*
ORDINARY F.D.I. POSTMARKS			
(21) Edinburgh - birthplace of Kenneth Graham	5		
(22) Hartfield - home of A. A. Milne	5		
(23) Oxford - Lewis Carroll	5		
(24) Stourbridge - Adrian Cresswell (designed PO cover)	5		
C.D.S. POSTMARKS			
(25) Child Okeford, Blandford Forum	30		
(26) Child's Hill, London N.W.2	30		
(27) Far Sawrey, Ambleside - home of Beatrix Potter	40		
(28) Hartfield, East Sussex - home of A. A. Milne	15		
(29) Playing Place, Truro	45		
SLOGAN POSTMARKS			
(30) Barnardo's Care about Children	60		
(31) Give a Child a Home Leeds Social Services	80		

Note - The date of issue was originally planned for 18th July 1979. Howerer, due to a shortage of stocks of definitive stamps at many Post Offices, resulting from an industrial dispute at the Post Office Supplies Deptartment, the date was brought forward by one week. This allowed for the early use of these commemorative stamps but caused a few headaches for cover producers!

PLEASE READ THE GENERAL NOTES
AT THE BEGINNING OF THIS CATALOGUE
These often provide the answers to enquiries received.

(1)

(3)

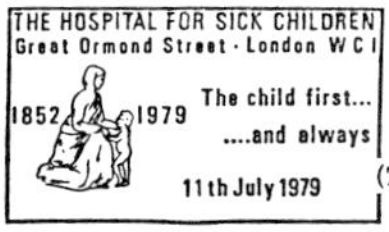

(7)

(16)

(15)

(18)

(22)

(5)

(20)

(31)

(30)

22nd August 1979 – CENTENARY OF THE DEATH OF SIR ROWLAND HILL

10p Sir Rowland Hill; 11½p General Post c 1839; 13p London Post c 1839; 15p Uniform Postage 1840

	ordinary covers	official covers
SPECIAL HANDSTAMPS	**£**	**£**
(1) First Day of Issue – Philatelic Bureau	2	– *Post Office*
(2) First Day of Issue – London EC	2	– *Post Office*
(3) London EC Chief Office (Rowland Hill Statue)	5	– *n.o.c.*
(4) National Postal Museum (Red Maltese Cross), EC4	5	– *n.o.c.*
(5) Bruce Castle Museum, Tottenham N17	5	15 *Haringey*
(6) Sir Rowland Hill, Kidderminster Art Gallery	5	– *n.o.c.*
(7) Bath Postal Museum, Centenary Exhib.	4	5 *BP Museum*
(8) Sir Rowland Hill, Mail Coach Run, Kidderminster	3	5 *BOCS 13*
(9) Sir Rowland Hill, Mail Coach Run, Birmingham	3	5 *BOCS 13*
(10) Rowland Hill, Commemorative Delivery, Rayleigh	5	60 *Wiggins Teape*
(11) Rowland Hill 1795-1879, Coventry	4	– n.o.c.
(12) Rowland Hill 1795-1879, Stratford	4	– *n.o.c.*
(13) Rowland Hill 1795-1879, Warwick	4	– *n.o.c.*
(14) Rowland Hill First Day of Issue, Kidderminster	4	– *n.o.c.*
(15) 1979 Anniversaries, British Library, WC	5	25 *BL 11*
(16) Military Tattoo, Edinburgh	6	20 *M Tattoo*
(17) York Races, Tote Ebor Handicap, York	6	5 *S.P.(s)*
(18) Pier Centenary, Bournemouth	6	20 *Philatex*
(19) Skirrid Energy Drive, SW1	6	20 *Skirrid*
(20) Haddo House, Aberdeen	6	12 *Scot N.T.*
ORDINARY F.D.I. POSTMARKS		
(21) Sanquhar – Britain's oldest Post Office	6	
C.D.S. POSTMARKS		
(22) Belsize Park – near to where Rowland Hill died	25	
(23) Hampstead Heath – near where Rowland Hill died	18	
(24) Hampstead – near to where Rowland Hill died	18	
(25) Bruce Grove – Rowland Hill lived at Bruce Castle	15	
(26) House of Commons, S.W.1	10	
(27) House of Lords, S.W.1	12	
(28) Kidderminster, Worcs – birthplace of Rowland Hill	7	
(29) PAQUEBOTS – introduced by Rowland Hill ... *from*	12	
(30) Rowlands Castle, Hants	16	
SLOGAN POSTMARKS		
(31) International Stamp Exhib., Earls Court, EC	70	
(32) Datapost D – a new postal service, Enfield	90	

(8)

(2)

(5)

(9)

(20)

(6)

(19)
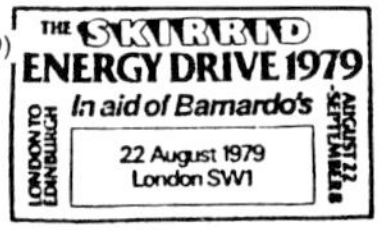

(32)

26th September 1979 – 150th ANNIVERSARY OF THE METROPOLITAN POLICE FORCE

10p Local 'bobby'; 11½p Traffic Control; 13p Mounted police; 15p Police Launch on the Thames

	ordinary covers	official covers
SPECIAL HANDSTAMPS		
(1) First Day of Issue – Philatelic Bureau	2	– *Post Office*
(2) First Day of Issue – London SW	2	– *Post Office*
(3) New Scotland Yard, Metropolitan Police	4	8 *Cotswold*
(4) Port of London Police, E16	6	100 *Port London*
(5) Devon & Cornwall Constabulary, Exeter	5	20 *D & C Const.*
(6) West Yorks Metropolitan Police, Wakefield	3	5 *BOCS 14*
(7) Sir Robert Peel, Tamworth	5	– *n.o.c.*
(8) Royal Air Force Police, Bruggen, BF 1665 PS	5	25 *RAF Police*
(9) 1979 Anniversaries, British Library, WC	6	20 *BL 12*
(10) Shooting First Enemy Aircraft, BF 1662 PS	6	– *n.o.c.*
(11) Zeppelin Mail Exhibition, NPC Warwick	6	15 *W & W*
(12) Sir John Gielgud at Blackpool	6	20 *Blk Theatre*
ORDINARY F.D.I. POSTMARKS		
(13) Bedford (Bedfordshire Police cover)	15	
(14) Bolton & Bury (Greater Manchester Police cover)	15	
(15) Lincoln (Lincolnshire Police cover)	15	
(15a) Norwich (Norfolk Constabulary cover)	15	
C.D.S. POSTMARKS		
(16) Bow Street, Dyfed – Bow Street Runners	50	
(17) Bury, Lancs – birthplace of Sir Robert Peel	20	
(18) Constable Burton, Leyburn North Yorks	30	
(19) Constable Road, Sheffield	40	

(5)

(8)

(11)

(6)

(7)

(4)

PRICES & CONDITION – PLEASE READ GENERAL NOTES

Police (contd.)

	ordinary covers £	official covers £
(20) Crook, Co. Durham	25	
(21) Hendon, N.W.4 - Police Training School	20	
(22) House of Commons, S.W.1	20	
(23) House of Lords, S.W.1 - highest court in the land	30	
(24) Law, Carluke	30	
(25) Tamworth - Home of Sir Robert Peel	15	
(26) Wapping, E.1 - River Police HQ (15p)	25	
(27) Eynsham (Police Training Centre cover)	25	
(28) Field Post Office 999 (North Yorks Police cover)	50	

SLOGAN POSTMARKS

(29) Durham 800 Years a City (Durham prison)	90	

24th October 1979 - CENTENARY OF THE DEATH OF SIR ROWLAND HILL

Miniature sheet

SPECIAL HANDSTAMPS

(1) First Day of Issue - Philatelic Bureau	2	- *Post Office*
(2) First Day of Issue - London EC	2	- *Post Office*
(3) London EC Chief Office (Rowland Hill Statue)	5	- *n.o.c.*
(4) National Postal Museum (Red Maltese Cross) EC	5	- *n.o.c.*
(5) Bruce Castle Museum, Tottenham N17	20	40 *Haringey*
(6) Sir Rowland Hill London & Brighton Rly Co	3	6 *BOCS 16*
(7) Cartoonists Club, Sir Rowland Hill, Gatwick Airport	3	5 *BOCS Sp 2*
(8) 1979 Anniversaries, British Library, WC	5	20 *BL 11a*
(9) PUC 1929 Exhibition NPC Warwick	6	- *n.o.c.*

ORDINARY F.D.I. POSTMARKS

(10) Kidderminster - birthplace of Rowland Hill	4	
(11) Sanquhar - Britain's oldest Post Office	6	

C.D.S. POSTMARKS

(12) Hampstead NW3 - near to where Rowland Hill died	12	
(13) House of Commons, S.W.1	10	
(14) House of Lords, S.W.1	12	
(15) Kidderminster, Worcs - birthplace of Rowland Hill	8	
(16) Rowlands Castle, Hants	15	

SLOGAN POSTMARKS

(17) Int. Stamp Exhib., Earls Court, London 1980, EC	45	

22nd August & 24th October 1979 - SIR ROWLAND HILL (DOUBLE DATED COVERS)

Prices can be summarised as follows:	£
(1) special handstamp (both dates on one cover)	40
(2) appropriate CDS (both dates on one cover)	50

21st November 1979 - CHRISTMAS

8p, 10p, 11½p, 13p, 15p The Nativity

SPECIAL HANDSTAMPS

(1) First Day of Issue - Philatelic Bureau	2	- *Post Office*
(2) First Day of Issue - Bethlehem, Llandeilo, Dyfed	2	- *Post Office*
(3) Christmas, British Library, WC	3	15 *BL 13*
(4) 25th Anniv After the Ball, Blackpool	4	15 *Blk Theatre*
(5) Cheriton & Morehall Traders, Christmas Lights	3	6 *CM Traders*
(6) Father Christmas Special, K. & E. S. Rly, Tenterden	3	5 *RH 10*
(7) Centenary of the War Cry, EC4	3	35 *H.R.*
(8) Rotary Club of Swansea	3	15 *Rotary*
(9) Year of the Child Stamp & Coin Exhib. Coventry	3	10 *D.F.*
(10) Official Naming Ceremony new Margate Lifeboat.	3	8 *Pilgrim*
(11) Air Mails, 1920-1950 NPC ,Warwick	5	15 *W & W*
(12) BIPEX, London SW	5	- *n.o.c.*
(13) England v. Bulgaria, Wembley	5	2 *Dawn(s)*

C.D.S. POSTMARKS

(14) Nasareth, Caernarfon	30	

In addition, covers are known with the following CDS pmks: Angel Hill, Holy Island, Kings Road, Star, Starcross, Shepherds Bush. Prices from £6 each.

SLOGAN POSTMARKS

(15) Milton Keynes, Xmas Shopping As It Should Be	75	

In addition: Barnardos Cares About Children; Postcode It. Prices from £30.

16th January 1980 - BRITISH BIRDS

10p Kingfisher; 11½p Dipper;
13p Moorhen; 15p Yellow Wagtail

SPECIAL HANDSTAMPS

	ordinary covers £	official covers £
(1) First Day of Issue - Philatelic Bureau	2	- *Post Office*
(2) First Day of Issue - Sandy, Beds	2	- *Post Office*
(3) Essex Field Club, Centenary, Chelmsford	3	5 *Havering 5*
(4) Leicestershire & Rutland Ornithological Society	3	15 *LFDC (f)*
(5) West Midlands Bird Club, 51st Anniversary	3	4 *P.P.S.*
(6) Wildfowl Trust, Arundel	3	6 *BOCS 17*
(7) Wildfowl Trust, Washington	3	6 *BOCS 17*
(8) Wildfowl Trust, Peakirk	3	6 *BOCS 17*
(9) Wildfowl Trust, Martin Mere	3	7 *BOCS 17*
(10) Wildfowl Trust, Slimbridge	3	5 *BOCS 17*
(11) Pioneers in Bird Protection, RSPB Sandy	3	8 *R.S.P.B.*
(12) Hull Natural History Society, Centenary Year	3	8 *MW School*
(13) NNT, 1880 Wild Birds Protection Act, Norwich	3	6 *Markton*
(14) 10th Anniv., Cotswold Wildlife Park, Burford	3	5 *Cotswold (g)*
(15) Wintertime, British Library, WC	9	40 *BL 14*
(16) The Salvation Army, 100, Harwich	9	50 *H.R.*
(17) The Royal Image Exhibition, NPC, Warwick	9	20 *W & W*
(18) Queens School Rheindahlen, BF 1671 PS	9	75 *Queens Sch*

C.D.S. POSTMARKS

(19) Fair Isle, Shetland - famous bird observatory	40
(20) House of Commons SW1 - Wild Bird Protection Act	25
(21) House of Lords SW1 - Wild Bird Protection Act	30
(22) Sandy, Beds. - R.S.P.B. Headquarters	40

In addition: Birds Edge, Cley, Eagle, Heron Cross, Hickling, Holme, Partridge Green, Ranworth, Swallownest, Wing, Wren's Nest. Prices range from £10 each.

SLOGAN POSTMARKS

(23) Dovecot Arts Centre (depicting doves), Stockton	350

In addition: Collect British Stamps £30.

12th March 1980 - THE LIVERPOOL & MANCHESTER RAILWAY

5 x 12p 'The Rocket' and various railway carriages

SPECIAL HANDSTAMPS

	ordinary covers £	official covers £
(1) First Day of Issue - Philatelic Bureau	2	- *Post Office*
(2) First Day of Issue - Manchester	2	- *Post Office*
(3) First Day of Issue - Liverpool	2	- *Post Office*
(4) Great Railway Exposition, Manchester	3	- *n.o.c.*
(5) Main Line Steam Trust, Loughborough	3	10 *LFDC (f)*
(6) Newton-le-Willows, Earlstown	3	20 *Newton 150*
(7) 80th Anniversary Rother Railway, Tenterden	3	12 *RH 11*
(8) The Railway Age, Coventry	3	20 *D.F.*
(9) To London 1980 by Rail, BF 1682 PS	4	2 *R.A.F.(s)*
(10) Havering's own Railway, 150 Years Mail by Rail	3	7 *Havering 6*
(11) Bressingham Steam Museum, Diss	3	7 *Markton*
(12) T.P.O. Exhibition, Crewe	4	15 *Dawn*
(13) Manchester (Kelloggs)	5	25 *Kelloggs*
(14) Austro-Hungarian Postal History, Warwick	10	25 *W & W*
(15) Volvo Diplomat Sales Consult the Experts, W1	12	80 *Volvo*
(16) LSP Ammeraal, Ware Herts	12	80 *LSP*
(17) Wintertime, British Library, WC	12	40 *BL 16*
(18) Daily Mail, Ideal Home Exhib., SW5	15	40 *Pilgrim*
(19) Codesort Comes to Manchester, or Liverpool *each*	15	- *Post Office*

ORDINARY F.D.I. POSTMARKS

(20) Bournemouth (Big Four Railway Museum cover)	10
(20a) Bradford (Worth Valley Railway cover)	15
(20b) Colchester (Stour Valley Railway cover)	15

C.D.S. POSTMARKS (inc. T.P.O. CANCELS)

(21) Crowthorne Stn - station Post Office	20
(22) Rainhill, Prescot - 'Rainhill Trials'	25
(23) The Rocket, Liverpool	35
(23a) Sheringham (North Norfolk Railway cover)	10
(24) NW TPO Night Down - the most appropriate	15
(25) Any other TPO (travelling post office) *from*	15
(26) TPO 'A.M.' pmks - these have to be handed over early on the morning of the stamp issue	20

SLOGAN POSTMARKS

(27) 150 Years of Mail by Rail - Manchester	40
(28) 150 Years of Mail by Rail - Liverpool	40

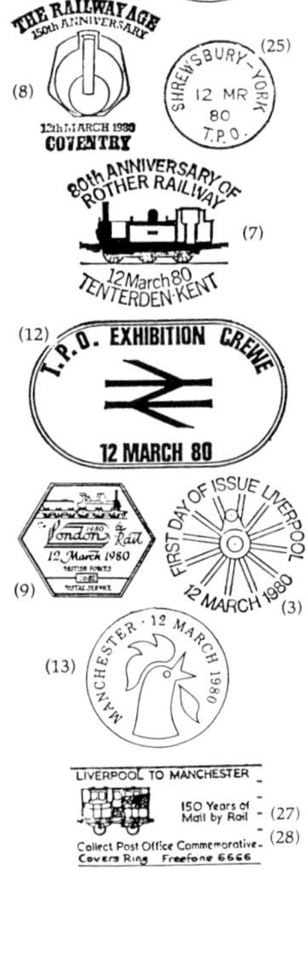

9th April 1980 - LONDON 1980 INTERNATIONAL STAMP EXHIBITION

50p Montage of London Buildings

	ordinary covers £	official covers £	
SPECIAL HANDSTAMPS			
(1) First Day of Issue - Philatelic Bureau	2	-	*Post Office*
(2) First Day of Issue - London S.W	2	-	*Post Office*
(3) Stampway to London 1980, Cameo Stamp Centre	3	5	*Cameo*
(4) London Tourist Board, London 1980, Victoria	3	5	*BOCS 19*
(5) West Country-Liverpool, Inaugural Flight	4	10	*Royal Mail Air*
(6) Manchester (Kelloggs)	4	-	*n.o.c.*
(7) Trafalgar Square Branch Office (Nelson's Column)	8	-	*n.o.c.*
(8) G.B. Major Errors Exhibition, Warwick	6	10	*W & W*
(9) Springtime, British Library, WC	6	20	*BL 17*
(10) C.S./R.I.C. Annual Congress, Durham	6	25	*CS/RIC*
C.D.S. POSTMARKS			
(11) Earls Court B.O., London S.W.5	50		
(12) House of Commons, S.W.1	12		
(13) House of Lords, S.W.1	15		
SLOGAN POSTMARKS			
(14) Collect British Stamps World's Greatest Hobby	35		
(15) Int. Stamp Exh. Earls Court London 1980 - Leeds	45		

(2)

(5)

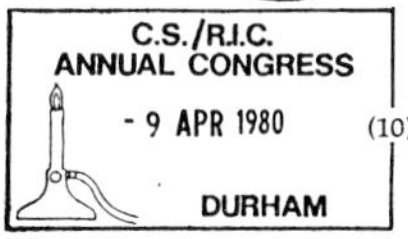

(10)

(9)

7th May 1980 - LONDON 1980 INTERNATIONAL STAMP EXHIBITION

50p Miniature Sheet

	ordinary covers £	official covers £	
SPECIAL HANDSTAMPS			
(1) First Day of Issue - Philatelic Bureau (Eros)	2	-	*Post Office*
(2) First Day of Issue - Philatelic Bureau (London 1980)	2	-	*Post Office*
(3) First Day of Issue - Kingston-upon-Thames	2	-	*Post Office*
(4) First Day of Issue - London SW	2	-	*Post Office*
(5) Stamps Magazine/London 1980, Brentwood	3	-	*n.o.c.*
(6) Supersonically to London 1980, BF 7580 PS	3	8	*BOCS 20*
(7) Centenary Appeal, London Union of Youth Clubs	3	-	*n.o.c.*
(8) Leicester Philatelic Society	3	30	*LFDC Sp 1*
(9) London Stamp Fair, London SW1	3	3	*Showpiece*
(10) Post Office Day, London 1980, SW	3	3	*PO Comm Cvr*
(11) Royal Opera House, Covent Garden, WC	3	-	*n.o.c.*
(12) Warwick Penny Post Postal History Exhibition,	8	-	*n.o.c.*
(13) Festival Fringe, Brighton	8	-	*n.o.c.*
(14) Salvation Army, 1880-1980, Belfast	8	15	*Sal Army*
(15) Freedom of Plymouth, BF 1694 PS	8	-	*n.o.c.*
(16) Manchester (Kelloggs)	8	-	*n.o.c.*
(17) Parish Church, Hampton-in-Arden	15	-	*n.o.c.*
(18) Springtime, British Library, London WC	10	25	*BL 17a*
C.D.S. POSTMARKS			
(19) Earl's Court B.O., London S.W.5	50		
(20) Earl's Court Exhibition B.O., S.W.5	50		
(21) House of Commons, S.W.1	12		
(22) House of Lords, S.W.1	15		
(23) Little London, Basingstoke	20		
SLOGAN POSTMARKS			
(24) Collect British Stamps - World's Greatest Hobby	30		

(6)

(15)

(5)

(14)

(3)

(2)

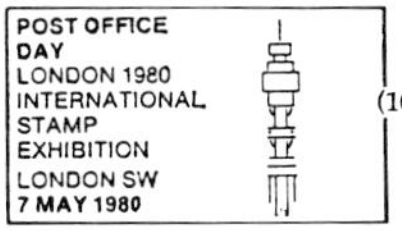

(10)

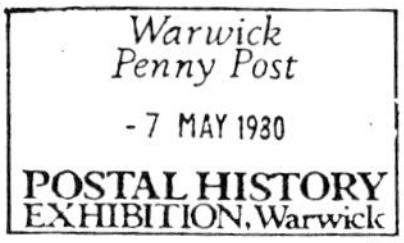

(12)

(18)

9th April & 7th May 1980 - LONDON 1980 (DOUBLE DATED COVERS)

Some double-dated covers exist with both the 50p stamp postmarked 9th April and the miniature sheet postmarked 7th May. Prices from £30.

PLEASE READ THE GENERAL NOTES
AT THE BEGINNING OF THIS CATALOGUE
These often provide the answers to enquiries received.

SLOGAN POSTMARKS

Prices in the catalogue (from 1980) are for covers with stamps sited to advantage so that the slogan is clearly legible.
Please refer to the General Notes.

7th May 1980 - LONDON LANDMARKS

10½p Buckingham Palace; 12p Albert Memorial; 13½p Royal Opera House; 15p Hampton Court; 17½p Kensington Palace

SPECIAL HANDSTAMPS	ordinary covers £	official covers £
(1) First Day of Issue - Philatelic Bureau (Eros)	2	- *Post Office*
(2) First Day of Issue - Philatelic Bureau (London 1980)	2	- *Post Office*
(3) First Day of Issue - Kingston-upon-Thames	2	- *Post Office*
(4) First Day of Issue - London SW	2	- *Post Office*
(5) Stamps Magazine/London 1980, Brentwood	3	- *n.o.c.*
(6) Supersonically to London 1980, BF 7580 PS	3	2 *RAF Mus.(s)*
(7) Centenary Appeal, London Union of Youth Clubs	3	5 *S.P. (Card)*
(8) Leicester Philatelic Society	3	6 *LFDC 1*
(9) London Stamp Fair, London SW1	3	4 *Showpiece*
(10) Post Office Day London 1980, London SW	3	4 *PO Commem Cvr*
(11) Royal Opera House, Covent Garden, WC	3	10 *Cotswold*
(12) Warwick Penny Post, Postal History Exhibition	5	10 *W & W*
(13) Festival Fringe, Brighton	6	3 *Brighton FF(s)*
(14) Salvation Army, 1880-1980, Belfast	6	10 *S. Army*
(15) Freedom of Plymouth, BF 1694 PS	6	3 *R. Marine(s)*
(16) Manchester (Kelloggs)	6	- *n.o.c.*
(17) Parish Church, Hampton-in-Arden	6	30 *H-i-A Church*
(18) Springtime, British Library, London WC	6	20 *BL 18*
C.D.S. POSTMARKS		
(19) Buckingham Palace, S.W.1	90	
(20) Earl's Court - posted at the Exhibition	50	
(21) Little London, Basingstoke	20	
(22) Piccadilly, Tamworth	20	

(17)

(8)

(11)

(13)

(7)

9th July 1980 - FAMOUS PEOPLE

12p Charlotte Brontë - Jane Eyre; 13½p George Eliot - Mill on the Floss; 15p Emily Brontë - Wuthering Heights; 17½p Mrs. Gaskell - North & South

SPECIAL HANDSTAMPS	ordinary covers £	official covers £
(1) First Day of Issue - Philatelic Bureau	2	- *Post Office*
(2) First Day of Issue - Haworth, Keighley	2	- *Post Office*
(3) International Society, Mrs Gaskell	3	10 *Int. Society*
(4) Elizabeth Gaskell Chelsea, SW3	3	30 *Hawkwood*
(5) Leicester Writers' Club	3	6 *LFDC 2*
(6) The Elms, Country Home of George Eliot	3	10 *The Elms*
(7) George Eliot Centenary, Nuneaton	3	10 *D.F.*
(8) Dent/Charlotte & Emily Brontë, Haworth	3	10 *BOCS 22*
(9) World's Women Christian Temperance Union	10	- *n.o.c.*
(10) Rush & Tompkins, Swindon	10	75 *R & T*
(11) Summertime, British Library, WC	6	20 *BL 19*
(12) William Shakespeare, Stratford	10	- *n.o.c.*
(13) Manchester (Kelloggs)	5	- *n.o.c.*
(14) Channel Isles Occupation Exhibition, Warwick	7	10 *W & W*
(15) Llangollen International Musical Eisteddfod	7	25 *Eist 2 cvrs*
(16) Royal Tournament Centenary, BF 1980 PS	7	15 *BFPS*
ORDINARY F.D.I. POSTMARKS		
(17) Altrincham (with official Knutsford P.O. cachet)	10	
C.D.S. POSTMARKS		
(18) Chilvers Coton - birthplace of George Eliot	20	
(19) Cranford, Kettering - Mrs Gaskell's 'Cranford'	15	
(20) Haworth - home of Brontë sisters	20	
(21) Inkpen, Newbury, Berks	18	
(22) Knutsford - Mrs Gaskell's 'Cranford'	15	
(23) Thornton - birthplace of Brontë sisters	18	
SLOGAN POSTMARKS		
(24) Knutsford, Mrs Gaskell's 'Cranford' - Altrincham	40	
(25) Central Library & Museum, Sunderland	125	

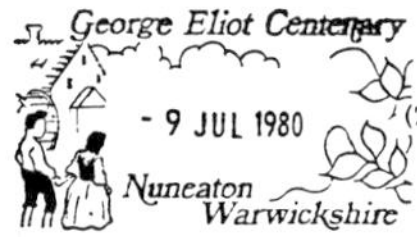

(7)

(1)

(4)

(2)

(24)

(8)

(11)

(14)

PLEASE READ THE GENERAL NOTES
AT THE BEGINNING OF THIS CATALOGUE
These often provide the answers to enquiries received.
C.D.S. = COUNTER DATE STAMP
These are everyday operational postmarks available
at all Post Office Counters.
Please refer to the General Notes for more details.

4th August 1980 – 80th BIRTHDAY HER MAJESTY QUEEN ELIZABETH THE QUEEN MOTHER

12p Portrait of the Queen Mother

SPECIAL HANDSTAMPS	ordinary covers £	official covers £
(1) First Day of Issue – Philatelic Bureau	2	– *Post Office*
(2) First Day of Issue – Glamis, Forfar	2	– *Post Office*
(3) Queen Mother's 80th Birthday, BF 8080 PS	6	20 *BFPS*
(4) Queen Mother's 80th Birthday, Clarence House	3	6 *Havering 11*
(5) St. Paul's Walden Flower Festival, Hitchin	3	15 *Hawkwood*
(6) St. Mary's Church, Ware	3	25 *St. Mary's*
(7) Grand Theatre Blackpool	3	10 *Blk Theatre*
(8) Queen Mother's 80th Birthday, Windsor	3	15 *Sumner*
(9) Queen Mother's 80th Birthday, York	3	15 *Sumner*
(10) First Day Covers of Royalty Exhibition, Leicester	3	4 *LFDC 3*
(11) Hitchin Salutes the Queen Mother	5	– *n.o.c.*
(12) Happy Birthday, British Library, WC	3	20 *BL 20*
(13) Lord Warden of Cinque Ports, Walmer	3	7 *BOCS 25*
(14) Queen Mother's 80th Birthday, St. Paul's Walden	3	15 *Sumner*
(15) 100 Years of GMT, Greenwich, SE10	3	15 *GMT*
(16) Poppy Appeal cares all year, Richmond	3	6 *Poppy Appeal*
(17) Forces Help Society/Lord Roberts Workshops, SW3	3	6 *Cotswold*
(18) Hull Kingston Rovers, Hull	3	6 *MW School*
(19) RNLI Station Calshott	3	6 *Pilgrim*
(20) Great Railway Exposition, Manchester	3	– *n.o.c.*
(21) Paramins 50 Years, Southampton	5	50 *Paramins*
(22) Rother Railway, Tenterden	3	3 *RH 11*
(23) 1980 Promenade Concerts, SW7	6	– *n.o.c.*
(24) Recro '80, Kenilworth	6	25 *D.F.*
(25) Manchester (Kelloggs)	6	– *n.o.c.*
(26) Anglo-Boer War Exhibition, Warwick	6	15 *W & W*
(27) Rochdale, Toad Lane	6	15 *Toad Lane*
(28) British Chess Congress, Brighton	6	10 *Chess Fed*

ORDINARY F.D.I. POSTMARKS	
(29) King's Lynn ('Estate Office Sandringham' cachet)	10
(29a) Windsor, Berks	5

C.D.S. POSTMARKS	
(30) Bowes – Bowes-Lyon (family name)	15
(31) Buckingham Palace, S.W.1	120
(32) Glamis – Queen Mother's ancestral home	30
(33) House of Commons, S.W.1	25
(34) House of Lords, S.W.1	30
(35) Mey – Castle of Mey belongs to Queen Mother	35
(36) Queen Elizabeth Avenue, Walsall	9
(37) Windsor Castle, Windsor, Berks	150

SLOGAN POSTMARKS	
(38) Isle of Man, Queen Mother Crowns	15

In addition: Elizabethan Banquets; Post Code It. Prices from £30.

(9)

(11)

(13)

(10)

(1)

(6)

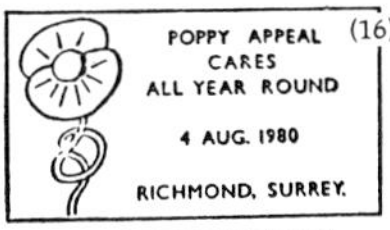

(16)

(4)

(8)

10th September 1980 – BRITISH CONDUCTORS

12p Sir Henry Wood; 13½p Sir Thomas Beecham;
15p Sir Malcolm Sargent; 17½p Sir John Barbirolli

SPECIAL HANDSTAMPS		
(1) First Day of Issue – Philatelic Bureau	2	– *Post Office*
(2) First Day of Issue – London SW	2	– *Post Office*
(3) Royal Opera House, WC2	3	10 *Cotswold*
(4) Guildhall School of Music & Drama, EC2	3	3 *Benham*
(5) Leicester Symphony Orchestra	3	6 *LFDC 4*
(6) Famous British Conductors, Bedford	3	20 *Bed Music Club*
(7) Conductors of the Halle, Manchester	3	10 *P.P.S.*
(8) 1980 Promenade Concerts, SW7	3	5 *BOCS 24*
(9) BBC Symphony Orchestra, SW7	3	5 *BOCS 24*
(10) Royal Philharmonic Orchestra, SE1	3	12 *S.P.*
(11) Anaesthesia 1980, Royal Festival Hall, SE1	3	8 *Hawkwood*
(12) Sir Malcolm Sargent Cancer Fund, SW3	3	6 *Havering 12*
(13) Birthplace Sir Thomas Beecham, St. Helens	3	15 *Th Beecham*
(14) CBSO (City of Birmingham Symp. Orch.)	3	3 *C.B.S.O.*
(15) TI Commemorates CBSO Birmingham	3	15 *C.B.S.O.*

(13)

(11)

(4)

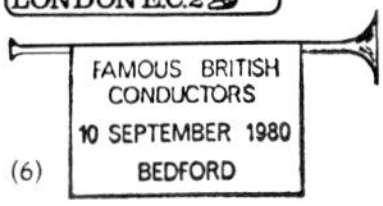

(6)

PRICES & CONDITION – PLEASE READ GENERAL NOTES

Conductors (contd.)

	ordinary covers £	official covers £	
(16) Sir Thomas Beecham Rossall School, Fleetwood	4	1	*Benham(s)*
(17) Fairfield, Croydon	3	10	*Fairfield*
(18) Manchester (Kelloggs)	5	-	*n.o.c.*
(19) Summertime, British Library, WC	5	25	*BL 21*
(20) Sponne School 550th Anniv., Towcester	6	20	*Sponne Sch*
(21) Nat. Festival of Flower Arrangement, Nottingham	6	15	*NFFA*
(22) Moorlands Festival, Leek	5	25	*Festival*
(23) From Tom-Tom to Telex , NPC Warwick	6	20	*W & W*
(24) Sir Geoffrey De Havilland, Hatfield	8	25	*Mosquito Mus*
(25) England v. Norway, World Cup, Wembley	10	20	*Dawn*
(26) Great Railway Exposition, Manchester	10	-	*n.o.c.*

C.D.S. POSTMARKS

(27) Hitchin, Herts - Sir Henry Wood died here	10
(28) Marylebone, W1 - Royal Academy of Music	10
(29) New York - N.Y. Philharmonic (Barbirolli)	10
(30) Southampton Row, W.C.1 - birthplace of Barbirolli	10
(31) Stamford - birthplace of Sir Malcolm Sargent	10
(32) St. Helens - birthplace of Sir Thomas Beecham	10

SLOGAN POSTMARK

B.P.E. Wembley. Prices range from £50.

10th October 1980 - SPORTING ANNIVERSARIES

12p Athletics; 13½p Rugby; 15p Boxing; 17½p Cricket

SPECIAL HANDSTAMPS

(1) First Day of Issue - Philatelic Bureau	2	-	*Post Office*
(2) First Day of Issue - Cardiff	2	-	*Post Office*
(3) W.R.U. Centenary, Cardiff Arms Park	4	15	*W.R.U.*
(4) The Saints 1880-1980, Northampton	4	15	*Saints RFC*
(5) King Henry VIII, Rugby Centenary, Coventry	3	10	*D.F.*
(6) Leicester Football Club	3	6	*LFDC 5*
(7) Norfolk County F. A. Centenary, Norwich	3	6	*Markton*
(8) Middlesex CCC, NW8	3	6	*Havering 13*
(9) PO XI v Cricket Writers/Vic Lewis XI Lord's, NW8	5	-	*n.o.c.*
(10) Centenary Tour, 1880-1980, Lord's, NW8	3	8	*S.P.*
(11) Century of Tests, England v Australia, Oval, SE11	3	8	*Hawkwood*
(12) London Union of Y.C./London Sportsmen, SE5	5	-	*n.o.c.*
(13) Amateur Athletic Assoc., Crystal Palace, SE19	3	6	*BOCS 23*
(14) Amateur Boxing Assoc., Wembley, Middlesex	3	7	*BOCS Sp 3*
(15) St. John Ambulance 1880-1980, Manchester	6	25	*Cotswold*
(16) Autumntime, British Library, WC	5	25	*BL 22*
(17) New Zealand Exhibition, Warwick	5	10	*W & W*
(18) Manchester (Kelloggs)	6	-	*n.o.c.*
(19) Post Office Philatelic Centre, Plymouth	6	-	*n.o.c.*
(20) Nearest & Dearest, Blackpool	6	15	*Blk Theatre*

ORDINARY F.D.I. POSTMARKS

(21) Oxford - Amateur Athletics Assoc founded here	4
(22) Rugby - Rugby Football originated here	5
(23) Twickenham - English Rugby Union ground	5

C.D.S. POSTMARKS

(24) Hambledon - birthplace of English cricket	30
(25) Kennington, SE11 - The Oval	20
(26) Llanelli - one of the founding WRU members	12
(27) Marylebone, W1 - Marylebone Cricket Club (MCC)	25
(28) Murrayfield - Scottish Rugby Football ground	25
(29) Neath - Welsh Rugby Union formed here	25

In addition: Boycott, Bowling, Box, Brecon, Lampeter, Jump, Llandovery, Rugby, The Oval, Welford Road, Wells. Prices from £10.

SLOGAN POSTMARKS

Leicester Speedway. £150.

PLEASE READ THE GENERAL NOTES
AT THE BEGINNING OF THIS CATALOGUE
These often provide the answers to enquiries received.
SLOGAN POSTMARKS
Prices in the catalogue (from 1980) are for covers with stamps sited to advantage so that the slogan is clearly legible.

(25)

(7)

(24)

(22)

(23)

(13)

(7)

(5)

(12)

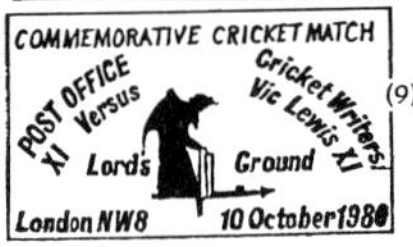

(9)

(8)

(19)

19th November 1980 - CHRISTMAS

10p, 12p, 13½p, 15p, 17½p Christmas decorations

SPECIAL HANDSTAMPS	ordinary covers £	official covers £	
(1) First Day of Issue - Philatelic Bureau	2	-	*Post Office*
(2) First Day of Issue - Bethlehem, Llandeilo, Dyfed	3	-	*Post Office*
(3) 950 Years of Worship, Waltham Abbey	3	8	*Hawkwood*
(4) 1980 Christmas, British Library, WC	3	15	*BL 23*
(5) Regent Street Association, W1	3	5	*Havering 14*
(6) Christmas Carols, Ivybridge	4	-	*n.o.c.*
(7) Merry Christmas, Hollybush	4	-	*n.o.c.*
(8) Norway's Christmas Gift, Trafalgar Square, WC	3	5	*BOCS 26*
(9) Commonwealth Christmas Stamps, Warwick	4	15	*W & W*
(10) Fire Service Charity Appeal, Leicester	3	6	*LFDC 6*
(11) Salvation Army, Mount Cross, Bramley	8	45	*H.R.*
(12) England v. Switzerland World Cup, Wembley	10	12	*Dawn*
(13) W.R.U. Centenary, Cardiff Arms Park	10	20	*W.R.U.*
(14) Manchester (Kelloggs)	10	-	*n.o.c.*

C.D.S. POSTMARKS

(15) Bethlehem or Nasareth	*each*	20
(16) Glastonbury - conversions to Christianity		13

In addition, covers are known with the following CDS pmks: Fairy Cross, Holly Bush, Holly Hall, Holy Island, Ivybridge, Ivychurch, Magdalen, Star. Prices from £8 each.

SLOGAN POSTMARKS

Shopping By Post. £30.

(3)

(4)

(2)
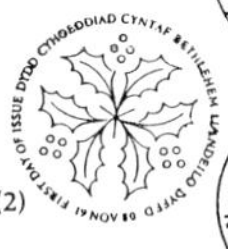

(8)

6th February 1981 - FOLKLORE

14p St. Valentine's Day; 18p Morris Dancers;
22p Lammastide; 25p Medieval Mummers

SPECIAL HANDSTAMPS			
(1) First Day of Issue - Philatelic Bureau	2	-	*Post Office*
(2) First Day of Issue - London WC	2	-	*Post Office*
(3) My Valentine, Lover, Salisbury	3	4	*Cotswold (g)*
(4) Valentines at the British Library, WC	3	35	*BL 25*
(5) Valentines Card Exhibition, Leicester	3	15	*LFDC 7*
(6) English Folk Song & Dance Society, SW1	3	4	*BOCS (2) 1*
(7) Headington Morris Dancers, Oxford	3	7	*Hawkwood*
(8) Thaxted Morris Men	3	10	*Havering 15*
(9) Dunmow Flitch, Little Dunmow	3	10	*Havering Sp 1*
(10) Robin Hood Society, Nottingham	3	10	*Bradbury*
(11) Radley College, St. Helens, Abingdon	3	15	*Radley Coll*
(12) Royal Mail Stampede, Hornsea Pottery	8	-	*n.o.c.*
(13) Aviation History at Hendon, BF 1725 PS	8	8	*RFDC 1*
(14) Orient F.C. Centenary, E10	8	15	*Hawkwood*
(15) Victoria Cross Exhib., Postal Museum	10	-	*n.o.c.*
(16) George VI, Sandringham	15	-	*n.o.c.*
(17) W.R.U. Centenary, Cardiff Arms Park	10	25	*W.R.U.*

C.D.S. POSTMARKS

(18) Gretna Green or Lover	*each*	30
(19) Headington Quarry - Morris Dancers		20
(20) Thaxted - Morris Ring meet here annually		20

In addition, covers are known with the following CDS pmks: Bampton, Chipping Campden, Davey Place, Honiton, Padstow, Robin Hood, St. George's, Tintagel, Widecombe-in-the-Moor. Prices from £10 each.

(2)

(4)

(5)

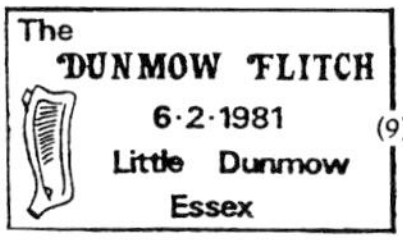

(9)

(6)

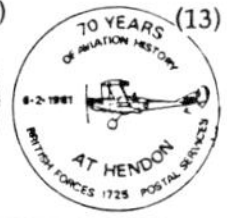

(13)

(12)

25th March 1981 - INTERNATIONAL YEAR OF DISABLED PEOPLE

14p Guide Dog; 18p Sign Language; 22p Wheelchair; 25p Foot Artist

SPECIAL HANDSTAMPS			
(1) First Day of Issue - Philatelic Bureau	2	-	*Post Office*
(2) First Day of Issue - Windsor	2	-	*Post Office*
(3) Oaklands PH School, Salford	4	35	*Oaklands*
(4) Guide Dogs Jubilee, Wallasey	3	6	*BOCS (2) 2*
(5) Menphys Celebrate IYDP, Leicester	3	15	*LFDC 8*
(6) MS, Exeter & District Branch	4	30	*Exeter MS*
(7) IYDP Toynbee Hall, D.I.G., E1	3	4	*Havering 16*
(8) Leicestershire Committee Commemorates IYDP	3	6	*P.P.S.*
(9) Le Court: First Cheshire Home, Petersfield	3	20	*Cotswold*
(10) Cambridge & District Hard of Hearing	3	20	*Cam. HHA*

(5)

(10)

Disabled (contd.)

	ordinary covers	official covers	
SPECIAL HANDSTAMPS	£	£	
(11) Arthritis Care, London SW1	5	50	*Arlington*
(12) RAF Headley Court, BF 1726 PS	3	7	*RFDC 2*
(13) Stoke Mandeville, Spinal Unit	3	6	*Hawkwood*
(14) Coventry Sports Association, Charity Walk	3	8	*D.F.*
(15) Disabled Drivers Motor Club, W3	3	10	*D.D.M.C.*
(16) The Royal British Legion, SW1	3	50	*Brit. Leg.*
(17) Stars for the Disabled, Peterborough	3	15	*Stars*
(18) Carters (J & A), IYDP, Westbury	6	15	*P.P.S.*
(19) Donington Park, 1931-1981, Derby	5	25	*Don. Park*
(20) W.R.U. Centenary, Cardiff Arms Park	5	20	*W.R.U.*
(21) Daily Mail Ideal Home, Earls Court, SW5	5	20	*Pilgrim*
(22) Swansea Philatelic Counter	6	30	*Cotswold*
(23) March Philatelic Displays British Library, WC	7	20	*BL 24*
(24) Victoria Cross Exhib., Postal Museum	7	-	*n.o.c.*
C.D.S. POSTMARKS			
(25) King Edward Vll Hospital, Midhurst	25		
(26) Stoke Mandeville - Spinal Injury Unit	25		
(27) Orthopaedic Hospital, Oswestry	25		

In addition, covers are known with the following CDS pmks: Bethesda, Guide, St. Dunstans, Stoke Charity, Tredegar, Wallasey. Prices from £8 each.

SLOGAN POSTMARKS		
(28) 'Can Disabled People Go Where You Go?'	35	
(29) St. Loyes College Exeter	50	
(30) The British Deaf Association, Carlisle	35	

(6)

(3)

(7)

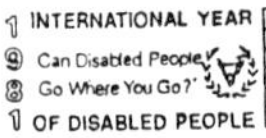

(28)

(29)

13th May 1981 - BUTTERFLIES

14p Small Tortoiseshell; 18p Large Blue; 22p Peacock; 25p Chequered Skipper

SPECIAL HANDSTAMPS			
(1) First Day of Issue - Philatelic Bureau	2	-	*Post Office*
(2) First Day of Issue - London SW	2	-	*Post Office*
(3) Large Blue,Quorn	4	10	*BOCS (2) 3*
(4) Chequered Skipper, Bourton	4	7	*BOCS (2) 3*
(5) Peacock, Sherborne	4	7	*BOCS (2) 3*
(6) Wildfowl Trust, Slimbridge	4	7	*BOCS (2) 3*
(7) World Wide Butterflies, Sherborne	4	6	*Havering Sp 2*
(8) Nottingham Trust, Eakring Meadows	4	4	*Bradbury*
(9) Margaret Fountaine Exhib., Norwich	4	6	*Markton*
(10) Leics. Museums British Butterflies Exhib.	4	5	*LFDC 9*
(11) British Naturalist Assoc., Woodwalton	4	10	*Hawkwood*
(12) National Butterfly Museum, Bramber	4	25	*S.P.*
(13) No 20 Mtce Unit Conservamus, BF 1738 PS	4	8	*RFDC 3*
(14) 25 Years Freedom, RAF Locking	5	2	*RAF(s)*
(15) Sub-Postmasters Conf., Scarborough	5	-	*n.o.c.*
(16) Victorian Postbox Postcards, Liverpool	5	-	*n.o.c.*
(17) Victorian Postbox Postcards, Keswick	5	-	*n.o.c.*
(18) Victorian Postbox Postcards, Buxton	5	-	*n.o.c.*
(19) Rochdale's Unique Pillar Box	5	-	*n.o.c.*
(20) May Philatelic Displays, British Library, WC	5	25	*BL 26*
(21) Inauguration Wood Green Shopping	5	20	*Havering 17*
(22) 25th Christian Aid Week, Preston	6	20	*Chr. Aid*
(23) Caldey Island, Tenby	6	20	*Caldey Isl.*
C.D.S. POSTMARKS			
(24) Peacock Cross, Hamilton	15		
(25) Quorn - HQ British Butterflies Conservation Society..	15		

In addition, covers are known with the following CDS pmks: Castle Acre, Dousland, Kings Norton, Nettlebed, Nettleham, Spring Gardens. Prices from £7 each.

SLOGAN POSTMARKS		
(26) National Butterfly Museum Bramber	30	

In addition: Whipsnade Zoo. Prices from £40.

(9)

(7)

(3)

(15)

(13)

(2)

(21)

PLEASE READ THE GENERAL NOTES
AT THE BEGINNING OF THIS CATALOGUE
These often provide the answers to enquiries received.

C.D.S. = COUNTER DATE STAMP

These are everyday operational postmarks available
at all Post Office Counters.

Please refer to the General Notes for more details.

24th June 1981 - NATIONAL TRUSTS

14p Glenfinnan; 18p Derwentwater; 20p Stackpole Head; 22p Giant's Causeway; 25p St. Kilda

SPECIAL HANDSTAMPS	ordinary covers £	official covers £
(1) First Day of Issue - Philatelic Bureau	3	- *Post Office*
(2) First Day of Issue - Keswick	4	- *Post Office*
(3) First Day of Issue - Glenfinnan	4	- *Post Office*
(4) National Trust, Derwentwater	4	5 *BOCS (2) 4*
(5) National Trust for Scotland, Glenfinnan	4	6 *BOCS Sp 4*
(6) National Trust for Scotland, St. Kilda	4	7 *BOCS Sp 5*
(7) National Trust, Stackpole Head	4	2 *Benham(s)*
(8) National Trust, Giants Causeway	4	2 *Benham(s)*
(9) N.T. Leicester, Sir Robert Shirley's Church	4	20 *LFDC 10*
(10) Oakham Castle, 800 Years, Rutland	4	8 *Oakham Castle*
(11) Lingholm Gardens, Open Day, Keswick	5	12 *Hawkwood*
(12) Geology of Causeway Coast, Nottingham	4	12 *Bradbury*
(13) Robin Hood Society, Nottingham Castle	4	12 *Bradbury*
(14) St. Kilda, 25 Years BF 1750 PS	4	15 *BFPS*
(15) The N.T. Scotland, Charlecote, Warwick	4	15 *Charlecote*
(16) London International Stamp Centre, WC2	5	15 *Stamp Centre*
(17) Lyke Wake Walk, BF 1739 PS	5	8 *RFDC 4*
(18) Friends of the Earth, Olympia W14	5	8 *Havering 18*
(19) Jaguar Drivers Club, 1956-1981, Luton	5	10 *Jaguar DC*
(20) Crane Schools Golden Jubilee, Nottingham	5	20 *Crane Sch.*
(21) Holkham Hall, Norfolk	5	6 *Markton*
(22) Lawn Tennis Museum, SW19	5	15 *Lawn Tennis*
(23) Christianity in Otley, Leeds	5	8 *Parish Church*
(24) June Philatelic Displays, British Library, WC	5	20 *BL 27*
(25) Scottish Council for Spastics Upper Springland	5	20 *Spastics*
(26) Caldey Island, Tenby	5	15 *Caldey Isl.*
(27) ANTAR Service in BAOR, BF 1724 PS	10	3 *Army (s)*
(28) Humber Bridge Hull, Open to Traffic	10	3 *Scarboro' (s)*
C.D.S. POSTMARKS		
(29) Alfriston - first building acquired by N.T	15	
(30) Barmouth - first site acquired by N.T.	10	
(31) Buckland Monachorum - Buckland Abbey (N.T.)	15	
(32) Culross - first building acquired by N.T. for Scotland	10	
(33) Glenfinnan, Stackpole, or Causeway Head *each*	15	
(34) Tintagel - PO is National Trust property	12	
(35) Haslemere - home of Sir Robert Hunter (founder)	20	
(36) Lower Shiplake - b/place Canon Rawnsley (founder)	20	
(37) Wisbech - b/place of Octavia Hill (founder)	20	
(38) Land's End & John O' Groats *pair*	70	

SLOGAN POSTMARKS

Bluebell Railway; Gawsworth Hall; Visit Sandwich; The Pantiles; Hagley Hall. Prices from £75.

(5)

(2)

(9)

(10)

(21)

(13)

(4)

(8)

(12)

(7)

(6)

(9)

22nd July 1981 - ROYAL WEDDING

14p, 25p Prince of Wales and Lady Diana Spencer

SPECIAL HANDSTAMPS		
(1) First Day of Issue - Philatelic Bureau	2	- *Post Office*
(2) First Day of Issue - London EC	2	- *Post Office*
(3) First Day of Issue - Caernarfon	2	- *Post Office*
(4) Royal Wedding Celebrations, Leicester	4	15 *LFDC 11*
(5) Royal Wedding, Chingford Old Church, E4	4	6 *Hawkwood*
(6) Royal Wedding, St. Paul's Cathedral, EC4	3	5 *Havering 19*
(7) Royal Wedding, Stamp Exhibition, Exeter	4	8 *Ex Stamp Centre*
(8) Royal Wedding, Cameo Stamp Centre, WC2	4	8 *Cameo*
(9) First Prince of Wales, Lincoln Cathedral	5	50 *Lin. Cath*
(10) Greetings from Watton-at-Stone, Hertford	5	40 *Watton Church*
(11) Prince of Wales & Lady Diana, Caernarfon	3	20 *BOCS (2) 6*
(12) Royal Wedding Greetings, Canterbury	6	- *n.o.c.*
(13) Canoe 81/Royal Wedding, Nottingham	3	10 *Bradbury*
(14) RAF St. Clement Danes, BF 1932 PS	4	15 *RFDC 5*
(15) Royal Wedding, Althorp, Northampton	4	20 *Althorp*

PLEASE READ THE GENERAL NOTES
AT THE BEGINNING OF THIS CATALOGUE
These often provide the answers to enquiries received.

(s) indicates covers are only known with a single stamp.

Royal Wedding (contd.)

	ordinary covers £	official covers £	
(16) Loyal Greetings, Lullingstone Silk Farm	4	80	*Benham L1*
(17) Royal Wedding, St. Pauls, EC4 (changeable date)	3	20	*H.R.*
(18) East of England Show, Peterborough	4	15	*S.P.*
(19) Congratulations, Todd Scales, Cambridge	4	20	*Todd Scales*
(20) Royal Tournament, BF 1805 PS	4	12	*BFPS*
(21) Mayors Charity, City of Exeter	4	6	*Mayors Charity*
(22) Centenary Postcard, Cornhill P.O., Ipswich	10	–	*n.o.c.*
(23) Keswick/National Trust	10	–	*n.o.c.*
(24) South Lakeland/National Trust	10	–	*n.o.c.*
(25) July Philatelic Displays, British Library, WC	8	20	*BL 28*
(26) East Midlands CBI, Head P.O., Leicester	8	–	*n.o.c.*
(27) Lifeboat Week 1981, Lyme Regis	8	15	*Pilgrim*
(28) Caldey Island, Tenby	8	15	*Caldey Isl.*
(29) Gredington Jamboree, Whitchurch	20	30	*Jamboree*
(30) Port Sunlight, Liverpool	8	50	*Lever Bros*
(31) Windsor, Berks	9	–	*n.o.c.*

ORDINARY F.D.I. POSTMARKS

(32) Chester – Prince Charles is Earl of Chester	6
(33) Gloucestershire (Highgrove House special cover)	15
(34) King's Lynn (Sandringham special cover)	20
(34a) Windsor	6

C.D.S. POSTMARKS

(35) Buckingham Palace, SW1	150
(36) House of Commons, SW1	25
(37) House of Lords, SW1	30
(38) Prince Charles Ave or Prince of Wales Ave ... *each*	15
(39) Princetown	15
(40) Romsey – honeymoon started at Broadlands	35
(41) Tetbury – Highgrove House	25
(42) Windsor Castle, Windsor, Berks	175

In addition: Caernarfon, Charlestown, Dartmouth, Diss, Duffus, Highgrove, Sevenoaks, Spencers Wood, St. Paul's, Trinity Street. Prices from £8 each.

SLOGAN POSTMARKS

(43) Prince Charles/Lady Diana, Isle of Man Crowns	30
(44) Exhibition of Royal Pagentry, Hagley Hall	75
(45) Royal Westminster Exhibition	100

In addition: The Pantiles. £25.

NOTE: **Double dated covers** *exist with 22 July handstamp and 29 July (Wedding Day) handstamp. Each handstamp cancelling both stamps.* ***Prices from £13***
In addition, **triple dated covers** *were serviced with 22 July, 28 July (Royal Wedding Fireworks) and 29 July (Wedding Day) handstamps. Each handstamp cancelling both stamps.* ***Prices from £15***

Doubt has arisen to the authenticity of some of these covers – particularly those with all London handstamps. Whilst the handstamps are genuine, it is understood that many were unofficially back-dated.

12th August 1981 – 25th ANNIVERSARY OF THE DUKE OF EDINBURGH'S AWARD SCHEME

14p Expeditions; 18p Skills; 22p Service; 25p Recreation

SPECIAL HANDSTAMPS

(1) First Day of Issue – Philatelic Bureau	2	–	*Post Office*
(2) First Day of Issue – London W2	3	–	*Post Office*
(3) Duke of Edinburgh's Award, Belfast	3	10	*Cotswold*
(4) Duke of Edinburgh's Award, Cardiff	3	10	*Cotswold*
(5) Duke of Edinburgh's Award, Edinburgh	3	10	*Cotswold*
(6) Duke of Edinburgh's Award, EC4	3	10	*Cotswold*
(7) Duke of Edinburgh's Award, SW1	3	10	*Cotswold*
(8) Duke of Edinburgh's Award, County of Devon	3	3	*Devon DoEAS*
(9) Duke of Edinburgh's Award, Winchmore Hill, N24	3	4	*Havering 20*
(10) RAF Canadian Rockies, BF 1740 PS	3	9	*RFDC 6*
(11) Duke of Edinburgh's Award, Hull	3	10	*Hull DoEAS*
(12) Leics Girl Guides Association	3	7	*LFDC 12*
(13) August Philatelic Displays, British Library, WC	4	20	*BL 29*
(14) Royal Mail House, Wakefield	4	10	*Wakefield*
(15) Cardiff Searchlight Tattoo, BF 1747 PS	4	20	*BFPS*

(21)

(11)

(15)

(8)
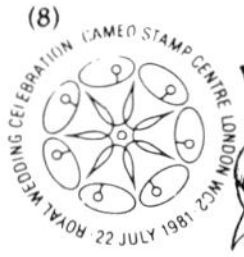

(4)

(25)

(20)

(45)

(5)

(11)

(8)

(7)

(10)

1981

Duke of Edinburgh Awards (contd.)

	ordinary covers £	official covers £	
(16) Stoke Mandeville Games, Aylesbury	6	10	*Hawkwood*
(17) Military Tattoo,Edinburgh	6	20	*M Tattoo*
(18) Caldey Island, Tenby	6	15	*Caldey Isl.*
(19) Keswick/National Trust	7	-	*n.o.c.*
(20) South Lakeland/National Trust	7	-	*n.o.c.*
(21) Port Sunlight, Liverpool	8	-	n.o.c.
(22) Royal Wedding, St. Pauls Cathedral, EC4	6	35	*H.R.*

C.D.S. POSTMARKS

(23) Buckingham Palace, S.W.1	100	
(24) Pathfinder Village, Exeter	20	
(25) Windsor Castle, Windsor, Berks	10	

In addition, covers are known with the following CDS pmks: Calshot, Duffus, Edinburgh, Gateshead, Holyrood, House of Lords, Okehampton, Phillipstown. Prices from £8 each.

SLOGAN POSTMARKS

(26) Duke of Edinburgh's Award Crowns 25

In addition: Cardiff Tattoo; Highland Games; Royal Westminster Exhib. Prices from £25

(26)

(13)

(9)

(8)

23rd September 1981 - FISHING

14p Cockle dredging; 18p Hauling in a Trawl Net; 22p Lobster Potting; 25p Hoisting a Seine Net

SPECIAL HANDSTAMPS

(1) First Day of Issue - Philatelic Bureau	2	-	*Post Office*
(2) First Day of Issue - Hull	3	-	*Post Office*
(3) Catch '81, Falmouth	3	10	*Catch '81*
(4) Manchester Weather Centre	3	10	*Dawn*
(5) Royal Nat. Mission Deep Sea Fishermen, Aberdeen	3	5	*BOCS (2) 5*
(6) Heart of Scotland's Fishing Industry, Buckie	3	12	*Fish.Mut.Ass.*
(7) Fishing Fleets of Brixham	3	10	*Pandora Press*
(8) Leics. Amalgamated Society of Anglers	3	15	*LFDC 13*
(9) Centuries of Trading, Billingsgate, EC3	3	10	*Hawkwood*
(10) Ocean Tapestry, BF 1741 PS, RAF St. Mawgan	5	10	*RFDC 7*
(11) Fishmonger's Company, EC4	4	5	*S. Petty 1*
(12) Sept. Philatelic Displays, British Library, WC	7	20	*BL 30*
(13) Transporter Bridge, Newport	7	40	*Newport BC*
(14) Travelling Tram Post Office, Blackpool	7	-	*n.o.c.*
(15) Langley Grammar School, Slough	9	20	*Langley Sch*
(16) Port Sunlight, Liverpool	10	-	*n.o.c.*

ORDINARY F.D.I. POSTMARKS

(17) Grimsby or Lowestoft - fishing ports .... *each* 5

C.D.S. POSTMARKS

(18) Lighthouse. Fleetwood		50
(19) Six Bells or The Wharf	*each*	25

In addition, covers are known with the following CDS pmks: Crab Lane, Dousland, Eyemouth, Fisherie Turriff, Fisherow, Fisher's Pond, Fishpool, Fishguard, Fleetwood, The Harbour, Hull, Milford Haven, Stafford, St. Peter's St., The Salmon Leap, Whale Hill, Whiting Bay. Prices from £7 each.

SLOGAN POSTMARKS

(20) Hastings - A resort for all seasons (depicts boat) 60

In addition: Visit Sandwich. Price from £35

(2)

(11)

(9)

(6)

(7)

18th November 1981 - CHRISTMAS

11½p, 14p,18p, 22p, 25p Childrens Paintings

SPECIAL HANDSTAMPS

(1) First Day of Issue - Philatelic Bureau	2	-	*Post Office*
(2) First Day of Issue - Bethlehem, Llandeilo, Dyfed	3	-	*Post Office*
(3) Children First Canterbury	3	5	*BOCS (2) 8*
(4) Children's Christmas Book Show Blackwells	3	12	*Hawkwood*
(5) Friends of Leicester Cathedral	3	25	*LFDC 14*
(6) Church of St. Mary-at-Hill, EC3	3	7	*S. Petty 2*
(7) Stamp Magazine Link House, Croydon	3	1	*Benham(s)*
(8) Happy Xmas from Big C Appeal Norwich	3	10	*Big C Appeal*
(9) Princess of Wales Regent St., W1	3	10	*Havering 22*
(10) Pillar Box Postcards - Preston	3	-	*n.o.c.*

(4)

(9)

(3)

(6)

1981 Christmas (contd.)

	ordinary covers £	official covers £
(11) Pillar Box Postcards - Oldham	4	- *n.o.c.*
(12) Pillar Box Postcards - Manchester	4	- *n.o.c.*
(13) Pillar Box Postcards - Blackpool	4	- *n.o.c.*
(14) November Philatelic, Displays British Library, WC	7	20 *BL 31*
(15) Manchester (sponsored by Kelloggs)	7	8 *Kelloggs*
(16) England v. Hungary, Wembley	7	10 *Dawn*
(17) Port Sunlight, Liverpool	10	- *n.o.c.*

C.D.S. POSTMARKS

(18) Bethlehem, Llandeilo, Dyfed	12	
(19) Nasareth, Gwynedd	8	
(20) Rhoose, Ramridge, Clutton, Horsham or Fulwood - homes of stamp designers *each*	6	

In addition, covers are known with the following CDS pmks: Angel Hill, Holy Island, Kings Road, Star, Starcross, St. Nicholas, Trinity. Prices from £5 each.

10th February 1982 - CHARLES DARWIN

15½p Giant Tortoises; 19½p Iguanas; 26p Finch; 29p Skulls

SPECIAL HANDSTAMPS

(1) First Day of Issue - Philatelic Bureau	2	- *Royal Mail*
(2) First Day of Issue - Shrewsbury	2	- *Royal Mail*
(3) Darwin Centenary, RSPB, Sandy	3	10 *R.S.P.B.*
(4) Maer Hall Tribute to Charles Darwin	4	50 *Maer Hall*
(5) Charles Darwin 1809-1882, Slimbridge	3	5 *BOCS(2)9*
(6) Charles Darwin 1809-1882, Cambridge	3	5 *BOCS(2)9*
(7) Charles Darwin 1809-1882, Shrewsbury	3	5 *BOCS(2)9*
(8) Down House, Charles Darwin Memorial	3	6 *S. Petty 3*
(9) Charles Darwin, Westminster Abbey, SW1	3	10 *Hawkwood*
(10) Voyage of HMS Beagle, Plymouth	3	6 *BLS 1*
(11) Man of Vision, London, SW7	3	10 *Havering 23*
(12) HMS Beagle, BF 1762 PS	3	10 *RFDC 9*
(13) 1809-1882 Charles Darwin Centenary, NW1	4	25 *London Zoo*
(14) Leicester University Jubilee Year	7	15 *LFDC 15*
(15) February Philatelic Displays, British Library, WC	7	25 *BL 32*
(16) Valentines at Harrods, SW1	6	25 *Pilgrim*
(17) Manchester (Kelloggs)	8	- *n.o.c.*
(18) Port Sunlight, Liverpool	8	- *n.o.c.*

C.D.S. POSTMARKS

(19) Downe - Darwin's home	12	
(20) Frankwell - near to Darwin's birthplace	30	
(21) The Lizard - lizards (19½p)	15	

In addition, covers are known with the following CDS pmks: Atcham, Falmouth, Frog Island, Oxford, Piltdown, Sandown, Shrewsbury, Slimbridge, Stonehouse (Plymouth), Whipsnade. Prices from £7 each.

24th March 1982 - YOUTH ORGANISATIONS

15½p Boys' Brigade; 19½p Girls' Brigade; 26p Scouts; 29p Girl Guides

SPECIAL HANDSTAMPS

(1) First Day of Issue - Philatelic Bureau	2	- *Royal Mail*
(2) First Day of Issue - Glasgow	2	- *Royal Mail*
(3) First Day of Issue - London SW	2	- *Royal Mail*
(4) St. Mary's 8th Hendon, NW4	3	7 *Havering 24*
(5) Year of the Scout Celebrations, Peterborough	3	15 *Peteb. Scouts*
(6) Lord Baden Powell, Westminster Abbey	3	10 *Hawkwood*
(7) Loughborough, Year of Scout	3	10 *Loughb. Scouts*
(8) Scout Movement W. Europe, BF 1742 PS	3	15 *Forces*
(9) 75th Anniversary of Scouting, Glasgow	3	15 *Glasgow Scouts*
(10) Scouting for Boys, Baden-Powell House, SW7	3	25 *Scouts Council*
(11) 75th Anniversary of Scouting, Caterham	3	25 *Cat'm Scouts*
(12) The Girls Brigade, SW6	3	10 *BOCS (2) 10b*
(13) Girl Guides Association, SW1	3	10 *Cotswold*
(14) First for Boys, SW6	3	10 *BOCS (2) 10a*
(15) Young Enterprise, Folkestone	3	25 *S. Kent Coll.*
(16) National Association of Youth Clubs, Leicester	3	20 *Bradbury*
(17) National Youth Bureau, Leicester	3	9 *LFDC 16*
(18) 1982 (Huyton) Sqd ATC, BF 5282 PS	8	9 *RFDC 10*
(19) Youth Activities, St. Donats Castle, Llantwit Major	8	10 *S. Petty 4*
(20) Yorkshire County Bowling Assoc., York	8	10 *Yorks CBA*
(21) Motorway Sub P.O., Rank M6 Forton	8	50 *Rank M6*

Youth (contd.)

	ordinary covers £	official covers £
SPECIAL HANDSTAMPS		
(22) First Postbus in Yorkshire, Masham	8	– *n.o.c.*
(23) Four Marks Golden Jubilee, Alton	8	35 *Four Marks PO*
(24) March Philatelic Displays, British Library, WC	8	20 *BL 33*
(25) Norwich Union, Mail Coach to Rayleigh	8	30 *Norwich Un.*
(26) Daily Mail, Ideal Home, Earls Court, SW5	8	30 *Pilgrim*
(27) Manchester (Kelloggs)	8	– *n.o.c.*
(28) Port Sunlight, Liverpool	8	– *n.o.c.*
C.D.S. POSTMARKS		
(29) Bentley, Farnham – home of Baden-Powell	9	
(30) Euston Centre B.O. – birthplace Baden-Powell	6	
(31) Fleur-de-lis – the scout's emblem	75	
(32) Guide, Blackburn	15	
(33) Pathfinder Village, Exeter	25	
(34) The Camp, St. Albans	15	
(35) West Hampstead – girl guide on 29p value	15	

In addition: Chingford, Pinkneys Road, Poole, Sandbanks, Scouthead, Scout Hill, Thurso. Prices from £6 each.

SLOGAN POSTMARKS		
(36) Scouts help others – Chingford (Gilwell Park)	20	
(37) Scouts help others – SW1 (HQ of scouts and guides)	17	
(38) Scouts help others – any other office	12	

(15)

(12)

(18)

(16)

(25)

28th April 1982 – BRITISH THEATRE

15½p Ballet; 19½p Harlequin; 26p Drama; 29p Opera

	ordinary covers £	official covers £
SPECIAL HANDSTAMPS		
(1) First Day of Issue – Philatelic Bureau	2	– *Royal Mail*
(2) First Day of Issue – Stratford-upon-Avon	2	– *Royal Mail*
(3) John Gay, Westminster Abbey	3	8 *Hawkwood*
(4) Royal Shakespeare Theatre, Stratford	3	7 *BOCS (2) 11*
(5) Royal Opera House, Covent Garden	3	5 *BLS 3*
(6) Arts Theatre, Cambridge	3	25 *Arts Theatre*
(7) Theatre Royal Restoration, Bath	3	20 *Cotswold*
(8) Queens Theatre, Hornchurch	3	10 *Havering 25*
(9) Tavistock Repertory Co., London N1	3	10 *Tav. Rep.*
(10) Leicester Drama Society	3	50 *LFDC 17*
(11) Theatre Royal, Norwich	3	20 *Th. Royal*
(12) Mercury Theatre, Colchester	3	7 *Mercury Th.*
(13) Shakespeare, Southwark Cathedral, SE1	3	5 *S. Petty 5*
(14) New Theatre, Hull	3	25 *New Theatre*
(15) Worthing Operatic Society	3	15 *S.P.*
(16) Barbican Centre, EC2	3	50 *Barbican*
(17) S.C.D.A., Pitlochry	3	20 *S.C.D.A.*
(18) Theatr Clwyd, Ebrill, Yr Wyddgrug, Mold	6	– *n.o.c.*
(19) William Shakespeare, Stratford	10	– *n.o.c.*
(20) Royal Air Force Central Band, BF 1773 PS	8	10 *RFDC 11*
(21) Centenary, Forces Postal Service BF 8282 PS	8	15 *Forces*
(22) Army Bag, National Postal Museum	8	– *n.o.c.*
(23) Rating & Valuation Association, SW1	8	25 *Bradbury*
(24) Queen Victoria's Visit of Epping Forest	8	15 *Hawkwood*
(25) Manchester (Kelloggs)	10	– *n.o.c.*
(26) Port Sunlight, Liverpool	10	– *n.o.c.*
ORDINARY F.D.I. POSTMARKS		
(26a) Basingstoke (Horseshoe Theatre Company cover)	20	
(26b) Northampton (Royal Theatre & Opera House cover)	20	
C.D.S. POSTMARKS		
(27) Barnstaple – birthplace of John Gay	8	
(28) Ben Jonson Road, E1	15	
(29) Great Yarmouth – first theatre	10	
(30) Shakespeare Street, Padham	15	
(31) Stratford-upon-Avon	8	
(32) The Harlequin – harlequin (19½p)	20	

In addition: Aldeburgh, Amesbury, Barbican, Bishopgate, Blackfriars, Broadway, Globe Road, Hereford, Macduff, Shoreditch, Stafford, The Circle. Prices from £6 each.

SLOGAN POSTMARKS		
(33) Eden Court – The Theatre of the Highlands	30	
(34) Dickens Festival – Rochester	90	

In addition: Dunfermline Abbey Festival; Congleton Carnival. Prices from £60.

(17)

(3)

(12)

(5)

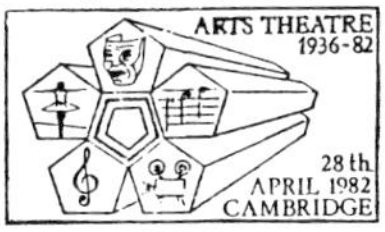

(6)

(15)

(23)

(13)

(34)

16th June 1982 – MARITIME HERITAGE

15½p Henry VIII/Mary Rose; 19½p Admiral Blake/Triumph; 24p Lord Nelson/HMS Victory; 26p Lord Fisher/HMS Dreadnought; 29p Viscount Cunningham/HMS Warspite

SPECIAL HANDSTAMPS	ordinary covers £	official covers £	
(1) First Day of Issue – Philatelic Bureau	3	–	*Royal Mail*
(2) First Day of Issue – Portsmouth	3	–	*Royal Mail*
(3) Birthplace of Nelson, Burnham Thorpe	5	10	*Hawkwood*
(4) National Maritime Museum, Greenwich, SE10	5	10	*BLS 4*
(5) Lloyds Register of Shipping, EC3	5	15	*S. Petty 6*
(6) Maritime Heritage, L!oyds, EC3	5	15	*Cotswold*
(7) Britannia's Maritime Heritage, Dartmouth	5	35	*B.R.N.C.*
(8) Maritime Heritage Stamp Exhibition, Exeter	5	10	*Exeter Cvrs*
(9) Maritime England Year, Poole	5	40	*Poole Mar Tr*
(10) Nottinghamshire Lifeboat Appeal	5	10	*Pilgrim*
(11) Axe Valley Maritime 82, Seaton	5	25	*Fire Ser NBF*
(12) Weymouth & Portland Chamber of Commerce	5	25	*Ch. of Comm.*
(13) Capt Matthew Flinders, Port Lincoln	5	40	*Lincoln Cath 2*
(14) Cook's Endeavour Salutes Nelson's Victory	5	10	*B. Travers*
(15) Royal Mail Maritime Heritage Cruise, Penarth	5	10	*Post Office*
(16) Missions to Seamen, Stratford	5	25	*Eng. T. Board*
(17) Historic Ships, St. Katherines Dock, E1	5	10	*Havering 26*
(18) Missions to Seamen, Portsmouth	5	25	*S.P.*
(19) Cinque Ports Exhibition, Dover	5	25	*Cinque Ports*
(20) Mountbatten Memorial Trust, Broadlands	5	6	*S. Petty 7*
(21) Leicester Sea Cadets	5	30	*LFDC 18*
(22) RAF Marine Branch, BF 1779 PS	10	20	*RFDC 12*
(23) Peru Hovercraft Expedition, BF 1956 PS	10	25	*Forces*
(24) Worshipful Co. of Shipwrights, EC	10	7	*BOCS (2) 12*
(25) Army Bag, National Postal Museum	10	–	*n.o.c.*
(26) Centenary Forces Postal Service, BF 8282 PS	10	15	*Forces*
(27) Trafalgar Sq. Philatelic Counter (Nelson's Column)	12	–	*n.o.c.*
(28) Philatelic Counter Opening, Coventry	12	–	*n.o.c.*
(29) Royal Shakespeare, Barbican, EC2	12	45	*Barbican*
(30) Caldey Island, Pope John Paul, Wales	12	20	*Caldey Isl.*
(31) Manchester (Kelloggs)	10	–	*n.o.c.*

C.D.S. POSTMARKS

(32) Bridgwater – birthplace of Blake	10
(33) Buckingham Palace, S.W.1	75
(34) Burnham Thorpe – birthplace of Nelson	20
(35) Castle Rd. Southsea – Henry VIII saw Mary Rose sink	20
(36) Devonport, Plymouth	25
(37) Falkland	20
(38) Flotta, Orkney – Scapa Flow (Home Fleet)	20
(39) FPO – Fleet Mail Office Portsmouth or Devonport	35
(40) Greenwich, London S.E.10	15
(41) House of Lords, SW1	25
(42) Marazion – b/place of Sandy Woodward (Falklands)	25
(43) Naval Barracks, Chatham	20
(44) Nelson, Portsmouth	20
(45) The Quarterdeck, Millwall E14	15
(46) Trafalgar	15
(47) Victory Street, Devonport	15
(48) Westward Ho!, Bideford, Devon	10

In addition, covers are known with the following CDS pmks: Blakes Corner, Blake Street, Bridgwater, Britannia, The Chart, Clyde Submarine Base, Cunningham Crescent, Dartmouth, Deptford High Street, The Docks (Bridgwater), Fleet, Henry St., Marton-in-Cleveland, Nelson (Lancs), Portsmouth, Portsmouth Dock Yard, St. Andrew's Cross (Plymouth), Tavistock. Prices from £10 each.

SLOGAN POSTMARKS

(49) See the Tall Ships in Southampton	35
(50) Maritime Bristol, Start of Many an Adventure	50
(51) Tower Bridge Open to the Public	75

OFFICIAL COVERS OR ORDINARY COVERS
Do you know the difference?
Please read the General Notes at the beginning of this catalogue for guidance.

(10)

(13)

(23)

(20)

(22)

(8)

(2)

(1)

(21)

(5)

(7)

(14)
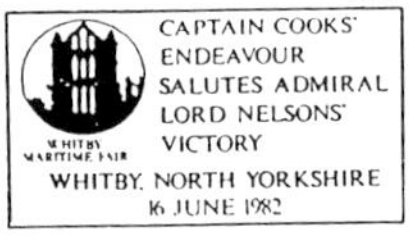

(50)

(51)

(49)

23rd July 1982 – BRITISH TEXTILES

15½p 'Strawberry Thief' (Morris); 19½p 'Scarlet Tulips' (Steiner); 26p 'Cherry Orchard' (Nash); 29p 'Chevrons' (Foster)

SPECIAL HANDSTAMPS	ordinary covers £	official covers £	
(1) First Day of Issue – Philatelic Bureau	3	–	*Royal Mail*
(2) First Day of Issue – Rochdale	3	–	*Royal Mail*
(3) William Morris, Water House, E17	4	10	*Hawkwood*
(4) Sir Richard Arkwright, Preston	4	5	*BOCS (2) 13*
(5) Hockley Mill, Nottingham	4	15	*Cotswold (g)*
(6) Textile Institute, Manchester	4	8	*Pilgrim*
(7) School of Textiles, Leicester	4	50	*Bradbury*
(8) Textile Exhibition, Bradford	4	10	*Peter Scot*
(9) Leek, Centre of Textile Industry	4	30	*Staffs C.C.*
(10) Textile Design, Huddersfield Polytechnic	4	30	*Hudd.Poly*
(11) Textiles on Stamps, Liberty, W1	4	6	*BLS 5*
(12) Coldharbour Mill, Uffculme	4	30	*Coldhbr. Mill*
(13) Leicester & District Knitting Industry	4	50	*LFDC 19*
(14) Royal School of Needlework, SW7	4	6	*S. Petty 8*
(15) No.2 Squadron RAF Regiment, BF 1781 PS	6	10	*RFDC 13*
(16) Arkwright Anniv., Cromford Mills, Matlock	4	10	*Ark. Soc.*
(17) British Philatelic Federation, Southampton	6	10	*B.P.F.*
(18) European Floral City, Exeter	6	10	*Exeter C.C.*
(19) Centenary, Forces Postal Service, BF 8282 PS	7	10	*Forces*
(20) BAE, National Postal Museum	7	–	*n.o.c.*
(21) Travelling Tram Post Office, Blackpool	8	10	*Blackpool*
(22) Papal Visits in Philately, SW1	8	10	*Bradbury*
(23) Royal Tournament, BF 1840 PS	8	15	*Forces*
(24) International Scout Camp, Blair Atholl	8	15	*Scot Scouts*
(25) Life Boat Week, Lyme Regis	8	15	*Pilgrim*
(26) Open Days, RNLI HQ, Poole	8	15	*Pilgrim*
(27) Caldey Island, Pope John Paul, Wales	10	15	*Caldey Isl.*

C.D.S. POSTMARKS	
(28) Cherry Orchard – 'Cherry Orchard' on 26p	10
(29) Forest Rd., E17 – birthplace of Wm. Morris	10
(30) Hall-ith-Wood – later named Spinning Mule	15
(31) Hammersmith W6 – home of Wm. Morris	10
(32) Preston – birthplace of Richard Arkwright	10
(33) Silk Street, Paisley	10
(34) Stanhill – James Hargreaves ('Spinning Jenny')	15
(35) Walthamstow, E17 – birthplace of Wm. Morris	9

In addition, covers are known with the following CDS pmks: All Saints (Derby), Arkwright Town, Axminster, Bobber's Mill, Coat, Coggeshall, Cotton Tree, Draperstown, Fair Isle, Harris, Lechlade, Merton, Milltown, New Invention, Shaftesbury, Tweed Road, Weaver Lodge, Wilton, Wool, Worstead. Prices from £6 each.

SLOGAN POSTMARKS

Collect British Stamps, Hull. £15.

(2)

(1)

(3)

(13)

(5)

(16)

(10)

(22)

8th September 1982 – INFORMATION TECHNOLOGY

15½p History of Communications; 26p Technology Today

SPECIAL HANDSTAMPS			
(1) First Day of Issue – Philatelic Bureau	2	–	*Royal Mail*
(2) First Day of Issue – London WC	2	–	*Royal Mail*
(3) Intelpost Head Post Office, E1	3	10	*Hawkwood*
(4) Computertown, Croydon	3	25	*Croy. Lib.*
(5) World Trade Centre	3	5	*Havering 28*
(6) Information Technology Year, Bedford	3	25	*Texas Instr.*
(7) RAF Supply Centre, BF 1787 PS	3	10	*RFDC 14*
(8) Best of Prestel, Martlesham	3	6	*Prestel*
(9) Artificial Earth Satellites, Jodrell Bank	3	5	*BLS 6*
(10) Information Technology, UMIST, Manchester	3	5	*BOCS (2) 14*
(11) University of Leicester	3	25	*LFDC 20*
(12) Ashville College, Computer Age, Harrogate	5	–	*n.o.c.*
(13) Centenary, Forces Postal Service, BF 8282 PS	6	10	*Forces*
(14) Exercise British Prince, 82 BF 1882 PS	6	10	*Forces*
(15) Travelling Tram Post Office, Blackpool	6	10	*Blackpool*
(16) Open Days Broadlands, Romsey	6	10	*S. Petty 9*
(17) Anaesthesiology, Royal Festival Hall, SE1	6	15	*Assoc Anaesth*
(18) 1982 Museum of the Year, Stoke	7	15	*Stoke Museum*
(19) Military Tattoo, Edinburgh	7	10	*Mil. Tattoo*

(12)

(4)

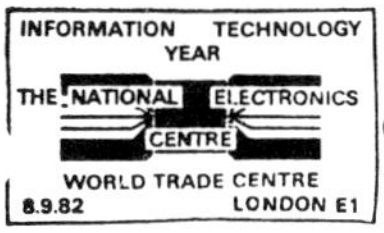

(5)

(1)

(6)

Information Technology (contd.)

	ordinary covers £	official covers £
(20) Trishaw Marathon, Kent Fire Brigade	7	10 *Kent Fire B.*
(21) King's Cup Air Race, BF 1788 PS	7	10 *Mosquito Mus.*
(22) Manchester (Kelloggs)	7	– *n.o.c.*

C.D.S. POSTMARKS

(23) Helston, Mawgan or Mullion – Goonhilly Downs	10
(24) Martlesham – British Telecom Research	20
(25) New Invention, Willenhall	10

In addition: Bletchley, Bracknell, Caversham, Cheltenham, Edinburgh, Felixstowe, Helensburg, Lovelace Road (Norwich), Mount Pleasant, National Insurance Blgs (Newcastle), Newton Street (Manchester), Oldland Common, Oxford, The Rocket, Rosetta, South Kensington, Stock Exchange, Taunton, Telephone House, Totnes, Walworth Road. Prices range from £6 each.

SLOGAN POSTMARKS

(26) Get the Most from your Post – Post Code It, Norwich ... 25

In addition: Radio Gwent; Beat Crime Dial 999; Collect British Stamps; any other Postcode slogans; Senders Name & Address etc. Prices range from £15.

13th October 1982 – BRITISH MOTOR CARS

15½p Metro & Austin Seven; 19½p Ford Escort & Model T; 26p Jaguar XJ6 & SS1; 29p Rolls-Royce Silver Spirit & Silver Ghost

SPECIAL HANDSTAMPS

	ordinary	official
(1) First Day of Issue – Philatelic Bureau	3	– *Royal Mail*
(2) First Day of Issue – Birmingham	3	– *Royal Mail*
(3) First Day of Issue – Crewe	3	– *Royal Mail*
(4) National Motor Museum, Beaulieu	5	5 *Beaulieu*
(5) Metro, World Trade Centre, E1	5	6 *Havering 29*
(6) Year of the Car, Woodford Green	5	15 *Havering*
(7) Millionth New Ford Escort, Halewood	5	15 *Ford*
(8) Nuffield College, Oxford	5	8 *Univ. Covers*
(9) Royal Flying Corps, BF 1789 PS	5	20 *RFDC 15*
(10) Worshipful Company of Coachmakers, WC	5	10 *S. Petty 10*
(11) Ford Sierra, Launch Day, Chippenham	5	20 *Cotswold*
(12) Cycle & Car Museum, Stanford Hall, Leicester	5	25 *LFDC 21*
(13) Austin 7, Brooklands, Weybridge	5	5 *BLS 7*
(14) Transport Centenary, Chesterfield	5	10 *Dawn*
(15) Heritage Collection, Syon Park, Brentford.	5	6 *Hawkwood*
(16) Dagenham, Home of Ford	5	25 *Dag. Motors*
(17) Sixty Years of Jaguar Cars, Coventry	5	8 *BOCS (2) 15*
(18) 35 Years of Silverstone Circuit	5	15 *Silverstone*
(19) Rolls-Royce Enthusiasts', Paulerspury	5	30 *Bradbury*
(20) Manchester (Kelloggs)	8	– *n.o.c.*
(21) Centenary, Forces Postal Service, BF 8282 PS	8	15 *Forces*
(22) Wiltshire Radio, Wootton Bassett	8	25 *Wilts Radio*
(23) Tile Hill Wood School, Coventry	8	25 *Tile Hill*

ORDINARY F.D.I. POSTMARKS

(24) Manchester – where Rolls met Royce ... 6

C.D.S. POSTMARKS

(25) Amersham – birthplace of Sir Herbert Austin	6
(26) Alwalton – birthplace of Henry Royce	10
(27) Austin, Plymouth	7
(28) Brighton & Knightsbridge – car rally ... *pair*	20
(29) Dagenham – Dagenham Motors (Ford)	9
(30) Foleshill – original Jaguar SS production	7
(31) Ford, Liverpool	7
(32) Halewood – Ford Escort	9
(33) Leyland – birthplace of Leyland Motors	9
(34) Longbridge – Mini Metro	10
(35) Mount Street, W1 – birthplace of Charles Rolls	10
(36) N.E.C. Birmingham – Motor Show	45
(37) R.A.C. London SW1	375
(38) Rank Forton Services – first motorway Post Office	50
(39) Trafford Park – U.K. assembly for Model T	35

In addition, covers are known with the following CDS postmarks: Allesley, Beaulieu, Bentley, Crewe, Dunlop, Hulme (Manchester), Lanchester, Lewisham, Milton, Rockfield, Saltley (Birmingham), Silverstone, Sparkbrook (Birmingham), St. James' St., Tooting, Vauxhall, Walthamstow. Prices range from £7 each.

SLOGAN POSTMARKS

(40) Hella of Banbury, Motor Show ... 30

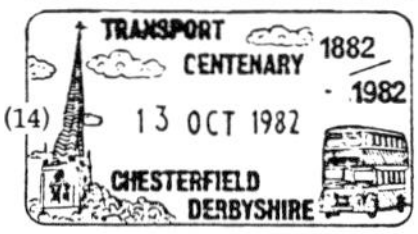

17th November1982 - CHRISTMAS

12½p, 15½p, 19½p, 26p, 29p Christmas Carols

SPECIAL HANDSTAMPS	ordinary covers £	official covers £
(1) First Day of Issue - Philatelic Bureau	3	- *Royal Mail*
(2) First Day of Issue - Bethlehem	3	- *Royal Mail*
(3) We Three Kings, Star, Glenrothes	4	5 *BLS 8*
(4) I Saw Three Ships, Hythe	4	6 *BOCS (2) 16*
(5) Good King Wenceslas, Salisbury	4	4 *Benham*
(6) Seasons Greetings, Norwich Cathedral	4	10 *Nor. Cath.*
(7) Seasons Greetings, Cutty Sark, SE10	4	10 *Havering 30*
(8) Salvation Army, Leicester	4	25 *LFDC 22*
(9) Christmas Carol, Dickens House, WC1	4	15 *Hawkwood*
(10) St. John Ambulance, Leicester	4	10 *St. John Am.*
(11) Sir Christopher Wren, East Knoyle	8	20 *S. Petty 11*
(12) 1st Highams Park Girl Guides, E4	8	15 *Girls Brig.*
(13) Centenary, Forces Postal Service, BF 8282 PS	8	15 *Forces*
(14) North Atlantic Assembly, SW	8	- *n.o.c.*
(15) HMS Brilliant, Freedom of Tunbridge Wells	8	15 *H.R.*
(16) Manchester (Kelloggs)	8	- *n.o.c.*
(17) BAE, National Postal Museum	8	- *n.o.c.*
C.D.S. POSTMARKS		
(18) Bethlehem, Llandeilo, Dyfed	10	
(19) Nasareth, Caernarfon, Gwyned	10	

In addition: Chipping Campden, East Grinstead, Fleet Street, Holly Bank, Hollybush, Holy Island, Holytown, Ivy Bush, Ivychurch, Kingsway, Kingsworthy, London SE1, Noel Road, Orient Road, St. Erth, St. Nicholas, St. Stephen, Shepherds Hill, Shepherdswell, Star, Starcross, Theobalds Road BO, Three Kingham. Prices from £6 each.

26th January 1983 - BRITISH RIVER FISH

Izaak Walton 'The Compleat Angler' 1593-1683

15½p Salmon; 19½p Pike; 26p Trout; 29p Perch

SPECIAL HANDSTAMPS	ordinary covers £	official covers £
(1) First Day of Issue - Philatelic Bureau	2	- *Royal Mail*
(2) First Day of Issue - Peterborough	2	- *Royal Mail*
(3) Fishing the Teign, Newton Abbot	7	- *Royal Mail*
(4) Display of River Fish, Salisbury	7	- *Royal Mail*
(5) 400 years of Fishing Tackle, Redditch	7	- *Royal Mail*
(6) British Waterways Board	5	10 *D. Taylor*
(7) Cinque Ports Angling Society, Hythe	5	8 *BOCS (2) 17*
(8) Pike Anglers Club, Norwich	5	15 *Pike Anglers*
(9) London Anglers Association, E17	5	10 *Havering 1*
(10) Izaak Walton, River Itchen, Winchester	5	10 *S. Petty 12*
(11) RAF Stafford Angling Club, BF 1798 PS	5	20 *RFDC 17*
(12) Tisbury Fish Farm, Romford	6	12 *Havering*
(13) National Anglers Council, EC4	5	12 *NAC*
(14) House of Hardy Exhibition, Pall Mall, SW1	5	12 *Hawkwood*
(15) Return of the Salmon, Thames Water, EC	5	15 *Thames Water*
(16) 100 years of Salmon Fishing, Salmon Leap	5	7 *BLS (83) 1*
(17) Douglas Bader Angling Club, Leicester	6	30 *Bradbury*
(18) Birmingham Anglers Association	6	30 *Bradbury*
(19) Izaak Walton Tercentenary, Stafford	6	25 *Staff. Museum*
(20) Izaak Walton, 1593-1683, Stafford	5	15 *LFDC 23*
(21) I.E.W. National Postal Museum	6	- *n.o.c.*
C.D.S. POSTMARKS		
(22) Fleet Street - 'The Compleat Angler' published here	6	
(23) Itchen - Izaak Walton's favourite fishing spot	6	
(24) Kingsgate St., Winchester - Walton's burial place	7	
(25) The Salmon Leap, Coleraine	5	
(26) Stafford - Izaak Walton's birthplace	5	
(27) Troutbeck: Windermere or Penrith *each*	5	
(28) Walton, Stafford	7	
(29) Winchester, Hants	5	

In addition: Alnwick, Angle, Bream, Coldstream, Fishbourne, Fishguard, Fishers Pond, Fishlake, Fishponds, Freshwater, Hook, Lochawe, Newton Solney, Norton Bridge, Oulton Broads, Pike Hill, Pike Road, River, Potters Heigham, Romsey, Salmon Lane, Walton-on-Thames. Prices from £4.

PRICES & CONDITION - PLEASE READ GENERAL NOTES

9th March 1983 - COMMONWEALTH

15½p Topical Island; 19½p Arid Desert;
26p Temperate Climate; 29p Mountainous Region

SPECIAL HANDSTAMPS	ordinary covers £	official covers £	
(1) First Day of Issue - Philatelic Bureau	2	-	*Royal Mail*
(2) First Day of Issue - London SW	2	-	*Royal Mail*
(3) Commonwealth Institute, W8	3	15	*LFDC 24*
(4) Capt. Cook's Voyages of Discovery, Whitby	3	6	*B. Travers*
(5) William Wilberforce, Hull	3	15	*Wilb. Council*
(6) World Trade Centre, E1	3	6	*Havering 2*
(7) Royal Commonwealth Society, WC2	3	7	*D. Taylor*
(8) Romsey, Mahatma Gandhi, 1869-1948	3	8	*S. Petty 13*
(9) No 24 Squadron, BF 1799 PS	4	15	*RFDC 18*
(10) British Airways, London Airport	4	10	*BOCS (2) 18*
(11) Geographical Magazine, London	4	8	*Hawkwood*
(12) Association of Cricket Umpires, Leicester	8	15	*Assoc. C.U.*
(13) Dunsmore Boy's School, Rugby	8	15	*Dunsmore Sch.*
(14) Daily Mail Ideal Home Exhibition, SW	8	15	*Pilgrim*
(15) I.E.W., National Postal Museum	8	-	*n.o.c.*
(16) Sixty years of Jaguar Cars, Coventry	8	7	*Benham*

C.D.S. POSTMARKS

(17) Buckingham Palace, S.W.1	80
(18) Gleneagles Hotel - 1977 'Gleneagles Agreement'	50
(19) House of Commons, S.W.1	30
(20) House of Lords, S.W.1	35
(21) Parliament Street BO. SW1	13
(22) Marldon - birthplace of Sir Humphrey Gilbert	10

In addition, covers are known with the following CDS pmks: The Beach, Blantyre, Dartmouth, Falklands, Forest Town, Hull, India St., Kensington High Street, Marton-in-Cleveland, Melbourne, Mountain Ash. Queen Elizabeth Ave., Queen Victoria Road, Romsey, Toronto, Windsor, Whitby. Prices from £6.

SLOGAN POSTMARKS

(23) House of Commons - wavy line	25

25th May 1983 - BRITISH ENGINEERING ACHIEVEMENTS

16p Humber Bridge; 20½p Thames Barrier; 28p Energy Support Vessel - Iolair

SPECIAL HANDSTAMPS	ordinary	official	
(1) First Day of Issue - Philatelic Bureau	2	-	*Royal Mail*
(2) First Day of Issue - Hull	2	-	*Royal Mail*
(3) Institution of Civil Engineers, SW1	3	25	*LFDC 25*
(4) Eng. Achievement, Thames Flood Barrier, SE7	3	10	*G & P*
(5) CTH, Thames Flood Barrier, SE7	3	10	*Havering 3*
(6) GLC Thames Barrier, Woolwich Reach	3	15	*Des. Enc.*
(7) Engineering Achievements, AUEW, SE15	3	20	*AUEW*
(8) British Shipbuilders Iolair, SW7	3	7	*BOCS (2) 19*
(9) BP Contribution Iolair, Aberdeen	3	5	*BOCS (2) 19*
(10) Technology to greater depths, UDI, Aberdeen	4	10	*UDI*
(11) Humber Bridge, Longest Single Span	3	10	*Hawkwood*
(12) Humber Bridge, Opened 17 July 1981, Barton	3	4	*BLS (83) 3*
(13) Institute of Mechanical Engineers, SW1	4	10	*Pilgrim*
(14) Printing Shares the fruits of Human Genius	4	15	*Havering*
(15) RAF Cosford, BF 1806 PS	3	10	*RFDC 19*
(16) The Harrier, Kingston upon Thames	4	10	*S. Petty 14*
(17) 30 Years experience, Dan Air, London Airport	3	10	*Benham*
(18) Post Office Philatelic Counter, Grimsby	5	15	*Royal Mail*
(19) Telecom Technology Showcase, EC4	6	-	*n.o.c.*
(20) Chester-le-Street Co. Durham	6	15	*C. leS. Council*
(21) The Wilberforce Council, Hull	6	15	*Wilb. Council*
(22) Children's Hospital, Chippenham	6	15	*Rotary*
(23) I.E.W., National Postal Museum	6	-	*n.o.c.*

C.D.S. POSTMARKS

(24) Coalbrookdale - birthplace of Ind. Revolution	8
(25) Eagle - 'Iolair' is gaelic for eagle	8
(26) Hessle & Barton - N. & S. of Humber Bridge *pair*	12
(27) Ironbridge - the world's first iron bridge	12
(28) New Bridge Road, Hull	13
(29) Port Glasgow - 'Iolair' was built here	35
(30) Silvertown & Woolwich - N. & S. of Barrier *pair*	12
(31) Silvertown & Charlton - N. & S. of Barrier *pair*	12

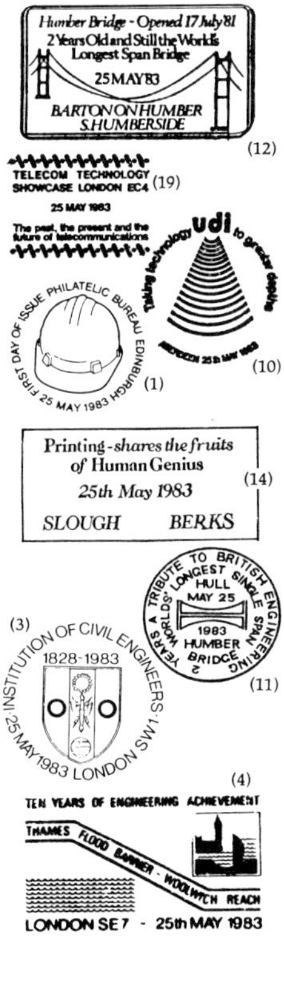

Engineering (contd.)

	ordinary covers £	official covers £

In addition, covers are known with the following CDS pmks: Bacton, Bridge, Clydebank, Cleveland, Cruden Bay, Dundee, Hatfield, Langholm, Portsmouth, Rigside, Rotherham, Saltash, Stock Exchange, Telford. Prices range from £5.

SLOGAN POSTMARKS

(32) GLC Thames Barrier - Charlton, SE7	18	
(33) GLC Thames Barrier - Woolwich, SE18	18	
(34) Collect British Stamps Humberside	25	

In addition: Middlesbrough Philatelic Counter; Royal Mail Helping Business on Merseyside; World Communications Year. Prices from £20.

(31) (32)

6th July 1983 - THE BRITISH ARMY

16p The Royal Scots; 20½p Royal Welch Fusiliers; 26p Royal Green Jackets; 28p Irish Guards; 31p Parachute Regiment

SPECIAL HANDSTAMPS

(1) First Day of Issue - Philatelic Bureau	3	-	*Royal Mail*
(2) First Day of Issue - Aldershot	3	-	*Royal Mail*
(3) Regimental Stamp Display, Glasgow	6	-	*Royal Mail*
(4) The British Army Series, BF 1983 PS	6	20	*Army*
(5) The Royal Scots, BF 0350 PS	6	20	*Army*
(6) The Royal Welch Fusiliers, BF 0294 PS	6	20	*Army*
(7) The Royal Greenjackets, BF 1800 PS	6	20	*Army*
(8) The Irish Guards, BF 1900 PS	6	20	*Army*
(9) The Parachute Regiment, BF 2000 PS	6	20	*Army*
(10) 75th Anniversary of the TA in Wales, BF 1908 PS	6	40	*Forces*
(11) Rheindahlen Allied Marches, BF 1810 PS	6	25	*Forces*
(12) Royal Military Academy, Sandhurst	6	12	*G & P*
(13) Queen's Own Hussars, Warwick	6	25	*LFDC 26*
(14) Duke of York's Royal Military School, Dover	6	9	*Benham L2*
(15) Blenheim Palace, Woodstock	6	10	*Havering 4*
(16) Soldier Print Soc., Worthing	6	25	*S.P.*
(17) National Army Museum 1971-1983, SW3	6	7	*BOCS (2) 20*
(18) Ensign Model Soldier Exhib., Boston	6	10	*Hawkwood*
(19) Duke of Edinburgh's Reg. Museum, Salisbury	6	15	*S. Petty 15*
(20) Ancient Order of Foresters, Rugeley	6	20	*A.O.F.*
(21) Richard III 500th Anniv., Middleham	6	30	*R III Soc*
(22) Llangollen International Eisteddfod	8	25	*Eist'd*
(23) Telecom Technology Showcase, EC4	8	25	*Brit Tele*
(24) Royal Show, Kenilworth	8	-	*n.o.c.*

C.D.S. POSTMARKS

(25) Aldershot - Parachute Regiment HQ	15	
(26) Battle, or Battlefield *each*	12	
(27) Broadway, SW1 - Irish Guards Regimental HQ	15	
(28) Buckingham Palace, SW1	75	
(29) Catterick Garrison, N Yorks	15	
(30) Duke of York's School, Dover - Military School	20	
(31) Edinburgh - Royal Scots Regimental HQ	15	
(32) Hightown - Royal Welch Fusiliers Regimental HQ	15	
(33) Marlborough, Wilts	15	
(34) Sandhurst - Royal Military Academy	15	
(35) Wilton, Salisbury - HQ UK Land Forces	15	
(36) Winchester - Royal Greenjackets Regimental HQ	15	
(37) Army POs (Bassingbourn, Worthy Down, etc)	15	
(38) Any Field or Forces Post Office cancellations	20	

In addition, covers are known with the following CDS pmks: Athelstaneford, Bannockburn, Barracks, Brunswick Road (Pirbright Camp), Bunkers Hill, Chelsea Royal Hospital, Falkland, Guard House, Gunhill, Huntingdon, Montgomery, Naseby, St. Andrews, Sentry Corner, Terriers, Tidworth, Waterloo, Wellington, Woodstock, Woolwich, York, Yorktown. Prices from £7.

SLOGAN POSTMARKS

(39) Join Territorial Army 75th Anniversary	475	
(40) National Army Museum - London SW	25	

OFFICIAL COVER ABBREVIATIONS:
BOCS = Benham Official Cover Series
LFDC = Leicester First Day Covers series
Please read about Official Covers in the General Notes at the beginning of this catalogue.

(16)

(4)

(5)

(6)

(7)

(8)

(9)

(15)

(2)

(21)

(14)

(18)

(39)

(40)

24th August 1983 - BRITISH GARDENS
'Capability' Brown, Landscape Gardener 1716-1783

16p Sissinghurst; 20½p Biddulph Grange;
28p Blenheim; 31p Pitmedden

SPECIAL HANDSTAMPS

	ordinary covers £	official covers £	
(1) First Day of Issue - Philatelic Bureau	3	-	*Royal Mail*
(2) First Day of Issue - Oxford	3	-	*Royal Mail*
(3) Capability Brown at Bowood, Calne	6	-	*Royal Mail*
(4) Queen's Gardens, Croydon	6	25	*Croydon BC*
(5) Capability Brown, Kew Gardens	5	13	*LFDC 27*
(6) National Trust, Sissinghurst Castle	5	7	*BOCS (2) 21*
(7) League of Friends, The Grange, Biddulph	5	15	*League of F*
(8) Blenheim Palace, Woodstock	5	6	*Havering 5*
(9) National Trust for Scotland, Pitmedden	5	5	*BLS (83) 5*
(10) Capability Brown, Esher, Claremont	5	20	*Arlington*
(11) Roses in August, Syon Park, Brentford	5	5	*Hawkwood*
(12) Lancelot Capability Brown, Fenstanton	5	15	*Fenst Par Ch*
(13) National Trust for Scotland, Crathes Castle	5	7	*Benham L4*
(14) National Trust, Lyme Park, Disley	5	5	*Benham L3*
(15) Capability Brown, Kirkharle, Newcastle	5	15	*Landscape Ins.*
(16) Capability Brown, GRBS, Hampton Court	5	18	*S. Petty 16*
(17) Celebration of English Gardens, SW1	5	10	*DGT*
(18) RAF Gardens, Runnymede, BF 1814 PS	10	10	*RFDC 21*
(19) International camp, BB 83, Perth	10	30	*Boys Brig.*
(20) Travelling Tram Post Office, Blackpool	10	-	*n.o.c.*
(21) Military Tattoo Edinburgh	10	15	*Mil. Tattoo*
(22) Hornchurch Cricket Club	20	25	*H.C.C.*

C.D.S. POSTMARKS

(23) Biddulph - featured on 20½p value	10
(24) Botanic Gardens, Belfast	25
(25) Fenstanton - Capability Brown is buried here	12
(26) Kew Gardens, Richmond	35
(27) Kirkwhelpington - birthplace of Capability Brown	10
(28) Mayfair BO., W1 - Capability Brown died here	10
(29) Sissinghurst - featured on 16p value	7
(30) Udny, Ellon - Pitmedden (31p)	8
(31) Woodstock - Blenheim Palace (28p)	8

In addition, covers are known with the following CDS pmks: Garden Suburb, Garden Village, Glamis, Harewood, Headstone Gardens, Petworth, Rake, Royal Hospital Chelsea, Sledmere, The Allotments, Trentham, Welwyn Garden City. Prices from £6.

SLOGAN POSTMARKS

(32) Back Beautiful Britain	25
(33) Chamber of Commerce - Devizes in Bloom	30
(34) Your Garden Isle is Beautiful - Isle of Wight	35

In addition: Beautiful Bath. £20.

(12)

(14)

(2)

(5)

(7)

(18)

(15)

(29)

(30)

(34)

5th October 1983 - BRITISH FAIRS
16p Merry-go-round; 20½p Menageries and rides;
28p Side shows; 31p Early trade and produce fairs

SPECIAL HANDSTAMPS

	ordinary covers £	official covers £	
(1) First Day of Issue - Philatelic Bureau	3	-	*Royal Mail*
(2) First Day of Issue - Nottingham	3	-	*Royal Mail*
(3) St. Bartholomew the Great, EC	5	6	*Havering 6*
(4) Butchers Charitable Institution, EC1	5	6	*Hawkwood*
(5) Showmen's Guild, Staines	5	25	*S. Guild*
(6) Goose Fair, Tavistock	5	15	*S. Petty 17*
(7) Chipperfield's Circus, EC	5	10	*BLS (83) 6*
(8) NABMA (Markets Authority) Birmingham	5	6	*Des. Enc.*
(9) Fairfield, Croydon	5	15	*F. Field Halls*
(10) Turner's Musical Merry-go-Round, Northampton	5	7	*BOCS (2) 22*
(11) Goose Fair 1983, Nottingham	5	25	*LFDC 28*
(12) World's First Air Fair, BF 1815 PS	7	8	*RFDC 22*
(13) Rowell Lions, Rothwell, Kettering	6	25	*Rothwell Lions*
(14) British Philatelic Federation, Bath	9	12	*BPF*
(15) Travelling Tram Post Office, Blackpool	8	-	*n.o.c.*
(16) Samuel Pepys, Cambridge	8	10	*Univ. Covers*
(17) The Boys Brigade Centenary, Cardiff	8	20	*BB Wales*
(18) MMB (Milk Marketing Board) Newcastle	8	15	*MMB*
(19) Exhibition Garden City, Letchworth	8	-	*n.o.c.*

(13)

(10)

(18)

(8)

British Fairs (contd.)

	ordinary covers £	official covers £
C.D.S. POSTMARKS		
(20) Borough High Street, S.E.1 – Southwark Fair	10	
(21) Cambridge or Chesterton – Sturbridge Fair ....*each*	10	
(22) Horse Fair	8	
(23) London Chief Office – Bartholomew Fair	10	
(24) St. Giles, Oxford – largest surviving wake	12	
(25) Scarborough	15	
(26) Tavistock – Goose Fair	12	
(27) Widecombe-in-the-Moor	25	
(28) Winchester – Bishops Fair, oldest Charter Fair	7	

In addition: Abingdon, Alford, Appleby-in-Westmorland, Barrus Bridge, Big Top, Brigg, Elephant and Castle, Exeter, Frome, Greenwich, Honiton, Hyson Green, King's Lynn, Marlborough, Market Sidmouth, Mayfair, North End, St. Ives, Stow-on-the-Wold, Stratford-upon-Avon, Ulverston, Warwick, Wookey Hole, Woodkirk, Yarm. Prices from £8 each.

SLOGAN POSTMARKS

Wonderland of Wales; Magnum World of Entertainment. Prices from £85.

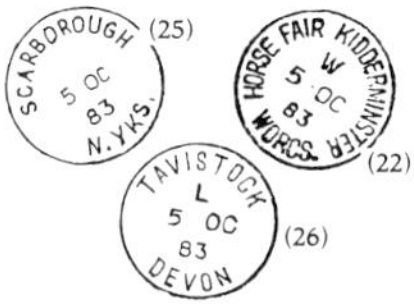

16th November 1983 – CHRISTMAS

12½p, 16p, 20½p, 28p, 31p Peace and Goodwill

SPECIAL HANDSTAMPS		
(1) First Day of Issue – Philatelic Bureau	3	– *Royal Mail*
(2) First Day of Issue – Bethlehem	3	– *Royal Mail*
(3) Peace and Goodwill, Nasareth	4	15 *LFDC 29*
(4) Minster Gatehouse, Sheppey	6	10 *Hawkwood*
(5) Leicestershire Society for the Blind	4	4 *L. Blind Soc*
(6) Winchester Cathedral	4	15 *S. Petty 18*
(7) Peace on Earth, Peacehaven	4	6 *BLS (83) 7*
(8) St. Mary le Strand, WC2	4	8 *Havering 7*
(9) Telecom Technology Showcase, EC4	4	20 *Brit Tele*
(10) Lyminge Parish Church, Festival Year	4	7 *BOCS (2) 23*
(11) T.C. (Tandy Corporation), Walsall	10	35 *T.C.*
C.D.S. POSTMARKS		
(12) Bethlehem, Llandeilo, Dyfed	10	
(13) Nasareth, Gwynedd	10	

In addition, covers are known with the following CDS pmks: Birdsall, Blackbird Leys, Canterbury, Chapel, Chester-le-Street, Christchurch, Dovecot, Dove Holes, Dove House Lane, Holy Island, Kingsworthy, Minster, Peacehaven, Quakers Rd., St. Augustine's, St. Nicholas, Star. Prices from £6.

SLOGAN POSTMARKS

(14) Hastings – Resort for All Seasons (Xmas scene)	90	

In addition: Royal Mail Special Services, Hull. £30.

17th January 1984 – HERALDRY

16p College of Arms; 20½p Richard III;
28p The Earl Marshal; 31p City of London

SPECIAL HANDSTAMPS		
(1) First Day of Issue – Philatelic Bureau	3	– *Royal Mail*
(2) First Day of Issue – London EC	3	– *Royal Mail*
(3) Heraldry Guildhall, City of London, EC	6	– *Royal Mail*
(4) College of Arms, London EC4	6	25 *Cotswold*
(5) The Heraldry Society, WC	6	10 *BOCS (2) 24*
(6) Richard III Society, Leicester	6	35 *LFDC 30*
(7) Richard III, Fotheringhay Castle	6	35 *LFDC 30*
(8) Richard III Celebration, Scarborough	6	25 *Pilgrim*
(9) The City of London, The Square Mile, EC	6	15 *G&P*
(10) Deputy Norroy, King of Arms, York	6	10 *Hawkwood*
(11) Friary Meux Kings Arms, Godalming	6	10 *Hawkwood*
(12) Coat of Arms Granted in 1890, Belfast	6	20 *BLS (84) 1*
(13) Coat of Arms Granted in 1906, Cardiff	6	20 *BLS (84) 1*
(14) Coat of Arms Granted in 1975, Edinburgh	6	20 *BLS (84) 1*
(15) Spencer of Althorp	6	20 *Althorp*
(16) Heirlooms, 1 Hayhill, Berkeley Sq., W1	7	10 *Havering*
(17) Arthurian Legend, Camelot, Tintagel	8	15 *S. Petty 19*
(18) 1st RAF Badge, BF 1826 PS	10	12 *RFDC 24*
(19) NSPCC Centenary, EC4	10	25 *NSPCC*
(20) High Wycombe, Stamp Printing	10	10 *Harrisons*

Heraldry (contd.)

	ordinary covers £	official covers £
(21) Lincoln Philatelic Counter Opened	15	- *n.o.c.*
(22) Marks & Spencer, 100 Years, W1	8	8 *DGT*
(23) London FS, Air Mail, National Postal Museum	10	- *n.o.c.*
(24) Berkswell Parish Church	10	20 *Par. Ch.*
(25) Good News People, Martins, Aylesbury	10	35 *Martins*
(26) Story of the Poppy, British Legion, Maidstone	10	25 *Brit. Leg.*
(27) London SW1 (Buckingham Palace)	10	- *n.o.c.*

C.D.S. POSTMARKS

(28) Arundel - home of the Earl Marshal	[illegible]	
(29) Cannon St., EC4 - near to College of Arms	8	
(30) Fore St., EC2 - near to the Guildhall	8	
(31) Market Bosworth - Richard III, Bosworth Field	10	
(32) Middleham - Richard III's castle	10	

In addition covers are known with the following CDS pmks: Barony, Chester, College Town, Coneysthorpe, Fleur-de-Lis, Godalming, Gloucester, Harewood, King Arthur's Way, Leadenhall St., Lombard St., Ludgate Circus, Ludlow, Queen Elizabeth Ave., Richmond, St. Georges Cross, Sloane Square, Stock Exchange, York. Prices from £7.

(27)

(22)

(18)

(15)

6th March 1984 - BRITISH CATTLE

16p Highland Cow; 20½p Chillingham Wild Bull; 26p Hereford Bull; 28p Welsh Black Bull; 31p Irish Moiled Cow

SPECIAL HANDSTAMPS

(1) First Day of Issue - Philatelic Bureau	4	- *Royal Mail*
(2) First Day of Issue - Oban Argyll	4	- *Royal Mail*
(3) Highland Cattle Society, Edinburgh	5	10 *BOCS (2) 25*
(4) Chateau Impney, Highland Cattle, Droitwich	15	- *Royal Mail*
(5) Last Stronghold of the Chillingham Bull	5	6 *BLS (84) 2*
(6) Home of the Chillingham Wild Cattle	5	10 *CWC Assoc*
(7) Hereford Herd Book Society	5	10 *DGT*
(8) Welsh Black Cattle Society, Caernarfon	5	10 *DGT*
(9) Irish Moiled Cattle Society, Ballynahinch	5	10 *DGT*
(10) British Friesian Cattle Society, Rickmansworth	5	10 *DGT*
(11) Livestock Show, Tring	15	- *Royal Mail*
(12) Farming the Backbone of Britain, SW1	5	10 *DGT*
(13) Rare Breeds Survival Trust, Stoneleigh	5	8 *LFDC 31*
(14) Butcher's Charitable Institute, Smithfield EC1	5	6 *Hawkwood*
(15) Earl's Court - Royal Smithfield Show, SW5	6	6 *Havering*
(16) Royal Veterinary College, NW1	6	7 *S. Petty 20*
(17) Farmers Weekly Golden Jubilee, Sutton	6	30 *Des. Enc.*
(18) Dairy Crest Honours British Cattle, Crewe	8	15 *MMB*
(19) RAF Hereford, BF 1828 PS	8	10 *RFDC 25*
(20) The Martyrs, Tolpuddle	10	15 *TUC*
(21) Stampex, London, SW1	10	15 *Stampex*
(22) London FS, National Postal Museum	10	- *n.o.c.*
(23) Colchester Castle Restoration	25	- *n.o.c.*
(24) Daily Mail, Ideal Home Exhibition, SW	15	18 *Pilgrim*
(25) 767 Another 1st from Britannia	20	50 *Brit. Airw.*

A special handstamp 'Maiden Flight Skyship 600, Cardington' was used on 6th March, but no covers are known to exist with the British Cattle Stamps affixed.

C.D.S. POSTMARKS

(26) Ballynahinch, or Saintfield - Irish Moiled Cow .. *each*	15
(27) Black Bull St., Leeds	15
(28) Bull Farm, Mansfield	15
(29) Caernarfon - Welsh Black Cattle	8
(30) Cattle Market, Preston	25
(31) Chillingham - Chillingham Wild Cattle	10
(32) Hereford	7
(33) Kyle, Kyleakin or Oban - Highland Cattle ...*each*	15
(34) Red Cow, Exeter	25

In addition: Bull Bay, Bull Brook, Cowfold, Cowplain, Dolgellau, Heriot, Lavenham, Lincoln, Moy, Oxen Park, Royal College St., Stoneleigh, Terling, Thames Ditton, The Markets, Thirsk. Prices from £6.

SLOGAN POSTMARKS

Collect British Stamps; Any Royal Mail slogans. Prices from £10.

(9)

(2)

(1)

(8)

(17)

(15)

(14)

(16)

(3)

(19)

(10)

(12)

10th April 1984 - URBAN RENEWAL

16p Liverpool Garden Festival; 20½p Milburngate Centre, Durham; 28p City Docks, Bristol; 31p Commercial St. Redevelopment, Perth

SPECIAL HANDSTAMPS	ordinary covers £	official covers £
(1) First Day of Issue - Philatelic Bureau	3	- *Royal Mail*
(2) First Day of Issue - Liverpool	3	- *Royal Mail*
(3) International Garden Festival, Liverpool	5	10 *BOCS (2) 26*
(4) Abbey National Building Society	5	6 *G&P*
(5) Urban Renewal, City of Durham	5	10 *C of Durham*
(6) Laing Development, Durham	5	10 *Laing*
(7) Urban Renewal, BDP, W1	5	10 *BDP*
(8) Bush House, Arnolfini Gallery, Bristol	5	10 *C of Bristol*
(9) Commercial Street Redevelopment, Perth	5	10 *G&P*
(10) Landscape Institute, Liverpool	5	10 *Lans. Inst.*
(11) RIBA, Festival of Architecture, York	5	25 *Cotswold*
(12) RIBA, Festival of Architecture, W1	5	25 *Cotswold*
(13) St. John the Evangelist, (RIBA), E15	5	5 *Hawkwood*
(14) Festival of Architecture, Guildhall, EC2	7	- *Royal Mail*
(15) Year of Building, CIOB, Ascot	5	9 *DGT*
(16) DIADEM, Dundee Inst. of Architects	7	15 *D.I.A.*
(17) Letchworth the First Garden City	5	10 *LFDC 32*
(18) London Docklands, Isle of Dogs, E14	6	9 *Havering*
(19) Covent Garden Market, WC	6	10 *S. Petty 21*
(20) Cheshire Gibson, Surveyors, Birmingham	10	- *n.o.c.*
(21) Wigan Pier Project	10	20 *Wigan Coun.*
(22) Bristol Scout, BF 1835 PS	12	15 *RFDC 26*
(23) London FS, National Postal Museum	15	- *n.o.c.*
(24) Colchester Castle Restoration	25	- *n.o.c.*

C.D.S. POSTMARKS

(25) Aigburth, or Cockburn St. - near to the IGF	7
(26) Ascot - Chartered Inst. of Building	7
(27) Brigend, Perth - Commercial St. Redevelopment	10
(28) Letchworth - First Garden City	7
(29) New Buildings, Londonderry	45
(30) North Rd., Durham - near to Milburngate Centre	10
(31) Prince St., Bristol - near to Arnolfini Gallery	10

In addition covers are known with the following CDS pmks: Fore Street, Isle of Dogs, Red House, Southampton Street, Telford, Tingley, Welwyn Garden City. Prices from £6.

SLOGAN POSTMARKS

(32) International Garden Festival Liverpool 84	15

In addition: Royal Mail, Hull; Beautiful Bath; Sunderland. Prices from £20.

(3)

(19)

(12)

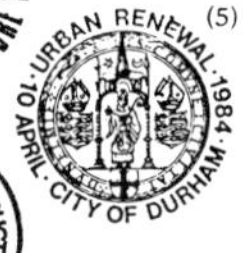

(5)

(6)

(4)

(11)

(2)

(1)

(16)

(8)

15th May 1984 - EUROPA

2 x 16p; 2 x 20½p CEPT 25th anniversary logo and the abduction of Europa

SPECIAL HANDSTAMPS		
(1) First Day of Issue - Philatelic Bureau	3	- *Royal Mail*
(2) First Day of Issue - London SW	3	- *Royal Mail*
(3) European Elections, London, SW	4	4 *Havering*
(4) Second British European Elections, SW1	4	7 *BLS (84) 4*
(5) Sealink, Bridge with Europe, Folkestone	4	10 *BOCS (2) 27*
(6) 1606-1984 Dover Harbour Board	4	8 *LFDC 33*
(7) Hawkwood Covers, Europa E1	4	5 *Hawkwood*
(8) D-Day + 40 Portsmouth	4	12 *S. Petty 22*
(9) 35th Anniv. Formation of NATO, BF 1949 PS	12	20 *RFDC 27*
(10) International Garden Festival, Liverpool	8	- *n.o.c.*
(11) London FS, National Postal Museum	8	- *n.o.c.*
(12) Mosquito Aircraft Museum, Hatfield	10	20 *M.A. Mus.*
(13) Colchester Castle Restoration	20	- *n.o.c.*

C.D.S. POSTMARKS

(14) Bridge or Postbridge ...*each*	7
(15) Dover, Folkestone, Harwich, Newhaven, Weymouth	7
(16) House of Commons, SW1	15
(17) House of Lords, SW1	20
(18) Mark Cross, Crowborough	40
(19) Newhaven plus PAQUEBOT	12
(20) Boulogne, Calais or Dieppe plus PAQUEBOT ...*each*	15
(21) Parliament Street	15

(1)

(13)

(2)

(5)

(6)

Europa (contd.)

In addition covers are known with the following CDS pmks: Felixstowe, Holland Fen, Montgomery, Normandy, Northern Parliament, Poling Corner, Portsmouth, Portsmouth Dockyard, York. *Prices from £6.*

SLOGAN POSTMARKS

Milk on your Doorstep; Historic Sandwich; Any Royal Mail slogans; Collect British Stamps. Prices from £20.

(1)

(2)

(10)

(14)

-5 JUN'84

5th June 1984 - LONDON ECONOMIC SUMMIT 1984

31p Lancaster House

SPECIAL HANDSTAMPS	ordinary covers £	official covers £	
(1) First Day of Issue - Philatelic Bureau	2	-	*Royal Mail*
(2) First Day of Issue - London SW	2	-	*Royal Mail*
(3) Economic Summit, SW1 (50p shaped globe)	4	5	*LFDC 34*
(4) London Economic Summit, SW1	4	4	*Havering*
(5) London Welcomes the Economic Summit, EC1	4	5	*BOCS (2) 29*
(6) Sterling Travellers Cheques, Croydon	4	-	*Post Office*
(7) TSB, Chingford	6	8	*Hawkwood*
(8) Brit. Philatelic Cover Producers Assoc., SW1	4	5	*BPCPA*
(9) London Underwriters Centenary, EC3	4	10	*Cotswold*
(10) 1924 Wembley Exhibition, NW10	5	8	*DGT*
(11) 75th Rotary Convention, Birmingham	5	8	*Int. Rotary*
(12) The Queen Embarks Britannia, Portsmouth	10	35	*Rembrandt*
(13) UPU Exhibition, National Postal Museum	10	-	*n.o.c.*
(14) International Garden Festival, Liverpool	10	-	*n.o.c.*
(15) Colchester Castle Restoration	15	-	*n.o.c.*
C.D.S. POSTMARKS			
(16) Dollar	40		
(17) Lombard St. B.O. - London's 'banking street'	25		
(18) Pound or Summit ... *each*	15		
(19) St. James's St. - near to Lancaster House	8		
(20) Stock Exchange	25		

-5 JUN'84
(11)

(7)

(5)

In addition covers are known with the following CDS pmks: Bretton, The Forum, Lancaster, Moneyhill, Parliament Street BO. Prices from £6.

SLOGAN POSTMARKS

Sunderland Loans & Grants; Shopping by Post; Any Royal Mail slogans; Inverness Conference Capital; Sandwell Industrial. Prices from £30.

(19)

(12)

26th June 1984 - GREENWICH MERIDIAN

16p Astronomy; 20½p Navigation; 28p The Observatory; 31p Time

SPECIAL HANDSTAMPS	ordinary covers £	official covers £	
(1) First Day of Issue - Philatelic Bureau	3	-	*Royal Mail*
(2) First Day of Issue - Greenwich	3	-	*Royal Mail*
(3) World's Prime Meridian, Greenwich, SE10	4	8	*BOCS (2) 28*
(4) Greenwich Mean Time, EC4	8	-	*n.o.c.*
(5) Geographical Magazine	5	8	*Hawkwood*
(6) Royal Naval College	5	15	*RNC*
(7) Meridian Road 0° 00' 00" Longitude, Boston	7	-	*Royal Mail*
(8) Greenwich Meridian, East Lindsey, Louth	5	15	*L. Rotary*
(9) Royal Naval Staff College, BF 1838 PS	5	12	*RFDC 28*
(10) Longitude Zero, Somersham, Huntingdon	7	-	*Post Office*
(11) Meridian County School, Comberton	5	15	*MCP Sch.*
(12) Meridian Day, 0° MG GM, Swavesey	5	15	*MG Owners*
(13) Peacehaven, Newhaven	5	15	*P'haven P.O.*
(14) British Horological Institute, Newark	5	8	*LFDC 35*
(15) John Longitude Harrison, Barrow	7	25	*Lincoln Cath.*
(16) British Astronomical Association, W1	5	8	*DGT*
(17) National Physical Laboratory, Teddington	5	20	*NPL*
(18) Captn. Cook Study Unit, Whitby	6	10	*B. Travers*
(19) Lloyds List, Greenwich, SE10	6	15	*Lloyds*
(20) UPU Exhibition, National Postal Museum	10	-	*n.o.c.*
(21) 1924 Wembley Exhibition, NW10	10	12	*DGT*
(22) National Federation of Women's Institutes, W14	10	15	*Arlington*
(23) Steve Davis Embassy World Champion	10	15	*Havering*
(24) Ladies Centenary Year, Lawn Tennis Museum	15	18	*AELTC*
(25) Colchester Castle Restoration	15	-	*n.o.c.*
(26) International Garden Festival, Liverpool	15	-	*n.o.c.*

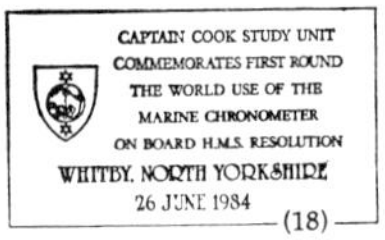

(18)

(23)

(15)

(3)

(6)

Greenwich Meridian (contd.)

C.D.S. POSTMARKS	ordinary covers £	official covers £
(27) Alnwick - birthplace of Sir George Airy	6	
(28) Chingford - longitudinal obelisk	8	
(29) Clock Face, St. Helens	20	
(30) Hartland - Magnetic Observatory	20	
(31) Herstmonceux - new observatory	7	
(32) Greenwich	10	
(33) Meridian Centre, Peacehaven	100	
(34) Playford, Ipswich - home of Sir George Airy	15	
(35) The Chart, Oxted	10	

In addition: Cleethorpes, Comberton, Globe Rd, Great Ayton, Great Portland St., Louth, Macclesfield, Swavesey, Washington, World's End. Prices from £6.

SLOGAN POSTMARKS
Magyar Philatelic Society. £65.

31st July 1984 - THE ROYAL MAIL

5 x 16p: The Bath Mail Coach 1784; Attack on Exeter Mail Coach 1816; Norwich Mail Coach in a thunderstorm 1827; Holyhead & Liverpool Mail Coaches 1828; Edinburgh Mail Coach Snowbound 1831

SPECIAL HANDSTAMPS	ordinary	official	
(1) First Day of Issue - Philatelic Bureau	3	-	*Royal Mail*
(2) First Day of Issue - Bristol	3	-	*Royal Mail*
(3) Bath Mail Coach Commemorative Run	3	10	*BOCS (2) 30*
(4) Golden Age of Coaching, Bath	3	13	*LFDC 36*
(5) Interlink Express Parcels Co, Bristol	3	5	*Hawkwood*
(6) Royal Mail Transport, Leicester	3	15	*Mus. of Tech.*
(7) Manchester - Altrincham Mail Coach Run	3	5	*BLS (84) 7*
(8) Liverpool Mail Coach	3	5	*BLS (84) 7*
(9) British Airways Mail Service, BF 1845 PS	5	10	*RFDC 30*
(10) The Islington Society, N1	5	8	*Havering*
(11) Worshipful Company of Coachmakers, WC2	5	12	*Cotswold*
(12) Royal Mail Commemoration, Holyhead Mail	5	-	*Royal Mail*
(13) North Eastern Parcel Centre, Washington	10	-	*Royal Mail*
(14) Worlds First Post Office Tram, Blackpool	10	-	*Royal Mail*
(15) St. James's Church Piccadilly, W1	10	15	*St. J. Church*
(16) Colchester Castle Restoration	12	-	*n.o.c.*
(17) International Garden Festival, Liverpool	10	-	*n.o.c.*
(18) UPU Exhibition, National Postal Museum	12	-	*n.o.c.*
(19) 1924 Wembley Exhibition, NW10	12	15	*DGT*
(20) Island of Portland Heritage Trust	12	20	*PHT*
(21) International Essex Jamboree, Chelmsford	15	20	*Scouts*

ORDINARY F.D.I. POSTMARKS	
(21a) Bromley (Bromley Post Office cover) *each*	15

C.D.S. POSTMARKS	
(22) Bath, Bristol, Edinburgh, Exeter, Holyhead, Liverpool or Norwich *each*	7
(23) Fleet Street, EC4 - 'Bolt-in-Tun' Inn	10
(24) Holyhead or Dun Laoghaire PAQUEBOTS *each*	17
(25) Islington, N1 - 'The Angel Inn'	7
(26) London Chief Office, EC1	7
(27) Marlborough - provided Bath Mail Coach horses	10
(28) Moffat - snowbound Edinburgh Mail	8
(29) Newmarket - Norwich Mail in thunderstorm	7
(30) Thatcham - provided Bath Mail Coach horses	12
(31) Winterslow or Lopcombe Corner - scene of the attack on the Exeter Mail *each*	7

In addition: Black Horse, Coach Road, Devonport. Prices from £6.

SLOGAN POSTMARKS	
(32) Collect British Stamps	30
(33) Be Properly Addressed, Post Code It	40
(34) First Day of Issue (Envelope design), Bristol	8(s)
(35) Magyar Philatelic Society	75
(36) Take a Break in Beautiful Bath	50

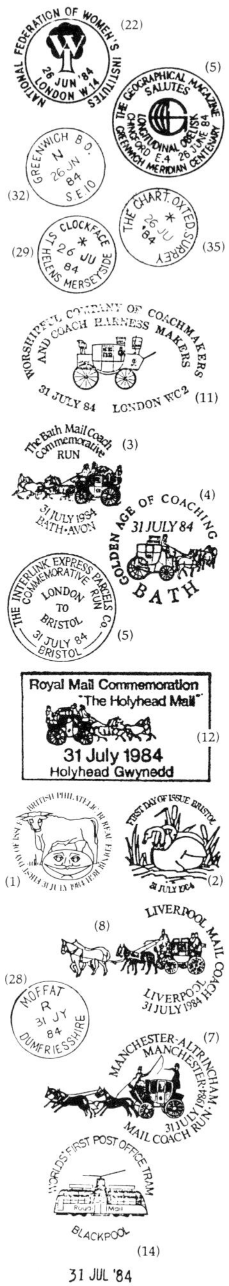

Prices are for unaddressed covers in good condition with the full set of postage stamps.

25th September 1984 - THE BRITISH COUNCIL

17p Medicine; 22p Arts;
31p Construction; 34p Language

SPECIAL HANDSTAMPS	ordinary covers £	official covers £
(1) First Day of Issue - Philatelic Bureau	3	- *Royal Mail*
(2) First Day of Issue - London SW	3	- *Royal Mail*
(3) The British Council, SW	4	12 *G&P*
(4) Oxford Dictionary Exhibition	4	8 *Hawkwood*
(5) Ausipex 84, Melbourne	4	10 *BOCS (2) 31*
(6) RBPD, Sutton	7	5 *Des. Enc.*
(7) Samuel Johnson, Lichfield	4	10 *LFDC 37*
(8) Battle of Britain, BF 1850 PS	6	10 *RFDC 31*
(9) Worlds First Post Office Tram, Blackpool	6	- *Royal Mail*
(10) St. James's Church, Piccadilly, W1	5	- *Royal Mail*
(11) Colchester Castle Restoration	8	- *n.o.c.*
(12) International Garden Festival, Liverpool	8	- *n.o.c.*
(13) Mail Coach Service, National Postal Musuem	10	- *n.o.c.*
(14) Beagles Congratulate Daley Thompson, E13	10	15 *Havering*

C.D.S. POSTMARKS

(15) Southampton St. - 1st Meeting of British Council	10
(16) St. James's St. - inaugurated at St. James's Palace	9
(17) Trafalgar Sq. BO - near to British Council	10
(18) Wadhurst - Tippett's 'The Midsummer Marriage'	10
(19) Walton St., Oxford - Oxford English Dictionary	7
(20) Westminster Bdg. Rd. - Tippett, Morley College	7

In addition: Aberystwyth, Burgh, Dundee, King Edward VII Hospital, Lichfield, Limpsfield, Lower Broadheath, Melbourne, Oxford. Prices from £7.

SLOGAN POSTMARKS

Doctor Johnson, Lichfield; Collect British Stamps. Prices from £20.

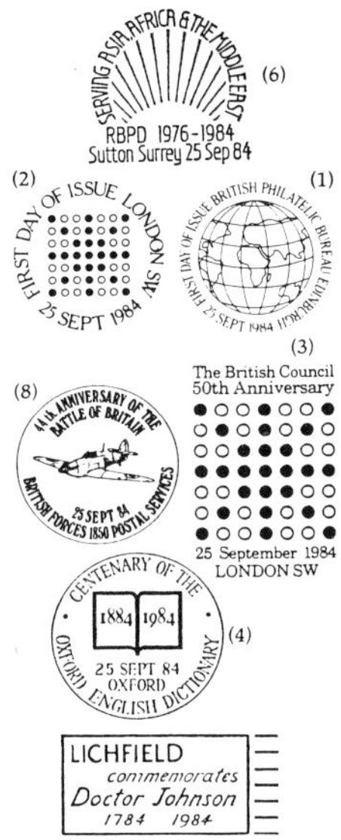

20th November 1984 - CHRISTMAS

13p, 17p, 22p, 31p, 34p the Nativity

SPECIAL HANDSTAMPS	ordinary covers £	official covers £
(1) First Day of Issue - Philatelic Bureau	3	- *Royal Mail*
(2) First Day of Issue - Bethlehem	3	- *Royal Mail*
(3) Christian Heritage Year - Durham	5	7 *BOCS (2) 32*
(4) Christian Heritage Year - Ely	5	12 *BOCS (2) 32*
(5) Christian Heritage Year - Norwich	5	6 *BLS (84) 6*
(6) Christian Heritage Year - Liverpool	5	6 *BLS (84) 6*
(7) Christmas, Isle of Iona	6	15 *Pilgrim*
(8) Glastonbury Abbey	6	15 *Fine Arts 1*
(9) Christmas Greetings, World Trade Centre, E1	6	8 *Havering*
(10) Christmas, Weybridge	7	15 *S. Petty 25*
(11) Christmas, Theatre Royal, Stratford, E15	4	7 *Hawkwood*
(12) Telecom Technology Showcase, EC4	8	- *n.o.c.*
(13) John Wycliffe, Lutterworth	6	9 *LFDC 38*
(14) The Lindisfarne Gospels, Holy Island	6	7 *S. Muscroft*
(15) Samuel Johnson, Lichfield	8	15 *Bradbury*
(16) Mail Coach Service, National Postal Museum	10	- *n.o.c.*

C.D.S. POSTMARKS

(17) Bethlehem, Llandeilo, Dyfed	7
(18) Nasareth, Gwynedd	9

In addition: Canterbury, Glastonbury, Holy Island, Holytown, Horbury Bridge, Jarrow, Lutterworth, Shepherd's Bush, Shepherd's Hill, Three Kingdom. £5 each.

SLOGAN POSTMARKS

(19) Hastings - A Resort for All Seasons (snowman)	40
(20) Halfpenny Green - Christmas 1984	50

In addition: Late Night Shopping, Exeter. Prices from £20.

CHRISTMAS DISCOUNT BOOKLET: Covers bearing a pair or block of 4 x 13p Christmas stamps from booklet with relevant postmark 5

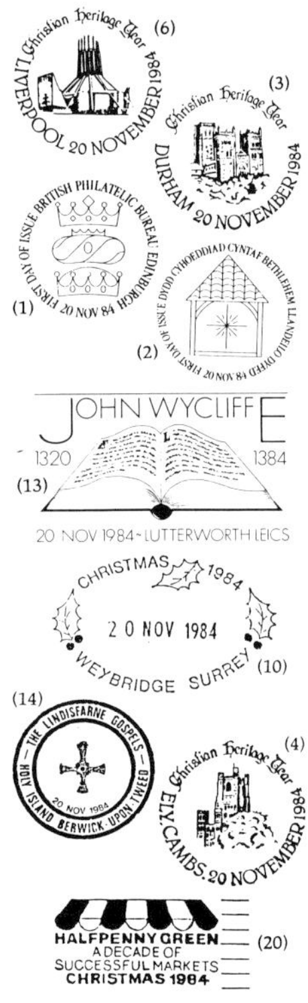

> PLEASE READ THE GENERAL NOTES
> AT THE BEGINNING OF THIS CATALOGUE
> **C.D.S. = COUNTER DATE STAMP**
> These are everyday operational postmarks available
> at all Post Office Counters.
> *Please refer to the General Notes for more details.*

22nd January 1985 – FAMOUS TRAINS

17p Flying Scotsman; 22p Golden Arrow; 29p Cheltenham Flyer; 31p Royal Scot; 34p Cornish Riviera

SPECIAL HANDSTAMPS	ordinary covers £	official covers £
(1) First Day of Issue – Philatelic Bureau	5	– *Royal Mail*
(2) First Day of Issue – Bristol	5	– *Royal Mail*
(3) Steamtown Railway Museum, Carnforth	10	15 *LFDC 39*
(4) Flying Scotsman, Doncaster	10	15 *LFDC 39*
(5) Flying Scotsman, King's Cross, N1	10	30 *Benham L6*
(6) Flying Scotsman, Scotrail, Edinburgh	15	– *n.o.c.*
(7) Golden Arrow, Dover	10	30 *Benham L8*
(8) Golden Arrow, VSOE, Victoria, SW1	10	25 *G&P*
(9) VSOE Stops at Denham Station.	15	– *Royal Mail*
(10) GWR 150, Paddington Stn., London, W2	10	35 *CoverCraft*
(11) Great Western Hotel, Paddington, W2	10	25 *Fine Arts 2*
(12) Cheltenham Flyer, Cheltenham	10	75 *B'ham 500 (1)*
(13) Great Western Town, Swindon	10	20 *Hawkwood*
(14) GWR Didcot, Oxon	10	25 *814 TPO Gp*
(15) GWR Preservation Group, Southall Rly Centre	10	25 *DGT*
(16) Firefly Project, Swindon	10	25 *Cotswold*
(17) King George V, Hereford	15	– *Royal Mail*
(18) Royal Scot, Scotrail, Glasgow	15	– *n.o.c.*
(19) Royal Scot, Euston, NW1	10	30 *Benham L7*
(20) Cornish Riviera, Paddington	10	50 *BLCS 1*
(21) Cornish Riviera, Penzance	10	50 *BLCS 1*
(22) National Railway Museum, York	15	– *Royal Mail*
(23) York Station, Rail Riders	10	12 *DGT*
(24) North Staffs Rly. Co. Ltd., Leek	10	50 *NSRly*
(25) Railway Loco's, British Legion, Maidstone	10	15 *Brit. Leg.*
(26) Hendon Spitfire, BF 1857 PS	15	30 *RFDC 33*
(27) Rowland Hill Loco, Crewe	20	– *Royal Mail*
(28) National Assoc'n Boys' Clubs, Blenheim	20	45 *NABC*

C.D.S. POSTMARKS (inc. T.P.O. CANCELS)

(29) Carnforth – home of Flying Scotsman 25
(30) Cheltenham, Penzance or Swindon .... *each* 15
(31) Didcot – GWR centre 15
(32) Doncaster – Flying Scotsman was built here 20
(33) Euston, King's Cross or Paddington. .... *each* 25
(34) Railway Place, Coleraine 25
(35) Saltash – Brunel's famous GWR bridge 20
(36) Any 'station' pmk (Auchterless, Bosham, Carstairs Junction, Central Stn., Edinburgh, Crowthorne, Martin Mill, Meopham, Murton, Nigg, Nunthorpe, Timperley, Trimdon) .... *each* 20
(37) Any connected T.P.O. (same route or part thereof):
Flying Scotsman: North Eastern T.P.O. Night Up and Down; London-York-Edinburgh; Edinburgh-York.
Golden Arrow: South Western Night Up and Night Down.
Cheltenham Flyer: Midland Going South and North; Bristol-Derby; Derby-Bristol.
Royal Scot: Up and Down Specials; Up Special Glasgow Section; North Western Night Down; Crewe-Glasgow Sorting Carriage; Caledonian Up and Day Up Edinburgh Section.
Cornish Riviera: Great Western Up and Down ......*each* 25
(38) Any other T.P.O. cancellations 20

In addition covers are known with the following C.D.S. pmks: City of Bristol, Edinburgh, Glasgow, Portsmouth, Silver Link, The Rocket. Prices from £15.

PLEASE READ THE GENERAL NOTES
AT THE BEGINNING OF THIS CATALOGUE
These often provide the answers to enquiries received.

SLOGAN POSTMARKS

Prices in the catalogue are for covers with stamps sited to advantage so that the slogan is clearly legible.
Please refer to the General Notes.

1985

(13)

(20)

(9)

(8)
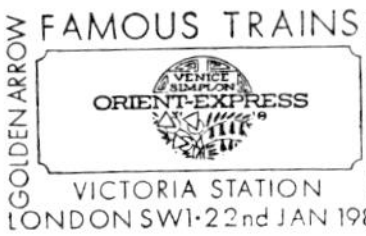

(4)

(23)

(1)

(2)

(14)

(16)

(11)

(18)

(22)

12th March 1985 - BRITISH INSECTS

17p Buff Tailed Bumble Bee; 22p Seven Spotted Ladybird; 29p Water-Biter Bush-Cricket; 31p Stag Beetle; 34p Emperor Dragonfly

SPECIAL HANDSTAMPS	ordinary covers £	official covers £
(1) First Day of Issue - Philatelic Bureau	4	- *Royal Mail*
(2) First Day of Issue - London SW	4	- *Royal Mail*
(3) Royal Entomological Soc., Meadow Bank	5	20 *B'ham 500 (2)*
(4) Royal Entomological Soc., SW7	5	6 *BLCS 2*
(5) A.E.S. Golden Jubilee, Feltham	5	20 *LFDC 40*
(6) Selborne Society Centenary, Alton	6	20 *Cotswold*
(7) Writhlington School, Radstock	5	25 *Writh. Sch.*
(8) British Museum, Natural History, SW7	5	10 *BLCS 2*
(9) Stamp Bug Club, High Wycombe	7	40 *SB Club*
(10) Bugford, I AM FIVE	10	50 *SB Club*
(11) Nature Conservation, Hummer Sherborne	7	- *Post Office*
(12) Enfield Butterfly Centre	5	10 *Hawkwood*
(13) Robert Hooke, Freshwater	5	20 *Fine Arts 3*
(14) Scottish Wildlife Trust, Edinburgh	5	15 *Pilgrim*
(15) Mosquito Aircraft, BF 1862 PS	6	8 *RFDC 34*
(16) Pestalozzi Children's Village	25	- *n.o.c.*
(17) National Assoc'n Boys' Clubs, Abercrave	15	25 *NABC*

C.D.S. POSTMARKS	
(18) Buckfastleigh - Abbey monks, famous bee-keepers	7
(19) Nettleham - Society for Nature Conservation	8
(20) St. Bees	7
(21) St. James's St., SW1 - inaugural meetings of R.E.S.	7
(22) Selborne - 'Natural History of Selborne'	7
(23) South Kensington SW7 - Royal Entomological Soc.	7

In addition: Alexandra Park, Alexandra, Beeston, Bugthorpe, Church St., Enfield, Dunkeld, Duns, Feltham, Fleet St., Kingsstag, Lady, Meadow Bank, Northam, Sedgfield, Sheerness, Wickham, Writhlington. Prices from £6.

SLOGAN POSTMARKS

Collect British Stamps. £10.

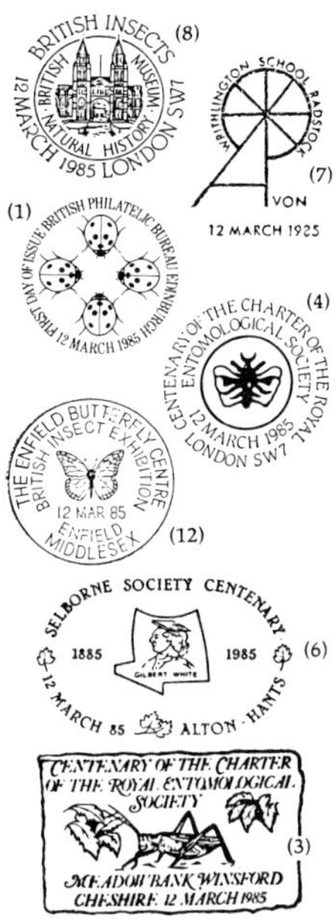

14th May 1985 - BRITISH COMPOSERS

17p Handel - Water Music; 22p Holst - The Planets; 31p Delius - The First Cuckoo; 34p Elgar - Sea Pictures

SPECIAL HANDSTAMPS	ordinary covers £	official covers £
(1) First Day of Issue - Philatelic Bureau	3	- *Royal Mail*
(2) First Day of Issue - Worcester	3	- *Royal Mail*
(3) Handel's Birthday, Royal Opera House	5	10 *BLCS 3*
(4) Handel, Westminster Abbey, SW1	5	10 *LFDC 41*
(5) St. Paul's Cathedral, 850 Years of Music	5	15 *St. Paul's*
(6) Holst Birthplace Museum, Cheltenham	5	15 *H.B. Museum*
(7) Holst, European Music Year, Cheltenham.	5	20 *B'ham 500 (3)*
(8) Stagenhoe Park, Centenary of Mikado, Hitchin	5	8 *Hawkwood*
(9) Delius Festival, Bradford	5	10 *P. Scott*
(10) Sir Edward Elgar, Birmingham	7	- *n.o.c.*
(11) Sir Michael Tippett, Bournemouth	5	15 *Pilgrim*
(12) British Composers, Royal Festival Hall, SE1	5	6 *G.L.C.*
(13) European Music Year, High Wycombe	7	- *n.o.c.*
(14) Scottish National Orchestra, Aberdeen	5	12 *Benham L9*
(15) Scottish National Orchestra, Dundee	5	12 *Benham L10*
(16) Royal Military School of Music, BF 2128 PS	5	8 *RFDC 35*
(17) Music Year, National Postal Museum, EC1	7	- *n.o.c.*
(18) Leicester Philharmonic Society	5	10 *L.P.O.*
(19) 1st Ruislip Guides	6	15 *Ruislip GG*
(20) St. David's Hall, Cardiff	6	20 *Pilgrim*
(21) Haddo House, Aberdeen	8	20 *Pilgrim*
(22) Lennon & McCartney, Composers of Today	8	10 *Fine Arts 4*
(23) Philatelic Counter - Worcester	8	- *n.o.c.*
(24) Centenary of SSAFA, SW1	10	15 *SSAFA*
(25) North Norfolk Railway, Sheringham	10	15 *NNR*
(26) Royal Visit, The Princess of Wales, E13	10	12 *Havering*
(27) Ultramar Fifty Years, EC	10	75 *CoverCraft*
(28) National Assoc'n Boys' Clubs, Edinburgh	10	35 *NABC*
(29) 700th Mayoral Anniversary, High Wycombe	10	15 *High Wycombe DC*

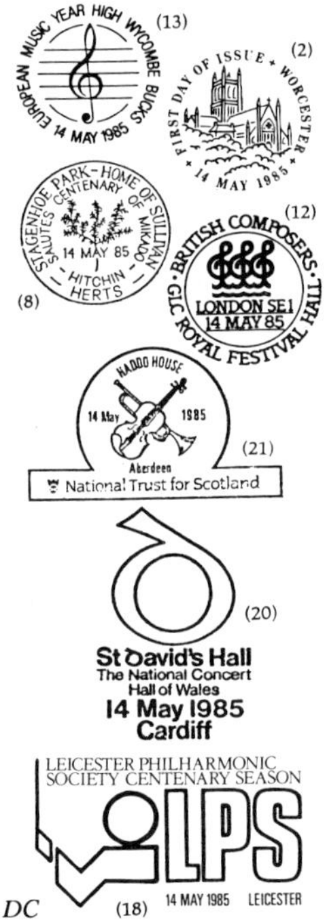

PRICES & CONDITION - PLEASE READ GENERAL NOTES

British Composers (contd.)

	ordinary covers £	official covers £
C.D.S. POSTMARKS		
(30) Chichester – Holst buried in Chichester Cathedral	8	
(31) Hammersmith – Holst wrote 'Planets' here	8	
(32) Limpsfield – Delius is interred here	8	
(33) Lower Broadheath – Elgar's birthplace	12	
(34) Lowesmoor – Elgar died here	9	
(35) Pittville – Holst's birthplace	9	
(36) South Molton St., W1 – Handel lived here	8	
(37) Thaxted – Holst lived here	12	
(38) University, Bradford – near to Delius's birthplace	10	
(39) Malvern – Elgar buried nearby	9	

In addition: Brigg, Chelsea, Hereford, Whitwell. Prices from £5.

SLOGAN POSTMARKS

(40) CBSO Proms, Birmingham *(on two covers)*	40	
(41) Delius Festival, Bradford *(on two covers)*	40	

In addition: Hereford Cathedral; North Wiltshire Entertains. Prices from £50.

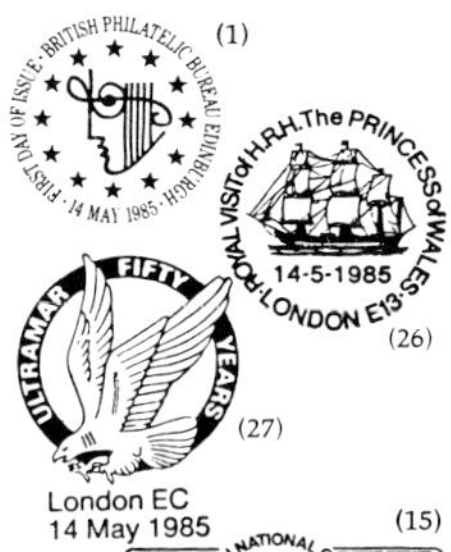

18th June 1985 – SAFETY AT SEA

17p Lifeboat; 22p Lighthouse; 31p Satellite; 34p Buoy

SPECIAL HANDSTAMPS		
(1) First Day of Issue – Philatelic Bureau	3	– *Royal Mail*
(2) First Day of Issue – Eastbourne, E. Sussex	3	– *Royal Mail*
(3) The Plimsoll Line, Bristol	4	– *Royal Mail*
(4) Spurn Head Lifeboat, Hull	4	– *Royal Mail*
(5) Lifeboat Dedication, Cromer	4	15 *RNLI*
(6) Lifeboat Display, Poole, Dorset	4	15 *RNLI*
(7) Berwick-upon-Tweed Lifeboat	4	35 *B.u.T. Lifeboat*
(8) Appledore, RNLI Lifeboat Station	4	15 *Appledore LS*
(9) Earliest Lifeboat Design, Lowestoft	4	20 *B'ham 500 (4)*
(10) Grace Darling Museum, Bamburgh	4	8 *LFDC 42*
(11) Lukin's Patent for Lifeboat Design, Hythe	4	10 *BLCS 4*
(12) Lighthouse Club, Whitley Bay	4	15 *Light. Club*
(13) Nore Lightship, E1	4	15 *Fine Arts 5*
(14) Global Maritime, Safety at Sea, WC2	4	20 *Global*
(15) Maritime Museum, SE10	4	5 *BLCS 4*
(16) Schermuly, Greenwich, SE10	4	15 *Schermuly*
(17) Sealion Shipping, City of London	4	15 *Sealion*
(18) The Geographical Magazine, SW7	5	7 *Hawkwood*
(19) No. 22 Squadrom, RAF BF 1890 PS	7	12 *RFDC 36*
(20) British Film Year, Bristol	8	20 *CoverCraft*
(21) The Ashes Tour, NW8	8	15 *S.P.*
(22) London Welsh Rugby, Richmond	8	15 *London Welsh*
(23) Lawn Tennis Museum, Wimbledon, SW19	8	12 *AELTA*
(24) North Norfolk Railway, Sheringham	8	15 *NNR*
(25) Nat. Assoc. of Boys' Clubs, Worcester	8	30 *NABC*
(26) GWR 150 Exhibition Train, Shrewsbury	8	10 *BLCS 4*
(27) Scottish National Orchestra, Glasgow	8	– *n.o.c.*
C.D.S. POSTMARKS		
(28) Anstruther or Cromer – both lighthouse & lifeboats	6	
(29) Austhorpe – b/place of Smeaton (Eddystone)	6	
(30) Bamburgh – first lifeboat station	6	
(31) Cawsand, Toward Point, Whitley Bay – lighthouses	6	
(32) Daventry – first successful radar experiments	9	
(33) Dover – lighthouse built by the Romans	8	
(34) East Dean or Grand Hotel Blgs. – Beachy Head	8	
(35) Hawes – birthplace of RNLI founder	6	
(36) Hythe – Lionel Lukin is buried here	8	
(37) Lighthouse, Fleetwood	10	
(38) Little Dunmow – birthplace of Lionel Lukin	9	
(39) Poole – Headquarters of RNLI	7	
(40) Redcar – The 'Zetland' oldest lifeboat	7	
(41) Richmond – H. Greathead – builder of 'Zetland'	7	
(42) Seething Lane, EC3 – near to Trinity House	6	
(43) Culdrose or Yeovilton RN Air Stns (Air-Sea Rescue)	18	
(44) Any RAF (Air-Sea Rescue) Station – Finningley, Lindholme, Valley, St. Athan Main Site or St. Athan	15	
(45) Cottishall, Leuchars, Manston, Portland, or Prestwick Airport – RN or RAF Stations (Air-Sea Rescue)	12	

In addition: Beacon, Camborne, Marton-in-Cleveland, Sheerness, Six Bells, The Rocket, Thorpe Esplanade, Yeovil. Prices from £5.

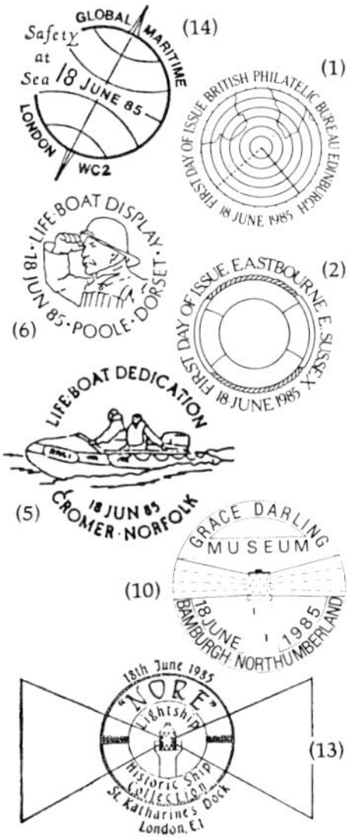

	ordinary covers £	official covers £
SLOGAN POSTMARKS		
(46) Relax at Sunny Weymouth	75	

30th July 1985 - 350th ANNIVERSARY OF THE ROYAL MAIL

17p Datapost; 22p Postbus; 31p Parcel Post; 34p Letter Post

	ordinary covers £	official covers £
SPECIAL HANDSTAMPS		
(1) First Day of Issue - Philatelic Bureau	3	- *Royal Mail*
(2) First Day of Issue - Bagshot	3	- *Royal Mail*
(3) P.O. Archives, 23 Glass Hill St., SE1	5	20 *Fine Arts 6*
(4) National Postal Museum, 350 Years Service	5	- *Royal Mail*
(5) Thomas Witherings Postmaster, 1635	5	15 *St. Andrew's*
(6) Royal Mail London Post, 1635-1985, EC1	5	- *Post Office*
(7) UCWA Public Service Union, SW4	5	8 *BLCS 5*
(8) Royal Mail 350 Years of Service, EC	5	- *Royal Mail*
(9) Royal Mail SEPR Postcards, Bagshot	5	- *Royal Mail*
(10) Royal Mail SEPR Postcards, Windsor	5	- *Royal Mail*
(11) Royal Mail 350 Exhibition, Bristol	5	- *Royal Mail*
(12) Post Paid, Healey & Wise, EC4	5	15 *H & W*
(13) Intelpost, Head Post Office, E1	5	10 *Hawkwood*
(14) Postal Museum, Bath	5	15 *B'ham 500 (5)*
(15) National Postal Museum (Red Maltese Cross)	10	- *Royal Mail*
(16) North Eastern Parcels Centre	10	- *Royal Mail*
(17) 10 Downing Street, SW1	8	35 *LFDC 43*
(18) British Legion, SW1	9	15 *Brit. Leg.*
(19) The Cardiff Tattoo, BF 1879 PS	9	14 *Forces*
(20) Norton 100, 1885-1985, Leicester	10	35 *N. Clipper*
(21) GWR 150 Steam Special, Gloucester	10	- *n.o.c.*
(22) M.C.C. Cricket Festival, Uxbridge	10	25 *MCC*
(23) The Ashes Tour, NW8	10	12 *S.P.*
(24) North Norfolk Railway, Sheringham	10	14 *NNR*
(25) Nat. Assoc. of Boys' Clubs, Trentham Gdns	10	35 *NABC*
(26) Ptarmigan Equipment, BF 3254 PS	10	10 *RFDC 37*
C.D.S. POSTMARKS		
(27) Aberfeldy - postbus	12	
(28) Bagshot - Charles I Proclamation	10	
(29) Buckingham Palace, SW1	40	
(30) Cannon Street, EC1	10	
(31) Hornchurch - Thomas Witherings, first postmaster	10	
(32) Letter, Enniskillen	20	
(33) Llangurig or Llandloes - first ever postbus *each*	30	
(34) Lombard Street EC3 - General Letter Office	15	
(35) Mount Pleasant - Britain's major sorting office	15	
(36) Sanquhar - Britain's oldest Post Office	15	
(37) Stock Exchange, EC2 - Royal Exchange (17p)	15	

In addition covers are known with the following C.D.S. pmks: Brighton, Dunfermline, Edinburgh, FPO postmarks, Henfield, House of Commons, Kidderminster, Kingstanding, Postbridge. Prices from £8.

SLOGAN POSTMARKS		
(38) Royal Mail 350 Years of Service to the Public	12	
(39) Make any Post Office in Cleveland, etc	40	
OTHER POSTMARKS		
(40) Parcel Post cancellation - Chingford, London E4	50	
ROYAL MAIL DISOUNT BOOKLET		
Covers bearing a pair or block of 4 x 17p 'Datapost' stamps from booklet with relevant postmark	4	
Covers with complete pane and relevant postmark	10	

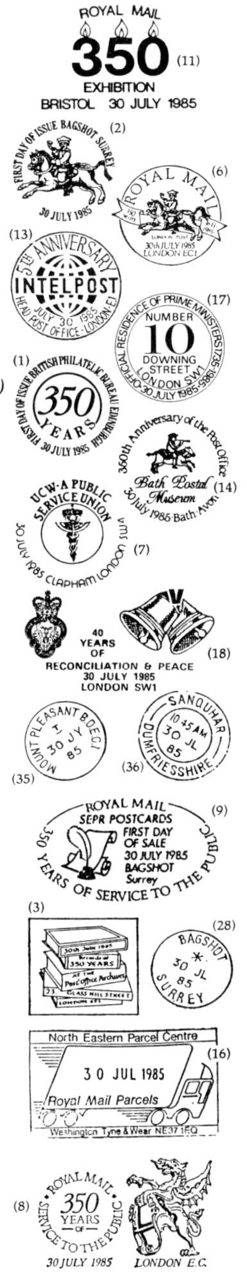

PLEASE READ THE GENERAL NOTES
AT THE BEGINNING OF THIS CATALOGUE
These often provide the answers to enquiries received.
C.D.S. = COUNTER DATE STAMP
These are everyday operational postmarks available
at all Post Office Counters.
Please refer to the General Notes for more details.

3rd September 1985 - ARTHURIAN LEGEND

17p King Arthur & Merlin; 22p The Lady of the Lake; 31p Guinevere & Lancelot; 34p Sir Galahad

SPECIAL HANDSTAMPS	ordinary covers £	official covers £
(1) First Day of Issue - Philatelic Bureau	3	- *Royal Mail*
(2) First Day of Issue - Tintagel	3	8 *Royal Mail*
(3) The Sword & The Stone, St. Paul's, EC4	5	10 *Fine Arts 7*
(4) Legendary Camelot, Old Post Office ,Tintagel	5	10 *Benham L12*
(5) The Legendary Camelot, Winchester.	5	7 *BLCS 6*
(6) Morte D'Arthur, Mere, Warminster	5	20 *B'ham 500 (6)*
(7) The Great Hall, Winchester.	5	10 *Hants CC*
(8) Exhibition of Celtic Legend, Glastonbury	5	10 *Arth. Exh.*
(9) St. Margaret's Church, SW1	5	6 *Hawkwood*
(10) King Arthur's Avalon, Glastonbury	5	8 *LFDC 44*
(11) Royal Fleet Auxiliary, BF 1880 PS	6	8 *RFDC 38*
(12) Leith Hall, Huntly	6	6 *Pilgrim*
(13) Stockton on Tees, Town Hall	8	15 *Town Counc.*
(14) Nat. Assoc. of Boys' Clubs, Guildhall, EC3	8	35 *NABC*
(15) BI Centenary Cricket, Schaw Park	8	10 *Scot. Cricket*
(16) Nat. Post. Museum, 350 Years Service	8	- *Royal Mail*
(17) North Norfolk Railway, Sheringham	8	8 *NNR*
(18) 23 BASE WKSP REME, BF 2340 PS	8	10 *Forces*

ORDINARY F.D.I. POSTMARKS

(19) Cardiff or Newport - Arthur was King of Glamorgan and Gwent	6	

C.D.S. POSTMARKS

(20) Amesbury - Guinevere became a nun here	10	
(21) Bamburgh - Lancelot's Castle of 'Joyous Gard'	8	
(22) Bodmin - Dozmary Pool where Excalibur was cast	8	
(23) Camelford - Arthur mortally wounded by Mordred	10	
(24) Glastonbury - the legendary 'Isle of Avalon'	6	
(25) King Arthur's Way, Andover	10	
(26) Lancelot Place, SW7	10	
(27) Merlin's Bridge	12	
(28) Silchester - where Arthur was crowned	10	
(29) South Cadbury - most probable site of 'Camelot'	10	
(30) Stretton-under-Fosse - birthplace of Malory	9	
(31) Tintagel - birthplace of Arthur	8	
(32) Winchester - the Round Table	8	

In addition: Caxton, Corfe Castle, Knight's Road, Tregaron. Prices from £7.

SLOGAN POSTMARKS

Carlisle - worth a closer look. £50.

(2)

(1)

(9)

(29)

(27)

(18)

(5)

(8)

(10)

(4)

(15)

8th October 1985 - BRITISH FILM YEAR

17p Peter Sellers; 22p David Niven; 29p Charles Chaplin; 31p Vivien Leigh; 34p Alfred Hitchcock

SPECIAL HANDSTAMPS		
(1) First Day of Issue - Philatelic Bureau	4	- *Royal Mail*
(2) First Day of Issue - London WC	4	- *Royal Mail*
(3) British Film Year, MCMLXXXV, W1	7	15 *LFDC 45*
(4) British Film Year, Bradford	7	25 *BLCS 7*
(5) British Film Year, Richmond	7	40 *B'ham 500 (7)*
(6) British Film Year, Leicester Sq., WC2 (rectangular)	7	10 *Arlington*
(7) British Film Year, Goldcrest London W1	7	12 *G&P*
(8) British Film Year, David Niven	7	25 *Cotswold*
(9) British Film Year, Leicester Sq., WC2 (Pink Panther)	7	25 *BLCS 7*
(10) Equity, Harley Street, W1	7	15 *Fine Arts 8*
(11) 50 Years, National Film Archives, W1	10	20 *N.F.A.*
(12) Dambusters, BF 2101 PS	8	30 *RFDC 39*
(13) Alfred Hitchcock, Leytonstone, E11	8	10 *Hawkwood*
(14) Charrington Bass, LVNH Denham	6	10 *Havering*
(15) Nat. Post. Museum, Film Festival, EC1	8	- *n.o.c.*
(16) Brian Reeve New Stamp Shop, WC2	8	8 *DGT*
(17) Perth Theatre	8	15 *Perth*
(18) Opening Arndale Centre, Luton	10	- *n.o.c.*
(19) National Postal Museum, 350 Years Royal Mail	10	- *n.o.c.*
(20) Nat. Assoc. of Boys' Clubs, Belfast	12	35 *NABC*

PRICES & CONDITION
Please remember that prices quoted are for good clean covers, unaddressed and with the full set of stamps.

(8)

(6)
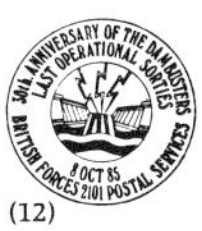
(12)

(5)

(1)

(14)

	ordinary covers	official covers
C.D.S. POSTMARKS	£	£
(21) Bray; Denham; Hammersmith; Shepherd's Bush; St. Margaret's, Twickenham; St. Mary's Road, Ealing; Walton; Welwyn or Wembley - film studios .... *each*	12	
(22) Castle Road, Southsea - birthplace of Peter Sellers	8	
(23) Down Special T.P.O. - P.O. film 'Night Mail'	25	
(24) East St., Walworth - birthplace of Charles Chaplin	7	
(25) Elstree - famous film studios	15	
(26) Hollywood, Birmingham	15	
(27) Iver Heath - Pinewood film studios	10	
(28) Kirriemuir - home of David Niven	8	
(29) Lacock - Fox Talbot (photographic negative)	8	
(30) Leytonstone - birthplace of Alfred Hitchcock	8	
(31) Maida Vale - Friese Green (inventor of cine)	8	
(32) Shepperton - famous film studios	15	
(33) Victoria St., SW1 - birthplace of David Niven	15	

In addition covers are known with the following C.D.S. pmks: Chancery Lane, Goonhaven, Queens Rd., Shamley Green, Sloane Square, Star. Prices from £6.

SLOGAN POSTMARKS
Eden Court Theatre. £45.

19th November 1985 - CHRISTMAS

12p, 17p, 22p, 31p, 34p - pantomime characters

SPECIAL HANDSTAMPS			
(1) First Day of Issue - Philatelic Bureau	3	-	*Royal Mail*
(2) First Day of Issue - Bethlehem, Llandeilo, Dyfed	3	-	*Royal Mail*
(3) Telecom Technology Showcase, EC4	5	-	*n.o.c.*
(4) Aladdin, Nottingham Theatre	5	8	*LFDC 46*
(5) English Pantomime, Drury Lane, WC2	5	12	*B'ham 500 (8)*
(6) Peace on Earth, Sewardstone Church, E4	5	6	*Hawkwood*
(7) Mother Goose, Biddenden	5	8	*BLCS 8*
(8) Cinderella at the Palladium, W1	5	12	*Fine Arts 9*
(9) Nat. Postal Museum, 350 Years Royal Mail	8	-	*n.o.c.*
(10) Nat. Assoc. of Boys' Clubs, Althorp	8	25	*NABC*
C.D.S. POSTMARKS			
(11) Bethlehem, Llandeilo, Dyfed	8		
(12) Nasareth, Gwynedd	15		
(13) Shrewsbury - John Weaver (father of pantomime)	8		
(14) The Harlequin	10		

In addition covers are known with the following C.D.S. pmks: Holy Island, Lilliput, Old Whittington, Robin Hood, Star, The Circle, Whittington. Prices range from £6.

SLOGAN POSTMARKS
Eastgate Shopping; Eden Court Theatre; Exeter Late Shopping; Explorer Bus Tickets. Prices from £20.

CHRISTMAS BOOKLET: Covers bearing a pair or block of 4 x 12p stamps from booklet with special handstamp...... 5

14th January 1986 - INDUSTRY YEAR

17p Energy; 22p Health; 31p Leisure; 34p Food

SPECIAL HANDSTAMPS			
(1) First Day of Issue - Philatelic Bureau	3	-	*Royal Mail*
(2) First Day of Issue - Birmingham	3	-	*Royal Mail*
(3) Birthplace of Industry, Ironbridge	5	12	*LFDC 47*
(4) Rank Taylor Hobson, Leicester	5	15	*RTH*
(5) Osram, A Leading Light, Wembley	6	125	*G&P*
(6) British Steel, Industry Year, SE1	6	25	*CoverCraft*
(7) Purveyors of Flour, Hovis, Windsor	6	150	*CoverCraft*
(8) The Workers Playground, Blackpool	5	8	*BLCS 9*
(9) Farming Feeds the Nation, Wheatacre	5	12	*B'ham 500(9)*
(10) British Steel Smelters Assoc'n, WC1	6	20	*BSSA*
(11) Ulcer Therapy, Welwyn	5	50	*Smith K. F.*
(12) All Industrious People are Happy, Blackwells	5	7	*Hawkwood*
(13) Industry Year, BP, EC	5	7	*BP*
(14) World Leading Energy Technology, Aberdeen	7	-	*n.o.c.*
(15) British Aerospace Companies BF 2105 PS	8	25	*RFDC 41*
(16) The Salvation Army, Hoxton, N1	10	25	*H.R.*
(17) Nat. Postal Museum, 350 Years Royal Mail	10	-	*n.o.c.*

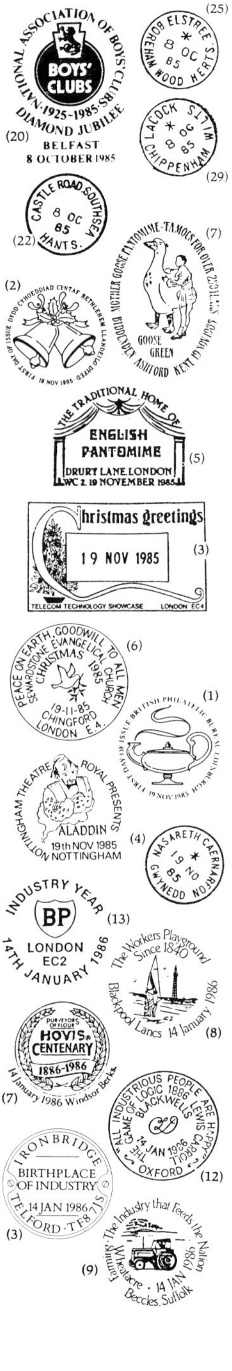

Industry Year (contd.)

C.D.S. POSTMARKS

	ordinary covers £	official covers £
(18) Aycliffe; Slough or Team Valley – Trading Estates	20	
(19) Bridgend; Kirby or Treforest – Ind. Estates *each*	20	
(20) Clydebank – shipbuilding	10	
(21) Cruden Bay – North Sea oil pipeline	8	
(22) Furnace or Furnace End *each*	10	
(23) Greenock – birthplace of James Watt	8	
(24) Ironbridge – 'Birthplace of Industry'	10	
(25) Oxford St., Sunderland – Joseph Swan (light bulb)	7	
(26) Steel or Steel City House *each*	20	

In addition: Bacton, Bakewell, NEC, New Invention, Pill. Prices from £7.

SLOGAN POSTMARKS

Clydebank; Sedgemoor has the Edge; Nissan Sunderland. Prices from £35.

18th February 1986 – HALLEY'S COMET

17pDr. Edmond Halley; 22p Giotto; 31p Twice in a Lifetime; 34p Comet Orbiting the Sun.

SPECIAL HANDSTAMPS

	ordinary	official	
(1) First Day of Issue – Philatelic Bureau	4	–	*Royal Mail*
(2) First Day of Issue – London SE10	4	–	*Royal Mail*
(3) Old Royal Observatory, SE10	4	8	*BLCS 10*
(4) A Return of Halley's Comet, Star	4	15	*B'ham 500(10)*
(5) Giotto, Halley's Comet Interceptor, Bristol	4	12	*CoverCraft*
(6) Halley's Comet Society, SE10	4	15	*HC Soc.*
(7) Islington Home of Halley, N1	4	7	*Hawkwood*
(8) London Planetarium, NW1	4	10	*LFDC 48*
(9) Interplanetary Society, SW	4	6	*DGT*
(10) Edmund Halley born 1656, Haggerston,, E2	4	12	*Fine Arts 11*
(11) Royal Greenwich Observatory, Herstmonceux	4	7	*K&D*
(12) Skynet 4A Satellite, BF 2109 PS	4	20	*RFDC 42*
(13) Royal Mail Fiveways, Tunbridge Wells	8	–	*Royal Mail*
(14) Royal Mail SEPR Postcards, Brighton	8	–	*Royal Mail*
(15) Ripon 1100 AD 886-1986	8	10	*Ripon Counc.*
(16) Nat. Postal Museum, 350 Years Royal Mail	8	–	*n.o.c.*

C.D.S. POSTMARKS

	ordinary
(17) Battle – Bayeux Tapestry features Halley's Comet	6
(18) Filton – Giotto Project Team	8
(19) Greenwich or Herstmonceux – observatories *each*	10
(20) Hartland – Magnetic Observatory	10
(21) Helston – Goonhilly Downs	7
(22) Islington – home of Edmund Halley	7
(23) Lower Withington or Macclesfield – Jodrell Bank	6
(24) Seven Sisters or Star *each*	8
(25) Shoreditch – birthplace of Edmund Halley	7

SLOGAN POSTMARKS

Shop at any Post Office; Zone Tickets etc.; Industry Year. Prices from £18.

21st April 1986 – H.M. THE QUEEN'S 60th BIRTHDAY

2 x 17p; 2 x 34p: HM The Queen in 1928, 1942, 1952, 1958, 1973 and 1982

SPECIAL HANDSTAMPS

	ordinary	official	
(1) First Day of Issue – Philatelic Bureau	4	–	*Royal Mail*
(2) First Day of Issue – Windsor	4	–	*Royal Mail*
(3) Birthday Greetings, London SW1 (square)	5	12	*LFDC 49*
(4) Queen's Birthday, Sandringham, Norfolk	5	7	*BLCS 11B*
(5) Queen's Birthday, London SW1 (circular)	5	7	*BLCS 11A*
(6) Lombard North Central, 17 Bruton St., W1	5	7	*G&P*
(7) Queen's Birthday, Windsor	5	30	*B'ham 500(11)*
(8) Radio Times, W1	5	15	*Arlington*
(9) Queen's 60th Birthday, SW1 (rectangular)	5	15	*Arlington*
(10) Southend Pier Train	5	7	*Hawkwood*
(11) Queen's Flight, BF 2106 PS	5	20	*RFDC 43*
(12) Queen's 60th Birthday Bruton St., W1	5	7	*K&D*
(13) Queen's Birthday, Balmoral	5	20	*Benham S.G.1*

PLEASE READ THE GENERAL NOTES
AT THE BEGINNING OF THIS CATALOGUE
These often provide the answers to enquiries received.

H.M. The Queen's 60th Birthday (contd.)

SPECIAL HANDSTAMPS *(contd.)*	ordinary covers £	official covers £
(14) Loyal Greetings, City of London	5	– *n.o.c.*
(15) Many Happy Returns Nat. Postal Museum	5	– *n.o.c.*
(16) Lord High Admiral, BF 2113 PS	5	30 *Royal Navy*
(17) Royal British Legion, SW1	5	8 *Brit. Leg.*
(18) London SW1 (Palace) – permanent h/s	8	– *n.o.c.*
(19) Windsor (Castle) Philatelic Counter h/s	8	– *n.o.c.*
(20) Tower Hill (Tower) – permanent h/s	8	– *n.o.c.*
(21) Royal Academy of Dancing, SW11	7	25 *CoverCraft*
(22) N. Ireland £1 Coin, Royal Mint	7	– *n.o.c.*
(23) Women's Institutes, Denham College	7	8 *Fed. WI*
(24) Durham County Spastics Society	10	10 *DCSS*
(25) Licensed Victuallers Soc., Horsham	12	65 *Rum Merchants*
(26) G&J Swingler Ltd., Birmingham	10	20 *G&J Sw.*
(27) BNAI Brith District 15, London WC1	10	20 *B.B.*
(28) Austin Rover, Birmingham	10	25 *A. Rover*
(29) Open Days Broadlands	10	10 *Broadlands*
(30) Thames Barrier Visitors Centre, SE18	8	30 *CoverCraft*
(31) Nat. Postal Museum, 350 Years Royal Mail	8	– *n.o.c.*
C.D.S. POSTMARKS		
(32) Aldershot – HM Queen enroled in A.T.S	8	
(33) Badminton – Horse Trials	8	
(34) Buckingham Palace, SW1	100	
(35) Camberley, Surrey	8	
(36) Crathie – near to Balmoral	8	
(37) House of Commons, SW1	15	
(38) House of Lords, SW1	17	
(39) Mount Street, W1 – near to Queen's birthplace	10	
(40) Romsey – honeymoon at Broadlands	15	
(41) Queen Elizabeth Ave	10	
(42) Queen's Parade or Queensway *each*	10	
(43) Windsor Great Park or Windsor *each*	15	
(44) Windsor Castle, Berks	120	
(45) RAF Benson – The Queen's Flight	12	

20th May 1986 – NATURE CONSERVATION

17p Barn Owl; 22p Pine Marten; 31p Wild Cat; 34p Natterjack Toad

SPECIAL HANDSTAMPS	ordinary covers £	official covers £
(1) First Day of Issue – Philatelic Bureau	4	– *Royal Mail*
(2) First Day of Issue – Lincoln	4	– *Royal Mail*
(3) Ramblers' Association, SW8	5	15 *LFDC 50*
(4) Barn Owl, Endangered Species, Owlsmoor	5	30 *B'ham 500(12)*
(5) RSPB, Endangered Species, Sandy	5	7 *BLCS 12*
(6) Life & Landscape, Norfolk Broads	5	15 *Brs.Inf.Ltd.*
(7) The Wildfowl Trust, Slimbridge	5	7 *BLCS 12*
(8) Friends of the Earth, EC1	5	6 *F.o.t.E.*
(9) Royal Society for Nature Conservation, EC4	5	10 *Arlington*
(10) Species at Risk, Hants & IOW	5	10 *H&IOW NT*
(11) Herpetological Society, Studland	5	8 *Hawkwood*
(12) Cornish Wildlife, CTNC, Truro	5	5 *CTNC*
(13) Royal Society for Nature Conservation, W1	5	10 *Arlington*
(14) Lady's Slipper Orchid, Grassington	5	12 *Fine Arts 13*
(15) Garden Festival, Stoke on Trent	6	10 *NGF*
(16) Friends of Arundel Castle CC	10	15 *FACCC*
(17) Big Ack, BF 2111 PS	10	15 *RFDC 44*
(18) British Naval Anniversary, Plymouth	10	– *n.o.c.*
(19) England v. India, NW8	10	12 *S.P.*
(20) Caring & Sharing, Colchester Co-op	10	– *Col. Co-op*
(21) Thames Barrier Visitor Centre, SE18	8	30 *CoverCraft*
(22) Hawk 200, First Flight, Godalming	10	15 *V.A.F.A.*
C.D.S. POSTMARKS		
(23) Aviemore, Kinloch, or Tummel Bridge – Wildcat	8	
(24) Beddgelert or Kilnlochewe – Pine Marten	8	
(25) Lincoln or Nettleham – Royal Soc. Nature Conserv.	9	

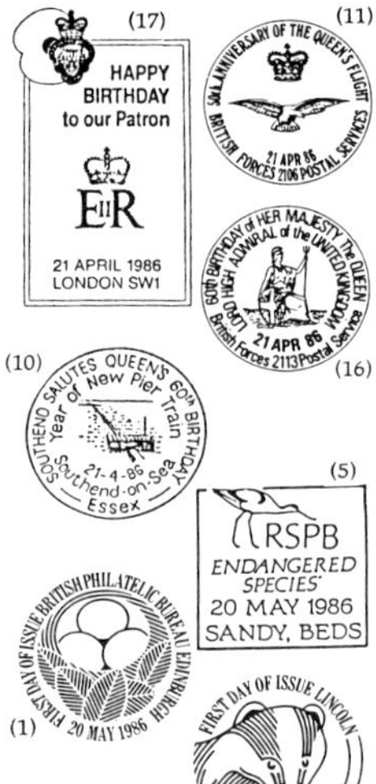

Nature Conservation (contd.)

	ordinary covers £	official covers £
(26) Park Road, Regents Park - London Zoo	10	
(27) Selbourne - Gilbert White (famous naturalist)	7	

In addition: Cheltenham; Ecclestone St., SW1; Eagle; Eaglescliffe; Fair Isle; Frog Island; Isle of Rhum; Otterburn; Otterferry; Owlsmoor; Paddock Wood; Studland and Willsbridge. Prices from £6.

SLOGAN POSTMARKS

(28) Lincs. & Humberside Trust Nature Conservation.	70	
(29) Natureland Marine Zoo Skegness.	70	

In addition: Stoke Garden Festival (2 versions). Prices from £40.

17th June 1986 - MEDIEVAL LIFE

17p Serf; 22p Freeman; 31p Knight; 34p Baron

SPECIAL HANDSTAMPS

	ordinary	official	
(1) First Day of Issue - Philatelic Bureau	4	-	*Royal Mail*
(2) First Day of Issue - Gloucester	4	-	*Royal Mail*
(3) Domesday Book MLXXXVI, Winchester	5	8	*LFDC 51*
(4) Freemen of England, Oswestry	5	15	*Bradbury*
(5) Cub Scouts Medieval Pageant, Worthing	5	10	*Worthing Cubs*
(6) Crofters Act, Inverness	6	40	*Crofters Comm.*
(7) Crofters Act, Edinburgh	6	40	*Crofters Comm.*
(8) Medieval Life Stamps/Tayburn, Edinburgh	6	-	*n.o.c.*
(9) Medieval Life Stamps/Tayburn, W14	6	-	*n.o.c.*
(10) Domesday, 900th Anniversary, WC2	5	12	*Cotswold*
(11) Charter Celebrations, Port of Penryn	5	15	*Penryn*
(12) Domesday Survey 900 Years, Battle	5	12	*B'ham 500(13)*
(13) Hereward Country, Isle of Ely	5	15	*E.Cambs DC*
(14) Hereward Country, Peterborough	5	15	*E.Cambs DC*
(15) The Great Hall, Domesday 900, Winchester	5	12	*Cotswold*
(16) 900th Anniversary, Domesday Survey, Exeter	5	7	*BLCS 13*
(17) Chapter House, Abbey of St. Peter, Gloucester	5	12	*Fine Arts 14*
(18) Blackwells Childrens Bookshop, Oxford	5	10	*Hawkwood*
(19) Battle, East Sussex (permanent handstamp)	10	-	*n.o.c.*
(20) Hastings, East Sussex (permanent handstamp)	10	-	*n.o.c.*
(21) Ripon 1100, AD 886-1986	6	15	*Ripon*
(22) Harrow Heritage Trust	5	15	*HHT*
(23) Tattershall Castle, BF 2116 PS	8	15	*RFDC 45*
(24) Legal & General, London EC4	8	50	*CoverCraft*
(25) Stamplink '86, Portsmouth	8	20	*Brit. Ferries*
(26) Blair Castle, Pitlochry	8	20	*Pilgrim*
(27) Commonwealth Games, Edinburgh	8	20	*Pilgrim*
(28) England v. India Tour Match, NW8	8	15	*DGT*
(29) Thames Barrier Visitors Centre, SE18	8	20	*S.P.*
(30) Friends of Arundel Castle	8	25	*CoverCraft*
(31) Garden Festival, Stoke on Trent	8	20	*S.P.*

ORDINARY F.D.I. POSTMARKS

For this issue only, many Post Offices used special F.D.I. postmarks. These were non-pictorial and incorporated both the modern and medieval spelling of the town name. Such covers (unaddressed) are valued at £6 each.

C.D.S. POSTMARKS

(32) Battle - sites of William's battle with Harold	15
(33) Bosham - the only Manor reserved by William	20
(34) Braunton or Laxton - ancient methods of farming	40
(35) Chancery Lane, WC2 - Domesday Book	12
(36) Cherbourg PAQUEBOT - Duke of Normandy	15
(37) Kingsholm - William decreed the Domesday survey	50
(38) Winchester - Domesday Book compiled	12

In addition: Castle Acre, Castle Rising, Castleton, Chertsey, Egham, Ettington, Guernsey or Jersey Paquebots, Hastings, Knight's Road, Oswestry, Saxon Ave., The Barony, Westham. Prices from £6.

SLOGAN POSTMARKS

(39) Hereward Country - Fen Heritage	60

In addition: Crofter's Act. Prices from £35.

OFFICIAL COVERS OR ORDINARY COVERS
Do you know the difference?
Please read the General Notes at the beginning of this catalogue for guidance.

(29)

(7)

(19)

(16)

(12)

(14)

(11)

(22)

(30)

(17)

(15)

(18)

(23)

(3)

15th July 1986 – SPORTS

17p Athletics; 22p Rowing; 29p Weight Lifting; 31p Shooting; 34p Hockey

SPECIAL HANDSTAMPS	ordinary covers £	official covers £	
(1) First Day of Issue – Philatelic Bureau	4	–	*Royal Mail*
(2) First Day of Issue – Edinburgh	4	–	*Royal Mail*
(3) Amateur Rowing Association, W6	5	6	*LFDC 53*
(4) British Rowing, Henley-on-Thames	5	20	*B'ham 500(14)*
(5) Cosford Arena, BF 2119 PS	15	15	*RFDC 46*
(6) 6th World Hockey Cup, NW10	5	15	*Cotswold*
(7) Scottish Brewers, Edinburgh	5	6	*DGT*
(8) The Royal British Legion, SW1	5	10	*Brit.Leg.28*
(9) Amateur Athletic Association, SW1	5	6	*DGT*
(10) Commonwealth Games, MAC, Edinburgh	5	6	*DGT*
(11) Waltham Forest, London Youth Games, E17	5	6	*Hawkwood*
(12) The Royal Tournament, BF 2118 PS	8	–	*n.o.c.*
(13) Garden Festival, Stoke on Trent	8	10	*NGF*
(14) England v. N. Zealand, NW8	8	10	*S.P.*
(15) England v. India, NW8	8	10	*S.P.*
(16) Medieval Life Stamps/Tayburn, Edinburgh	8	–	*n.o.c.*
(17) Medieval Life Stamps/Tayburn, W14	8	–	*n.o.c.*
(18) Domesday 900th Anniversary, WC2	8	–	*n.o.c.*
(19) Blair Castle, Pitlochry	8	10	*Pilgrim*
(20) Thames Barrier Visitors Centre, SE18	8	20	*CoverCraft*

C.D.S. POSTMARKS	
(21) Edinburgh, Jock's Lodge, Leith Walk, Murrayfield, Musselborough, Newbridge, North Motherwell or Norton Park – venues of Games events ... *each*	10
(22) Bisley – famous shooting venue	10
(23) Gleneagles Hotel – 'Gleneagles Agreement'	20
(24) Henley-on-Thames – 'Henley Royal Regatta'	10
(25) Mobile P.O. 2 Edinburgh – sited in Games Village	100
(26) Willesden – World Hockey Championships	15

In addition: Badminton, Bowling Green, Clarkston, Fulham Rd SW6, Gun Hill, and Shooting Common. Prices from £6.

(7)

(6)

(3)

(2)

(11) (2)

(8) (5)

(19) (3)

22nd July 1986 – ROYAL WEDDING

12p, 17p Prince Andrew & Sarah Ferguson

SPECIAL HANDSTAMPS	ordinary covers £	official covers £	
(1) First Day of Issue – Philatelic Bureau	2	–	*Royal Mail*
(2) First Day of Issue – London SW1	2	–	*Royal Mail*
(3) Dummer (depicts horseshoe and church)	3	8	*G&P*
(4) Westminster Abbey (circular - front of Abbey)	3	15	*LFDC 52*
(5) Royal Wedding Greetings, Windsor	3	20	*B'ham 500(15)*
(6) Loyal Greetings from York	3	15	*Benham S.G.2*
(7) The Royal Wedding, EC4	3	10	*Arlington*
(8) Westminster Abbey (circular - twin towers of Abbey)	3	10	*Arlington*
(9) Loyal Greetings from Lullingstone Silk Farm	3	15	*Benham L14*
(10) Debretts Recording Royal History, SW6	20	15	*Fine Arts 16*
(11) Westminster Abbey (vertical - front of Abbey))	3	5	*Havering*
(12) The Royal Wedding, London EC	3	–	*Royal Mail*
(13) Dummer (depicts bell)	3	6	*K&D*
(14) The Lewis Carroll Society	3	6	*Hawkwood*
(15) Royal Wedding, XIII Commonwealth Games	3	7	*DGT*
(16) Westminster Abbey (rectangular - four bells)	3	7	*DGT*
(17) Woman's Weekly, SE1	6	20	*CoverCraft*
(18) Open Days Broadlands, Romsey	6	8	*Broadlands*
(19) London SW1 (Palace) – permanent h/s	7	–	*n.o.c.*
(20) Windsor (Castle) Philatelic Counter h/s	7	–	*n.o.c.*
(21) Blair Castle, Pitlochry	6	10	*Pilgrim*
(22) Commonwealth Games, 1986 MAC, Edinburgh	6	7	*DGT*
(23) Wednesbury Sport Union	7	12	*Wed.Sports*
(24) Lifeboat Week, Lyme Regis	8	12	*Pilgrim*
(25) Brooklands, Daily Mail Air Race	8	25	*V.A.F.A.*
(26) Head Post Office, Hemel Hempstead	10	45	*H.H.P.O.*

(12) (9)

(16)

(23)

(27)

PLEASE READ THE GENERAL NOTES
AT THE BEGINNING OF THIS CATALOGUE
These often provide the answers to enquiries received.

1986 Royal Wedding (contd.)

SPECIAL HANDSTAMPS	ordinary covers £	official covers £	
(27) Royal Tournament, BF 2118 PS	7	–	*n.o.c.*
(28) Garden Festival, Stoke-on-Trent	8	15	*NGF*
(29) England v. N. Zealand, NW8	8	15	*S.P.*
(30) England v. India, NW8	8	15	*S.P.*
(31) Thames Barrier Visitors Centre, SE18	8	25	*CoverCraft*
(32) Amateur Athletic Association, SW1	8	10	*DGT*

C.D.S. POSTMARKS	
(33) Ascot – Andrew and Sarah, schools	8
(34) Buckingham Palace, SW1	100
(35) Dummer – home of Sarah Ferguson	12
(36) Great Portland St/Portman Sq – Sarah's birthplace	10
(37) House of Commons, SW1	20
(38) House of Lords, SW1	25
(39) Kelso – where Andrew proposed to Sarah	12
(40) Windsor or Windsor Great Park *each*	15
(41) Windsor Castle, Berks	120

In addition: Culdrose RNAS, Dartmouth, Duffus, Duke of York's School, Ferguson's Lane, Princetown, Romsey, St. Aldates, St. Andrews, Yeovilton RNAS. Prices from £6.

SLOGAN POSTMARKS

St. Anne's Church, Naval Base Portsmouth; Collect British Stamps; Victorian Rose Garden. Prices from £15.

(5)

(2)

(10)

(1)

19th August 1986 – COMMONWEALTH PARLIAMENTARY ASSOCIATION CONFERENCE

34p Stylised Cross and Ballot Paper

SPECIAL HANDSTAMPS	ordinary	official	
(1) First Day of Issue – Philatelic Bureau	2	–	*Royal Mail*
(2) First Day of Issue – London SW1	2	–	*Royal Mail*
(3) Common'lth Parl. Conf., Houses of Parliament	3	6	*LFDC 54*
(4) Common'lth Parl. Assoc., 32nd Conf., SW1	3	7	*BLCS 16*
(5) St. Margaret's Parish Church, SW1	3	5	*Hawkwood*
(6) London SW1 (Palace) permanent h/s	5	–	*n.o.c.*
(7) Dumfries Octocentenary 1186-1986	5	10	*Dumfries*
(8) World Chess Championship, W1	10	20	*H.Murray*
(9) Garden Festival, Stoke-on-Trent	5	15	*NGF*
(10) England v. N. Zealand, NW8	5	10	*S.P.*

C.D.S. POSTMARKS	
(11) Buckingham Palace, SW1	60
(12) Gleneagles Hotel – 'Gleneagles Agreement'	15
(13) House of Commons, SW1	25
(14) House of Lords, SW1	35
(15) Huntingdon – birthplace of Oliver Cromwell	12
(16) Kensington High St. W8 – Commonwealth Institute	7
(17) Queen Elizabeth Ave., Walsall	7
(18) Westminster Bridge Rd., SE1 – venue of Conference	8

SLOGAN POSTMARKS

Inverness Conference Capital; British Presidency. Prices from £15.

(8)

(3)

(4)

(1)

(2)

(5)

16th September 1986 – THE ROYAL AIR FORCE

17p Lord Dowding/Hurricane; 22p Lord Tedder/Typhoon; 29p Lord Trenchard/DH 9A; 31p Sir Arthur Harris/Lancaster; 34p Lord Portal/Mosquito

SPECIAL HANDSTAMPS	ordinary	official	
(1) First Day of Issue – Philatelic Bureau	5	–	*Royal Mail*
(2) First Day of Issue – Farnborough	5	–	*Royal Mail*
(3) 46th Anniversary Battle of Britain, Uxbridge	7	10	*LFDC 55*
(4) Hawkinge Aerodrome, Spitfire	7	40	*B'ham 500(17)*
(5) RAF Scampton, Lincoln	7	20	*BLCS 17*
(6) Spitfire, 1936-1986, Eastleigh	7	20	*Bradbury*
(7) RAFA, Andover, Hants	7	15	*Cotswold*
(8) Kenley Aerodrome	8	20	*Fine Arts 18*
(9) Re-organisation of RAF, BF 2114 PS	9	15	*RFDC 49*
(10) The Battle of Britain, BF 2123 PS	9	15	*Forces*

(1)

(2)

(3)

16 SEP '86
(12)

PRICES & CONDITION – PLEASE READ GENERAL NOTES

R.A.F. (contd.)

	ordinary covers £	official covers £	
(11) Newark on Trent, RAF	9	25	*Newark*
(12) Duxford Aviation Society	9	15	*Havering*
(13) England v. N. Zealand, NW8	9	20	*S.P.*
(14) British Philatelic Federation, Norwich	9	–	*n.o.c.*
(15) Marx Memorial Library, EC1	9	10	*Hawkwood*
(16) Garden Festival, Stoke-on-Trent	9	15	*NGF*
(17) High Wycombe, Bucks	9	–	*n.o.c.*

C.D.S. POSTMARKS

(18) RAF Biggin Hill *(for Biggin Hill village see below)*		100
(19) Any other RAF station postmark	*each*	15
(20) Any Field or Forces Post Office	*each*	20
(21) House of Lords, SW1		15
(22) Moffat, Killearn, Taunton, Cheltenham or Hungerford – birthplaces of Commanders on stamps	*each*	12
(23) Gravesend, Hawkinge, Digby Aerodrome, Manston, Kenley or Oakington – connected with aircraft featured on stamps	*each*	20
(24) Biggin Hill, Cosford Camp, Cranwell, Duxford, Honington Camp or Leuchars – RAF connections	*each*	15

In addition: Churchill, Eastleigh, Gatenby, The Hyde, Hendon, Lancaster, Middle Wallop, Northolt, Pathfinder Village, Stanmore. Prices from £7.

(4)

(6)

(8)

(14)

18th November 1986 – CHRISTMAS

13p The Glastonbury Thorn; 18p The Tanad Valley Plygain; 22p The Hebrides Tribute; 31p The Dewsbury Church Knell; 34p The Hereford Boy Bishop

SPECIAL HANDSTAMPS

(1) First Day of Issue – Philatelic Bureau	3	–	*Royal Mail*
(2) First Day of Issue – Bethlehem, Llandeilo	3	–	*Royal Mail*
(3) The Hebrides Tribute, Stornaway	4	12	*B'ham 500(18)*
(4) The Devil's Knell, Dewsbury	4	15	*Dewsbury PC*
(5) Christmas Greetings, Folkestone	4	8	*Benham L15*
(6) St. Margaret's, Westminster, SW1	4	5	*Hawkwood*
(7) The Glastonbury Thorn	4	8	*LFDC 56*
(8) English Folk, Dance & Song Soc., Sheffield	4	5	*BLCS 18*
(9) Telecom Technology Showcase, EC1	4	–	*n.o.c.*
(10) Seasons Greetings/Railway Societies, WC1	4	–	*n.o.c.*
(11) Christmas, Hereford	4	5	*BLSC 18*
(12) NE Parcels Centre, Washington	10	–	*Royal Mail*
(13) Thames Barrier Visitors Centre, SE18	10	25	*CoverCraft*
(14) Lloyd's of London, EC3	10	20	*CoverCraft*
(15) Battle of the Somme, BF 2124 PS	10	–	*n.o.c.*
(16) High Wycombe, Bucks	8	–	*n.o.c.*
(17) Leicester Circuits	10	20	*L. Circuits*

C.D.S. POSTMARKS

(18) Bethlehem or Nasareth	*each*	8
(19) Dewsbury, Glastonbury or Hereford	*each*	10
(20) Llanrhaeadr-ym-Mochnant (Welsh Plygain)		12
(21) Lochboisdale or Lochmaddy (Hebrides Tribute)	*each*	12

In addition: Holy Island, St. Nicholas. Prices from £6.

SLOGAN POSTMARKS

10th Anniversary Codesort. Prices from £20.

(1)

(2)

(8)

(6)

(5)

(14)

(10)

(19)

2nd December 1986 – CHRISTMAS

12p The Glastonbury Thorn

SPECIAL HANDSTAMPS

(1) First Day of Issue – Philatelic Bureau	1	–	*Royal Mail*
(2) The Glastonbury Thorn (changeable date)	3	5	*LFDC 56*
(3) The Glastonbury Thorn, Glastonbury SC, Somerset	3	5	*Cotswold*
(4) Christmas, Glastonbury, Somerset	3	10	*B'ham 500(19)*
(5) Telecom Technology Showcase, EC1	5	–	*n.o.c.*
(6) Biggin Hill, BF 2130 PS	3	5	*RFDC 51*
(7) Thames Barrier Visitors Centre, SE18	4	10	*CoverCraft*
(8) High Wycombe, Bucks	4	–	*n.o.c.*
(9) Submarine 2400, Upholder, Barrow	4	15	*Vickers*

(4)

(6)

(3)

PLEASE READ THE GENERAL NOTES
AT THE BEGINNING OF THIS CATALOGUE

1986 Christmas (contd.)

	ordinary covers	official covers
C.D.S. POSTMARKS	£	£
(10) Bethlehem, Llandeilo, Dyfed	5	
(11) Nasareth, Gwynedd	5	
(12) Glastonbury, Somerset	5	

In addition: Holy Island. Prices from £4.

SLOGAN POSTMARKS		
(13) Happy Christmas The Post Office	6	

Note: On the same day of issue, 2nd December, a special Christmas stamp pack was issued containing 36 x 13p Glastonbury Thorn Christmas stamps. The stamps were printed in sheetlet form – 2 panes of 18 with a central double gutter and star underprint (to indicate the stamps were issued at a discount). In all other respects they were identical to the 18th November 13p issue. Many of the covers produced for this issue bore both 12p and 13p values – the prices quoted above reflect this. Some covers exist with a complete pane of 18 x 13p stamps and are valued at around £15.

Some double-dated covers exist with the set of Christmas stamps postmarked 18th November, and 12p value postmarked 2nd December. Prices from £30.

20th January 1987 – FLOWERS

18p Gaillardia; 22p Echinops; 31p Echeveria; 34p Colchicum

SPECIAL HANDSTAMPS			
(1) First Day of Issue – Philatelic Bureau	4	–	*Royal Mail*
(2) First Day of Issue – Richmond, Surrey	4	–	*Royal Mail*
(3) Flowers, Flore, Northampton	5	20	*B'ham 500(20)*
(4) Nat. Assoc. Flower Arrangement Soc., SW1	5	7	*LFDC 57*
(5) Chelsea Flower Shows, SW3	5	8	*BOCS (3) 1*
(6) Westminster Shows, SW1	5	8	*BOCS (3) 1*
(7) The Lindley Library, SW1	5	8	*BOCS (3) 1*
(8) Wisley Gardens, Royal Hort. Society,	5	8	*BOCS (3) 1*
(9) Royal Botanical Gardens, Kew	5	7	*BLCS 20*
(10) Stephen Thomas Flora & Fauna Exhib., Ovingdean	5	8	*G & P*
(11) KEB Horticultural Society, EC1A	5	8	*KEB H.S.*
(12) GQT BBC Manchester	5	20	*CoverCraft*
(13) Royal College of Art, SW1	8	35	*CoverCraft*
(14) Reformation 77 Squadron, BF 2150 PS	10	10	*RFDC 52*
(15) Bradbury Blinds, Northampton	10	20	*Brad Blinds*
(16) Queen Victoria's Jubilee, Postal Museum	10	–	*n.o.c.*
(17) High Wycombe, Bucks	8	–	*n.o.c.*
C.D.S. POSTMARKS			
(18) Botanic Gardens, Belfast	20		
(19) Flowery Field or Spring Gardens *each*	10		
(20) Kew or Kew Gardens *each*	20		
(21) Royal Hospital, Chelsea – Flower Show	12		
(22) Sissinghurst or Ripley – Wisley Gardens *each*	8		

In addition: Ipswich, Mickleton, Ovingdean, Saffron Walden, St. Bees, Thistle Hill, Tresco. Prices from £6.

24th March 1987 – SIR ISAAC NEWTON

18p Principia; 22p Motion of Bodies in Ellipses; 31p Opticks; 34p The System of the World

SPECIAL HANDSTAMPS			
(1) First Day of Issue – Philatelic Bureau	3	–	*Royal Mail*
(2) First Day of Issue – Woolsthorpe, Lincs	3	–	*Royal Mail*
(3) Isaac Newton, Woolsthorpe, Grantham	4	8	*LFDC 58*
(4) Sir Isaac Newton, Trinity College, Cambridge	4	12	*B'ham 500(21)*
(5) The Old Royal Observatory, SE10	4	7	*BLCS 21*
(6) Weston Favell Upper School, Northampton	4	9	*WF School*
(7) Isaac Newton, Grantham	4	15	*Maths Assoc*
(8) The George, Newton's Tercentenary, Grantham	4	25	*George Hotel*
(9) Apple's Tenth Anniversary, Hemel Hempstead	4	40	*Arlington*
(10) Sir Isaac Newton, Science Museum, SW7	4	10	*Cotswold*
(11) Sir Isaac Newton, Royal Society, EC4	4	–	*n.o.c.*
(12) London College of Music, W1	6	25	*CoverCraft*
(13) Parachute Descent, BF 2151 PS	6	10	*RFDC 53*
(14) Holmfirth Postcard Museum	6	–	*n.o.c.*
(15) Queen Victoria's Jubilee, Postal Museum	6	–	*n.o.c.*

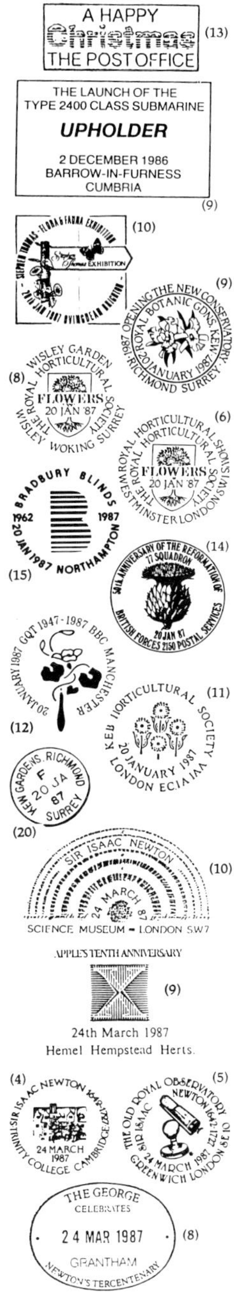

PRICES & CONDITION – PLEASE READ GENERAL NOTES

Sir Isaac Newton (contd.)

C.D.S. POSTMARKS

	ordinary covers £	official covers £
(16) Colsterworth, Lincs. - Woolsthorpe Manor	10	
(17) Grantham - Newton attended King's School	7	
(18) Greenwich - reflecting telescope, Royal Observatory	7	
(19) House of Commons - MP for Cambridge University	12	
(20) Kensington - where Newton died	7	
(21) Newton - Cambridge, Swansea or Wisbech ... *each*	10	
(22) Regent St., SW1 - Newton's home	7	
(23) Trinity St., Cambridge - Trinity College	8	

In addition: Globe Road and Seething Lane EC3. Prices from £6.

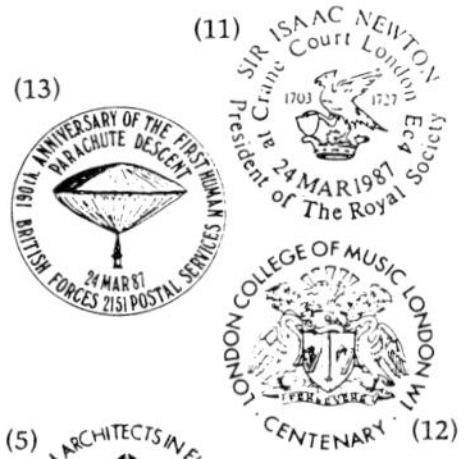

12th May 1987 - BRITISH ARCHITECTS IN EUROPE

18p Ipswich (Foster); 22p Paris (Rogers & Piano);
31p Stuttgart (Stirling & Wilford); 34p Luxembourg (Lasdun)

SPECIAL HANDSTAMPS

(1) First Day of Issue - Philatelic Bureau	3	-	*Royal Mail*
(2) First Day of Issue - Ipswich	3	-	*Royal Mail*
(3) British Architects in Europe, W1	4	5	*LFDC 59*
(4) The Clore Gallery, SW1	4	12	*B'ham 500(22)*
(5) R.I.B.A., Macclesfield	4	6	*BLCS 22*
(6) R.I.B.A., Royal Charter, W1	4	25	*CoverCraft*
(7) Willis Faber, Heritage & Progress, Ipswich	4	10	*CoverCraft*
(8) Clinical Biochemists, Eastbourne	8	13	*A.C.B.*
(9) Royal Engineers, BF 1876 PS	8	12	*RFDC 54*
(10) Holmfirth Postcard Museum	8	-	*n.o.c.*
(11) Queen Victoria's Jubilee, Postal Museum	8	-	*n.o.c.*
(12) Gallantry Awards RNLI, SE1	8	10	*Pilgrim*
(13) London - Venice, Orient Express, Folkestone	8	50	*Benham S.G.3*

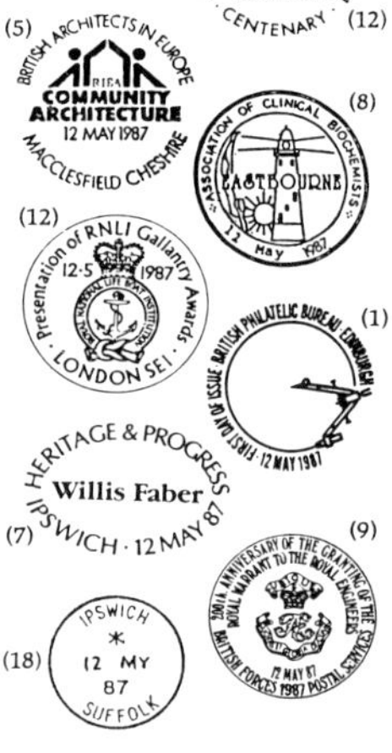

C.D.S. POSTMARKS

(14) Ascot - Chartered Institute of Building	6
(15) Euston Centre BO - James Stirling & Associates	6
(16) Gt. Portland St. - Foster Associates & R.I.B.A.	6
(17) Hammersmith W6 - Richard Rogers Partnership	6
(18) Ipswich - Willis Faber Building	6
(19) New Buildings, Londonderry	25
(20) Vauxhall Bridge Rd. - Denys, Lasdun & Associates	6

In addition: Buxton Road, Macclesfield; Kirkwall; Paris Ave.; Stirling; Town Centre. Prices from £5.

SLOGAN POSTMARKS

St. Magnus Cathedral; The Copthorne; Arndale Centre; Collect British Stamps; Nissan. Prices from £35.

16th June 1987 - ST. JOHN AMBULANCE

18p Early First Aid Duties 1887; 22p First Aid in Wartime 1940;
31p First Aid at Pop Concert 1965; 34p Transplant Organ Flights 1987

SPECIAL HANDSTAMPS

(1) First Day of Issue - Philatelic Bureau	3	-	*Royal Mail*
(2) First Day of Issue - London EC1	3	-	*Royal Mail*
(3) St. John's Gate, SJA Exhibition, EC1	4	9	*LFDC 60*
(4) 2nd Oldest Div. SJA Brigade, Heywood	4	6	*Cotswold*
(5) St. John Ambulance, Hyde Park, SW1	4	20	*B'ham (500)23*
(6) St. John Ambulance, Stansted	4	10	*BLCS 23*
(7) St. John Ambulance Brigade, SW1	4	10	*Arlington*
(8) St. Margaret;s Hospital, Epping	4	15	*Arlington*
(9) Thames Barrier Visitors Centre, SE18	7	15	*CoverCraft*
(10) Holmfirth Postcard Museum	7	-	*n.o.c.*
(11) Queen Victoria's Jubilee, Postal Museum	8	-	*n.o.c.*
(12) Maiden Voyage, Waverley, Glasgow	7	9	*Benham*
(13) London - Venice, Orient Express, Folkestone	8	75	*Benham S.G.3*

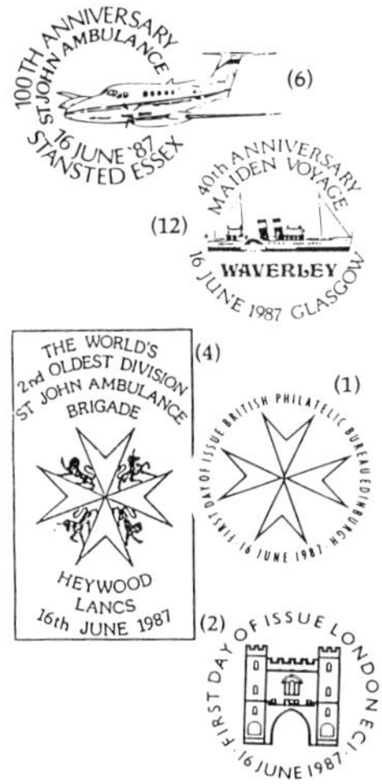

PLEASE READ THE GENERAL NOTES
AT THE BEGINNING OF THIS CATALOGUE
C.D.S. = COUNTER DATE STAMP
These are everyday operational postmarks available
at all Post Office Counters.
Please refer to the General Notes for more details.

St. John Ambulance (contd.)

C.D.S. POSTMARKS

	ordinary covers £	official covers £
(14) Ashford – Birthplace of founder Sir John Furley	8	
(15) Bow or Coventry – The Blitz (22p) *each*	7	
(16) Epping or Stansted – The Airwing (34p)	10	
(17) Farringdon Rd. or London EC – St. John's Gate *each*	6	
(18) Harrow – First road accident attended by SJA	6	
(19) Margate – First Ambulance Corp.	7	
(20) Mount St., W1 – Hyde Park (31p)	6	
(21) Papworth – Transplant surgery (34p)	9	
(22) RAF Benson – First flight of Air Wing (34p)	20	
(23) St. John's – Bradford, Ipswich or Worcester *each*	12	
(24) St. John's Chapel, Bishop Auckland	12	
(25) Woolwich – First Centre of the Association	6	

In addition: GWR TPO 'Up', House of Commons, House of Lords, Muswell Hill, Oldham, Orthopaedic Hospital, Royal Hospital School, and Windsor Great Park. Prices from £5.

SLOGAN POSTMARKS

British Deaf Association (s); Postcode your Property. Prices from £5.

(5)

(23) (24)

21st July 1987 – SCOTTISH HERALDRY

18p Lord Lyon King of Arms; 22p HRH The Duke of Rothesay; 31p Royal Scottish Academy; 34p Royal Society of Edinburgh

SPECIAL HANDSTAMPS

(1) First Day of Issue – Philatelic Bureau	4	–	*Royal Mail*
(2) First Day of Issue – Rothesay, Isle of Bute	4	–	*Royal Mail*
(3) Order of the Thistle, Edinburgh	5	18	*B'ham 500(24)*
(4) Drum Castle, Banchory	5	8	*BLCS 24*
(5) Crathes Castle, Banchory	5	8	*BLCS 24*
(6) Dunkeld, Perthshire	5	8	*BLCS 24*
(7) Bannockburn, Stirling	5	8	*BLCS 24*
(8) Mary Queen of Scots, Fotheringhay	5	12	*LFDC 61*
(9) Royal Scottish Academy, Edinburgh	5	15	*CoverCraft*
(10) Lord Cameron of Balhousie, BF 2144 PS	5	7	*RFDC 56*
(11) Glasgow Herald	7	20	*Pilgrim*
(12) Duke & Duchess of York	7	20	*Y. Minster*
(13) Thames Barrier Visitors Centre, SE18	8	15	*CoverCraft*
(14) Queen's School Rheindahlen, BF 21787 PS	9	15	*Queens Sch*
(15) The Royal Tournament, BF 2142 PS	9	15	*Forces*

C.D.S. POSTMARKS

(16) Banff – home of Lord Lyon King of Arms	8
(17) Bannockburn – famous battle	15
(18) Edinburgh	8
(19) Frederick St., Edinburgh – Royal Soc. of Edinburgh	8
(20) Holyrood – Royal residence in Edinburgh	16
(21) House of Lords, SW1	15
(22) Largs or Luncarty – adoption of Thistle (battles)	12
(23) Rothesay – arms of Duke of Rothesay (22p)	8
(24) Scone – Scone Palace	35
(25) St. Andrews – Patron Saint of Scotland	20
(26) St. Mary St., Edinburgh – Royal Scottish Academy	7

In addition: Dingwall, Elgin, Gordon, Kintore, Prince Charles Ave, Selkirk, Thistle Hill, Ullapool. Prices from £6.

SLOGAN POSTMARKS

Etterick & Lauderdale: Aberdeen Youth Festival; Inverness Conference Capital; St. Magnus Cathedral. Prices from £20.

(4) (8) (6)

(12)

(10)

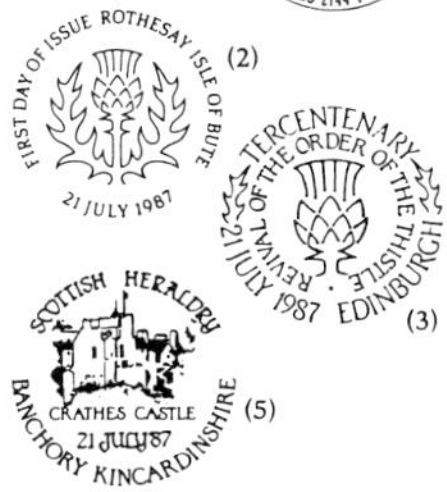

(2) (3) (5)

8th September 1987 – VICTORIAN BRITAIN

18p Great Exhibition: 'Monarch of the Glen'; Grace Darling
22p 'Great Eastern'; Prince Albert; Mrs. Beeton
31p Albert Memorial; Benjamin Disraeli; Ballot Box
34p Relief of Mafeking; Marconi Wireless; Diamond Jubilee

SPECIAL HANDSTAMPS

(1) First Day of Issue – Philatelic Bureau	4	–	*Royal Mail*
(2) First Day of Issue – Newport, Isle of Wight	4	–	*Royal Mail*
(3) N.T. for Scotland, Edinburgh	5	10	*BLCS 25*
(4) Victorian Britain VA, SW7	5	10	*BLCS 25*

(8)

(15)

(11)

(14)

Victorian Britain (contd.)

	ordinary covers £	official covers £	
(5) Queen Victoria, 1837-1901, SW1	5	10	*LFDC 62*
(6) Victorian Britain, Balmoral	5	20	*B'ham 500 (25)*
(7) Victorian Britain, Windsor	5	40	*Benham S.G.4*
(8) Southampton Victorian Post Office	8	-	*Royal Mail*
(9) Historic Worcester Postmarks Picture Card	8	-	*Royal Mail*
(10) Mrs. Beeton's, W1	10	8	*Arlington(s)*
(11) Calderdale's Victorian Inheritance, Halifax	10	-	*Post Office*
(12) Marconi Philatelic Society, Gt Baddow	6	10	*G & P*
(13) Victorian Britain, Edensor, Bakewell	6	20	*CoverCraft*
(14) Henry Archer, Festiniog Rly., Porthmadog	6	25	*Benham L16*
(15) National Postal Museum, 1966 -1987, EC1	6	-	*n.o.c.*
(16) Ballooning in British Army, BF 2156 PS	8	9	*RFDC 57*
(17) Ballymena Rugby Football Club	7	15	*Bally RFC*
(18) Royal Navy Equip. Exhib., BF 2187 PS	8	12	*Forces*

C.D.S. POSTMARKS

(19) Balmoral Castle	300
(20) Bamburgh – Grace Darling	10
(21) Beaconsfield – Disraeli was Lord Beaconsfield	10
(22) Buckingham Palace, SW1	100
(23) East Cowes – near to Osborne House	10
(24) Fleet St., – 'Mafeking' on newspaper hoarding	15
(25) Hatch End, Pinner – Mrs. Beeton	10
(26) House of Commons, SW1 – Ballot Act, 1972	15
(27) House of Lords, SW1 – Lord Beaconsfield	20
(28) Hughenden Valley – home of Disraeli	25
(29) Kensington – V & A, Albert Memorial etc	10
(30) Maida Vale – Landseer 'Monarch of the Glen'	10
(31) Old Windsor or Windsor Great Park *each*	10
(32) Prince Consort Rd., Queen Victoria Rd., Victoria Rd.	15
(33) St. Margaret's Bay, Dover – wireless transmission	20
(34) Theobald's Road – birthplace of Disraeli	10
(35) West Ferry Rd., Millwall – 'The Great Eastern'	10
(36) Westow St., Norwood – resited Crystal Palace	10

In addition: Britannia, Paddington, Nelson, Woburn. Prices from £6.

SLOGAN POSTMARKS

Church of Latter Day Saints. Prices range from £20.

13th OCTOBER 1987 – STUDIO POTTERY

Pots by: 18p Bernard Leach; 26p Elizabeth Fritsch; 31p Lucie Rie; 34p Hans Cope

SPECIAL HANDSTAMPS

(1) First Day of Issue – Philatelic Bureau	3	-	*Royal Mail*
(2) First Day of Issue – St. Ives, Cornwall	3	-	*Royal Mail*
(3) Craftsmen Potters Assoc'n, W1	5	8	*LFDC 63*
(4) Studio Pottery, Potters Corner, Ashford	5	10	*B'ham 500(26)*
(5) Studio Pottery, VA, SW7	5	6	*BLCS 26*
(6) Designed by Tony Evans, Shrewsbury	5	10	*Tony Evans*
(7) Stoke-on-Trent, Philatelic Counter	8	-	*n.o.c.*
(8) Battle of Britain, BF 2154 PS	9	12	*RFDC 58*

C.D.S. POSTMARKS

(9) Carbis Bay, St. Ives – home of Bernard Leach	25
(10) Chelsea, London SW3 – annual Craft Fair	10
(11) Frome, Somerset – Hans Coper's studio	8
(12) Marble Arch, W1 – Lucie Rie's studio	8
(13) Poplar, E14 – Elizabeth Fritsch's studio	8
(14) South Kensington – Victoria & Albert Museum	8
(15) St. Ives – home of studio pottery	12
(16) Stennack, St. Ives – Leach's pottery	25
(17) Welwyn Garden – Elizabeth Fritsch – first studio	8
(18) Whitchurch – birthplace of Elizabeth Fritsch	8

In addition: Barlaston, Bathwick St., Dartington, Digswell, Euston Centre, Leach Lane, Potters Bar, Pottery Road. Prices from £6.

SLOGAN POSTMARKS

Redhill Philatelic Soc.; Royal Mail Code Show. Prices from £15.

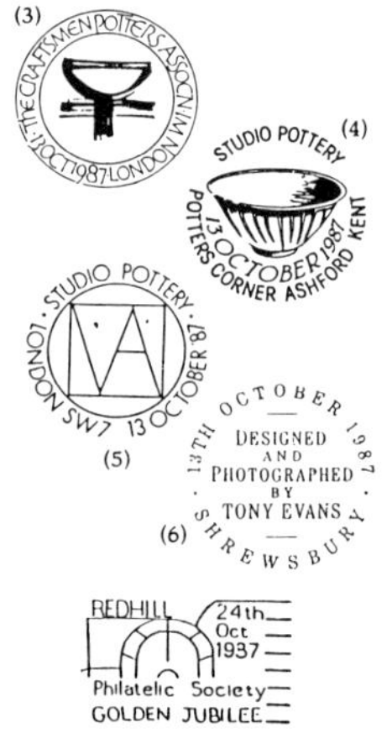

Do you know the difference between commemorative covers and first day covers?
If not, please refer to the General Notes

17th November 1987 - CHRISTMAS

13p, 18p, 26p, 31p, 34p A child's view of Christmas

SPECIAL HANDSTAMPS	ordinary covers £	official covers £	
(1) First Day of Issue - Philatelic Bureau	4	-	*Royal Mail*
(2) First Day of Issue - Bethlehem, Llandeilo	4	-	*Royal Mail*
(3) Christmas, Toys Hill, Westerham	4	10	*B'ham 500(27)*
(4) 175th Anniv. Birth of Charles Dickens	4	8	*LFDC 64*
(5) Hamley's Toy Shop, W1	5	9	*CoverCraft*
(6) Christmas Common, Oxford	5	7	*BLCS 27*
(7) Holy Cross Church, Pattishall	5	10	*HC Church*
(8) Christmas, Christleton, Chester	5	6	*Benham*
(9) Christmas 1987, Star Underprint, Star	5	7	*B'ham 500(28)*
(10) Telecom Technology Showcase, EC4	9	-	*n.o.c.*
(11) RFA Argus, BP 2157 PS	10	15	*FAA Museum*
(12) Age of Chivalry Exhibition, W1	10	15	*Pilgrim*

C.D.S. POSTMARKS

(13) Bethlehem, Dyfed	20
(14) Nasareth, Gwynedd	9
(15) Regent Street, W1 - near to Hamley's Toy Shop	6

In addition: Child Okeford, Childs Hill, Fir Tree, Holy Island, Noel Road, Playing Place, St. Nicholas, Snowshill, Star, Sidmouth. Prices from £5.

SLOGAN POSTMARKS

(16) Gold Angels for Xmas - Pobjoy Mint	10(s)
(17) The Church of Jesus Christ of Latter Day Saints	25
(18) Christmas Shopping is Fun, Nottingham	95
(19) Gold Angels available from Jewellers	10(s)

CHRISTMAS DISCOUNT 13P MINIATURE SHEET

Covers with gutter pair from sheet and special h/s	4
Covers with whole miniature sheet and special h/s	20

19th January 1988 - THE LINNEAN SOCIETY

18p Bull-rout (fish); 26p Yellow Waterlily;
31p Bewick's Swan; 34p Morel (fungus)

SPECIAL HANDSTAMPS	ordinary covers £	official covers £	
(1) First Day of Issue - Philatelic Bureau	3	-	*Royal Mail*
(2) First Day of Issue - Burlington House, W1	3	-	*Royal Mail*
(3) 1788-1988 The Linnean Society, W1	5	18	*LFDC 65*
(4) British Natural History, Waterside	5	15	*B'ham (500)29*
(5) The Wildfowl Trust, Welney	5	10	*BLCS 29*
(6) The Wildfowl Trust, Swan Lake	5	7	*BLCS 29*
(7) Sir Thomas Sopwith, BF 2158 PS	8	10	*RFDC 60*
(8) Age of Chivalry Exhibition, W1	8	12	*Pilgrim*
(9) The Emperor's Warriors Exhibition, SW1	8	12	*Pilgrim*
(10) Railways and the Post, Postal Museum	8	-	*n.o.c.*

C.D.S. POSTMARKS

(11) Broadwick St., W1 - first meeting place of Society	7
(12) Norwich - B/place of founder Sir J. E. Smith	8
(13) Fleur-de-lis - flower of the lily	15
(14) Gotenburg, Sweden PAQUEBOT	50
(15) Heddon St., Albemarle St., Regent St., - near to Burlington House, W1 *each*	7
(16) Holloway - Edward Lear (illustration 31p)	7
(17) Kew Gardens or Slimbridge *each*	15
(18) Lambeth SE11 - James Sowerby (illustration 34p)	7
(19) Ovingham and Mickley Sq., North'land - Bewick	7
(20) Polperro - Dr. Jonathan Couch (manuscript 18p)	20

In addition: Abbotsbury, Badger's Mount, Bosherton, House of Commons, Lillies Leaf, Nettleham, Selbourne, Swanpool, Waterside, Welney. Prices from £6.

(1)

(2)

(3)

(4)

(6)

(21)

1st March 1988 - THE WELSH BIBLE 1588-1988

18p William Morgan; 26p William Salesbury;
31p Richard Davies; 34p Richard Parry

SPECIAL HANDSTAMPS	ordinary covers £	official covers £	
(1) First Day of Issue - Philatelic Bureau	4	-	*Royal Mail*
(2) First Day of Issue - Ty Mawr Wybrnant, Gwynedd	4	-	*Royal Mail*
(3) Bible Society, St. David's Day, St. Asaph	5	6	*LFDC 66*
(4) Welsh Bible, Caernarfon Castle	5	20	*B'ham (500)30*
(5) Y Beibl Yn Gymraeg, 1588-1988, Llanrhaeadr	5	10	*BLCS 30*

(1)

(2)

Welsh Bible (contd.)

	ordinary covers £	official covers £	
(6) Translators of Welsh Bible, St. Asaph	5	13	*BLCS 30*
(7) Soldiers' & Airmen's Scripture Assoc., BF 2159 PS	6	9	*RFDC 61*
(8) 1588-1988 Ty Mawr Wybrnant, Gwynedd	6	8	*CoverCraft*
(9) Spring Stampex, SW1	8	-	*Post Office*
(10) Railways and the Post, Postal Museum	8	-	*n.o.c.*
(11) Age of Chivalry Exhibition, W1	8	12	*Pilgrim*

C.D.S. POSTMARKS

(12) Abergwili – Richard Davies buried here	7
(13) Bala – associated with the story of Mary Jones	8
(14) Bethlehem, Dyfed	10
(15) Conway – birthplace of Richard Davies	6
(16) Cwm – birthplace of Richard Parry	8
(17) Dyserth – where Parry worked on his translation	6
(18) House of Commons – Act of 1563 Welsh translation	15
(19) House of Lords – Act of 1563 Welsh translation	20
(20) Llandaff – Morgan was Bishop here	6
(21) Llanrhaeadr Ym – Morgan translated Bible here	6
(22) Llansanffraid – Richard Davies associations	6
(23) Llansannan – birthplace of William Salesbury	6
(24) Penmachno – birthplace of William Morgan	6
(25) St. Asaph – Morgan, Davies, Parry all Bishops here	6
(26) St. David's – stamps issued on St. David's Day	9
(27) Welshpool – Morgan was vicar here	10

In addition: Ruthin, Trinity St. Prices from £5.

SLOGAN POSTMARKS

(28) Jesus is Alive!	45

In addition: Oldham Education Week. Prices from £60.

(7)

(4)

(3)

(9)

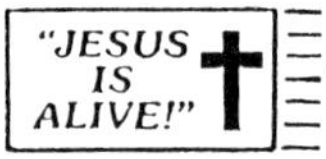

(28)

(2)

22nd March 1988 – SPORT

18p Gymnastics; 26p Skiing; 31p Lawn Tennis; 34p Association Football

SPECIAL HANDSTAMPS

(1) First Day of Issue – Philatelic Bureau	4	-	*Royal Mail*
(2) First Day of Issue – Wembley	4	-	*Royal Mail*
(3) 100 Years Ago Accrington	6	30	*Dawn*
(4) 100 Years of League Football, Aston Villa	6	30	*Dawn*
(5) 100 Years of League Football, Wolves	6	30	*Dawn*
(6) 100 Years of League Football, Everton	6	30	*Dawn*
(7) Record Holders, Liverpool FC	6	30	*Dawn*
(8) Manchester United	6	30	*Dawn*
(9) Record Holders, Tottenham Hotspur	6	12	*BLCS 31*
(10) Record Holders, Arsenal FC	6	15	*BLCS 31*
(11) Preston North End Football Club, Preston	6	10	*LFDC 67*
(12) Lawn Tennis at Edgbaston	6	15	*B'ham (500)31*
(13) The Lawn Tennis Association, W14	6	8	*Cotswold*
(14) Amateur Gymnastics Assoc., Slough	6	8	*Cotswold*
(15) 'A Question of Sport', Manchester	6	7	*CoverCraft*
(16) Physical Training Corps, BF 2161 PS	8	10	*RFDC 62*
(17) Railways and the Post, Postal Museum	9	-	*n.o.c.*

C.D.S. POSTMARKS

(18) Accrington, Blackburn, Bolton, Burnley, Derby, Preston, Stoke – founder members of Football League *each*	10
(19) Aviemore – ski centre	10
(20) Deepdale Rd., Preston – Preston North End FC	10
(21) Eccleston St., SW1 – HQ of Ski Association	7
(22) Edgbaston – first lawn tennis court marked out	10
(23) Fleet St. – first meeting of Football League	10
(24) Inner Park Rd., Wimbledon Park or Wimbledon B.O.	10
(25) Leamington Spa – world's first tennis club	8
(26) Lilleshall, Salop – National Gymnastics Centre	10
(27) Liverpool – most successful League Club	8
(28) Lytham St. Annes – HQ of the Football League	8
(29) Meadow Lane, Nottingham – Notts County FC	20
(30) Slough – HQ of the Amateur Gymnastics Assoc'n	7
(31) Villa Road – near to Aston Villa FC	40
(32) Wembley B.O.	7
(33) Wembley Park	20

In addition: Highbury, North End Road W14. Prices from £8.

(14)

(8)

(10)

(9)

(6)

1988

10th May 1988 - TRANSPORT AND COMMUNICATIONS

18p 'Mallard' and T.P.Os; 26p R.M.S. 'Queen Elizabeth'; 31p Glasgow Tram; 34p Handley Page

SPECIAL HANDSTAMPS	ordinary covers £	official covers £	
(1) First Day of Issue - Philatelic Bureau	3	-	*Royal Mail*
(2) First Day of Issue - Glasgow	3	-	*Royal Mail*
(3) Railways and the Post, Postal Museum	6	-	*n.o.c.*
(4) Mallard, National Rly. Museum, York	5	20	*BLCS 32*
(5) Mallard, Rail Riders, York	5	35	*CoverCraft*
(6) T.P.O. 150 Anniversary, Peterborough	5	30	*Nene V. Rly*
(7) The Jessop Collection, Diss	5	20	*P.P.S.*
(8) Sheffield & Rotherham Railway	5	50	Br. Rail
(9) Video Cinecosse Film, Ellen	5	60	*Cinecosse*
(10) R.M.S. Queen Elizabeth, SW1	5	10	*Arlington*
(11) R.M.S. Queen Elizabeth, Southampton	5	12	*LFDC 68*
(12) First Atlantic Convoy, BF 2165 PS	5	20	*FAA Museum*
(13) The Museum of Transport, Glasgow	5	12	*BLCS 32*
(14) Imperial Airways, Rochester	5	15	*B'ham 500(32)*
(15) Croydon Airport Terminal, BF 2162 PS	5	8	*RFDC 63*
(16) National Postal Museum (AirMail routes)	5	-	*n.o.c.*
(17) TGWU, SW1	5	20	*CoverCraft*
(18) Laser, 1973-1988, Hythe	8	10	*G&P*
(19) Illustrated by Andrew Davidson, Bromley	8	-	*n.o.c.*
(20) Designed by Carroll Dempsey & Thirkell, WC1	8	-	*n.o.c.*
(21) Lloyd's of London, EC3	8	10	*CoverCraft*
(22) 19th Century Post Box Discovery, Spilsby	8	15	*Spilsby C of T*
(23) Transams By Technology, WC1	10	125	*Transams*
(24) W. Indian Tour, NW8	10	14	*S.P.*

C.D.S. POSTMARKS (inc. T.P.O. CANCELS)	
(25) Berkhamsted - first use of T.P.O. apparatus	7
(26) Central Stn., Edinburgh; or Nunthorpe Stn *each*	12
(27) Croydon or Purley - Croydon Airport *each*	30
(28) Clydebank - where 'Queen Elizabeth' was built	12
(29) Cricklewood, NW2 - Handley Page HP42 built here	7
(30) Doncaster - where 'Mallard' was built	7
(31) Essendine - where 'Mallard' broke the speed record	10
(32) Garden Festival - Glasgow's trams operated here	8
(33) Hong Kong BFPO 1 - RMS 'Queen Elizabeth'	80
(34) Mosspark, Glasgow - tram destination (31p)	10
(35) Southampton - home port of 'Queen Elizabeth'	8
(36) Springburn, Glasgow - first tram route	8
(37) Tiverton - where HP42 ended its days	8
(38) York - home of 'Mallard'	8
(39) Crewe-Peterborough TPO - 'Mallard's' record	15
(40) Up or Down Special, or N.W. Night Down TPOs - the first TPOs *each*	15
(41) London-York-Edin: N.E. Night Up or Down TPOs - route of 'Mallard' *each*	15
(42) Any other TPO postmark	12

In addition: Crich, Forton Services, Heathrow Airport, Hope St., New York, Queen Elizabeth Ave. Prices from £6.

SLOGAN POSTMARKS	
(43) Only Fools Play on Railway Lines	20
(44) Paisley 500 (Paisley's last tram No. 146)	20
(45) Royal Mail Supports Glasgow Garden Festival	20
(46) Grampians - Going Places - Aberdeen	30
(47) West Midlands 100 Great Days Out - Shropshire	35

In addition: Postcode your Property; Tobormory. Prices from £15.

(2)

(1)

(16)

(19)

(17)

(23)

(9)

(4)

(7)

(11)

(10)

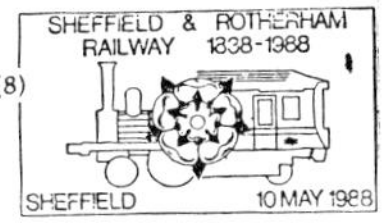

(8)

(14)

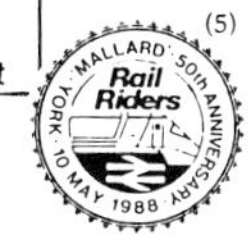

(5)

21st June 1988 - AUSTRALIAN BICENTENARY (Double Postmarked Covers)

This issue was the first 'joint issue' involving the British Post Office. Arrangements were made for British collectors to send their British first day covers to Australia where the Australia stamps were affixed and cancelled on 21st June 1988. The prices below are in respect of covers with the FULL SET of both British and Australian stamps affixed.

(1) Any British handstamp + Australian handstamp	35
(2) Any British C.D.S. + Australian handstamp	40
(3) Any other covers	25

PRICES & CONDITION - PLEASE READ GENERAL NOTES

21st June 1988 - AUSTRALIAN BICENTENARY

18p Historical - Early Settler and Clipper Ship;
18p Constitutional - HM The Queen and Parliament Buildings;
34p The Arts - John Lennon, Shakespeare, Sydney Opera House;
34p Sports - W.G. Grace and Tennis.

SPECIAL HANDSTAMPS	ordinary covers £	official covers £	
(1) First Day of Issue - Philatelic Bureau	3	-	*Royal Mail*
(2) First Day of Issue - Portsmouth	3	-	*Royal Mail*
(3) Bicentenary of Australia, SW1	5	12	*LFDC 69*
(4) Australian Bicentenary, Portsmouth	5	30	*Benham S.G.5*
(5) Capt. James Cook Museum, Marton-in-Cleveland	5	9	*S. Muscroft*
(6) Links with Australia, Amy Johnson, Hull	5	40	*Bradbury*
(7) GB Cricketing Links, Old Trafford	5	30	*S.P.*
(8) GB Cricketing Links, Edgbaston	5	30	*S.P.*
(9) GB Cricketing Links, Trent Bridge	5	30	*S.P.*
(10) GB Cricketing Links, The Oval, SE11	5	30	*S.P.*
(11) GB Cricketing Links, Headingley	5	30	*S.P.*
(12) GB Cricketing Links, Lords	5	30	*S.P.*
(13) Wedgwood, Australian Bicentenary, Barlaston	5	20	*Arlington*
(14) Botany Bay, Enfield	5	15	*B'ham (500)33*
(15) Bombardment of Bardia, BF 2178 PS	8	15	*FAA Museum*
(16) Australian Bicentennial, EC	7	12	*CoverCraft*
(17) Lawn Tennis Museum, SW19	9	15	*H.R.*
(18) Railways and the Post, Postal Museum, EC1	10	-	*n.o.c.*
(19) Thames Barrier Visitors Centre, SE18	10	15	*CoverCraft*
(20) W. Indian Tour, NW8	10	12	*S.P.*
(21) R.A.F. Cottesmore, TTT3, BF 2177 PS	10	12	*RFDC 64*

C.D.S. POSTMARKS	
(22) Bathampton - Capt. Phillip (first Gov. of NSW)	7
(23) Botany Bay	15
(24) Downend - birthplace of W.G. Grace	8
(25) Hambledon - birthplace of English Cricket	8
(26) House of Commons, SW1	20
(27) House of Lords, SW1	35
(28) Penny Lane, Liverpool - famous Beatles' record	10
(29) Portsmouth - from where the First Fleet sailed	6
(30) Ryde, Isle of Wight - First Fleet gathered here	6
(31) Stratford-upon-Avon - William Shakespeare	6
(32) Whitby - Home of Captain James Cook	6
(33) Windsor	6

In addition: Buckingham Palace, Croydon, Headingley, Kennington Park, Marton-in-Cleveland, Melbourne, Queen Elizabeth Ave., St. Bravels, Sydney Road, Wimbledon. Prices from £5.

SLOGAN POSTMARKS	
(34) 1588-1788-1988 Tobormory 200, Oban	175

In addition: Royal Mail/Glasgow G.F.; Ullapool Bicentenary. Prices from £15.

(3)

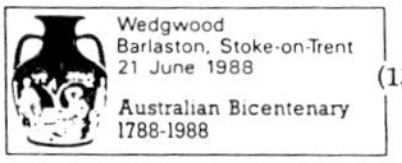

(13)

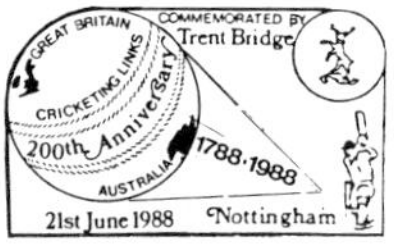

(9)

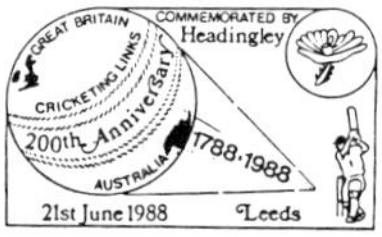

(11)

(5)

(6)

(28)

(34)

19th July 1988 - THE ARMADA 1588

5 x 18p stamps show the progress of the Armada, viz:
The Lizard; Plymouth; Isle of Wight; Calais; and North Sea.

SPECIAL HANDSTAMPS			
(1) First Day of Issue - Philatelic Bureau	3	-	*Royal Mail*
(2) First Day of Issue - Plymouth	3	-	*Royal Mail*
(3) Royal Naval College, SE10	6	20	*CoverCraft*
(4) Spanish Armada, Tilbury (Elizabeth I on horse)	6	15	*Benham S.G. 6*
(5) Spanish Armada, Effingham	6	15	*B'ham (500)34*
(6) Sighting of Armada, BF 2179 PS	6	9	*RFDC 65*
(7) Armada 400 Plymouth (circular)	6	9	*PlyPhilSoc*
(8) Armada 400 Years, Plymouth (rectangular)	8	-	*n.o.c.*
(9) Armada Anniversary, Tavistock	6	15	*TavBookShop*
(10) First Armada 400 Beacon, The Lizard	6	20	*Benham L19*
(11) Armada 400, Battle of Gravelines, Dover	6	7	*BLCS 34*
(12) Spanish Armada, Tilbury (Tudor Rose)	6	15	*LFDC 70*
(13) John Hurleston, Mariner, Chester	6	10	*Havering*
(14) Royal Tournament, BF 2181 PS	8	15	*Forces*
(15) Scout Camp, Blair Atholl, Pitlochry	6	12	*Scouts*
(16) 'K' Blackburn	8	15	*Kelloggs*
(17) Merriott Mouldings Ltd	8	15	*Cotswold*
(18) W. Indian Tour, NW8	10	7	*S.P.*
(19) Thames Barrier Visitors Centre, SE18	8	40	*CoverCraft*
(20) Railways and the Post, Postal Museum	10	-	*n.o.c.*

(3)

(4)

(13)

(9)

(14)

(17)

The Armada (contd.)

	ordinary covers £	official covers £
C.D.S. POSTMARKS		
(21) Altofts – birthplace of Sir Martin Frobisher	8	
(22) Buckland Monachorum – home of Drake	25	
(23) Calais or Dover + PAQUEBOT markings *each*	25	
(24) Drake, Plymouth	175	
(25) Effingham – b/place of Lord Howard of Effingham	10	
(26) Greenwich – b/place of Queen Elizabeth I	10	
(27) Maritime Mail I.S. London	100	
(28) Paquebot, London	50	
(29) Portland, Southwell, or Bonchurch – battle sites	10	
(30) Plymouth	15	
(31) Sandwich – prepared to meet invasion on beaches	10	
(32) Santander PAQUEBOT	60	
(33) St. Mary's, Isle of Scilly – first sighting	10	
(34) Tavistock – birthplace of Sir Francis Drake	10	
(35) The Lizard and Berwick – first and last beacons ...*each*	12	
(36) Tilbury – where Elizabeth rallied her troops	10	
(37) Tobomory, Hope and Fair Isle – wreck sites *each*	20	
(38) West Hoe, Plymouth	20	

In addition: Beacon, Drakes Broughton, House of Commons, House of Lords. Prices from £6.

SLOGAN POSTMARKS

(39) 400th Anniv. of Spanish Armada	50	
(40) Tobomory 200, 1588-1788-1988	275	

In addition: Isle of Skye; Royal Mail Letters Supports G.G.F. Prices from £25.

6th September 1988 – EDWARD LEAR – VERSE FOR CHILDREN

19p 'The Owl and the Pussycat'; 27p Pen Sketch; 32p Alphabet 'C'; 35p Rhyme

SPECIAL HANDSTAMPS

(1) First Day of Issue – Philatelic Bureau	4	–	*Royal Mail*
(2) First Day of Issue – London N7	4	–	*Royal Mail*
(3) Edward Lear, Foss Rampant, Learmouth	6	12	*B'ham (500)35*
(4) Edward Lear Centenary, Knowsley	6	8	*LFDC 71*
(5) Hull Schools Reorganization	7	7	*Hull Schools*
(6) Birthplace of Edward Lear, Holloway, N7	6	6	*BLCS 35*
(7) Designed by the Partners, Edward Lear, EC1	6	–	*n.o.c.*
(8) Knowsley, from Menagerie to Safari Park	6	12	*CoverCraft*
(9) Coeliac Symposium, St. Batholomew's, EC1	9	30	*St. Barts*
(10) Railways and the Post, Postal Museum	9	–	*Royal Mail*
(11) Farnborough International, BF 2173 PS	9	12	*RFDC 66*
(12) 'K' Blackburn, Lancs	9	–	*n.o.c.*

C.D.S. POSTMARKS

(13) Camden Town, or Theobald's Rd. – homes of Lear	10
(14) Chester, Gretna, Portree, Ryde – Lear's rhymes	10
(15) Holloway, N7 – birthplace of Lear	10
(16) Knowsley – where Lear wrote his nonsense verse	10
(17) Regents Park Rd. etc – Lear drew birds and animals at the Zoological Gardens	12

In addition: Catsfield, Catshill, Derry Hill, East Cowes, Foss Mount, Freshwater, Luimneach, Owlsmoor, Petworth, Victoria Street, Winchelsea. Prices from £5.

SLOGAN POSTMARKS

Visit Isle of Skye; Brighton Guide; Guide Dog Week; Tobomory. Prices from £15.

(1)

(2)

(12)

(39)

(15)

(1)

(3)

(5)

(4)

(2)

(9)

(7)

(11)

GENERAL NOTES

The General Notes at the beginning of this catalogue includes examples and descriptions of all covers and postmarks.

COVERS: ORDINARY and OFFICIALS

Do you know in which year the Post Office first started issuing their own first day covers?

POSTMARKS: SPECIAL HANDSTAMPS, CDS and SLOGANS

Do you know why the House of Commons and Lords CDS postmarks are included under some issues and not others?

27th September 1988 - EDWARD LEAR - VERSE FOR CHILDREN

Miniature Sheet

SPECIAL HANDSTAMPS	ordinary covers £	official covers £	
(1) First Day of Issue - Philatelic Bureau	5	-	*Royal Mail*
(2) First Day of Issue - London, N22	5	-	*Royal Mail*
(3) Edward Lear, Foss Rampant, Learmouth	7	12	*BLCS 36*
(4) Edward Lear Centenary, Knowsley	7	10	*LFDC 72*
(5) Edward Lear Centenary, Stampex, SW	7	12	*BLCS 36*
(6) Birthplace of Edward Lear, Holloway, N7	7	12	*B'ham (500)36*
(7) Stampway to the World, Liverpool	10	-	*n.o.c.*
(8) Autumn Stampex/BPE, SW1	9	12	*Stampex*
(9) Royal Mail Exhibition Card, Stampex/BPE	9	-	*Royal Mail*
(10) Cancer & Leukaemia, BF 2182 PS	9	10	*RFDC 67*
(11) Railways and the Post, Postal Museum	9	-	*Post Office*
(12) 150 Wolverton, Milton Keynes	9	-	*n.o.c.*
(13) 'K' Blackburn, Lancs	9	-	*n.o.c.*
(14) HMS Leamington, BF 2189 PS	9	12	*FAA Museum*
(15) RMS Queen Elizabeth, Clydebank	9	20	*Clydebank*
(16) Royal Academy of Arts, Henry Moore, W1	9	15	*Pilgrim*

C.D.S. POSTMARKS

(17) Alexandra Park Rd, N10 - 'Stamp World 1990'		10
(18) Chester, Gretna, Portree, Ryde - Lear's rhymes		10
(19) Holloway, N7 - birthplace of Lear		10
(20) Knowsley - where Lear wrote his nonsense verse		10
(21) Park Rd. and Regent's Park - Lear drew birds and animals at the Zoological Gardens	*each*	12
(22) Portman Square - home of Lear		10

In addition: Catsfield, Catshill, Derry Hill, East Cowes, Foss Mount, Freshwater, Luimneach, Owlsmoor, Petworth, Victoria St., Winchelsea. Prices from £5.

SLOGAN POSTMARKS

(23) Autumn Stampex/BPE	20
(24) Great Ormonde St. Candle	15
(25) Philatelic Bulletin 25th Anniversary	25

In addition: Isle of Skye; Brighton Guide; Guide Dog Week. Prices from £12.

Some double-dated covers exist with the set of stamps postmarked 6th September and the miniature sheet postmarked 27th September. Prices from £35.

(5)

(9)

(10)

(6)

(8)

(12)

(24)

15th November 1988 - CHRISTMAS

14p, 19p, 27p, 32p, 35p Christmas Cards

SPECIAL HANDSTAMPS			
(1) First Day of Issue - Philatelic Bureau	4	-	*Royal Mail*
(2) First Day of Issue - Bethlehem, Llandeilo	4	-	*Royal Mail*
(3) St. Alban The Martyr, Northampton	5	10	*Ch. of St. A.*
(4) Guinea Pig Club, BF 2184 PS	5	6	*RFDC 67*
(5) York Minster Commemoration	5	15	*CoverCraft*
(6) Christmas Card Mailcoach Run, Box	5	7	*BLCS 37*
(7) Christmas Card Mailcoach Run, Luton	5	10	*BLCS 37*
(8) Christmas Card Mailcoach Run, Bath	5	12	*BLCS 37*
(9) Victorian Christmas Cards Postling, Hythe	5	10	*B'ham (500)37*
(10) Saint Dunstan Millennium, Canterbury	7	8	*LFDC 73*
(11) Cartmel Priory, Grange, Cumbria	8	10	*Bradbury*
(12) Telecom Technology Showcase, EC4	10	-	*n.o.c.*
(13) Scanner, HRH Princess Margaret, Romford	9	10	*OldchurchHosp*
(14) Royle, Royle, Royle, N1	8	75	*Arlington*
(15) Stampway to the World, Liverpool	9	-	*n.o.c.*
(16) Royal Academy of Arts, Henry Moore, W1	9	9	*Pilgrim*
(17) The Green Howards, BF 2183 PS	9	35	*Forces*
(18) Railways and the Post, Postal Museum	9	-	*Royal Mail*
(19) Holmfirth Postcard Museum	15	-	*n.o.c.*

C.D.S. POSTMARKS

(20) Kensington Ch. St. - first Xmas card designed here	10
(21) Nasareth, Gwynedd	10

In addition: Angel Hill, Bath, Holy Island, Lancelot Place SW7, Noel Road W3, St. Nicholas, Shepherds Bush W12, Shepherds Hill, Star. Prices from £5.

SLOGAN POSTMARKS

(22) Washington Apples, Bigger Christmas Crunch	20

In addition: Stampway; BBC Children in Need. Prices from £15.

(1)

(2)
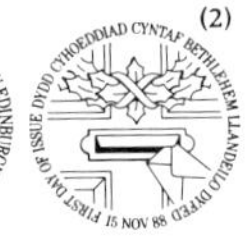

(7)

(8)

(6)

(15)

(4)
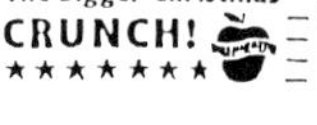
(22)

1989

17th January 1989 – SEA BIRDS

19p Puffin; 27p Avocet; 32p Oyster Catcher; 35p Gannet

SPECIAL HANDSTAMPS

	ordinary covers £	official covers £	
(1) First Day of Issue – Philatelic Bureau	4	–	*Royal Mail*
(2) First Day of Issue – Sandy, Bedfordshire	4	–	*Royal Mail*
(3) Famous Gannet Colony, Bass Rock	5	10	*Benham S.G.8*
(4) Leics. & Rutland Ornithological Society	5	15	*LFDC 74*
(5) Lundy Island, Bideford	5	40	*Lundy P.B.*
(6) British Sea Birds, Dungeness	5	10	*B'ham (500)38*
(7) St. Kilda – Puffin Colony	5	12	*BLCS 38*
(8) RSPB, Action for Birds, Sandy.	5	15	*CoverCraft*
(9) No. 201 Squadron, BF 2193 PS	8	12	*RFDC 69*
(10) HMS Quorn, BF 2194 PS	8	15	*FAA Museum*
(11) Italian Art in the 20th Century, WI	8	12	*Pilgrim*

C.D.S. POSTMARKS

(12) Balivanich, Bempton, Papa Westray or Rathlin Is. – Puffin colonies *each*	12
(13) Didsbury Village – RSPB founded here	9
(14) Fair Isle or Ness – Gannet colonies *each*	15
(15) Orford – near to Minsmere (Avocet)	9
(16) Sandy – RSPB	12
(17) Slimbridge – Wildfowl Trust	10
(18) Snettisham or Westleton – Oystercatcher *each*	10
(19) Tring – British Trust for Ornithology	35

In addition: Bideford, Birdsedge, Heron Cross, Kinlochleven, Redhill, Swallow's Nest, Wren's Nest. Prices from £6.

SLOGAN POSTMARK

Visit the Isle of Skye. Prices from £25.

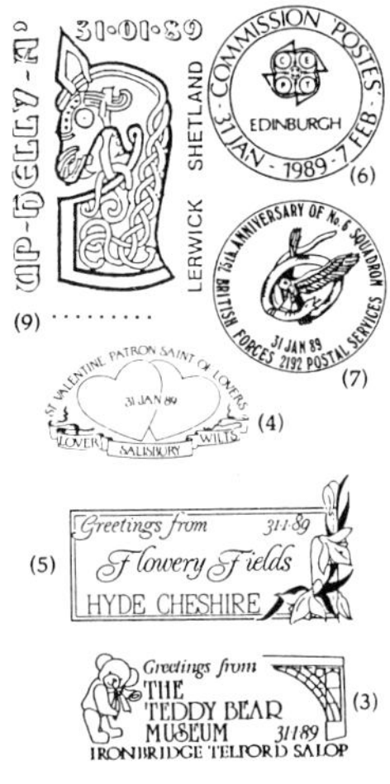

31st January 1989 – GREETING STAMPS

5 x 19p: rose, cupid, sailing boat, bowl of fruit and teddy bear.

SPECIAL HANDSTAMPS

(1) First Day of Issue – Philatelic Bureau	8	–	*Royal Mail*
(2) First Day of Issue – Lover, Salisbury	8	–	*Royal Mail*
(3) Teddy Bear Museum, Ironbridge	10	12	*BLCS 39*
(4) St. Valentine's, Lover	10	12	*B'ham (500)39*
(5) Flowery Field, Hyde	10	12	*BLCS 39*
(6) Commission 'Postes' CEPT, Edinburgh	15	–	*n.o.c.*
(7) No. 6 Squadron, BF 2192 PS	15	20	*RDFC 70*
(8) Italian Art in 20th Century, W1	12	15	*Pilgrim*
(9) Up-Helly-A, Lerwick	12	25	*UpHellyA*
(10) Wish you were here, Holmfirth Postcard Museum	15	–	*n.o.c.*

C.D.S. POSTMARKS

(11) Bearpark, Cowes, Flowery Field, Greet, Greetland, Gretna Green, Kew Gardens, Lover, Orchard, Pudsey, Rose, Rosehearty, Seaside, or Strawberry Hill *each*	17

SLOGAN POSTMARK

Burns, Dumfries; Visit the Isle of Skye. Prices from £20.

***N.B.** Prices quoted above are for covers with a strip of five stamps. These stamps were issued in booklets of ten stamps, i.e. two strips of the same five designs. Covers with the complete pane of ten stamps command a £2/£4 premium.*

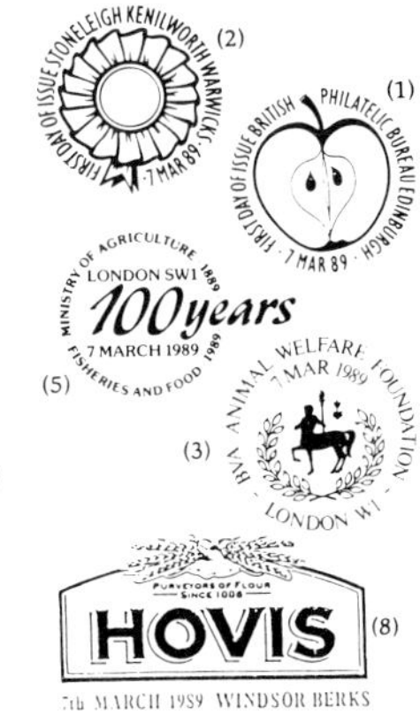

7th March 1989 – FOOD & FARMING YEAR

19p Fruit and vegetables; 27p Meat and Fish produce; 32p Dairy produce; 35p Cereal produce

SPECIAL HANDSTAMPS

(1) First Day of Issue – Philatelic Bureau	4	–	*Royal Mail*
(2) First Day of Issue – Kenilworth	4	–	*Royal Mail*
(3) BVA Animal Welfare Foundation, W1	5	10	*LFDC 75*
(4) British Food & Farming, Isle of Grain	5	10	*B'ham (500) 40*
(5) Min. of Agriculture, Fisheries and Food, SW1	5	15	*CoverCraft*
(6) Women's Land Army, BF 2195 PS	5	8	*RFDC 71*
(7) Royal Agricultural Soc., Stoneleigh	5	7	*BLCS 40*
(8) Purveyors of Flour, Hovis, Windsor	5	2	*Arlington(s)*
(9) Italian Art 20th Century, W1	10	15	*Pilgrim*
(9a) Taunton tourist h/s (features apple)	20	–	*n.o.c.*

Food and Farming (contd.)

	ordinary covers	official covers	
C.D.S. POSTMARKS	£	£	
(10) Any Farm Post Offices	20		
(11) Cheddar, Stilton or Wensley *each*	15		
(12) Corn Exchange or Market Place *each*	10		
(13) Farmers, Dyfed	12		
(14) Ham or Melton Mowbray – pork pies *each*	10		
(15) Isle of Grain, Rochester	10		
(16) Leek or Bramley *each*	10		
(17) Ivymeade, High Wycombe – shopping centre P.O.	20		
(18) Savacentre – Supermarket Post Office	40		
(19) Stoneleigh – Royal Show	15		
(20) Tile Farm, Orpington	15		

In addition: The Allotments, Bakers Lane, Bakewell, Butterton, Evesham, The Orchard, Wheatley, Prices from £8.

SLOGAN POSTMARKS

(21) 'Collect British Stamps' – Bradford (sheep's head) 25

In addition: York Collect British Stamps; Wild about Worcestershire; Hooked on Herefordshire; County Councils; Industry Matters. Prices from £12.

11th April 1989 – ANNIVERSARIES

19p Public Education (150th Anniversary);
19p European Parliament (3rd Direct Elections);
35p Postal Telegraph & Telephones Congress;
35p Inter-Parliamentary Union Centenary Conference

SPECIAL HANDSTAMPS			
(1) First Day of Issue – Philatelic Bureau	4	–	*Royal Mail*
(2) First Day of Issue – SW London	4	–	*Royal Mail*
(3) Strasbourg – Leicester's Twin City	5	10	*LFDC 76*
(4) 26th World Congress PTTI, W1	5	15	*B'ham (500)41*
(5) Inter Parliamentary Union, SW1	5	10	*BLCS 41*
(6) Direct Elections, Downing St.	5	10	*BLCS 41*
(7) Operation Sunfish, S.E.A.C., BF 2202 PS	5	20	*FAA Museum*
(8) RAFLET, BF 2179 PS	7	10	*RFDC 72*
(9) Centenary Derbyshire County Council, Matlock	7	35	*DerbysCC*
(10) Stampway to the World, Manchester	8	15	*S.P.Board*
(11) Weston Favell School, Northampton	8	15	*WFUS*
(12) Evesham Corps, Centenary Blood & Fire	8	12	*H.R.*
C.D.S. POSTMARKS			
(13) Brighton – PTTI Conference	10		
(14) Brighton Centre, Brighton – PTTI Conference	50		
(15) Broadway, SW1 – site of IPU Congress	7		
(16) Dover or Calais with PAQUEBOT markings *each*	15		
(17) Hope Street, Edin. – b/place Alexander Graham Bell	7		
(18) House of Commons, SW1	20		
(19) House of Lords, SW1	30		
(20) Mark Cross, Crowborough	20		
(21) Northern Parliament, Belfast	15		
(22) Duke of York's School or Royal Hospital School	15		
(23) Telephone House, Birmingham	10		
(24) Temple Hill, Dartford – Unwin Pyrotechnics	6		
(25) Heathrow – main UK airport serving Europe	30		
(26) University pmks: Bath, Bradford, Essex, Lancaster, Liverpool, Norwich and Swansea *each*	10		

In addition: Clapham Common, College Rd, Eton, Fareham, Grange Hill, Harwich, Regent St, Rochdale, Scholar Green, Sussex Coast, World's End. Prices from £7 each.

SLOGAN POSTMARKS	
(27) University of Durham, Dept. of Geography	20
(28) Mailing and Communications Show, London EC1	20
(29) Liverpool Mechanised Office – use postcodes	20
(30) Remember to use the Postcode – Ipswich	15
(31) Edinburgh Festival of Science & Technology	20
(32) NATO Fortieth Anniversary	60

In addition: Lead Free; Derbyshire C.C.; Inverness Conference Capital; BBC Wilts Sound; Stampway. Prices from £14.

PRICES & CONDITION
Values should be taken as a guide, and are for covers in good clean condition with the full set of stamps

(7)

(4)

(1)

(2)

(6)

(5)

(3)

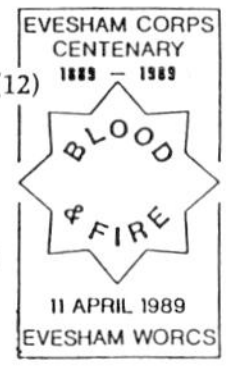

(12)

(4)

(27)

(28)

(17)

(23)

(32)

16th May 1989 – GAMES AND TOYS

19p train and plane; 27p building blocks; 32p board games; 35p boat, robot and doll's house

SPECIAL HANDSTAMPS	ordinary covers £	official covers £	
(1) First Day of Issue – Philatelic Bureau	4	–	*Royal Mail*
(2) First Day of Issue – Leeds	4	–	*Royal Mail*
(3) Putting Children First, NSPCC, EC	5	5	*CoverCraft*
(4) Lewis Carrol, 1832-1898, Oxford	5	15	*Zanders*
(5) The Teddybears' Picnic, Ironbridge	5	12	*BLCS 42*
(6) Pollock's Toy Museum, W1	5	10	*LFDC 77*
(7) Toys Hill, Westerham	5	10	*B'ham(500)42*
(8) Stampway to the World, Manchester	6	15	*S.P.Board*
(9) Postal Museum, Uniform Exhibition, EC	7	–	*n.o.c.*
(10) Rotary Diamond Charter, Newcastle	8	15	*Rotary*
(11) Guisborough Priory	8	10	*S. Muscroft*
(12) Royal Naval Air Service, BF 2200 PS	8	12	*RFDC 73*
(13) RNLI Gallantry Awards, SE1	8	10	*Pilgrim*
(14) History of the Royal Navy, Plymouth	8	–	*n.o.c.*
C.D.S. POSTMARKS			
(15) Fforestfach, Swansea – 'Corgi' toys	10		
(16) Hornby or Waddington *each*	12		
(17) Mount Pleasant, Liverpool – b/place Frank Hornby	8		
(18) Old Swan, Liverpool – 'Hornby' factory	12		
(19) Playing Place, Truro	12		
(20) Regent St., W1 – Hamley's Toy Shop	8		
(21) Any TPO postmark	10		
(22) Woodlesford or Rothwell – Waddington Games	8		

In addition: Bathampton, Bethnal Green, Bowling, Bunny, Butlin's Holiday Camp, Child's Hill, Ironbridge, Kirton, Market, Mulberry Parade, Paddington. Prices from £4

SLOGAN POSTMARKS		
(23) 'Chess board' – Bradford	60	
(24) Save the Children Week	40	

In addition: Medway & Swale Child Safety; 40 Years Council of Europe; Lead Free; Spotless; Robin Hood; Train slogans; The Archers. Prices from £12.

4th July 1989 – INDUSTRIAL ARCHAEOLOGY

19p Ironbridge; 27p Tin mine, St. Agnes; 32p New Lanark Mills; 35p Pontcysyllte Aqueduct

SPECIAL HANDSTAMPS	ordinary covers £	official covers £	
(1) First Day of Issue – Philatelic Bureau	4	–	*Royal Mail*
(2) First Day of Issue – Telford	4	–	*Royal Mail*
(3) Isambard Kingdom Brunel, Bristol	5	20	*Zanders*
(4) Water Powered Mills at New Lanark	5	10	*B'ham (500)43*
(5) Pontcysyllte Aqueduct, Llangollen	5	10	*Benham L21*
(6) New Lanark Conservation	5	10	*LFDC 78*
(7) Our Industrial Heritage, St. Agnes	5	10	*BLCS 43*
(8) Birthplace of British Industry, Ironbridge	5	10	*BLCS 43*
(9) Aberdulais Falls, W. Glam	5	6	*CoverCraft*
(10) Penfold Box Waterways Museum, Gloucester	5	–	*n.o.c.*
(11) Philatelic Counter, Bolton ('Spinning Mule')	12	–	*n.o.c.*
(12) Philatelic Counter, Bradford (industiral mills)	12	–	*n.o.c.*
(13) Yorkshire Museum, York	7	–	*n.o.c.*
(14) Killiecrankie, National Trust Scotland	8	–	*n.o.c.*
(15) Trenchard-Keyes Agreement, BF 2208 PS	9	20	*FAA Museum*
(16) Lawn Tennis Museum	9	12	*H.R.*
(17) The Royal Show, Stoneleigh	9	–	*n.o.c.*
(18) No. 72 Squadron, BF 2201 PS	9	10	*RFDC 74*
C.D.S. POSTMARKS			
(19) Froncysyllte or Trevor – Pontcysyllte aqueduct *each*	10		
(20) Ironbridge (19p)	12		
(21) Langholm – birthplace of Thomas Telford	10		
(22) New Lanark (32p)	12		
(23) St. Agnes (27p)	12		

In addition: Arkwright Town, Bolton, Camborne, Chirk, Highway, Illogen, Liverton Mines, Newtown, Preston, Saltaire, Shrewsbury, Stewarton. Prices from £5.

PRICES & CONDITION – PLEASE READ GENERAL NOTES

Industrial Archaeology (contd.)

	ordinary covers	official covers	
SLOGAN POSTMARKS	£	£	
(24) Aveling Barford - The Earthmovers	20		
(25) Collect British Stamps - Bradford (industrial mills)	25		

In addition: Marine Engineers; Teesside Talent Ability; Richmond Festival; Post Code; Post Early; York, the Distinct Advantage. Prices from £10.

25th July 1989 - INDUSTRIAL ARCHAEOLOGY

Miniature Sheet

SPECIAL HANDSTAMPS

(1) First Day of Issue - Philatelic Bureau	4	-	*Royal Mail*
(2) First Day of Issue - New Lanark	4	-	*Royal Mail*
(3) Water Powered Mills at New Lanark	5	8	*Benham L22*
(4) Pontcysyllte Aqueduct, Llangollen	5	25	*B'ham (500)44*
(5) Assoc'n for Industrial Archaeology, Ironbridge	5	10	*LFDC 79*
(6) Our Industrial Heritage, Redruth	5	15	*BLCS 44*
(7) Birthplace of British Industry, Ironbridge	5	15	*BLCS 44*
(8) National Postal Museum, SWL90, EC	7	-	*n.o.c.*
(9) Killiecrankie, National Trust Scotland	7	15	*Scot.N.T.*
(10) International Scout Camp, Gosford	7	20	*Scouts*
(11) Aircraft Archaeology, BF 1968 PS	9	12	*RFDC 75*
(12) Royal Tournament, BF 2198 PS	9	12	*Forces*
(13) Philatelic Counter, Bolton ('Spinning Mule')	15	-	*n.o.c.*
(14) Philatelic Counter, Bradford (industrial mills)	15	-	*n.o.c.*

C.D.S. POSTMARKS

(15) Froncysyllte or Trevor - Pontcysyllte aqueduct	12
(16) Ironbridge (19p)	15
(17) Langholm - birthplace of Thomas Telford	8
(18) New Lanark (32p)	15
(19) St. Agnes (27p)	15

In addition: Alexandra Park Road, Arkwright Town, Camborne, Chirk, Illogen, Liverton Mines, Muswell Hill, Newtown, Preston, Saltaire, Shrewsbury, Stewarton. Prices from £7.

SLOGAN POSTMARKS

(20) Aveling Barford - The Earthmovers	25
(21) Collect British Stamps - Bradford (industrial mills)	20

In addition: Marine Engineers; Teesside Talent Ability; Please Post Early; Post Code. Prices from £10.

Some double-dated covers exist with both the sets of stamps postmarked 4th July and the miniature sheet postmarked 25th July. Prices range from £25.

5thSeptember 1989 - MICROSCOPES

19p Snowflake; 27p Blue Fly; 32p Blood Cells; 35p Microchip

SPECIAL HANDSTAMPS

(1) First Day of Issue - Philatelic Bureau	4	-	*Royal Mail*
(2) First Day of Issue - Oxford	4	-	*Royal Mail*
(3) Royal Microscopical Society, Oxford	5	20	*Bradbury*
(4) Royal Microscopical Society 1839-1989 Oxford	5	20	*Bradbury*
(5) Cambridge Instruments	5	30	*Bradbury*
(6) 1989 The Year of the Microscope, SW7	5	12	*LFDC 80*
(7) 1989 The Year of Microscope Exh. Science Museum	5	10	*BLCS 45*
(8) Year of the Microscope, Cambridge	5	10	*B'ham (500)45*
(9) Marconi Electronic Devices, Lincoln	5	7	*Cotswold*
(10) Dr. Robert Hooke, Freshwater	5	20	*B'ham (Zanders)*
(11) IMLS Conference, Warwick University	7	14	*H.R.*
(12) Stampway to the World, Newcastle	7	15	*S.P. Board*
(13) UK North Sea Oil, Aberdeen	7	30	*Arlington*
(14) Jeol (UK), NW9	7	35	*Arlington*
(15) Dormeuil, The World's Best Cloths, SW1	10	15	*Dormeuil*
(16) Battle of Britain, BF 2209 PS	10	12	*RFDC 65*
(17) Inter-Parliamentary Union Conf., SW1	9	9	*BLCS 41*

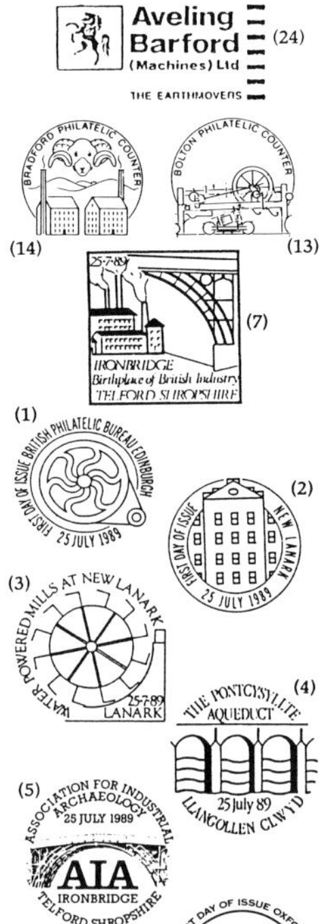

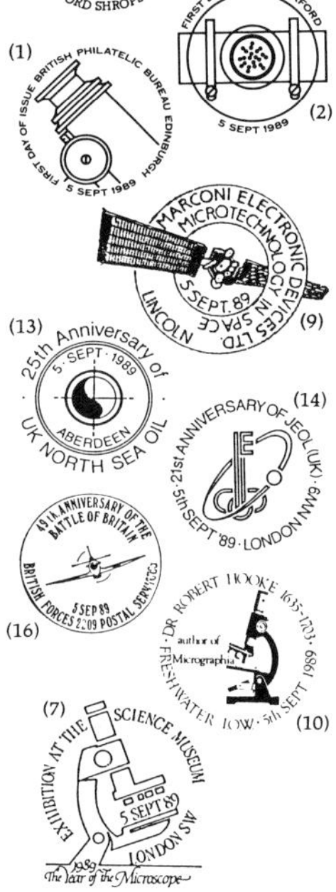

OFFICIAL COVERS OR ORDINARY COVERS
Do you know the difference?
Please read the General Notes at the beginning of this catalogue for guidance.

Royal Microscopical Society (contd.)

	ordinary covers £	official covers £	
C.D.S. POSTMARKS			
(18) Church, Freshwater – birthplace of Robert Hooke	25		
(19) Freshwater – Robert Hooke	10		
(20) Regent St., W1 – first meeting of Society	6		
(21) St. Clements, Oxford – Society HQ	7		
(22) South Kensington, SW7 – Science Museum	9		
(23) Whitechapel – first meeting of Society	8		

In addition: Alnwick, Holloway, Houndsditch, Lancaster, London Chief Office, Rotherhithe Lower Road, Royal Hospital School, Snowhill, Stoke Newington, Wollaston. Prices from £5.

SLOGAN POSTMARKS

(24) Army – 50 Years of Blood Transfusion	20		
(25) CARE '89	18		
(26) Europe Against Cancer Year 1989	20		

In addition: Europe's Universities; Royal Mail in the Community, Winchester; Collect British Stamps. Prices from £10.

17th October 1989 – THE LORD MAYOR'S SHOW

5 x 20p Scenes from the procession

SPECIAL HANDSTAMPS

(1) First Day of Issue – Philatelic Bureau	4		*Royal Mail*
(2) First Day of Issue – London EC4	4		*Royal Mail*
(3) Richard Whittington's Birthplace, Pauntley	5	40	*Bradbury*
(4) Dick Whittington, Thrice Lord Mayor, EC	5	10	*LFDC 81*
(5) Lord Mayor's Show, EC (trumpet)	5	12	*Benham S.G. 9*
(6) The Lord Mayor, City of London, EC (crest)	5	10	*BLCS 46*
(7) Exhibition at the Museum of London, EC	6	12	*B'ham (500) 46*
(8) Stampway to the World, Newcastle	6	10	*S.P.Board*
(9) Royal Mail Open Day, WC1	6	–	*n.o.c.*
(10) Royal Mail Exhibition Card 3, Stampex/BPE	6	–	*n.o.c.*
(11) Autumn Stampex/BPE, 1989, SW1	6	–	*n.o.c.*
(12) National Postal Museum, SWL90, EC	8	–	*n.o.c.*
(13) Berlin Airlift, BF 2210 PS	9	12	*RFDC 77*
(14) Sevastopol, BF 1782 PS	9	12	*FAA Museum*
(15) Town Hall Centenary, Middlesbrough	9	9	*S.Muscroft*
(16) Art of Photography, W1	9	12	*Pilgrim*

C.D.S. POSTMARKS

(17) Bovingdon – Hugh Bidwell (1989 Lord Mayor)	9		
(18) Fore St.; Lombard St.; Stock Exchange; Cannon St.; London Chief Office; Fleet St. – nearest Post Offices to scenes on the stamps	7		
(19) Ludgate Circus or Moorgate – on the route ... *each*	7		
(20) Newent or Redmarley – b/place of Dick Whittington	7		
(21) Wimbledon Park – Chris Collet (1988 Lord Mayor)	7		
(22) Whittington, Lichfield	12		

In addition: Richmond, Wickham. Prices from £5.

SLOGAN POSTMARKS

Autumn Stampex; Cancer; Stampway; Gloucester Cathedral; Any Royal Mail slogans; Robin Hood; Aveling Barford; Collect British Stamps. Prices from £15.

14th November 1989 – CHRISTMAS

Ely Cathedral

SPECIAL HANDSTAMPS

(1) First Day of Issue – Philatelic Bureau	4	–	*Royal Mail*
(2) First Day of Issue – Bethlehem, Llandeilo	4	–	*Royal Mail*
(3) First Day of Issue – Ely	4	–	*Royal Mail*
(4) 'Thomas' Invites you to Nene Valley	8	15	*N.V.Rly*
(5) Christmas 1989, Gloucester	6	12	*Bradbury*
(6) Telecom Technology Showcase, EC4	6	–	*n.o.c.*
(7) Christmas 1989, Ely, Cambs	6	12	*LFDC 82*
(8) Norman Nave, Ely Cathedral, (Mitre)	6	12	*B'ham (500)47*
(9) Norman Nave, Ely Cathedral, (3 Keys)	6	10	*BLCS 47*
(10) Mailcoach Run, Cambridge – Ely Cathedral	6	20	*BLCS 47*
(11) Christmas Greetings, HM Ships, BF 2214 PS	6	15	*FAA Museum*
(12) Whitby Abbey	9	10	*S.Muscroft*
(13) RAF Gliding Assoc'n., BF 2212 PS	10	10	*RFDC 78*
(14) Stampway to the World, Newcastle	10	15	*S.P.Board*
(15) Art of Photography 1839-1989, W1	10	15	*Pilgrim*

(11)

(26)

(24)
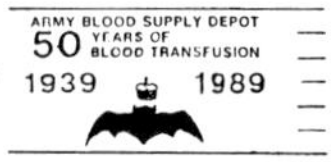

(11)

(3)

(7)

(6)

(9)

(15)

(8)

(1)

(2)

(5)

(11)

(6)

1989 Christmas (contd.)

C.D.S. POSTMARKS

	ordinary covers £	official covers £
(16) Barnack – Cathedral stone quarried from here	10	
(17) Ely, Cambs	12	
(18) Exning – B/place of Etheldreda, Cathedral Founder	10	
(19) Primrose Hill, Tonbridge – Charities Aid HQ	12	
(20) Stoke Charity	9	
(21) Walsingham – Alan de Walsingham, Ely architect	8	

In addition: Angel Hill, Canterbury, Holy Island, Nasareth, Northwold. Prices from £7.

SLOGAN POSTMARKS

(22) Gloucester Cathedral	20	
(23) Choose Charity Stamps	20	
(24) Luton Carol Aid '89	40	
(25) BBC Children in Need Appeal	16	

In addition: Unicef Cards; Beautiful Bath; Bath Royal Charter; Liverpool MLO; Collect British Stamps; Stampway. Prices from £10.

(13)

(12)

(17)
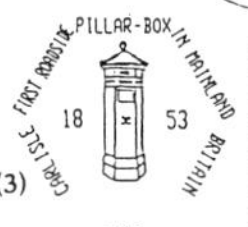
(3)

(12)

10th January 1990 – PENNY BLACK ANNIVERSARY

15p, 20p, 29p, 34p, 37p Queen Victoria & Queen Elizabeth II

SPECIAL HANDSTAMPS

(1) First Day of Issue – Philatelic Bureau	4	–	*Royal Mail*
(2) First Day of Issue – Windsor	4	–	*Royal Mail*
(3) First Roadside Pillar Box, Carlisle	10	35	*Carlisle P.O.*
(4) Postal Museum, 1840-1990, EC	7	–	*n.o.c.*
(5) Postal Museum, SWL90, Rowland Hill	7	–	*n.o.c.*
(6) Victorian Letterbox, Dean Heritage Museum	7	50	*CoverCraft*
(7) Uniform Penny Post, B.P.F., EC1	6	12	*CoverCraft*
(8) Uniform Penny Postage, Kidderminster	6	12	*CoverCraft*
(9) Sir Rowland Hill, Kidderminster	6	12	*LFDC 83*
(10) Perkins, Bacon & Co., Penny Black, Fleet St.	7	20	*Bradbury*
(11) 1840-1990 Uniform Penny Postage, SW1	8	20	*Bradbury*
(12) Etchingham Stamp Festival	9	35	*Et'ham P.C.*
(13) 150th Anniversaries, SG Plymouth	8	20	*BLCS 48*
(14) Windsor, Berks. (Maltese Cross)	8	20	*B'ham (500)48*
(15) Stampway to the World, Newcastle	10	35	*S.P.Board*

C.D.S. POSTMARKS

(16) Botchergate, Carlisle – first roadside postbox	30	
(16a) Buckingham Palace, SW1	50	
(17) Fleet Street – Perkins, Bacon (Penny Black)	15	
(18) House of Commons, SW1 – Postage Act	20	
(19) House of Lords, SW1 – Postage Act	30	
(20) Kidderminster – birthplace of Sir Rowland Hill	10	
(21) Sanquhar – oldest Post Office	15	
(22) Windsor, Berks.	25	
(23) Windsor Castle, Berks	75	

In addition: Arbroath, Bath, Birmingham, Holyrood, London Chief Office, Lordship Lane N17, Queen Elizabeth Avenue, Queensbury, Queen's Parade, Queen Victoria Rd, Scone, Seething Lane EC3, Stoke-on-Trent, Victoria Rd. Prices from £8.

SLOGAN POSTMARKS

(24) Collect British Stamps: Philatelic Counters	20	
(25) Collect British Stamps – World's Greatest Hobby	20	
(26) Be Properly Addressed, Postcode It	20	
(27) Pass on your Postcode	20	
(28) Get the Most From Your Post – Post Code It!	20	
(29) Remember to use the Postcode	20	
(30) Post Early in the Day	20	
(31) Liverpool is a Mechanised Letter Office	20	
(32) Senders Name & Address on the back of envelopes	20	
(33) Write Now! – Say it Better in a Letter	75	
(34) Stampway to the World – Newcastle	95	

Also available: Great Expectations; Beautiful Bath. Prices from £10.

(2)

(7)

(6)
(15)

(11)
(28)

(29)

23rd January 1990 – R.S.P.C.A.

20p Kitten; 29p Rabbit; 34p Duckling; 37p Puppy

SPECIAL HANDSTAMPS

(1) First Day of Issue – Philatelic Bureau	4	–	*Royal Mail*
(2) First Day of Issue – Horsham	4	–	*Royal Mail*
(3) Bunny, Nottingham	5	20	*Bradbury*
(4) Battersea, London SW8	5	15	*LFDC 84*

(1)

(2)

(5)

R.S.P.C.A. (contd.)

	ordinary covers £	official covers £	
(5) RSPCA, 150 Years, Horsham	5	15	*CoverCraft*
(6) RSPCA, Pett, Hastings	5	12	*B'ham (500)49*
(7) Cats Protection League, Middlesbrough	5	15	*S. Muscroft*
(8) Cat World Magazine, Shoreham	5	20	*BLCS 49*
(9) Provincial Grand Masters, Hadleigh	7	12	*Masons*
(10) Ekowe, Naval Brigade, BF 2215 PS	7	15	*FAAMuseum*
(11) No. 24 Squadron, BF 2216 PS	7	8	*RFDC 79*

C.D.S. POSTMARKS

(12) Battersea, or Battersea Park Road	*each*	10
(13) Bunny, Nottingham		12
(14) Dog & Gun, Dog Kennel Lane or Isle of Dogs	*each*	12
(15) Horsham – RSPCA headquarters		10
(16) Sidmouth – birthplace of founder of RSPCA		9
(17) Trafalgar Sq, WC2 – near to RSPCA's first meeting		9

In addition: Ballynahinch, Black Dog, Catfield, Catshill, Catsfield, Ducklington, Middlesbrough, Regent Street, SW1. Prices from £5.

SLOGAN POSTMARKS

(18) Collect British Stamps, Bradford (ram's head)	25
(19) Aveling Barford, the Earthmovers (horse)	70

Also: Collect British Stamps; Liverpool MLO; Write Now etc. Prices from £7.

6th February 1990 – GREETINGS STAMPS

10 x 20p Famous 'Smiles':
Teddy Bear; Dennis the Menace, Mr. Punch, Cheshire Cat, Man in the Moon, Laughing Policeman, Clown, Mona Lisa, Queen of Hearts, Stan Laurel.

SPECIAL HANDSTAMPS

(1) First Day of Issue – Philatelic Bureau	6	–	*Royal Mail*
(2) First Day of Issue – Giggleswick	8	–	*Royal Mail*
(3) Greetings, Clowne, Chesterfield	8	10	*Benham D135*
(4) Greetings, Puncheston, Haverfordwest	8	3	*Benham(s)*
(5) Greetings, The Teddy Bear Shop, Ironbridge	8	20	*B'ham (500)50 pair*
(6) Greetings, Hartford, Cheshire	8	25	*BLCS 50 pair*
(7) No.604 Squadron, BF 2217 PS	8	12	*RFDC 80*

C.D.S. POSTMARKS

(8) Bearpark, Catsfield, or Pudsey	*each*	15
(9) Bow St., Constable Rd., Constable Burton, or Law		15
(10) Fleet Street, EC4 – where 'Beano' is published		15
(11) Giggleswick		15
(12) Greet, Birmingham		15
(13) Oxford – Lewis Carrol wrote 'Alice in Wonderland'		15
(14) Ulverston – birthplace of Stan Laurel		15

Also: Colemore Circus, Greets Green, Big Top, Merry Hill, Laurel Lane, Puncheston, London E.C. Prices from £9.

SLOGAN POSTMARKS

(15) Take a Bite Out of Crime, Newcastle	30
(16) Collect British Stamps, Lincoln ('Lincoln Imp')	30

Also: Darlington Open Day; Stampex; Collect British Stamps. Prices from £15.

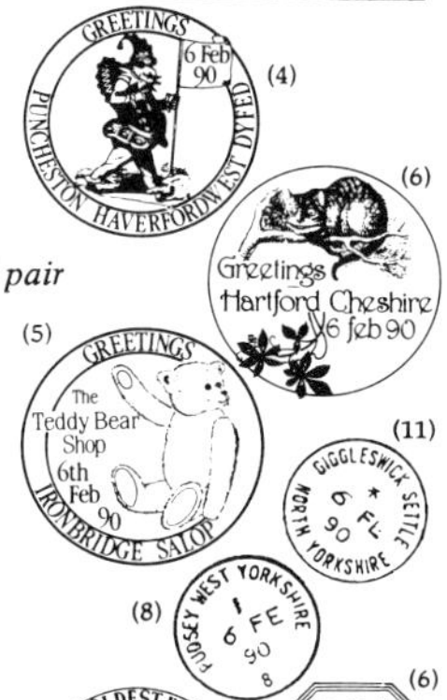

6th March 1990 – EUROPA

20p Alexandra Palace; 29p British Philatelic Bureau;
20p Glasgow School of Art; 37p Templeton Carpet Factory, Glasgow

SPECIAL HANDSTAMPS

(1) First Day of Issue – Philatelic Bureau	4	–	*Royal Mail*
(2) First Day of Issue – Glasgow	4	–	*Royal Mail*
(3) Cultural Capital, Glasgow	5	12	*Arlington*
(4) Europa, Stamp World, N22	5	10	*BLCS 51*
(5) Modern Movement Blg. in Europe, Glasgow	5	10	*B'ham (500)51*
(6) British Philatelic Bureau, Edinburgh	5	3	*Bureau (s)*
(7) 1st Int. Stamp Exhibition, BPF, N22	5	8	*BPF*
(8) Alexandra Palace, Victorian Heritage, N22	5	8	*CoverCraft*
(9) Europa 1990, Edinburgh	5	8	*LFDC 85*
(10) Alexandra Palace, Europa 1990, N22	5	15	*Bradbury*
(11) Oldest Post Office, Sanquhar	7	50	*Bradbury*
(12) Forth Bridge Centennial, S. Queensferry	7	15	*Bradbury*
(13) No.8 Squadron, BF 2219 PS	7	10	*RFDC 81*

PLEASE READ THE GENERAL NOTES
AT THE BEGINNING OF THIS CATALOGUE
These often provide the answers to enquiries received.

Europa (contd.)

	ordinary covers £	official covers £
C.D.S. POSTMARKS		
(14) Alexandra Park Rd., N10 – venue of Stamp World	8	
(15) Bridgeton, Glasgow – Templeton Carpet Factory	8	
(16) Cowcadden, City Branch, or Hope St. – near to Glasgow School of Art *each*	9	
(17) Warriston, Edinburgh – near to Philatelic Bureau	9	

In addition: Cove, Craigpark, Duke St., Edinburgh, Glasgow, Helensburgh, London EC1, Paisley, Sanquhar, Templeton, The Scotlands. Prices from £6.

SLOGAN POSTMARKS

(18) There's a lot of Glasgowing on	15	
(19) Collect British Stamps – World's Greatest Hobby	18	
(20) Collect British Stamps, Lincoln Philatelic Counter	18	
(21) Collect British Stamps, Bradford Philatelic Counter	18	

Also: Burgh of Lanark; Scottish Blood Transfusion; Liverpool MLO. Prices from £10.

10th April 1990 – QUEEN'S AWARDS TO INDUSTRY

2 x 20p, 2 x 37p Export & Technology Award emblems

SPECIAL HANDSTAMPS

(1) First Day of Issue – Philatelic Bureau	4	–	*Royal Mail*
(2) First Day of Issue – SW London	4	–	*Royal Mail*
(3) Queen's Awards to Industry, SW1	6	12	*B'ham (500)52*
(4) Queen's Award, SAGA, Folkestone	6	7	*BLCS 52*
(5) Laboratory of the Gov. Chemist	6	15	*CoverCraft*
(6) William Grant & Sons, Glenfiddich	8	2	*Arlington(s)*
(7) CBI, Silver Jubilee, Investing in Success, WC1	8	20	*LFDC 86*
(8) Paper for the Penny Black, Northampton	8	45	*D.Rutt*
(9) No. 10 Squadron, BF 2220 PS	8	10	*RFDC 82*
(10) Konigsberg, BF 2224 PS	8	10	*FAA Museum*

C.D.S. POSTMARKS

(11) Buckingham Palace, SW1	40	
(12) Dover, Gatwick or Heathrow – exports *each*	10	
(13) Golders Green – Abram Games (stamp designer)	8	
(14) New Invention, Willenhall	10	
(15) Queen Elizabeth Avenue	8	
(16) Tufton Street, SW1 – Queen's Award Office	7	
(17) Turnpike Estate, Newbury – Quantel Ltd., (Computer Graphic artwork for stamps)	15	

In addition: Aycliffe Trading Estate, Broadway SW1, Derby, Globe Road E1, House of Commons, Jubilee Crescent, Lombard St., London EC, NEC Birmingham, Newbury, Silver Link, South Lambeth SW8. Prices from £5.

SLOGAN POSTMARKS

(18) Invest in Sunderland – Enterprise Zone	20	

In addition: British Steel; Aveling Barford; Hastings Exhibition; Stamp World; Sure Plumber; Collect British Stamps; Penny Black Coin. Prices from £10.

3rd May 1990 – PENNY BLACK ANNIVERSARY

Miniature Sheet: 20p + Facsimile of Penny Black

SPECIAL HANDSTAMPS

(1) First Day of Issue – Philatelic Bureau	4	–	*Royal Mail*
(2) First Day of Issue – City of London	4	–	*Royal Mail*
(3) First Day of Issue – Alexandra Palace, N22	6	–	*Royal Mail*
(4) First Roadside Pillar Box, Carlisle	6	20	*Carlisle P.O.*
(5) Postal Museum, 1840-1990, EC	6	–	*n.o.c.*
(6) Royal Mail Exhibition Card No. 4, Edinburgh	6	–	*n.o.c.*
(7) Int. Stamp Exhibition, Stamp World, N22	6	–	*n.o.c.*
(8) Postal Museum, SWL90, EC	6	–	*n.o.c.*
(9) Penny Black, Rowland Hill, Kidderminster	6	8	*CoverCraft*
(10) Penny Black, William Wyon, Birmingham	6	8	*CoverCraft*
(11) 1d Black, Bruce Castle Museum, N17	6	8	*CoverCraft*
(12) Jacob Perkins, Printer of the Penny Black, SE1	6	8	*CoverCraft*
(13) British Philatelic Federation, N22	6	8	*CoverCraft*
(14) Sir Rowland Hill, Kidderminster	6	10	*LFDC 87*
(15) Perkins Bacon & Co., Fleet St.	6	15	*Bradbury*
(16) 'Rule Britannia', SW1	6	10	*Bradbury*
(17) Penny Black, Alexandra Palace, N22	6	15	*Benham SG10*
(18) The Penny Black, Bath	6	20	*B'ham (500)53*

OFFICIAL COVERS ABBREVIATIONS
BLCS = Benham Luxury Cover Series
LFDC = Leicester First Day Cover Series
Please refer to General Notes for full list

Penny Black (miniature sheet) contd.

	ordinary covers £	official covers £	
(19) Stanley Gibbons, Stamp World, N22	6	20	*BLCS53*
(20) Perkins, Bacon, Printers 1d Black, Southwark Bdge	6	12	*BLCS53*
(21) Etchingham Stamp Festival	7	8	*Etc'ham P.C.*
(22) The First Adhesive Stamp on Cover, Bath	7	10	*S. Muscroft*

C.D.S. POSTMARKS

(23) Alexandra Park Road, N10 – near to 'Stamp World'	10
(24) Britannia, Bacup or Porth *each*	10
(24a) Buckingham Palace, SW1	40
(25) Fleet Street – Perkins, Bacon (Penny Black)	10
(26) House of Commons, SW1 – Postage Act	20
(27) House of Lords, SW1 – Postage Act	30
(28) Kidderminster – birthplace of Sir Rowland Hill	7
(29) Sanquhar – oldest Post Office	10
(30) Wood Green – Mobile Post Office, 'Stamp World'	12
(31) Windsor, Berks.	65
(32) Windsor Castle	100

In addition: Cobham, Etchingham, Horsefair, London Chief Office, Lordship Lane N17, Queen Elizabeth Ave., South Kensington, Victoria Rd. Prices from £6.

SLOGAN POSTMARKS

(33) Visit Stamp World, Alexandra Palace	15
(34) Write Now! Say It Better in a Letter	30
(35) Remember to use the Postcode	30
(36) Please Post Early in the Day	30
(37) Senders name and address on back of envelopes	30
(38) New Sunday Collections, Royal Mail, Birmingham	15
(39) Be Properly Addressed Postcode It	40
(40) Pass on your Postcode	20
(41) Liverpool is a Mechanised Letter Office	20
(42) Postman of the Year	35
(43) Queen Victoria School	20

In addition: Aveling Barford; Cunard; 6 May Code Change; Help Police, Postcode Valuables. Prices from £7.

5th June 1990 – KEW GARDENS

20p Cycad + Joseph Banks Blg; 29p Stone Pine + Conservatory; 34p Willow Tree + Palm House; 37p Cedar + Pagoda

SPECIAL HANDSTAMPS

(1) First Day of Issue – Philatelic Bureau	4	–	*Royal Mail*
(2) First Day of Issue – Kew, Richmond	4	–	*Royal Mail*
(3) Arboricultural Assoc., Sevenoaks	5	7	*BLCS54*
(4) 150th Anniv. Royal Botanic Gardens, Kew	5	15	*B'ham (500)54*
(5) Royal Botanic Gdns, Given to the Nation, 1840	5	9	*LFDC 88*
(6) Royal Botanic Gdns, Kew 1840-1990	5	9	*LFDC 88*
(7) Botanical Society, SW7	5	8	*CoverCraft*
(8) The Conservation Trust, Reading	5	8	*CoverCraft*
(9) Nat. Garden Festival, Gateshead, (changeable date)	5	–	*Royal Mail*
(10) Nat. Garden Festival, Gateshead, Tyne and Wear	5	–	*Royal Mail*
(11) Church in the Wood, St. Leonards on Sea	7	15	*Bradbury*
(12) Forth Bridge Centennial	7	15	*Bradbury*
(13) 10th Anniversary, TTTE, BF 2247 PS	7	8	*RFDC 84*

C.D.S POSTMARKS

(14) Kew Gardens, Richmond, Surrey	20
(15) Ash, Beech, Cherry Tree, Elm, Hatfield Broad Oak, Fir Tree, Orange Tree, Pear Tree, Yew Tree *each*	8

In addition: Botanic Gdns, Broad Oak, Cedar Road, Chestnut Terrace, Forest Rd, The Firs, Glasshouses, Green Willows, Hawkhurst, Pinewoods, Sevenoaks, The Forest, The Green, The Willows, Wood End, Woodlands. Prices from £6.

SLOGAN POSTMARKS

(16) Royal Botanic Gardens, Kew	40
(17) Richmond, Twin Towns, Twickenham	20
(18) Dronfield & District Feast of Flowers	15

In addition: Steam Rally & Country Show; Royal Mail Derby/ESTF; Royal Mail Uxbridge New Sorting Office; Chester Business Park; Post Code; Collect British Stamps. Prices from £5.

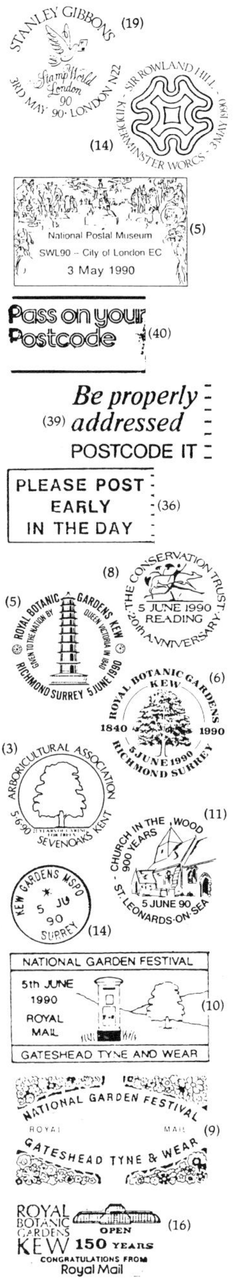

PLEASE MENTION THIS CATALOGUE WHEN REPLYING TO ADVERTISEMENTS

10th July 1990 - THOMAS HARDY

20p Portrait of Hardy with Clyffe Clump, Dorset

SPECIAL HANDSTAMPS	ordinary covers £	official covers £	
(1) First Day of Issue - Philatelic Bureau	2	-	*Royal Mail*
(2) First Day of Issue - Dorchester	2	-	*Royal Mail*
(3) Thomas Hardy Society, Higher Bockhampton	3	7	*LFDC 89*
(4) Marnhull, Tess of the D'Urbervilles	3	6	*Bradbury*
(5) Dorchester, Mayor of Casterbridge	3	6	*Bradbury*
(6) Thomas Hardy, Stinsford	3	6	*Bradbury*
(7) 150th Anniv. Thomas Hardy, Higher Bockhampton	3	8	*B'ham (500)55*
(8) Thomas Hardy, Wessex Poet & Novelist	3	6	*BLCS 55*
(9) Puddletown, Hardy's Weatherbury	3	6	*A. Pearce*
(10) Thomas Hardy, Dorchester	3	4	*Havering*
(11) Thomas Hardy, Higher Bockhampton	3	5	*CoverCraft*
(12) Nelson with Capt. Hardy, BF 2248 PS	4	5	*FAA Museum*
(13) Gibbons Stamp Monthly, Ringwood	4	5	*Benham L24*
(14) Royal Navy Series, Plymouth	4	6	*Marriott*
(15) RAF Station Northolt, BF 2250 PS	4	5	*RFDC 85*
(16) Wimbledon, Lawn Tennis Museum	4	7	*H.R.*
(17) National Garden Festival, Gateshead	4	-	*Royal Mail*

C.D.S. POSTMARKS

(18) Bere Regis (*Kingsbere*); Dorchester (*Casterbridge*); Maiden Newton (*Chalk Newton*); Puddletown (*Weatherbury*); Salisbury (*Melchester*); Shaftesbury (*Shaston*); Sherborne (*Sherton Abbas*); Sturminston Newton (*Stourcastle*); Weymouth (*Budmouth*); Winfrith (*Haggard Egden*) ....*each* 8

(19) Harrow Rd or Westbourne Park Rd - London home ... 8

(20) Fordington - Hardy wrote many of his works here 9

In addition: Amesbury, Hardy Lane, Owermoigne, Piddlehinton, Wimborne. Prices from £7.

SLOGAN POSTMARKS

Royal Mail Derby; Postcode, Dorchester; Say it Better in a Letter; Post Early; Various Post Code slogans; Uxbridge Sorting Office. Prices from £8.

(13) 

(12) 

(8) 

(20) 

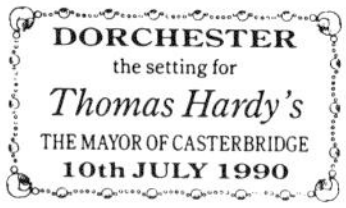 (5)

 (4)

 (10)

2nd August 1990 - THE QUEEN MOTHER'S 90th BIRTHDAY

20p Queen Elizabeth The Queen Mother; 29p Queen Elizabeth; 34p Elizabeth Duchess of York; 37p Lady Elizabeth Bowes-Lyon

SPECIAL HANDSTAMPS	ordinary covers £	official covers £	
(1) First Day of Issue - Philatelic Bureau	4	-	*Royal Mail*
(2) First Day of Issue - City of Westminster	4	-	*Royal Mail*
(3) St. Paul's, Walden, Herts - (square)	5	12	*LFDC 90*
(4) Clarence House, SW1 - (square)	5	12	*LFDC 90*
(5) Glamis, Tayside - (square)	5	12	*LFDC 90*
(6) Clarence House - (oval)	5	10	*BLCS 56*
(7) Glamis Castle - (oval)	5	12	*B'ham (500)56*
(8) Windsor Castle - (oval)	5	8	*BLCS 56*
(9) St. Paul's, Hitchin - (oval)	5	12	*Benham SG11*
(10) The Queen Mother, Woman & Home, SE1	5	20	*BLCS 56*
(11) Heartiest Congratulations, BF 1990 PS	5	10	*RFDC 86*
(12) Royal Mail, Birmingham	5	15	*RM B'ham*
(13) Queen Mother, Bowes Museum	5	6	*S. Muscroft*
(14) 90th Birthday of HM The Queen Mother, W1	5	20	*CoverCraft (RT)*
(15) Glamis Castle - (circle)	5	25	*CoverCraft*
(16) Clarence House - (circle)	5	25	*CoverCraft*
(17) Royal Wolverhampton School	5	8	*Bradbury*
(18) RNLI, Thurso Lifeboat	5	5	*Pilgrim*
(19) Royal Doulton, The Potteries	5	7	*P.Withers*
(20) National Garden Festival, Gateshead	6	-	*n.o.c.*

C.D.S. POSTMARKS	
(21) Barnard Castle - Bowes Museum	8
(22) Bowes - Lady Elizabeth Bowes-Lyon	8
(23) Buckingham Palace, SW1	100
(24) Glamis - Queen Mother's ancestral home	15
(25) House of Commons, SW1	15
(26) House of Lords, SW1	20
(27) Mey - Castle of Mey belongs to Queen Mother	12
(28) Queen Elizabeth Ave. or Queen's Rd.	8
(29) Whitwell, Hitchin - home of Bowes-Lyon family	7

(12) 

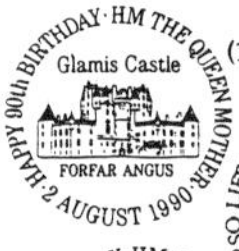 (15)

 (18)

 (16)

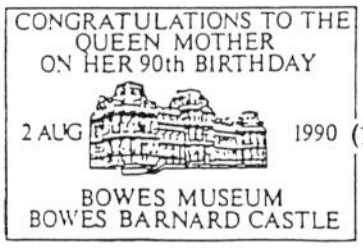 (13)

 (17)

 (24)

 (27)

Queen Mother (contd.)

	ordinary covers £	official covers £	
(30) Windsor, Berks., or Windsor Great Park ....*each*	8		
(31) Windsor Castle, Berks.	100		

In addition: Albemarle St, Crathie, Holyrood, Rose, Scone, Walmer, York. Prices from £5.

SLOGAN POSTMARKS

Queen Victoria School; Royal Engineers Museum; Cunard; Forres Europe in Bloom; Alder Hey 75th Birthday Appeal; Royal Mail - Car Secure; Royal Botanic Gardens. Prices from £7.

(19)

11th September 1990 - GALLANTRY

5 x 20p: Distinguished Service Cross & Medal; Distinguished Flying Cross & Medal; Military Cross & Military Medal; Victoria Cross; George Cross

SPECIAL HANDSTAMPS

(1) First Day of Issue - Philatelic Bureau	4	-	*Royal Mail*
(2) First Day of Issue - City of Westminster	4	-	*Royal Mail*
(3) St. George, Bristol	5	20	*Bradbury*
(4) The Spirit of Britain, SW1	5	10	*LFDC 91*
(5) Battle of Britain, Hawkinge	5	15	*BLCS 57*
(6) Battle of Britain, Westerham	5	20	*BLCS 57*
(7) Victoria Cross for Valour, SW..	5	20	*B'ham (500)57*
(8) George Cross for Gallantry, SW	5	15	*Benham SG 12*
(9) Military Medal for Bravery, Chichester	5	8	*Benham L26*
(10) Distinguished Service Medal, Liverpool..........................	5	12	*Benham L25*
(11) Battle of Britain, BF 2232 PS	5	15	*Forces*
(12) Royal Navy Series, Plymouth...	5	2	*Marriott(s)*
(13) Victoria Cross, National Postal Museum	8	-	*n.o.c.*
(14) World War II, Far East, BF 2251 PS	5	20	*FAA Museum*
(15) Defence of Rorke's Drift	5	18	*S. Muscroft*
(16) Battle of Britain, RAF Bentley Priory...............................	5	25	*CoverCraft*
(17) Battle of Britain, BBMF, RAF Coningsby	5	25	*CoverCraft*
(18) Battle of Britain, RAF Coltishall	5	10	*Markton*
(19) George Cross, Island Siege, Bell Fund, Malta...................	5	20	*Cam.S.C.*
(20) Baden-Powell House	5	8	*Havering*
(21) Sunderland AFC	6	12	*Dawn*
(22) Torquay, Birthplace of Agatha Christie	6	40	*CoverCraft*

C.D.S. POSTMARKS

(23) High Cross, Ware - b/place of first VC & Bar holder...	15
(24) Biggin Hill, or RAF Biggin Hill ....*each*	20
(25) Any Field Post Office..	15
(26) Portsmouth - Royal Navy	8
(27) Sandhurst - Royal Military Academy	9
(28) Royal Hospital Chelsea - Chelsea 'Pensioners'..............	12
(29) St. George, Bristol or St. Georges, Telford..............*each*	10
(30) St. George's Cross, Glasgow	15
(31) Hawkinge or Duxford ....*each*	8
(32) Any RAF Station ....*each*	10
(33) Maritime Mail	30

In addition: Albemarle St. W1, Battle, Battlefield, Battlefield Rd., Battlehill, Buckingham Palace, Churchill, Cove Bay, Duke of York School, Dunkirk, Falklands, Gun End, House of Commons, House of Lords, Immingham Dock, King George, Manor Park, Memorial Rd, Mount Ephriam, Normandy, Queen's Cross, Richmond, Sebastopol, Three Crosses, Victoria Rd, Walton-on-Thames, Wargrave, Waterloo, Wortley. Prices from £7.

SLOGAN POSTMARKS

(34) Royal Engineers Museum	12
(35) RAF Finningley Air Show..	12

In addition: North Yorks Police; Queen Victoria School. Prices from £8.

(1)

(2)

(8)

(19)

(11)

(6)

(10)

(9)

(12)
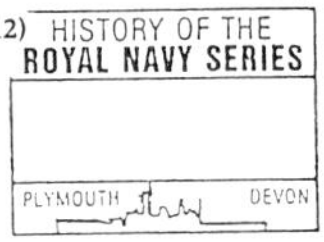

(20)

16th October 1990 - ASTRONOMY

22p Armagh Observatory; Jodrell Bank and La Palma telescopes;
26p Moon and tides; Herschel's telescope;
31p Greenwich Old Observatory and early Astronomical equipment;
37p Stonehenge: gyroscope and navigation by the stars

SPECIAL HANDSTAMPS

(1) First Day of Issue - Philatelic Bureau	4	-	*Royal Mail*
(2) First Day of Issue - Armagh	4	-	*Royal Mail*
(3) Jodrell Bank Science Centre	5	10	*LFDC 92*
(4) Old Royal Observatory, Greenwich	5	7	*BLCS 58*

(1)

(2)

(5)

Astronomy (contd.)

	ordinary covers £	official covers £	
(5) Heavens Declare the Glory of God, Armagh	5	7	*BLCS 58*
(6) Sir William Herschel, Slough	5	15	*B'ham (500)58*
(7) Woolsthorpe, Birthplace of Isaac Newton	5	40	*CoverCraft*
(8) Astronomical Alignments, Stonehenge	5	20	*Bradbury*
(9) Old Royal Observatory, Greenwich (globe)	5	15	*Arlington*
(10) British Astronomical Assoc., Burlington House	5	20	*Cam.S.C.*
(11) British Astronomical Assoc., Royal Observatory	5	20	*Cam.S.C.*
(12) Autumn Stampex/BPE, London SW1	6	-	*Royal Mail*
(13) Royal Mail Exhibition Card No. 4	6	-	*Royal Mail*
(14) No. 249 Squadron BF 2253 PS	6	8	*RFDC 88*

C.D.S. POSTMARKS

(15) Armagh - Armagh Observatory		9
(16) Chelford, Goostrey, Macclesfield etc - Jodrell Bank		8
(17) Greenwich, Herstmonceux, Cambridge - Royal Observatory	*each*	8
(18) Larkhill or Amesbury - Stonehenge		10
(19) Albemarle St. - Burlington House		7
(20) Meridian Centre, Peacehaven		15

In addition: Archer Road, Barnard Castle, Blackford Avenue Edinburgh, Ceres, Colsterworth, Comberton, The Crescent, Crown View, Denby, Five Points, Flamstead End, Globe Rd., Helston, Moore, Newton, North Pole, Oldland Common, The Rocket, Seven Sisters, Southern Cross, Starcross. Prices from £7.

SLOGAN POSTMARKS

Post Office Mercurycard; Stampex; New World Domestic Appliances; Car Secure; Smugglers Adventure; Isle of Skye; Royal Society of Chemistry. Prices from £7.

13th November 1990 - CHRISTMAS

17p Children building snowman; 22p Bringing home the Christmas tree; 26p Carol singers; 31p Tobogganing; 37p Skating

SPECIAL HANDSTAMPS

(1) First Day of Issue - Philatelic Bureau	4	-	*Royal Mail*
(2) First Day of Issue - Bethlehem, Llandeilo	4	-	*Royal Mail*
(3) Church Bell Ringers, St. Paul's, EC4	5	10	*Bradbury*
(4) Church Bell Ringers, Duffield	5	25	*Bradbury*
(5) Birmingham Cathedral	5	7	*Bradbury*
(6) 25 Years Christmas Stamps, Bethlehem	5	20	*LFDC 93*
(7) 150 Years of Stamps, Nasareth	5	15	*CoverCraft*
(8) 150 Years of Stamps, London EC1	5	8	*CoverCraft*
(9) Nat. Postal Museum, Post Early for Christmas	5	-	*n.o.c.*
(10) Benham, First Day Covers, Folkestone	5	7	*BLCS 59*
(11) Christmas Mailcoach Run, Windsor	5	7	*BLCS 59*
(12) Christmas Tradition, Snowdown, Dover	5	10	*B'ham (500)59*
(13) Stanley Gibbins Catalogue, Ringwood	5	15	*Benham L27*
(14) Christmas 1990, Cambridge	5	15	*Cam.S.C.*
(15) Stampway to the World, Glasgow	6	10	*S.P. Board*
(16) Bishop Vesey, Sutton Coldfield	6	12	*BVGS*
(17) Blood & Fire in Darkest England, EC1	6	8	*S.Army*
(18) Royal Navy Series, Plymouth	6	-	*n.o.c.*

C.D.S. POSTMARKS

(19) Church, Freshwater		10
(20) Hollybush or Fir Tree	*each*	7
(21) Nasareth, Caernarfon		8
(22) Playing Place, Truro		8

In addition: Aviemore, Churchfield, Church Hill, Church Village, Holy Island, Jericho, Jerusalem St., Merry Hill, Noel Road, St. Nicholas, Trafalgar Square, Winter Hey. Prices from £6.

SLOGAN POSTMARKS

(23) Birmingham Cathedral	15
(24) Happy Christmas - Please Post Early, Liverpool	40
(25) Nadolig Llawen - Happy Christmas	40

In addition: Stampway to the World; Candlelighters Fighting Children's Cancer; Control your Dog; Coventry Forward in Friendship; Alder Hey. Prices from £8.

CHRISTMAS BOOKLET

Covers bearing pair or block of 4 x 17p stamps from booklet with special handstamp (these have straight edges at top and bottom)	*each*	5
Full pane of ten stamps on cover	*each*	20

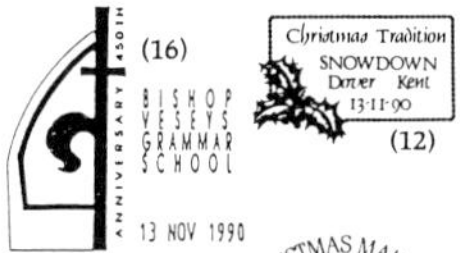

1991

8th January 1991 - DOGS (George Stubbs)

22p King Charles Spaniel; 26p A Pointer; 31p Two Hounds in a Landscape; 33p A Rough Dog; 37p Fino and Tiny

	ordinary covers	official covers	
SPECIAL HANDSTAMPS	£	£	
(1) First Day of Issue - Philatelic Bureau	4	-	*Royal Mail*
(2) First Day of Issue - Birmingham	4	-	*Royal Mail*
(3) PDSA, Telford	5	8	*LFDC 94*
(4) Tate Gallery, London, SW1	5	10	*Bradbury*
(5) Birmingham Dogs Home	5	8	*Bradbury*
(6) Best of British Dogs, Birmingham	5	10	*Bradbury*
(7) RVC, 200 Years, NW1	5	8	*Bradbury*
(8) Crufts Dog Show, Birmingham (badge)	5	8	*BLCS 60*
(9) Centenary Crufts Dog Show, Birmingham	5	15	*B'ham (500)60*
(10) Pawprints, Stoke-on-Trent	5	6	*P. Withers*
(11) Birthplace of George Stubbs, Liverpool	5	10	*CoverCraft*
(12) National Canine Defence League, NW1	5	10	*CoverCraft*
(13) Dog World, Crufts, NEC, Birmingham	5	7	*R. Skinner*
(14) Police Guard Dog School, BF 2257 PS	6	12	*RFDC 90*
(15) Stampway to the World, Glasgow	6	10	*S.P. Board*
C.D.S. POSTMARKS			
(16) Barking, Black Dog or Dogsthorpe *each*	6		
(17) Battersea, or Battersea Park Rd - Dogs' Home *each*	6		
(18) Dog & Gun, or Dog Kennel Lane *each*	10		
(19) Isle of Dogs, London E14	10		
(20) NEC - Crufts Centenary Show	10		
(21) Odiham - RVC founded by Odiham Agricultural Soc.	7		
(22) Portman Square - Stubb's studio	6		
(23) Royal College St, NW1 - Royal Veterinary College	7		
(24) Stubb's Cross	8		

In addition: Airedale, Corn Exchange, Houndsditch, Newmarket. Prices from £5.

SLOGAN POSTMARKS			
(26) Pawprints Appeal	15		
(27) Take a Bite out of Crime	15		

In addition: Stampway to the World. Prices from £8.

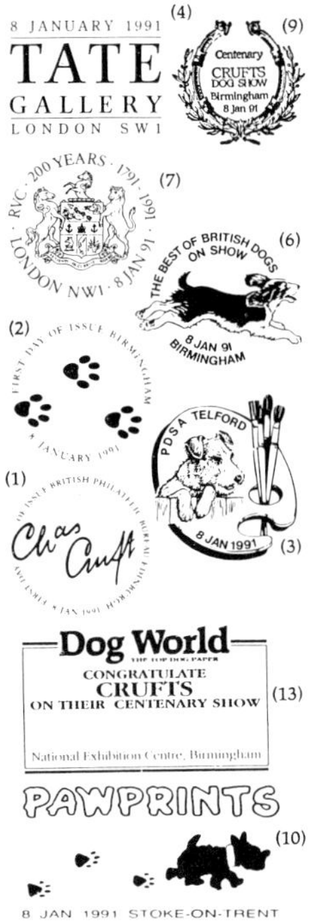

5th February 1991 - GREETINGS STAMPS

10 designs of '1st Class' stamps featuring good luck symbols

SPECIAL HANDSTAMPS			
(1) First Day of Issue - Philatelic Bureau	5	-	*Royal Mail*
(2) First Day of Issue - Greetwell, Lincs	5	-	*Royal Mail*
(3) Good Luck, Rainow, Macclesfield	6	8	*BLCS 61*
(4) Good Luck, Good Easter, Chelmsford	6	20	*B'ham (500)61*
(5) Good Luck, Wishford, Salisbury	6	8	*Benham D158*
(6) Good Luck, Glenrothes, Fife	6	20	*BLCS 61*
(7) Good Luck, Magpie, Yelverton	6	20	*BLCS 61*
(8) Good Luck, Luckington, Chippenham	6	12	*Bradbury*
(9) Rescue Services, BF 2258 PS	7	8	*RFDC 91*

C.D.S. POSTMARKS

(10) Acorn St., Bell Green, Boot, Branch End, Bridge, Catsfield, Clover Rd., Cross Keys, Drakes Broughton, Ducklington, Frog Island, Frogpool, Goldenacre, Greet, Greetland, Gretna Green, Jacob's Well, Keyworth, Klondyke, Luckington, Merlin's Bridge, Primrose Hill, Silverwell, Sky Crescent, Starcross, Swallow's Nest, Well, Wing, Wren's Nest *each* 10

POSTMARK SLOGANS

Pawprints Appeal; The Samaritans; Alder Hey; Magic of British Music; Royal Mail/Post Code slogans. Prices from £15.

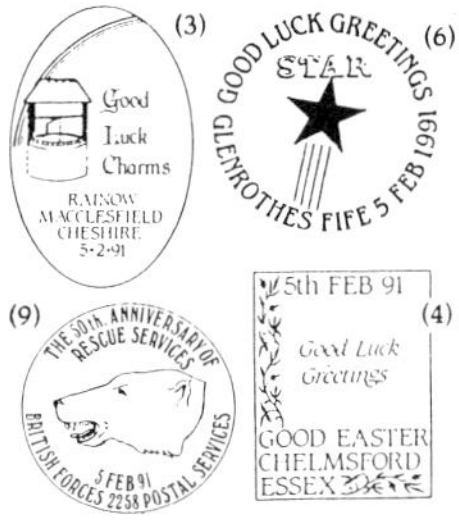

5th March 1991 - SCIENTIFIC ACHIEVEMENTS

22p Michael Faraday - electricity; 22p Charles Babbage - computers; 31p Robert Watson-Watt - radar; 37p Frank Whittle - jet engine

SPECIAL HANDSTAMPS			
(1) First Day of Issue - Philatelic Bureau	4	-	*Royal Mail*
(2) First Day of Issue - South Kensington, SW7	4	-	*Royal Mail*
(3) Charles Babbage, Science Museum, SW7	5	10	*Bradbury*
(4) Royal Society of Chemistry, W1	5	7	*Bradbury*
(5) Society British Aerospace Companies, SW1	5	10	*Bradbury*

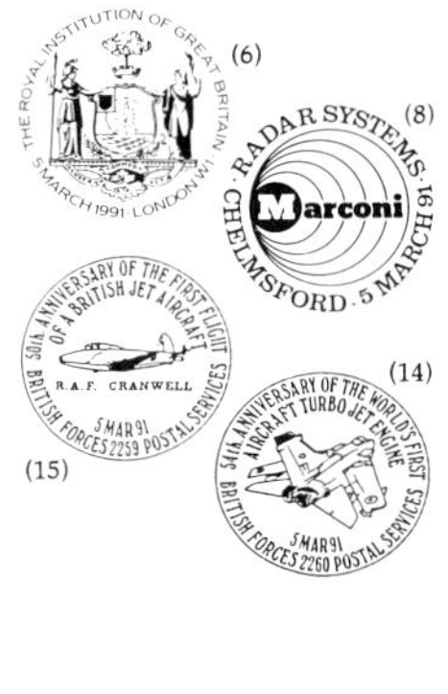

	ordinary covers £	official covers £	
(6) The Royal Institution, W1	5	10	*Bradbury*
(7) Sir Frank Whittle, Loughborough	5	8	*LFDC 95*
(8) Marconi Radar Systems, Chelmsford	5	7	*Bradbury*
(9) Michael Faraday, Electrical Discovery, SW	5	12	*B'ham (500)62*
(10) A.E.U. General Office, SE15	5	6	*R. Skinner*
(11) Loughborough University	5	6	*S. Muscroft*
(12) Michael Faraday/Charles Babbage, IEE	5	25	*Cam.S.C.*
(13) Industrial Soc., Peter Runge House	5	6	*P. Withers*
(14) First Aircraft Turbo Jet Engine, BF 2260 PS	5	10	*Forces*
(15) First Flight of Jet Aircraft, Cranwell, BF 2259 PS	5	10	*RFDC 92*
(16) Computer Innovation, Wembley	6	25	*Arlington*
(17) Electricity, Hove	6	2	*Arlington(s)*
(18) Royal Signals & Radar, Malvern	6	2	*Arlington(s)*
(19) RMA Woolwich, Sandhurst	6	2	*Arlington(s)*

C.D.S. POSTMARKS

(20) Albermarle Street, W1 - Royal Institution	7	
(21) Cranwell - first official flight of the jet engine	10	
(22) Daventry - radar experiments	8	
(23) Exhibition Road, SW7 - Science Museum	7	
(24) Hucclecote - Gloster Meteor was built here	20	
(25) Lutterworth - jet engine was built here	20	
(26) New Invention	12	
(27) Weedon - first successful radar demonstrated	20	

In addition: Alderton, Banbury, Brechin, Brockworth, Broomfield Rd, Caversham, Earlsden, Elephant & Castle, Faraday Street, Loughborough, Seascale, Southcliff, Totnes, Trinity St., Walworth Road. Prices from £6.

SLOGAN POSTMARKS

(28) Philips - a hundred years ahead	12	
(29) Loughborough University	12	

In addition: Sunderland Enterprise Zone £8.

26th March 1991 - GREETINGS STAMPS

Same 'smiles' designs as 6th Feb. 1990 - values changed from 20p to '1st Class'

SPECIAL HANDSTAMPS

(1) First Day of Issue - Philatelic Bureau	5	-	*Royal Mail*
(2) First Day of Issue - Laughterton, Lincs.	5	-	*Royal Mail*
(3) Puncheston, Haverfordwest, Dyfed	6	8	*Benham D159*
(4) Greetings, The Teddy Bear Shop, Ironbridge	6	12	*BLCS 63*
(5) Greetings, Clowne, Chesterfield	6	12	*BLCS 63*
(6) Greetings, Hartford, Cheshire	6	12	*B'ham (500)63*
(7) Birthplace of Stan Laurel, Ulverston	6	10	*Bradbury*
(8) Battle of Cape Matapan, BF 2262 PS	8	-	*n.o.c.*

C.D.S. POSTMARKS

(9) Bearpark, or Catsfield *each*	10	
(10) Constable Road, or Fleet Street *each*	10	
(11) Giggleswick, Greet or Laughterton *each*	10	
(12) Puncheston, Clowne or Queen's Head *each*	10	
(13) Ulverston - birthplace of Stan Laurel	10	

SLOGAN POSTMARKS

(14) Take a Bite out of Crime	12	

In addition: The Samaritans; Alder Hey. Prices from £7.

23rd April 1991 - EUROPE IN SPACE

2 x 22p Man looking into space; 2 x 37p Space looking at man

SPECIAL HANDSTAMPS

(1) First Day of Issue - Philatelic Bureau	4	-	*Royal Mail*
(2) First Day of Issue - Cambridge	4	-	*Royal Mail*
(3) Soft Moon Landing, Jodrell Bank	5	10	*BLCS 64*
(4) Vostok 1, Yuri Gargarin, The Rocket	5	10	*BLCS 64*
(5) First Man in Space, Harwell	5	10	*B'ham (500)64*
(6) Kettering Boys School	5	8	*P. Withers*
(7) Space: The Final Frontier, W1	5	12	*Bradbury*
(8) Hubble Space Telescope, Cambridge	5	15	*Bradbury*
(9) Royal Aeronautical Society, W1	5	10	*Bradbury*
(10) British Interplanetary Society, SW8 1SZ	5	7	*Bradbury*
(11) BNSC - Britain's Space Agency, SW1	5	10	*LFDC 96*
(12) Jodrell Bank Science Centre, Macclesfield	5	25	*CoverCraft*

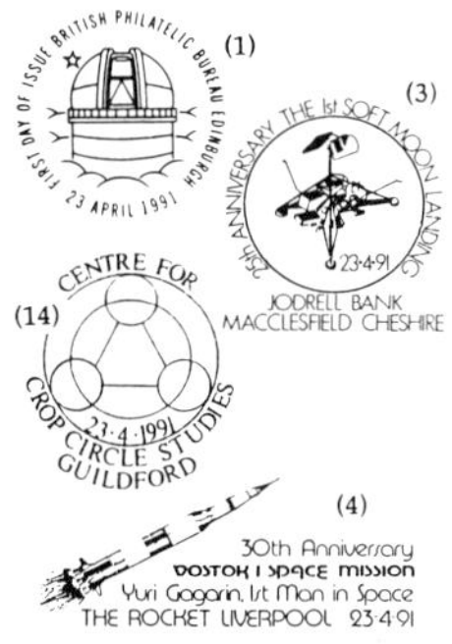

Space (contd.)

	ordinary covers £	official covers £	
(13) VC10 in Military Service, BF 2272 PS	6	9	*RFDC 93*
(14) Centre for Crop Circle Studies, Guildford	6	7	*S. Muscroft*
(15) Prince & Princess of Wales, Brazil, BF 2271 PS	6	40	*Forces*
(16) Salvation Army Match Factory, E3	6	15	*Army*

C.D.S. POSTMARKS

(17) Comberton – Mullard Radio Astron. Observatory		6
(18) Greenwich or Cambridge – Royal Observatory	*each*	6
(19) Helston – Goonhilly Downs Earth Station		6
(20) The Rocket		8
(21) Siddington, Goostrey, Macclesfield – Jodrell Bank		8
(22) South Lambeth Rd – British Interplanetary Soc		6
(23) Surbiton – Helen Sharman, Britain's first astronaut		8

In addition: Chilton, Eye, Farnborough, Neville's Cross, Oldland Common, South Wonston, Upton Lea. Prices from £5.

SLOGAN POSTMARKS

Loughborough University; BBC Radio; The Samaritans; Sunday Collections; Please Control your Dog; Beat the Burglar; Postcode it. Prices from £6.

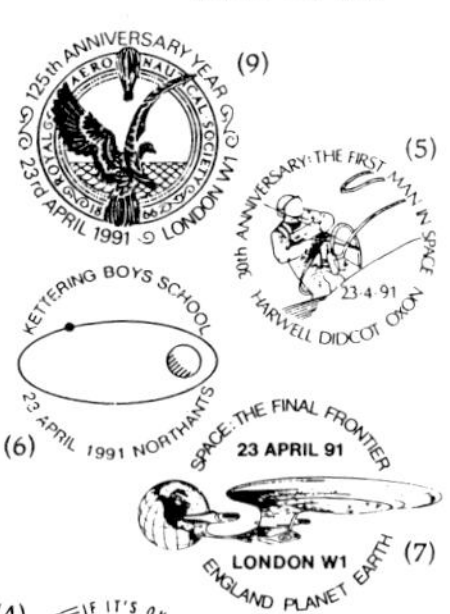

11th June 1991 – SPORTS

22p Fencing; 26p Hurdling; 31p Diving; 39p Rugby

SPECIAL HANDSTAMPS

(1) First Day of Issue – Philatelic Bureau	4	–	*Royal Mail*
(2) First Day of Issue – Sheffield	4	–	*Royal Mail*
(3) Rugby Football, 'Grand Slam', Twickenham	5	7	*Sajal Phil*
(4) If it's on, it's in Radio Times, W1	5	20	*Radio Times*
(5) Home of Welsh Rugby, Cardiff Arms Park	5	10	*BLCS 65*
(6) Home of Scottish Rugby, Murrayfield	5	7	*BLCS 65*
(7) Home of English Rugby, Twickenham	5	10	*BLCS 65*
(8) 1991 Year of Sport, Sheffield	5	12	*B'ham (500)65*
(9) Rugby School	5	10	*LFDC 97*
(10) William Webb Ellis: Game of Rugby	5	15	*Brad VP No59*
(11) Inter. Olympic Committee, Birmingham	5	7	*Bradbury*
(12) Sport for All, Wembley	5	10	*Bradbury*
(13) World Student Games, Sheffield	5	15	*WSGames*
(14) Avon Pride, 1977-1991, Bristol	10	50	*Avon Pride*
(15) Lawn Tennis Museum	5	10	*AELT*

C.D.S. POSTMARKS

(16) The Hayes (Cardiff); Kingsholm (Gloucester); Kneller Rd. (Twickenham); Murrayfield (Edinburgh); Ravenhill Park (Belfast); Sandygate (Llanelli); Welford Rd. (Leicester); Otley; Pontypool; Pontypridd – all venues for Rugby World Cup	*each*	12
(17) Cardiff, Gloucester, Leicester, Twickenham	*each*	10
(18) Rugby – Rugby School where the game started		7
(19) Sheffied – World Student Games		7

In addition: The University Bath, Fence, Jump, First Lane, Loughborough, University Bradford. Prices from £6.

SLOGAN POSTMARKS

(20) Birmingham Welcomes IOC Committee	15
(21) Cardiff Just Capital	12
(22) Federation Cup, Nottingham Tennis Centre	15

In addition: Loughborough University; Convention Centre B'ham; Cub Scouting. Prices from £7.

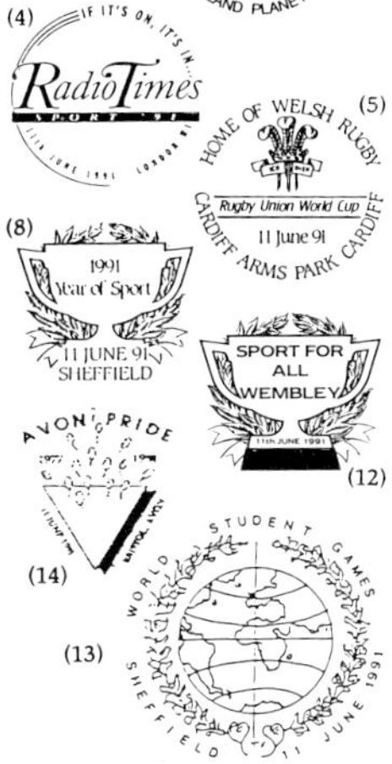

16th July 1991 – ROSES

22p Silver Jubilee; 26p Mme. Alfred Carriere; 31p Rosa Moyesii; 33p Harvest Fayre; 37p Rosa Mutabilis

SPECIAL HANDSTAMPS

(1) First Day of Issue – Philatelic Bureau	4	–	*Royal Mail*
(2) First Day of Issue – Belfast	4	–	*Royal Mail*
(3) Royal National Rose Society, St. Albans	5	10	*LFDC 98*
(4) Royal Botanic Gardens, Kew	5	10	*Bradbury*
(5) World Rose Convention, Belfast	5	10	*Brad VP No60*
(6) O, My Luve's Like a Red, Red Rose, Robert Burns	5	15	*Bradbury*
(7) Roses on Stamps, Rose, Truro	5	15	*Bradbury*

Roses (contd.)

	ordinary covers £	official covers £	
(8) The Gardener, Chelsea, SW3	5	10	*BLCS 66*
(9) Rosebush, Clynderwen, Dyfed	5	15	*B'ham (500)66*
(10) Rose Garden, Drum Castle, Banchory	5	12	*BLCS 66*
(11) Henry VIII, Hampton Court	5	12	*Benham SG13*
(12) Hampton Court Palace, Int. Flower Show	5	30	*CoverCraft*
(13) National Gallery, WC2	5	30	*CoverCraft*
(14) Royal Tournament, Earls Court, BF 2292 PS	6	10	*Forces*
(15) London Economic Summit, SW1	6	20	*Arlington*

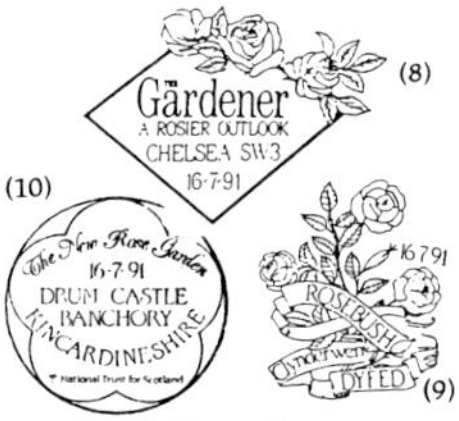

C.D.S. POSTMARKS

(16) Botanic Gardens, Belfast	12
(17) Kew Gardens, Richmond, Surrey	15
(18) Newtonards – 'Harvest Fayre' bred here	10
(19) Rose, Truro	15
(20) Roseacre, Rosebank, Rosebush, Rosedale Abbey, Rosehearty, Rose Hill, Roseland, Rosemarket, Roses Lane Ends ... *each*	10
(21) Royal Hospital, Chelsea – Chelsea Flower Show	12

In addition: Chipping Campden, Glamis, Leaves Green. Prices from £5.

SLOGAN POSTMARKS

(22) Beechwood Place – Shopping in full bloom 10

Also: Belfast 1991; Control your dog; Mansfield Show; Postcodes. Prices from £7.

20th August 1991 – DINOSAURS

22p Iguanodon; 26p Stegosaurus; 31p Tyrannosaurus; 33p Protoceratops; 37p Triceratops

SPECIAL HANDSTAMPS

	ordinary covers £	official covers £	
(1) First Day of Issue – Philatelic Bureau	4	–	*Royal Mail*
(2) First Day of Issue – Plymouth	4	–	*Royal Mail*
(3) Dinosaur Museum, Dorchester	6	10	*BLCS 67*
(4) The Last Dinosaur? The Loch Ness Monster	6	20	*BLCS 67*
(5) Iguanodon Mantelli , Maidstone	6	8	*Benham L28*
(6) First use of Word Dinosaur, Oxford	6	10	*B'ham (500)67*
(7) First Discovery of Iguanodon, Cuckfield	6	25	*Brad VP No61*
(8) Natural History Museum, Dinosaurs, SW7	6	12	*LFDC 99*
(9) First use of Word Dinosaur, Plymouth	6	20	*Bradbury*
(10) Farewell Shackletonsaurus, BF 2299 PS	6	9	*RFDC 96*
(11) Plymouth Museums & Art Gallery	6	15	*Arlington*
(12) Franklin & Andrew, London, EC4	6	30	*Arlington*

C.D.S. POSTMARKS

(13) Plymouth – first use of Word 'Dinosaur'	8
(14) Cuckfield, Lyme Regis, Maidstone, Stonesfield or Tilgate – locations where dinosaur remains found ... *each*	8
(15) Dorchester – Dinosaur Museum	8
(16) Exhibition Rd. – Natural History Museum	8
(17) The Lizard	10

In addition: Lancaster, Lewes, Ness, Stonewell, Sydenham. Prices from £6.

SLOGAN POSTMARKS

Pawprints; Control Your Dog; Royal Mail slogans; Guide Dogs. Prices from £10.

17th September 1991 – MAPS

24p, 28p, 33p, 39p – The Village of Hamstreet, Kent as depicted on Ordnance Survey maps in 1816, 1906, 1959 and present day.

SPECIAL HANDSTAMPS

	ordinary covers £	official covers £	
(1) First Day of Issue – Philatelic Bureau	4	–	*Royal Mail*
(2) First Day of Issue – Southampton	4	–	*Royal Mail*
(3) Visit the Nene Valley Railway	7	10	*N.V. Rly.*
(4) Maps and the Post Office, NPM, EC	5	–	*n.o.c.*
(5) Sir George Everest, Surveyor, Greenwich	6	25	*Bradbury*
(6) Birthplace of Tourism, Leicester	6	15	*Bradbury*
(7) RICS, London, SW1	6	7	*Bradbury*
(8) Ordnance Survey, Hamstreet	6	12	*LFDC 100*
(9) Ordnance Survey Act, Westminster, SW1	6	25	*Brad VP No62*
(10) Ordnance Survey, Hamstreet (oast house)	6	15	*B'ham (500)68*
(11) Hamstreet D490	6	12	*BLCS 68*
(12) Darling Buds of May, Hamstreet	6	10	*BLCS 68*
(13) Ordnance Survey Bicentenary OS, Southampton	6	50	*CoverCraft*
(14) Royal Observer Corps BF 2301 PS	6	10	*RFDC 97*
(15) Tower of London, EC3	4	4	*Sunday Mag.*
(16) Salvation Army, Hadleigh	5	15	*S. Army*

Maps (contd.)

	ordinary covers £	official covers £	
C.D.S. POSTMARKS			
(17) Hamstreet, Ashford	8		
(18) House of Commons, SW1 - Ordnance Survey Act	20		
(19) House of Lords, SW1 - Ordnance Survey Act 1841	30		
(20) John O'Groats/Land's End *pair*	35		
(21) Maybush, Southampton - Ordnance Survey HQ	8		
(22) Newlyn - OS Tidal Observatory	12		
(23) Pathfinder Village, Exeter	10		
(24) Seething Lane - original HQ of OS	7		

In addition: The Chart, Cross Roads, Hereford, Marshfield, Richmond, Roman Way, The Triangle, Tingley, World's End. Prices from £5.

SLOGAN POSTMARKS

(25) Royal Scottish Geographical Society	12		

In addition: New Postage Rates; Yellow Brick Road; Royal Mail in the Community; Please Control Your Dog. Prices from £7.

(15)

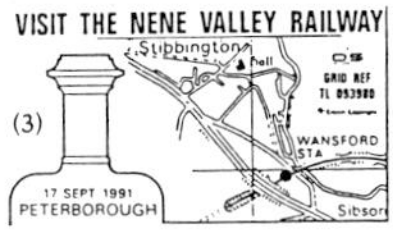

(3)

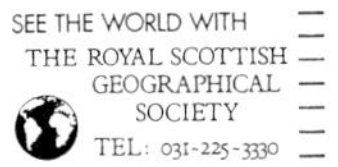

(25)

12th November 1991 - CHRISTMAS

18p, 24p, 28p, 33p, 39p Illuminated Manuscripts (Bodleian Library).

	ordinary	official	
SPECIAL HANDSTAMPS			
(1) First Day of Issue - Philatelic Bureau	4	-	*Royal Mail*
(2) First Day of Issue - Bethlehem, Llandeilo	4	-	*Royal Mail*
(3) Dean & Chapter Library, Durham Cathedral	5	8	*LFDC 101*
(4) Holy Island, Berwick	5	10	*Bradbury*
(5) Illuminated Manuscripts, Bodleian Library	5	15	*Bradbury*
(6) Illuminated Manuscripts, Bethlehem	5	12	*Brad VP No63*
(7) Cadfael Omnibus, Christmas, Shrewsbury	5	10	*BLCS 69*
(8) Christmas Manuscripts, Fountain's Abbey	5	10	*B'ham (500)69*
(9) Christmas, Jerusalem, Skellingthorpe	5	6	*C. Cooke*
(10) Lindisfarne Gospels, Holy Island	5	12	*S. Muscroft*
(11) Happy Christmas, Royal Mail, City of London	5	-	*n.o.c.*
(12) Nat. Postal Museum, Post Early for Christmas	5	-	*n.o.c.*
(13) Christmas 1991, Cambridge	5	15	*Cam. S.C.*
(14) Joy to the World, The Salvation Army, SW1	5	6	*S. Army*
(15) Hercules, BF 2304 PS	5	8	*RFDC 98*
(16) Henry VIII, Greenwich, SE1	5	12	*BLCS 69*
(17) New Hoylake Lifeboat, Liverpool	5	6	*Pilgrim*
C.D.S. POSTMARKS			
(18) Exeter - birthplace of Sir Thomas Bodley	8		
(19) Holy Island - Lindisfarne Gospels	7		
(20) Oxford - Bodleian Library	8		

In addition: Angel Hill, Bolton Abbey, Caldey Island, Jerusalem Street, Kings Road, Nasareth, St. Nicholas, Threekingham. Prices from £5.

SLOGAN POSTMARKS

Newcastle Brown; Clatterbridge Superscan; JVC Video Letter; Northsound Charity; Please Control Your Dog; Pulse Trust Appeal; Shopping in Full Bloom; Glasgow Court Hall; Alder Hey; Write Now etc. Prices from £7.

CHRISTMAS BOOKLET: Covers bearing pair or block of 4 x 18p stamps from booklet with special handstamp

(these have straight edges at top and bottom)	*each*	3
Full pane of ten stamps on cover	*each*	15

(4)

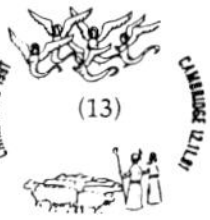

(13)

(6)

(10)

(7)

(17)

(16)

(5)

14th January 1992 - WINTERTIME

18p Deer; 24p Hare; 28p Fox; 33p Redwing; 39p Welsh Sheep.

	ordinary	official	
SPECIAL HANDSTAMPS			
(1) First Day of Issue - Philatelic Bureau	4	-	*Royal Mail*
(2) First Day of Issue - Brecon	4	-	*Royal Mail*
(3) Emmerdale, Arncliffe, Skipton	8	-	*n.o.c.*
(4) Wintertime, Richmond Park	5	10	*B. Reeve 1*
(5) Wintertime, Owlsmoor, Camberley	5	10	*LFDC 102*
(6) Wintertime, Haresfield	5	15	*Bradbury*
(7) Wintertime, New Forest	5	15	*Brad VP No64*
(8) The Monarch of the Glen, Glenbuck	5	12	*B'ham (500)70*
(9) Wildlife in Winter, Thrushwood, Keswick	5	10	*BLCS 70*
(10) Wild About Animals, EC	5	5	*Benham*
(11) World Wide Fund for Nature, Godalming	5	10	*BLCS 70*
(12) British Wintertime, Brecon	5	12	*BLCS 70*
(13) Wildlife in Winter, Foxearth, Suffolk (or Sufflok)	5	12	*Benham S.G. 14*

(1)

(11)

(6)

Wintertime (contd.)

	ordinary covers £	official covers £	
(14) Sittingbourne's New Postbus	5	-	*Royal Mail*
(15) Europe'92, City of London	4	-	*Royal Mail*
(16) Chester Cathedral	5	-	*n.o.c.*
(17) RAF Fylingdales, BF 2281 PS	5	15	*RFDC 99*

C.D.S. POSTMARKS

(18) Deerpark, New Deer or Old Deer	*each*	7
(19) Harefield, Harehills or Harewood	*each*	7
(20) Foxhole or Fox Lane	*each*	7
(21) Sheepridge or Sheepwash	*each*	7
(22) Sheepscombe - farm Post Office		15
(23) Brecon - design of sheep stamp set in Brecon area		7

Also: Coldridge, Frosterley, Freezywater, Godalming, Lairg, Lyndhurst, Nettleham, Wing, Winterbourne, Winter Hey, Winter Rd. Prices from £6.

SLOGAN POSTMARKS

Please control your dog; Ynys Mon Isle of Anglesey; Pawprints. Prices from £6.

28th January 1992 - GREETINGS STAMPS

10 designs of 1st Class stamps on the theme of Memories.

SPECIAL HANDSTAMPS

	ordinary covers £	official covers £	
(1) First Day of Issue - Philatelic Bureau	5	-	*Royal Mail*
(2) First Day of Issue - Whimsey	5	-	*Royal Mail*
(3) The Good Old Days, London Colney	6	9	*Benham D182*
(4) The Good Old Days, Surbiton	6	12	*B'ham (500)71*
(5) The Good Old Days, Brighton	6	15	*BLCS 71*
(6) The Good Old Days, Kings Cross	6	15	*BLCS 71*
(7) The Good Old Days, Oxford	6	15	*BLCS 71*
(8) Harrogate, Yorks	6	15	*BLCS 71*
(9) Portobello Road, W11	6	12	*Bradbury*
(10) Chester Cathedral	8	-	*n.o.c.*
(11) Up Helly AA Lerwick	8	20	*A. Moncrief*
(12) Eastbourne Judgement, Salvation Army	7	10	*S. Army*
(13) Europe '92, City of London	7	-	*Royal Mail*

C.D.S. POSTMARKS

(14) Bala - featured on the map on two of the stamps	10
(15) Greet, Birmingham	10
(16) Letter, Enniskillen - open letter features on stamps	12
(17) Lover, Salisbury	10
(18) Portobello Road, London - famous antiques market	10
(19) Rose, Truro	10
(20) Seaside - bucket and spade feature on stamps	12

In addition: Cargreen, Keyford, Kings Road, Chelsea, Market Place, Maypole, Ordnance Road, Penny Lane. Prices from £7.

SLOGAN POSTMARKS

(21) Southend on Sea Borough Centenary 1892-1992	20

In addition: Westmoreland; VW Audi; Please control your dog; Write Now etc. Prices from £12.

6th February 1992 - HAPPY & GLORIOUS

5 x 24p: Her Majesty as:- Head of State; Head of the Church of England; Head of the Royal Family; Head of Armed Forces; and Head of the Commonwealth.

SPECIAL HANDSTAMPS

	ordinary covers £	official covers £	
(1) First Day of Issue - Philatelic Bureau	3	-	*Royal Mail*
(2) First Day of Issue - Buckingham Palace	3	-	*Royal Mail*
(3) Happy & Glorious, National Postal Museum	4	-	*Royal Mail*
(4) Happy & Glorious, Brian Reeve, Windsor	4	10	*B. Reeve 2*
(5) Happy & Glorious, London, SW1	4	10	*Brad VP No65*
(6) Happy & Glorious, Church Bell Ringers, SW1	4	10	*LFDC 103*
(7) Happy & Glorious, Commonwealth Institute	4	9	*Bradbury*
(8) Happy & Glorious, Windsor	4	15	*Bradbury*
(9) Happy & Glorious, TV Times, SW1	4	5	*Benham*
(10) 40th Anniv. Accession, Sandringham	4	15	*BLCS 72*
(11) 40th Anniv. Accession, Windsor Castle	4	15	*BLCS 72*
(12) 40th Anniv. Accession, Buckingham Palace	4	10	*Benham SG 15*
(13) 40th Anniv. Accession, Balmoral Castle	4	10	*Benham SG 15*
(14) 40th Anniv. Accession, Westminster Abbey	4	20	*B'ham (500)72*

ORDINARY OR OFFICIAL COVERS?
Please read the General Notes

Happy & Glorious (contd.)

	ordinary covers £	official covers £	
(15) MAJESTY, London, W1	4	8	*CoverCraft*
(16) Long Live the Queen, SW1	4	8	*CoverCraft*
(17) Sooty World Museum	4	12	*Arlington*
(18) Queen's Flight, BF 1992 PS	4	12	*RFDC 100*
(19) City of London, 40 Happy & Glorious Years, EC	4	4	*MGN/SG/RMail*
(20) Europe '92, City of London EC	4	-	*Royal Mail*

C.D.S. POSTMARKS

(21) Buckingham Palace, SW1		75
(22) Canterbury or York - Head of Church	*each*	6
(23) Catterick Garrison - Head of Armed Forces		6
(24) Duke of Yorks School		7
(25) Any Field Post Office	*each*	8
(26) House of Commons, SW1		20
(27) House of Lords, SW1		25
(28) Kensington High St. - Commonwealth Institute		7
(29) Sandringham		100
(30) Scone - the Coronation Chair stone		12
(31) Terminal 2 or 4, Heathrow - H.M. first set foot on British soil as Queen		15
(32) West Newton - near to Sandringham House		10
(33) Windsor or Windsor Great Park	*each*	10
(34) Windsor Castle		80

In addition: Coronation Parade, Queen Elizabeth Ave., Queens Parade, Queens Road, Queen Street, Royal Parade, Trafalgar Square. Prices from £5.

SLOGAN POSTMARKS

Control your dog; Alder Hey; Royal School for Deaf Children; Post Code Windsor. Prices from £7.

(18)

(6)

(12)

(16)

(3)

(28)

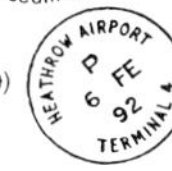

(30)

10th March 1992 - TENNYSON

Portraits of Tennyson together with characters from his poems, viz: 24p 'Vivien'; 28p 'The Miller's Daughter'; 33p 'The Lady of Shalott'; 39p 'Mariana'.

SPECIAL HANDSTAMPS

(1) First Day of Issue - Philatelic Bureau	3	-	*Royal Mail*
(2) First Day of Issue - Isle of Wight	3	-	*Royal Mail*
(3) Tennyson Centenary, Grange de Lings	4	9	*B'ham (500)73*
(4) Charge of the Light Brigade, Winchester	4	7	*BLCS 73*
(5) Tennyson, The Revenge, Bude	4	10	*BLCS 73*
(6) Idylls of the King, Tintagel	4	6	*Benham L29*
(7) Tennyson, Brian Reeve, Isle of Wight	4	10	*B Reeve 3*
(8) The Poetry Society, SW1	4	8	*CoverCraft*
(9) Lord Tennyson, Freshwater, Isle of Wight	4	10	*Brad VP No66*
(10) Lord Tennyson, Haslemere	4	10	*Bradbury*
(11) Lord Tennyson, Hagworthingham	4	20	*Bradbury*
(12) The Tennyson Society, Somersby	4	8	*LFDC 104*
(13) The Salvation Army, Newport	5	7	*S. Army*
(14) Europe '92, City of London	5	-	*Royal Mail*
(15) Number 60 Squadron, BF 2318 PS	5	6	*RAF FDC 1*

C.D.S. POSTMARKS

(16) Freshwater - Tennyson's home (Farringford)	10
(17) Haselmere - Tennyson's home (Aldworth)	7
(18) House of Lords, London SW1	20
(19) Louth - where he attended Grammar School	7
(20) Tetford - near to Somersby, his birthplace	9
(21) Tintagel - inspired 'Idylls of the King'	7
(22) Trinity St., Cambridge - he attended Trinity College	8

In addition: King Arthurs Way, Sebastopol, Tennyson Rd., Tennyson Ave., Trumpington and Winchester. Prices from £6.

SLOGAN POSTMARKS

Glasgow's Alive; Control your dog; Write Now!. Prices from £8.

(4)

(11)

(1)

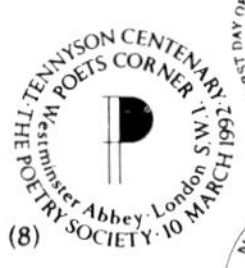

(8)

(15)

(12)

(19)

(3)

(18)

(6)

SLOGAN POSTMARKS
From 1980 prices in the catalogue are for covers with stamps sited to advantage so that the slogan is clearly legible.
Please refer to the General Notes.

7th April 1992 - EUROPA

24p Columbus; 24p Olympics; 24p Paralympics; 39p Operation Raleigh; 39p Expo.

SPECIAL HANDSTAMPS	ordinary covers £	official covers £	
(1) First Day of Issue - Philatelic Bureau	3	-	*Royal Mail*
(2) First Day of Issue - Liverpool	3	-	*Royal Mail*
(3) Landfall of the Americas, Columbus, Bristol	5	-	*n.o.c.*
(4) Columbus 500, Brian Reeve, Liverpool	4	10	*B Reeve 4*
(5) Columbus Quincentenary, Greenwich	4	10	*Bradbury*
(6) America, Yours to Discover, New York	4	15	*LFDC 105*
(7) America, Yours to Discover, California	4	15	*Brad VP No67*
(8) Columbus, Discovery of America, Portsmouth	4	12	*B'ham (500)74*
(9) Columbus, Discovery of America, Greenwich	4	7	*BLCS 74*
(10) Captain Cook's Endeavour, Whitby	4	6	*S. Muscroft*
(11) Peterborough, City of Europe	4	25	*N V Rly*
(12) King George's Fund for Sailors, SW1	4	15	*CoverCraft*
(13) Europe '92, City of London	4	-	*Royal Mail*
(14) 1992 Olympic Games, Manchester	4	12	*BLCS 74*
(15) No. 56 Squadron, BF 2319 PS	5	6	*RAF FDC 2*
(16) Royal Belfast Hospital for Sick Children	5	10	*R.B.H.S.C.*
(17) Walk Through Space, Jodrell Bank	5	12	*Bradbury*

C.D.S. POSTMARKS	
(18) Chelsea - Headquarters of 'Operation Raleigh'	6
(19) Croydon - Headquarters of British Paralympics	6
(20) Maritime Mail, London I.S.	15
(21) Raleigh	10
(22) Stoke Mandeville	7
(23) Wandsworth - British Olympic Assoc	6

In addition: Boston, Hagley Road, Birmingham, Lilleshall, Liverpool, Much Wenlock, New York, The Chart, The Quarterdeck, Washington, Westward Ho!, Whitechapel. Prices from £5.

SLOGAN POSTMARKS	
(24) Arcadian Festival, Birmingham	20

In addition: Please control your dog; Post Haste; Tenovus; Hearts of Oak; Railway History; PO Charter Croydon; Impact. Prices from £7.

(3)

(11)

(10)

(8)

(16)

(20)

16th June 1992 - ENGLISH CIVIL WAR

24p Pikeman; 28p Drummer; 35p Musketeer; 39p Standard Bearer

SPECIAL HANDSTAMPS	ordinary covers £	official covers £	
(1) First Day of Issue - Philatelic Bureau	3	-	*Royal Mail*
(2) First Day of Issue - Banbury, Oxfordshire	3	-	*Royal Mail*
(3) Civil War, The Sealed Knot, Edgehill	4	10	*Bradbury*
(4) Civil War, Edgehill Battle Museum, Banbury	4	9	*Bradbury*
(5) Civil War, The Commandery, Worcester	4	10	*Bradbury*
(6) Civil War, Cromwell Museum, Huntingdon	4	10	*LFDC 106*
(7) Civil War, Naseby	4	12	*Brad VP No68*
(8) Civil War, National Army Museum	4	6	*BLCS 75*
(9) Civil War, Robert Devereaux, Newbury	4	8	*Benham L30*
(10) Civil War, Oliver Cromwell, Huntingdon	4	5	*BLCS 75*
(11) Civil War, Prince Rupert, London EC	4	8	*Benham L30*
(12) Civil War, Raising of the Standard, Nottingham	4	10	*Benham SG17*
(13) Civil War, History Today, Kineton	4	10	*BLCS 75*
(14) Start & Finish Civil War, Bredon Covers	4	5	*Bredon Cvrs*
(15) Whitefriars, Coventry	4	7	*Coventry CC*
(16) English Civil War Society, Hull	4	15	*CoverCraft*
(17) Navy Goes Over to Parliament, Portsmouth	4	10	*Benham L30*
(18) Edgehill, Brian Reeve	4	10	*B Reeve 5*
(19) Lawn Tennis Museum	4	10	*L.T.Museum*
(20) Europe '92, City of London EC	4	-	*Royal Mail*
(21) 75th Anniversary of 101 Squadron	4	5	*RAF FDC 3*

C.D.S. POSTMARKS	
(22) Castle Boulevard - Raising of the Standard	9
(23) House of Commons, SW1	15
(24) House of Lords, SW1	20
(25) Huntingdon - Birthplace of Oliver Cromwell	10
(26) Kineton, Warks - near to Edgehill	10
(27) Marston - Battle of Marston Moor	10
(28) Naseby - Battle of Naseby	10
(29) Other sites of battles: Dunbar, Lostwithiel, Newbury, Powick, Ribbleton, Sidbury, Stow-on-the-Wold, Wash Common ... *each*	12

(1)

(2)

(13)

(10)

(11)

(5)

(17)

(22)

(27)

English Civil War (contd.)

	ordinary covers £	official covers £	
(30) Oliver's Battery, Winchester	12		
(31) Southwell - where Charles I surrendered	9		

In addition: Battlehill, Castle Donington, Charles St., Cropredy, Edgehill (Scarborough), Hull, Kingsland, Lichfield, Northern Parliament, Oxford, Preston, Ratley, Tragalgar Square, Worcester. Prices from £5.

SLOGAN POSTMARKS

(32) Storming of Preston - Battle and Pageant	15		
(33) Hull Festival 1992	15		

In addition: Guild Preston; Hearts of Oak; North Yorks Moors Rly. Prices from £8.

(28)

(30)

(32)

21st July 1992 - GILBERT & SULLIVAN

18p Yeoman of the Guard; 24p The Gondoliers; 28p The Mikado; 33p Pirates of Penzance; 39p Iolanthe

SPECIAL HANDSTAMPS

(1) First Day of Issue - Philatelic Bureau	3	-	*Royal Mail*
(2) First Day of Issue - D'Oyly Carte	3	-	*Royal Mail*
(3) D'Oyly Carte Opera Company, Birmingham	5	20	*LFDC 107*
(4) Lambeth Walk, SE11	5	10	*Brad VP No69*
(5) Royal Academy of Music, NW1	5	8	*Bradbury*
(6) The Gilbert & Sullivan Society, WC2	5	20	*Bradbury*
(7) Birthplace of Richard D'Oyly Carte, Soho	5	15	*Bradbury*
(8) Mikado, Savoy, WC2	5	15	*B'ham (500)76*
(9) Yeoman of the Guard, The Tower, EC1	5	7	*BLCS 76*
(10) Pirates of Penzance, Penzance	5	15	*BLCS 76*
(11) Iolanthe, The Sullivan Society, SW7	5	8	*Benham L32*
(12) Gondoliers, The Sullivan Society, Weybridge	5	8	*Benham L31*
(13) Sir Arthur Sullivan Sesquicentenary, Savoy	5	20	*CoverCraft*
(14) Ruddigore, etc., G & S Operas, Halifax	5	12	*Savoyards*
(15) Damart, Gilbert & Sullivan, Bingley	5	10	*Arlington*
(16) Gilbert & Sullivan Society, Paignton	5	10	*G&S Torbay*
(17) Symphony of Stamps, National Postal Museum	5	4	*N.P.M.(s)*
(18) The Salvation Army, Penzance	5	5	*H.R.*
(19) Sir Arthur Sullivan, 1842-1992, SE11	5	10	*B Reeve 6*
(20) No.47 Squadron, BF 2321 PS	5	6	*RAF FDC 4*
(21) Royal Tournament, BF 2330 PS	5	-	*n.o.c.*
(22) Europe '92, City of London	4	-	*Royal Mail*
(23) Hampton Court Palace	5	20	*CoverCraft*
(24) Shoreham-by-Sea Station	5	15	*Benham R7*
(25) Pad Cancelling Machine at SHC, Cardiff	5	-	*Royal Mail*

C.D.S. POSTMARKS

(26) Birmingham - D'Oyly Carte Opera Co.	7		
(27) House of Commons - Iolanthe 39p value	15		
(28) House of Lords - Iolanthe 39p value	20		
(29) Kingsway (TV House) - near to Savoy Theatre	8		
(30) Lambeth Walk - Birthplace of Sir Arthur Sullivan	7		
(31) Paignton - first performance of Pirates of Penzance	7		
(32) Penzance - Pirates of Penzance	7		
(33) Regent St - where Gilbert and Sullivan first met	8		
(34) Trafalgar Sq. - near to Birthplace of Gilbert	7		

In addition: Broadwick Street, Castle Green, The Circle, Gilbertstone, Harrow & Wealdstone, Haymarket, London EC, Old Windsor, Pindore Street, Seething Lane, Temple, West End. Prices from £6.

SLOGAN POSTMARKS

(35) Smugglers' Adventure, Hastings	10		

In addition: Maritime Mail; Belfast Harpers; PO Charter; BBC Radio Llandudno; Edinburgh Tattoo; Royal Mail Preston; Royal Mail Cardiff; Southend Borough Centenary. Prices from £6.

(1)

(12)

(7)

(2)

(11)

(15)

(13)

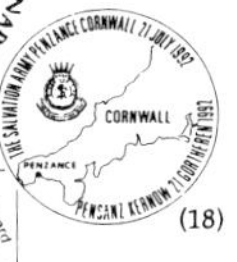
(18)

(9)

(8)

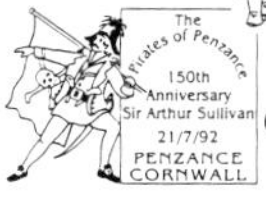
(10)

(17)

(16)

PLEASE READ THE GENERAL NOTES
AT THE BEGINNING OF THIS CATALOGUE
C.D.S. = COUNTER DATE STAMP
These are everyday operational postmarks available at all Post Office Counters.
Please refer to the General Notes for more details.

15th September 1992 - GREEN ISSUE

24p Acid Rain; 28p Ozone Layer; 33p Greenhouse Effect; 39p Bird of Hope

SPECIAL HANDSTAMPS	ordinary covers £	official covers £	
(1) First Day of Issue - Philatelic Bureau	3	-	*Royal Mail*
(2) First Day of Issue - Torridon	3	-	*Royal Mail*
(3) Without conservation..., Red Squirrel	4	15	*BLCS 77*
(4) Without conservation..., Cardigan	4	15	*BLCS 77*
(5) Without conservation..., Bristol Zoo	4	15	*BLCS 77*
(6) Without conservation..., Marsh Fritilary	4	15	*BLCS 77*
(7) Without conservation..., London Zoo	4	15	*BLCS 77*
(8) Without conservation..., The Osprey	4	15	*BLCS 77*
(9) Without conservation..., Howletts	4	15	*BLCS 77*
(10) Without conservation..., The Dormouse	4	15	*BLCS 77*
(11) Brownsea Island	4	9	*B'ham (500)77*
(12) Water Wildlife, Otterhampton	4	9	*BLCS 77*
(13) Sutton Ecology Centre	4	35	*SEC & RM*
(14) The Barn Owl Trust, Ashburton	4	20	*CoverCraft*
(15) Green Charter, City of Plymouth	4	15	*LFDC 108*
(16) Greenacres, Aylesford	4	10	*Brad VP No70*
(17) Preserve our Planet, Coventry Co-op	4	20	*Bradbury*
(18) Leicester on top of the World	4	12	*Bradbury*
(19) Carsington Water	4	15	*Bradbury*
(20) Green Issue, Fair Isle	4	10	*B Reeve 7*
(21) Manchester Metrolink	4	5	*Dawn*
(22) Europe '92, City of London EC	4	-	*Royal Mail*
(23) No.74 Squadron, BF 2322 PS	4	6	*RAF FDC 5*
(24) Shell UK, Cowdenbeath	4	8	*P.P.S.*
(25) Salvation Army, Greenford	4	5	*S. Army*
(26) National Postal Museum, London	4	-	*Royal Mail*

C.D.S. POSTMARKS	
(27) Balham, SW12 - Green Party Headquarters	10
(28) Glasshouses	9
(29) Greenacres, Greenhill, Greenfields, Green Island, Greenlands, Green St., Forest Green, The Green	7
(30) Islington, N1 - Green Peace Headquarters	10
(31) Kew Gardens - conservation and seed bank	10
(32) Leicester - first Environment City	8
(33) Paradise	15

In addition: Boat of Garton, Globe Road, Greeness, Greenlaw, Greenside, Hope, Hopes Green, Nettleham, Park Road, Rainhill, Shepherd's Bush, Slimbridge, Sunnyside, World's End, Wren's Nest. Prices from £5.

SLOGAN POSTMARKS	
(34) Leicester - Environment City	10
(35) Skegness is SO Bracing	15
(36) Enrico Fermi 50 Years Controlled Nuclear Fission	75
(37) Tropical Places - exotic holiday specialists	15

In addition: Wall's virtually fat free; Stamp Collecting Greatest Hobby; Please Control your Dog. Prices from £6.

13th October 1992 - SINGLE EUROPEAN MARKET

24p Artist's interpretation of British star on European flag

SPECIAL HANDSTAMPS			
(1) First Day of Issue - Philatelic Bureau	2	-	*Royal Mail*
(2) First Day of Issue - Westminster	2	-	*Royal Mail*
(3) First Day of Issue - Europe '92 City of London	3	-	*Royal Mail*
(4) Autumn Stampex, London SW1	3	-	*Royal Mail*
(5) British Presidency, Downing Street	3	12	*B'ham (500)78*
(6) The Single Market, Westminster, SW1	3	10	*BLCS 78*
(7) European Arts Festival, Edinburgh	3	6	*BLCS 78*
(8) CBI Investing for the New Europe, WC1	3	7	*LFDC 109*
(9) Single European Market, Dover	3	8	*Brad VP No71*
(10) Single European Market, Parliament Street	3	6	*B Reeve 8*
(11) European Commemorative 50 Pence	3	5	*Royal Mint*
(12) Liverpool FC - FA Cup Winners - In Europe	3	4	*Dawn*
(13) Manchester United in Europe, UEFA Cup	3	4	*Dawn*
(14) Leeds United - League Champions into Europe	3	4	*Dawn*
(15) Saltaire, 1853 Gallery	3	4	*1853 Gallery*
(16) No.111 Squadron, BF 2336 PS	3	4	*RAF FDC 6*
(17) HMC International	3	4	*HMC Int.*

Single European Market (contd.)

	ordinary covers £	official covers £
(18) Birmingham - venue for European Summit	6	
(19) House of Commons, SW1	10	
(20) House of Lords, SW1	15	
(21) Industrial and Trading Estates - various *each*	7	
(22) Lombard Street, or Stock Exchange *each*	7	
(23) Maritime Mail	9	
(24) Market, Market Place or Newmarket *each*	6	
(25) Newbridge, Dover or Aycliffe, Dover (Tunnel) *each*	8	
(26) Paquebot - various *each*	8	

In addition: Mastrick, Northern Parliament, Parliament Street, Pound, Runcorn (Shopping Centre), Saltaire, Starcross, Summit. Prices from £5.

SLOGAN POSTMARKS

(27) Birmingham (surrounded by circle of stars)	8	
(28) Europe for Workers Safety and Health	15	
(29) The Visaservice - Passports Renewed	8	
(30) Maritime Mail	10	

In addition: WHSmiths; Royal Mail Children in Cities; Post Haste, Postcode; Hearts of Oak. Prices from £4.

(27)

(28)

(29)

10th November 1992 - CHRISTMAS

Stained glass windows - Arts & Craft Movement:
18p St. James's, Pangbourne; 24p St. Mary's, Bibury;
28p & 39p Our Lady & St. Peter's, Leatherhead; 33p All Saint's, Porthcawl

SPECIAL HANDSTAMPS

(1) First Day of Issue - Philatelic Bureau	3	-	*Royal Mail*
(2) First Day of Issue - Bethlehem, Llandeilo	3	-	*Royal Mail*
(3) First Day of Issue - Pangbourne	3	-	*Royal Mail*
(4) Stained Glass at Canterbury Cathedral	4	7	*BLCS 79*
(5) Stained Glass, Castle Howard, York	4	7	*BLCS 79*
(6) All Saints, Middleton Cheney	4	7	*Benham L33*
(7) St. Peter & St. Paul, Cattistock	4	7	*Benham L33*
(8) St. Michaels Church, Forden	4	7	*Benham L34*
(9) All Hallows Church, Allerton	4	7	*Benham L34*
(10) St. Martin's Church, Brampton	4	7	*Benham L33*
(11) Christchurch, Cambridge	4	10	*B'ham (500)79*
(12) Bethlehem, Dyfed, Victorian Print No.72	4	7	*Brad VP No72*
(13) Church of the Lily Cross, Godshill	4	9	*LFDC 110*
(14) Our Lady & St. Peter's, Leatherhead	4	10	*Bradbury*
(15) St. Mary's Bibury, Glos	4	15	*CoverCraft*
(16) Peace on Earth, All Saint's, Porthcawl	4	15	*CoverCraft*
(17) Stained Glass Museum, Ely, Cambs	4	15	*CoverCraft*
(18) Christmas, Canterbury Cathedral	4	10	*B Reeve 9*
(19) Cambridge, Christmas 1992	4	6	*Cam. S.C.*
(20) Christmas Blessings, Salvation Army	4	6	*S. Army*
(21) National Postal Museum, EC	4	-	*n.o.c.*
(22) Happy Christmas, Royal Mail, EC1	4	-	*n.o.c.*
(23) Seasons Greetings from Liverpool FC	4	6	*Dawn*
(24) Seasons Greetings from Newcastle United	4	6	*Dawn*
(25) CEAC 7, COSAC, London	4	-	*n.o.c.*
(26) No.84 Squadron, BF 2338 PS	4	6	*RAF FDC 7*

(3)

(8)

(15)

(6)

(12)

(5)

(19)

(23)

(27)

C.D.S. POSTMARKS

(27) Bibury - 24p value	6	
(28) Leatherhead - 28p and 39 values	6	
(29) Pangbourne - 18p value	6	
(30) Porthcawl - 33p value	6	

Also: All Saints Church, Ely, Glasshouses, Holy Island, Jerusalem St., Nasareth, St. James, St. Marys, St. Nicholas, St. Peters, Threekingham. Prices from £4.

SLOGAN POSTMARKS

(31) Leeds Light Up - Illuminations	10	
(32) Happy Christmas, Please Post Early - Inverness	25	
(33) A Happy Christmas, The Post Office - Wick	25	
(34) Jesus is Alive! - Manchester	125	

In addition: Shetland for 93; Please control your Dog; Write now etc.; Senders Name and Address. Prices from £5.

(33)

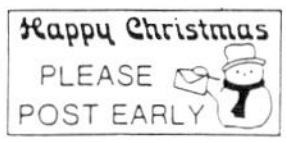

(32)

(31)

CHRISTMAS BOOKLET: Covers bearing pair or block of 4 x 18p stamps from booklet with relevant postmark

(these have margin at top and bottom) *each*	3	
Full pane of ten stamps on cover *each*	10	

19th January 1993 - SWANS

Abbotsbury Swannery:- 18p Mute Swan Cob; 24p Cygnets; 28p Mute Swan Breeding Pair; 33p Mute Swans Eggs; 39p 'First Winter' Mute Swans

SPECIAL HANDSTAMPS	ordinary covers £	official covers £	
(1) First Day of Issue - Philatelic Bureau	3	-	*Royal Mail*
(2) First Day of Issue - Abbotsbury	3	-	*Royal Mail*
(3) First Day of Issue - London	5	-	*Royal Mail*
(4) Wildfowl & Wetlands, Caerlaverock	5	12	*BLCS 80*
(5) Wildfowl & Wetlands, Castle Espie	5	10	*BLCS 80*
(6) Wildfowl & Wetlands, Martin Mere	5	12	*BLCS 80*
(7) Wildfowl & Wetlands, Slimbridge	5	7	*BLCS 80*
(8) Wildfowl & Wetlands, Llanelli	5	12	*BLCS 80*
(9) 600th Anniv. Abbotsbury Swannery	5	20	*Benham SG18*
(10) Bird Watching Magazine, Peterborough	5	6	*Benham*
(11) Stratford upon Avon	5	12	*B'ham (500)80*
(12) Dyers' Hall, London, EC4	5	10	*LFDC 111*
(13) Vintners' Company, London, EC4	5	12	*Brad VP No73*
(14) Swan Sanctuary, Egham	5	10	*Bradbury*
(15) Independent Chapel, Swanland	5	7	*S'land Priory*
(16) Old Swan Corps, Liverpool	5	6	*S. Army*
(17) Swan Lifeline, Eton	5	15	*CoverCraft*
(18) Swan Trust, Berwick	5	10	*CoverCraft*
(19) No.115 Squadron, BF 2347 PS	5	6	*RAF FDC 8*
(20) People in the Post, National Postal Museum	5	-	*n.o.c.*
(21) William Shakespeare, Stratford (swan in design)	7	-	*n.o.c.*

C.D.S. POSTMARKS

(22) Abbotsbury - Abbotsbury Swannery	9
(23) Egham - Swan Sanctuary	9
(24) Sandy - Headquarters of RSPB	9
(25) Slimbridge - Wildfowl Trust	9
(26) Swanland, Swanpool or Old Swan *each*	9
(27) Thetford - British Trust for Ornithology	9

In addition: Comber, Fleet, Hanley Swan, Henley-on-Thames, House of Lords, Ilchester, Mickley, Old Berwick, Swanmore, Swansea. Prices from £6.

SLOGAN POSTMARKS

Postcode, Doncaster; Colourful Greetings Stamps; Gloucester Citizen; Please Control your Dog. Prices from £6.

2nd February 1993 - GREETINGS

10 x 1st Class stamps 'Gift Giving', viz:- Long John Silver; Tweedledee and Tweedledum; Just William; Toad and Mole; Bash Street Kids; Peter Rabbit; the Snowman; Big Friendly Giant; Rupert Bear; Aladdin

SPECIAL HANDSTAMPS			
(1) First Day of Issue - Philatelic Bureau	5	-	*Royal Mail*
(2) First Day of Issue - Greetland	5	-	*Royal Mail*
(3) First Day of Issue - London	5	-	*Royal Mail*
(4) Badger	6	3	*Daily Express(s)*
(5) Daresbury, Warrington	6	15	*Bradbury*
(6) Scottish Literary Museum	6	8	*BLCS 81*
(7) Beatrix Potter, Kensington, W8	6	20	*BLCS 81*
(8) Big Friendly Giant, Great Missenden	6	20	*BLCS 81*
(9) Aladdin, Manchester	6	8	*Benham D191*
(10) Alice in Wonderland, Oxford	6	3	*Benham(s)*
(11) Rivers Corner, Sturminster Newton	6	10	*B'ham (500)81*
(12) Peter Rabbit Centenary, Near Sawrey	6	3	*CoverCraft(s)*
(13) Waterstone's, London	6	8	*Waterstone's*

C.D.S. POSTMARKS

(14) Far Sawrey - home of Beatrix Potter	9
(15) Fleet Street - where the 'Beano' is published	9
(16) Greet, Birmingham	9
(17) Oxford - home of Lewis Carroll	9

In addition: Badger's Mount, Bearpark, Blackfriars Road, Braemar, Bromley Common, Bunny, Cross Hands, Earls Court, Exchange, Fulham Palace Road, Great Missenden, Hassocks, Kensington High Street, Molehill Green, Portobello Road, Rupert Street, Stock Exchange, Tweedle, Waterstone, William Street, The Willows. Prices from £7.

SLOGAN POSTMARKS

(18) Use Colourful Greetings Stamps	15

In addition: Write Now, etc; Radio Nottingham. Prices from £5.

16th February 1993 - MARINE TIMEKEEPERS

24p, 28p, 33p, 39p: Four layer's of Harrison's 'H4' Clock celebrating the 300th anniversary of the birth of John Harrison

SPECIAL HANDSTAMPS	ordinary covers £	official covers £	
(1) First Day of Issue - Philatelic Bureau	3	-	*Royal Mail*
(2) First Day of Issue - Greenwich	3	-	*Royal Mail*
(3) First Day of Issue - John Harrison, London	3	-	*Royal Mail*
(4) Queen Elizabeth 2, Southampton	5	3	*Benham(s)*
(5) RMS Queen Mary, Southampton	5	3	*Benham(s)*
(6) The Cutty Sark, Greenwich	5	10	*BLCS 82*
(7) SS Great Britain, Bristol	5	10	*Benham L35*
(8) Marine Chronometer, Portsmouth	5	3	*Benham(s)*
(9) Marine Chronometer, Plymouth	5	10	*B'ham (500)82*
(10) HMS Belfast, London SE1	5	3	*Benham(s)*
(11) HMS Victory, Portsmouth	5	10	*BLCS 82*
(12) Antiquarian Horological Soc., Ticehurst	5	7	*Bradbury*
(13) British Watch & Clockmaker's Guild, Burnham	5	8	*LFDC 112*
(14) British Horological Institute, Newark	5	10	*Brad VP No74*
(15) John Harrison Tercentenary, Greenwich	5	6	*CoverCraft*
(16) British Sailors' Society, Southampton	5	6	*SP*
(17) No.1 Squadron, BF 2346 PS	5	6	*RAF FDC 9*
(18) Salvation Army, Medical Fellowship, EC4	5	6	*S. Army*
(19) First Day of Sale, Windsor	5	-	*n.o.c.*

C.D.S. POSTMARKS	
(20) Clockface or Clock House Parade *each*	8
(21) Greenwich	8
(22) Maritime Mail, London I.S.	10
(23) Meridian Centre, Newhaven	20
(24) Paquebot - various	10
(25) New Invention, Willenhall, West Midlands	7
(26) New Crofton - near to Birthplace of Harrison	7

In addition: The Chart, Cog Lane, Hampstead, Marton-in-Cleveland, The Quarterdeck, Theobalds Road, Watchet, Whitby. Prices from £6.

SLOGAN POSTMARKS	
(27) Maritime Mail, London I.S.	30
(28) SWATCH Swatch the World	100

In addition: Bedford Borough Council - Waste Watchers; Safeway, Plymouth; Royal Mail can help your Business. Prices from £6.

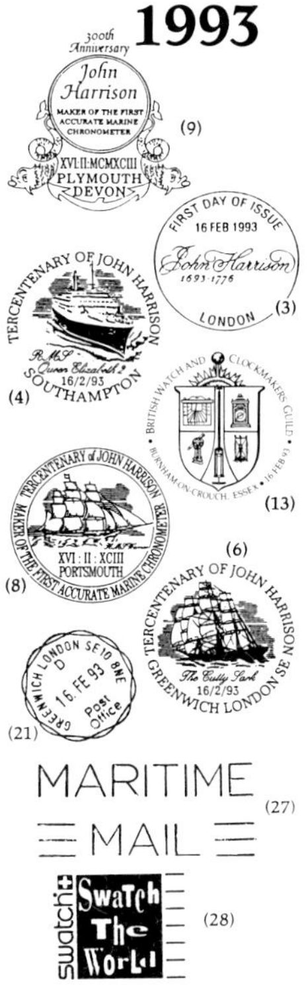

16th March 1993 - ORCHIDS

18p Dendrobium hellwigianum; 24p Paphiopedilum Maudiae *'Magnificum'; 28p Cymbidium lowianum; 33p Vanda* Rothschildiana; *39p Dendrobium vexillarious* var. *albiviride*

SPECIAL HANDSTAMPS			
(1) First Day of Issue - Philatelic Bureau	3	-	*Royal Mail*
(2) First Day of Issue - Glasgow	3	-	*Royal Mail*
(3) First Day of Issue - London	3	-	*Royal Mail*
(4) Royal Botanic Gardens, Kew	5	12	*BLCS 83*
(5) Botanical Gardens, Birmingham	5	15	*BLCS 83*
(6) Botanic Gardens, Glasgow	5	15	*BLCS 83*
(7) Botanic Gardens, Belfast	5	15	*BLCS 83*
(8) Royal Botanic Garden, Edinburgh	5	15	*BLCS 83*
(9) Oldest Botanic Gardens, Oxford	5	15	*BLCS 83*
(10) Royal Orchid Service, Thai Airways	5	15	*Benham SG20*
(11) World Orchid Conference, Glasgow	5	12	*B'ham (500)83*
(12) Worshipful Company of Gardeners, EC	5	15	*LFDC 113*
(13) Royal Botanic Garden, Edinburgh	5	12	*Brad VP No75*
(14) Orchid Society of Great Britain	5	20	*CoverCraft*
(15) No.30 Squadron, BF 2348 PS	5	6	*RAF FDC 10*
(16) Derwentside LDO, Consett	5	-	*n.o.c.*
(17) New Post Office, Southend-on-Sea	5	35	*Bradbury*

C.D.S. POSTMARKS	
(18) Botanic Gardens, Belfast	8
(19) Glasgow - World Orchid Conference	8
(20) Kew Gardens, Richmond	15
(21) Royal Hospital Chelsea - Chelsea Flower Show	10

In addition: Bloomfield, Flore, Flowery Field, Glasgow Airport, Glasshouses, Montague Terrace, Edinburgh, Queen Elizabeth Ave., Paradise, Ripley, Spring Gardens. Prices from £5.

SLOGAN POSTMARKS

Daffodil Day; Royal Concert Hall; Postcodes; Royal Mail. Prices from £5

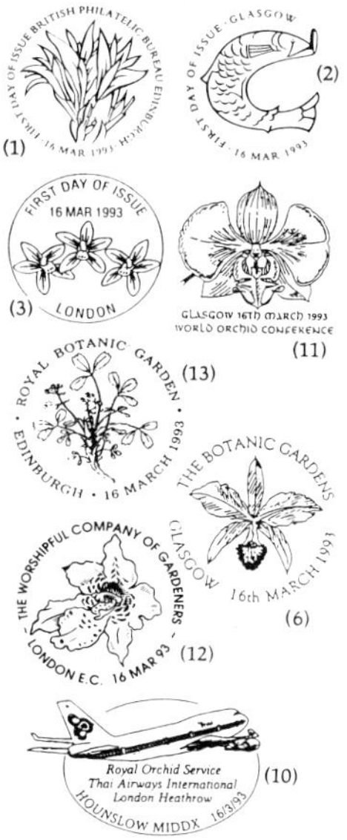

11th May 1993 - ART IN THE 20th CENTURY

24p Henry Moore - Family Group; 28p Edward Bawden - Kew Gardens;
33p Stanley Spencer - St. Francis and the Birds;
39p Ben Nicholson - Still Life, Odyssey 1

SPECIAL HANDSTAMPS	ordinary covers £	official covers £	
(1) First Day of Issue - Philatelic Burea	3	-	*Royal Mail*
(2) First Day of Issue - London SW	3	-	*Royal Mail*
(3) First Day of Issue - London	3	-	*Royal Mail*
(4) Courtauld Institute, WC2	4	6	*BLCS 84*
(5) Paul Nash, Dymchurch,	4	10	*B'ham (500) 84*
(6) Henry Moore, Leeds	4	10	*Benham SG21*
(7) Ben Nicholson, St. Ives,	4	3	*Benham(s)*
(8) Stanley Spencer, Cookham,	4	3	*Benham(s)*
(9) Edward Bawden, Saffron Walden,	4	3	*Benham(s)*
(10) National Portrait Gallery, London WC2	4	6	*Westminster Coll'n*
(11) Royal College of Art, SW7	4	9	*LFDC 114*
(12) Sir Joshua Reynolds, London W1	4	7	*Brad VP No.76*
(13) Swiss National Tourist Office	4	10	*CoverCraft*
(14) British Council, Promoting Britain Abroad	4	6	*CoverCraft*
(15) Frank Wootton Artist, Lympne	4	7	*BLCS 84*
(16) No.216 Squadron, BF 2349 PS	4	6	*RAF FDC 11*
(17) Cyprus, Malaya and Suez, BF 2368 PS	4	-	*n.o.c.*
(18) The Salvation Army, Sunbury,	4	6	*S. Army*

C.D.S. POSTMARKS	
(19) Albemarle Street - near to Royal Academy	6
(20) Braintree - birthplace of Edward Bawden	5
(21) Carbis Bay - home of Ben Nicholson	7
(22) Castleford - birthplace of Henry Moore	5
(23) Cookham - birthplace of Stanley Spencer	6
(24) Denham Green - birthplace of Ben Nicholson	7
(25) Great Bardfield - home of Edward Bawden	6
(26) Kew Gardens - 28p stamp	9
(27) Much Hadham - Henry Moore Foundation	8
(28) The Galleries	20

In addition: Pembroke St., Bedford; Plympton St. Maurice; Trafalgar Square, WC2; Tufton Street, SW1; Vauxhall Bridge Road, SW1. Prices from £4.

SLOGAN POSTMARKS	
(29) Barnes Cray School Arts Week	15
(30) Royal Mail Supports the Arts, Glasgow	10
(31) Milton Keynes, Festival Folk Art	50

In addition: Royal Mail Can Help Your Business; Postcodes. Prices from £5.

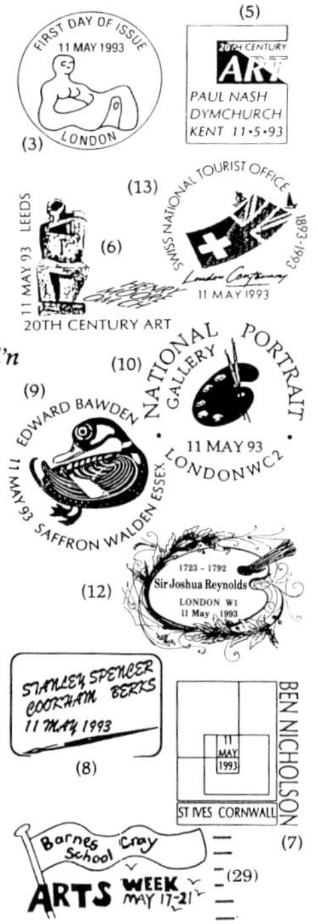

15th June 1993 - ROMAN BRITAIN

24p Claudius (Gold Coin, British Museum) found at Bredgar, Kent;
28p Hadrian (Bronze Sculpture, British Museum) found in the River Thames;
33p Roma (Gemstone, Legionary Museum, Caerleon) found at Caerleon;
39p Christ (Mosaic, British Museum) from a villa at Hinton St. Mary

SPECIAL HANDSTAMPS			
(1) First Day of Issue - Philatelic Bureau	3	-	*Royal Mail*
(2) First Day of Issue - Caerleon	3	-	*Royal Mail*
(3) First Day of Issue - London	4	-	*Royal Mail*
(4) Ermine Street Guard, York	4	10	*LFDC 115*
(5) Camulodunum, Roman Britain, Colchester	4	12	*Brad VP No77*
(6) Roman Britain, Caerleon	4	10	*Benham L37*
(7) Roman Britain, Chester	4	10	*Benham L37*
(8) Roman Britain, Newcastle	4	9	*Benham SG21*
(9) Roman Britain, Bath	4	9	*Benham SG21*
(10) Roman Britain, Colchester	4	10	*Benham L37*
(11) Roman Britain, Invasion A.D. 43, Canterbury	4	10	*Benham L37*
(12) White Cliffs Experience, Dover	4	5	*Benham L36*
(13) Largest Roman Palace in Britain, Fishbourne	4	7	*BLCS 85*
(14) Roman Villa, Chedworth	4	7	*BLCS 85*
(15) Roman Britain, Cirencester	4	10	*Benham L37*
(16) Roman Britain, Walbrook, EC4	4	10	*Benham L37*
(17) Roman Britain, St. Albans	4	10	*B'ham (500)85*
(18) Museum of Antiquities, Newcastle	4	12	*CoverCraft*
(19) Museum of London, London Wall	4	9	*CoverCraft*
(20) Lactodorum, Towcester,	4	15	*Sponne School*
(21) Royal Air Force Locking, Weston-super-Mare	4	25	*RAF Locking*
(22) New Relief Lifeboat, Fleetwood	4	8	*Pilgrim*
(23) Salvation Army, International Headquarters	4	6	*S. Army*

Roman Britain (contd.)

	ordinary covers	official covers
C.D.S. POSTMARKS	**£**	**£**
(24) Bowness or Heddon – Hadrian's Wall *each*	10	
(25) Bredgar – Claudius gold coin (24p)	6	
(26) Britannia – Roman name for Britain	10	
(27) Caerlon – Roma gemstone (33p)	6	
(28) London Bridge – Hadrian bronze sculpture (28p)	6	
(29) Roman Way, Caerlon – Roma gemstone (33p)	20	
(30) Sturminster – Mosaic of Christ (39p)	6	

In addition: Bacchus Road, Bath, Camp, Colchester, Eastgate, Ermine Street, Fisbourne, Fort Augustus, Garrison, High Holborn, Jerusalem, Micklegate, Occupation Road, Prettygate, Northgate, Roman Road, Russell Square, Sandwich, Southampton Row, Southgate, Temple, The Forum, Villa Road, Wall, Wallsend, Watling Street, Westgate, York. Prices from £5.

SLOGAN POSTMARKS

(32) Christian Aid Week	30	

In addition: Stenna Sealink; Any Royal Mail slogans. Prices from £5.

20th July 1993 – INLAND WATERWAYS

24p Grand Junction Canal; 28p Stainforth & Keadby Canal; 33p Brecknock & Abergavenny Canal; 39p Crinan Canal

SPECIAL HANDSTAMPS

(1) First Day of Issue – Philatelic Bureau	3	–	*Royal Mail*
(2) First Day of Issue – Gloucester	3	–	*Royal Mail*
(3) First Day of Issue – London	3	–	*Royal Mail*
(4) Inland Waterways Assoc'n, Market Harborough	5	25	*LFDC 116*
(5) Grand Union Canal, Foxton	5	20	*Brad VP No78*
(6) Canal Museum, Stoke Bruerne	5	10	*BLCS 86*
(7) Conserving..., The Wharf, Braunston	5	3	*Benham(s)*
(8) Conserving..., Lochgilphead, Argyll	5	10	*BLCS 86*
(9) Conserving..., Sheffield, Yorks.	5	10	*BLCS 86*
(10) Conserving..., Newport, Gwent	5	10	*BLCS 86*
(11) Canals 200, Grand Junction Canal	5	10	*BLCS 86*
(12) Canals 200, Crinan Canal	5	7	*BLCS 86*
(13) Canals 200, Stainforth & Keadby Canal	5	7	*BLCS 86*
(14) Canals 200, Brecknock & Abergavenny	5	7	*BLCS 86*
(15) Grand Junction Canal, London North	5	10	*B'ham (500)86*
(16) Canals Bicentenary, Regents Canal, London	7	–	*n.o.c.*
(17) Canals Bicentenary, Watford, Herts	7	–	*n.o.c.*
(18) New Lanark Visitor Centre, Lanark	12	–	*n.o.c.*
(19) The Mary-Anne Worsley Marina	5	6	*S. Army*
(20) No. 51 Squadron, BF 2383 PS	5	6	*RAF FDC 13*
(21) Royal Tournament, BF 2385 PS	5	10	*Forces*

ORDINARY F.D.I. POSTMARKS

(22) Milton Keynes (plus *Leighton Lady* PO cachet)	25	

C.D.S. POSTMARKS

(23) Abergavenny, Brecon or Pontymoile – – Brecknock & Abergavenny Canal (33p)	8	
(24) Ardrishaig or Bellanoch – Crinan Canal (39p)	8	
(25) Brentford or Braunston – Grand Junction (24p)	8	
(26) Stainforth or Keadby – (28p)	10	
(27) Ellesmere Port – Inland Waterways Museum	10	
(28) House of Commons, S.W.I – Canals Act, 1793	15	
(29) House of Lords, S.W.I – Canals Act, 1793	25	

In addition: Birchvale, Bridgwater, Lochgilphed, Locks Bottom, Locks Lane, Shelton Lock, Sugar Island, Towcester, Waterside. Prices from £6.

SLOGAN POSTMARKS

Postbus; Sixty Years Passenger Service; Royal Mail slogans; Sunbury Regatta. Prices from £4.

14th September 1993 – AUTUMN

18p Horse Chestnut; 24p Blackberry; 28p Hazel Nut; 33p Mountain Ash; 39p Pear

SPECIAL HANDSTAMPS

(1) First Day of Issue – Philatelic Bureau	3	–	*Royal Mail*
(2) First Day of Issue – Taunton	3	–	*Royal Mail*
(3) First Day of Issue – London	3	–	*Royal Mail*
(4) Autumn – Rowanburn	4	10	*Benham L38*
(5) Autumn – Pear Tree	4	10	*Benham L38*
(6) Autumn – Berry Hill	4	10	*Benham L38*
(7) Autumn – Nutfield	4	10	*B'ham (500)87*

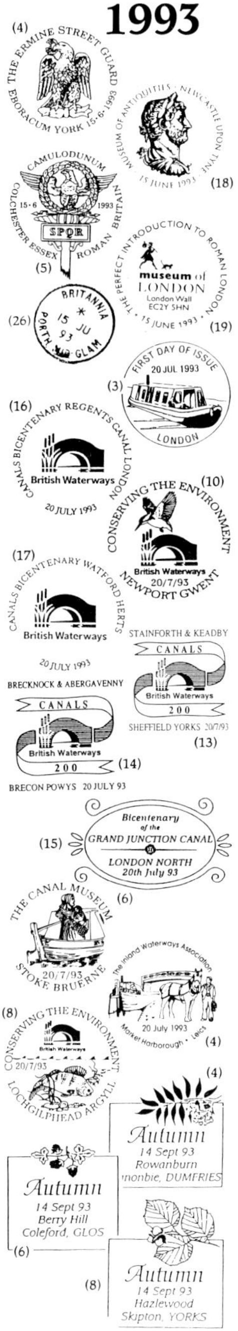

Autumn (contd.)

	ordinary covers £	official covers £	
(8) Autumn - Hazelwood	4	6	*BLCS 87*
(9) Stourhead House & Garden	4	6	*BLCS 87*
(10) Worshipful Company of Fruiterers	4	10	*LFDC 117*
(11) Worshipful Company of Gardeners, EC	4	7	*Brad VP No79*
(12) Battle of Britain, BF 2384 PS	4	6	*RAF FDC 14*
(13) Peterborough, NVR, Wansford Stn	4	-	*n.o.c.*
(14) National Postal Museum, 1793-1993	4	-	*n.o.c.*

C.D.S. POSTMARKS

(15) Chestnut Grove or Chestnut Terrace (18p) *each*	10
(16) Hazel Grove (28p), Mountain Ash (33p) *each*	10
(17) Kew Gardens, Richmond	15
(18) Pear Tree (39p)	10
(19) Savacentre - supermarket Post Office	15
(20) The Allotments, or The Orchards *each*	15

In addition: Berry Hill, Berrylands, Cherry Tree, Faversham, Forest Row, Garden Farm, Peel Green, Pershore, Plantation, Rowanburn, Woodlands, Woodside, Worcester. Prices from £6.

SLOGAN POSTMARKS

Autumn Concerts; £££s Paid for Stamp Collections; Philatelic Congress; Safeway; Any Royal Mail slogans. Prices from £5.

12th October 1993 - SHERLOCK HOLMES

5 x 24p stamps: The Reigate Squire; The Hound of the Baskervilles; The Six Napoleons; The Greek Interpreter; The Final Problem

SPECIAL HANDSTAMPS

	ordinary	official	
(1) First Day of Issue - Philatelic Bureau	3	-	*Royal Mail*
(2) First Day of Issue - 221B Baker St, NW1	3	-	*Royal Mail*
(3) First Day of Issue - London	3	-	*Royal Mail*
(4) First Day of Issue - Autumn Stampex, SW1	5	-	*Royal Mail*
(5) Conan Doyle Society (silhouette)	5	12	*Brad VP No80*
(6) Windlesham Manor, Crowborough	5	10	*Bradbury*
(7) Sherlock Holmes Museum (silhouette)	5	15	*LFDC 118*
(8) St. Bartholomew's Hospital	5	7	*H. Murray*
(9) Sherlock Holmes Society, London	5	15	*CoverCraft*
(10) Adventures of Sherlock Holmes, 221B Baker St.	5	15	*CoverCraft*
(11) POID Bicentenary, EC	5	7	*POID*
(12) Baker Street Post Office, W1	5	-	*n.o.c.*
(13) Radio Times, Sherlock Holmes, Baker St.	5	15	*Benham*
(14) Sherlock Holmes, Baker St., NW1 (silhouette)	5	3	*Benham(s)*
(15) Hound of the Baskervilles, Black Dog	5	12	*B'ham (500)88*
(16) Burial Place of Conan Doyle, Minstead	5	3	*Benham(s)*
(17) The Strand, WC2	5	3	*Benham(s)*
(18) Jeremy Brett is Sherlock Holmes, Granada TV	5	10	*BLCS 88*
(19) Sherlock Holmes, Granada TV, Manchester	5	10	*BLCS 88*
(20) Arthur Conan Doyle Society, ACD	5	15	*Benham L39*
(21) Conan Doyale Establishment, Crowborough	5	15	*Benham L39*
(22) Autumn Stampex, SW1 (changeable date)	5	-	*n.o.c.*
(23) Sherlock Holmes Memorabilia Company	5	10	*SHMCo*
(24) Province of Suffolk, Ipswich	5	10	*Masonic*
(25) No. 100 Squadron, BF 2388 PS	5	6	*RAF FDC 15*

C.D.S. POSTMARKS

(26) Baker Street - home of Sherlock Holmes	10
(27) Elm Row, Edinburgh - Birthplace of Conan-Doyle	9
(28) Beckenham, Kennington, Newhaven, Princetown, Reigate, Walkhampton, Widecombe-in-the-Moor: - locations connected with novels on stamps	8
(29) Crowborough, Hindhead, or South Norwood: - homes of Arthur Conan-Doyle	8
(30) Swiss Valley Park (The Final Problem)	15

In addition: Dog and Gun; Elm Grove, Southsea; Forest Row; Minstead; Nicholson St., Edinburgh; Stoneyhurst; The Strand. Prices from £7.

SLOGAN POSTMARKS

(31) Post Office Investigation Dept	10
(32) Autumn Stampex - features Sherlock Holmes	10
(33) Please Control your Dog - features a Hound	15

In addition: £££s Paid for Stamp Collections; Postbus Silver Jubilee; Exeter Automated Processing; Collect British Stamps; Any Royal Mail slogans. Prices from £5.

1993

9th November 1993 - CHRISTMAS

A Christmas Carol: 19p Bob Cratchit & Tiny Tim; 25p Mr & Mrs Fezziwig; 30p Scrooge; 35p Prize Turkey; 41p Mr Scrooge's Nephew

	ordinary covers £	official covers £	
SPECIAL HANDSTAMPS			
(1) First Day of Issue – Philatelic Bureau	3	–	*Royal Mail*
(2) First Day of Issue – Bethlehem	3	–	*Royal Mail*
(3) First Day of Issue – City of London (top hat)	3	–	*Royal Mail*
(4) First Day of Issue – London (cracker)	3	–	*Royal Mail*
(5) The Dickens Fellowship, London WC1	4	10	*LFDC 119*
(6) Birthplace of Dickens, Portsmouth	4	10	*Brad VP No81*
(7) Scrooge & Bob Cratchit, Rochester	4	10	*Bradbury*
(8) Dickens House Museum	4	10	*CoverCraft*
(9) Visit of Charles Dickens to Newcastle	4	–	*n.o.c.*
(10) A Christmas Carol – Rochester, Kent	4	10	*Benham L41*
(11) A Christmas Carol – Portsmouth	4	10	*B'ham (500)89*
(12) A Christmas Carol – Broadstairs	4	10	*Benham L41*
(13) A Christmas Carol – Pickwick	4	10	*Benham L41*
(14) A Christmas Carol – Chatham	4	10	*Benham L41*
(15) A Christmas Carol – Old Curiosity Shop	4	3	*Benham(s)*
(16) A Christmas Carol – Radio Times	4	8	*Benham*
(17) A Christmas Carol – Rochester, Medway	4	6	*BLCS 89*
(18) Scrooge's Mailcoach Run, Rochester	4	6	*BLCS 89*
(19) Gads Hill, Higham-by-Rochester	4	6	*Benham L40*
(20) The Salvation Army	4	5	*Southport Corps*
(21) Happy Christmas, Royal Mail, EC1	4	–	*n.o.c.*
(22) A Happy Christmas, News of the World	4	7	*CoverCraft*
(23) National Postal Museum, Christmas Postcards	4	–	*n.o.c.*
(24) No.10 Squadron, BF 2389 PS	4	6	*RAF FDC 16*
C.D.S. POSTMARKS			
(25) Broadstairs; Marylebone; Gad's Hill or Mid-Higham, Rochester; Sultan Road, Portsmouth; Theobalds Road, London – near to the homes of Dickens	8		
(26) Camden Town – 'home' of Bob Cratchit	8		

In addition: Holybush, Jerusalem Street, London Chief Office, Nasareth, St. Nicholas. Prices from £6.

SLOGAN POSTMARKS		
(27) Christmas Shopping at Rainbow Superstore		6

In addition: BT Payphone; Safeway; Postbus Silver Jubilee; Collect British Stamps; Any Royal Mail slogans. Prices from £5.

CHRISTMAS BOOKLETS		
£2.50	Covers with pair or block of 4 x 25p stamps	3
	Covers with complete pane of ten stamps	6
£3.80	Covers with pair or block of 4 x 19p stamps	3
	Covers with complete pane of 20 stamps	9

18th January 1994 – THE AGE OF STEAM

19p No. 61342 approaching Bridge of Orchy; 25p No. 60149 "Amadis" at King's Cross; 30p No. 43000 on turntable at Blyth North shed; 35p No. 42455 from Irlam into Wigan Central; 41p No. 7002 "Devizes Castle" across Worcester & B'ham Canal

SPECIAL HANDSTAMPS			
(1) First Day of Issue – Philatelic Bureau	3	–	*Royal Mail*
(2) First Day of Issue – York	3	–	*Royal Mail*
(3) First Day of Issue – Bridge of Orchy	5	–	*Royal Mail*
(4) First Day of Issue – London	5	–	*Royal Mail*
(5) The Age of Steam, Waterloo, SE1	5	15	*Brad VP No82*
(6) The Age of Steam, Derby	5	10	*LFDC 120*
(7) Peterborough NVR, Wansford Station	5	15	*Nene V. Rly*
(8) All Aboard Now, Collectors' Club, Northampton	5	–	*Royal Mail*
(9) North Yorkshire Moors Railway	5	6	*CoverCraft*
(10) Britain's Railway History, RMT, Euston	5	18	*CoverCraft*
(11) Britain's Railway Heritage, Ian Allen	5	18	*CoverCraft*
(12) Football Locomotives, Manchester United	5	7	*Dawn*
(13) Football Locomotives, Newcastle United	5	7	*Dawn*
(14) Great Central Railway, Loughborough	5	7	*Bradbury*
(15) Adventures of Sherlock Holmes, Paddington	5	7	*Bradbury*
(16) Midland Fox, Leicester	5	20	*Bradbury*

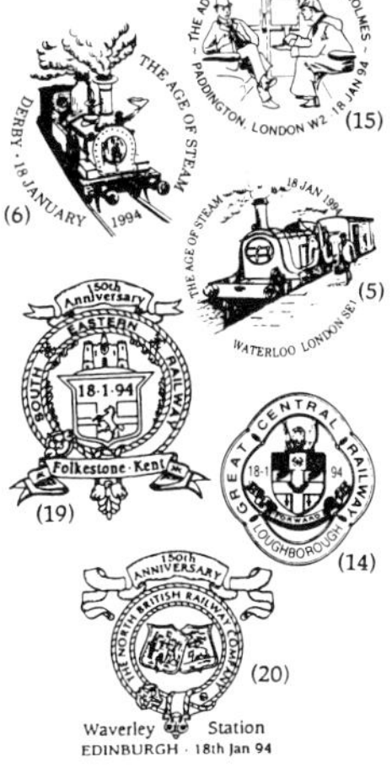

The Age of Steam (contd.)

	ordinary covers £	official covers £	
(17) Redhill, the Town and its Railway	5	10	*Redhill 150*
(18) Railway Mania, GWR Dainton Tunnel	5	8	*Benham SG22*
(19) South Eastern Railway, Folkestone	5	12	*B'ham (500)90*
(20) North British Rly., Edinburgh	5	12	*BLCS 90*
(21) Midland Railway, Euston	5	15	*BLCS 90*
(22) London, Brighton & South Coast Rly	5	20	*B'ham Gold 90a*
(23) Didcot, Great Western Railway Co.	5	15	*Benham L43*
(24) Great Eastern Railway, Great Yarmouth	5	15	*Benham L42*
(25) L.N.E.R., Railway Mania, Peterborough	5	15	*Benham L42*
(26) LXX Sqn. Est. LXXVII, BF 2393 PS	5	6	*RAF FDC 17*

C.D.S. POSTMARKS

(27) Any Station postmark (e.g. Crowthorne) 10
(28) Any TPO (Travelling Post Office) postmark 10
(29) Blyth (or Cambois); Bridge of Orchy; King's Cross; Wigan; Worcester (or Lowesmoor) – locations on stamps 10

In addition: Bright St. York, Carlisle, Carnforth, Darlington, Derby, Didcot, Euston, Gifford, Mallaig, Paddington, Quainton, Rainhill, The Rocket, Settle, Stephenson Square, Stockton, Swindon, Wylam. Prices from £7.

SLOGAN POSTMARKS

(29) Sixty Years Passenger Service for the Capital 35

In addition: British Philatelic Bulletin; Postbus. Prices from £5.

1st February 1994 – GREETINGS

10 x 1st Class – 'Messages', viz:- Dan Dare, The Three Bears, Rupert the Bear, Alice, Noggin the Nog, Peter Rabbit, Red Riding Hood, Orlando, Biggles, Paddington Bear.

SPECIAL HANDSTAMPS

(1) First Day of Issue – Philatelic Bureau	4	–	*Royal Mail*
(2) First Day of Issue – Penn, Wolverhampton	4	–	*Royal Mail*
(3) First Day of Issue – London	5	–	*Royal Mail*
(4) Greetings, Daresbury	5	10	*Bradbury*
(5) Greetings from Paddington Bear, W2	5	8	*BLCS 91*
(6) Greetings from Rupert, SE1	5	10	*BLCS 91*
(7) Orlando, the Marmalade Cat, W1	5	8	*Benham D223*
(8) Teddy Bear Times, Steyning	5	8	*Benham D223*
(9) The Tail of Peter Rabbit, Keswick	5	8	*Benham D223*
(10) Noggin the Nog, Canterbury	5	12	*B'ham (500)91*
(11) Little Red Riding Hood, Wolfsdale	5	8	*Benham D223*
(12) Bearsden	5	–	*Royal Mail*
(13) Evening Sentinel, Stoke on Trent	5	3	*Dawn (s)*

C.D.S. POSTMARKS

(14) Fleet St – newspapers characters 10
(15) Greet, Birmingham 10
(16) Letter – each stamp features a letter 10
(17) Oxford – home of Lewis Carroll 10
(18) Paddington – Paddington Bear 10

In addition: Bear Park, Bearsden, Biggleswade, Blackfriars Bridge Rd, Bunny, Catsfield, Catshill, Dunkeld, Eagle, Epsom Downs, Fulham Palace Road, Letterston, Mount Nod, Penn, Rupert Street, Wolf's Castle. Prices from £7.

SLOGAN POSTMARKS

(19) Write Now, Say it Better in a Letter 20

In addition: Octagon Theatre; Any Royal Mail slogans. Prices from £5.

1st March 1994 – 25th ANNIVERSARY OF THE INVESTITURE OF THE PRINCE OF WALES

19p Chirk Castle; 25p Ben Arkle; 30p Mourne Mountains; 35p Dersingham; 41p Dolwyddelan Castle

SPECIAL HANDSTAMPS

(1) First Day of Issue – Philatelic Bureau	3	–	*Royal Mail*
(2) First Day of Issue – Caernarfon	3	–	*Royal Mail*
(3) First Day of Issue – London	4	–	*Royal Mail*
(4) Caernarfon, St. David's Day	4	15	*Royal Mint*
(5) St. David's Day, Caernarfon Castle	4	10	*LFDC 121*
(6) St. David's Day, Caernarfon	4	10	*Brad VP No83*
(7) St. David's, Haverfordwest (daffodils)	4	–	*Royal Mail*

C.D.S. = COUNTER DATE STAMP
Please refer to the General Notes for more details.

	ordinary covers £	official covers £	
(8) Investiture, Caernarfon (circle)	4	6	*CoverCraft*
(9) Investiture, Caernarfon (oval)	4	12	*BLCS 92*
(10) Investiture, Highgrove	4	12	*BLCS 92*
(11) Investiture, Windsor	4	12	*BLCS 92*
(12) Radio Times, Buckingham Palace, SW1	4	12	*Benham*
(13) MAJESTY, Investiture, W1	4	15	*Benham*
(14) HRH Prince of Wales, Cardiff	4	10	*B'ham (500)92*
(15) Buckingham Palace, London, SW1A 1AA	4	10	*Prince's Trust*
(16) Prince Charles Ave. Post Office, Derby	4	–	*Royal Mail*
(17) Spring Stampex, SW1	4	–	*Royal Mail*
(18) Byddin Yr etc., Caernarfon	4	10	*S. Army*
(19) Football Locomotive Paintings, Sunderland	4	7	*Dawn*
(20) Richard I, Nottingham	4	6	*Benham SG23*
(21) New £2 Coin, Bank of England, EC2	4	6	*Westminster*
(22) 24 Squadron, BF 2409 PS	4	6	*RAF FDC 18*

C.D.S. POSTMARKS

(23) Achfary, Lairg – near to Ben Arkle (25p)	15
(24) Buckingham Palace, SW1	50
(25) Caernarfon – 1969 Investiture	7
(26) Chirk (19p) or Dersingham (35p) *each*	7
(28) Dolwyddelan – (41p)	20
(29) House of Commons, SW1	15
(30) House of Lords, SW1	20
(31) Nettleham – first Investiture	7
(32) Newcastle (or Donard St., Newcastle) – (30p)	8
(33) Prince Charles Ave., Derby	7
(34) St. David's – stamps issued on St. David's Day	8
(35) St. David's Road, Caernarfon	9
(36) Windsor, Berks	8
(37) Windsor Castle, Windsor	50

In addition: Mount Charles, Prince Consort Road, Princeville, Rhiconich, Tetbury, Wales (Sheffield). Prices from £7.

SLOGAN POSTMARKS

Newry 850; Any Royal Mail slogans. Prices from £15.

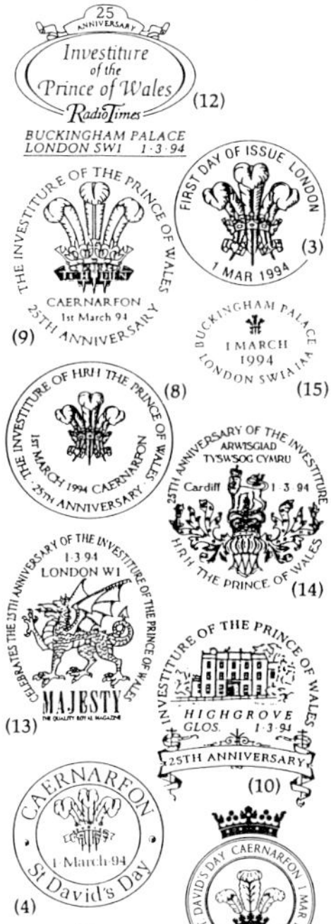

12th April 1994 – PICTORIAL POSTCARDS 1894–1994

19p Blackpool Tower; 25p "Where's my little lad"; 30p "Wish you were here!"; 35p Punch and Judy; 41p Tower Bridge.

SPECIAL HANDSTAMPS

(1) First Day of Issue – Philatelic Bureau	3	–	*Royal Mail*
(2) First Day of Issue – Blackpool	3	–	*Royal Mail*
(3) First Day of Issue – London	4	–	*Royal Mail*
(4) Wish you were here, Blackpool	4	12	*LFDC 122*
(5) Wish you were here, Broadstairs	4	12	*Brad VP No84*
(6) Wish you were here, Scarborough	4	15	*Bradbury*
(7) Blackpool Tower Centenary Year	4	7	*Bradbury*
(8) Picture Postcard Centenary, SW1	4	8	*BLCS 93*
(9) Tower Bridge Centenary, SE1	4	6	*BLCS 93*
(10) Picture Postcards Centenary, Brighton	4	10	*B'ham (500)93*
(11) Football Locomotive Postcards, Arsenal	4	7	*Dawn*
(12) FA Cup Winners, Arsenal in Europe	4	10	*Dawn*

C.D.S. POSTMARKS

(13) Any Seaside town, e.g. Broadstairs, Scarborough	8
(14) Butlin's Holiday Camp	20
(15) Grand Hotel Buildings, Eastbourne	8
(16) North Shore, or South Shore Blackpool *each*	8
(17) Sands or Sandy *each*	8
(18) Seaside: Combe Martin, Eastbourne or Llanelli *each*	10
(19) Seaview, Isle of Wight	10
(20) The Beach, The Pier or The Strand *each*	10
(21) Whitecliff, Poole	10

In addition: Bare, Blackheath, Broadbottom, Crab Lane, Freezywater, Giggleswick, Holmfirth, Littlehampton, Pratt's Bottom, Rock, Seething Ln, Tower Hill. Prices from £7.

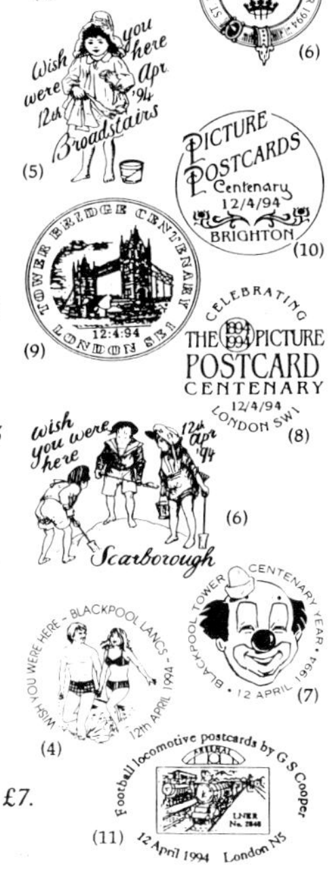

OFFICIAL COVERS OR ORDINARY COVERS ?
Please read the General Notes for explanation.

Pictorial Postcards (contd.)

SLOGAN POSTMARKS

	ordinary covers £	official covers £	
(22) Le Shuttle, Folkestone to Calais	10		
(23) Portsmouth 800	12		

In addition: Collect British Stamps; Isle of Skye; Postcodes. Prices from £6.

3rd May 1994 – CHANNEL TUNNEL

25p, 41p British Lion and Le Coq greeting over the Channel;
25p, 41p Joined hands over a speeding train.

SPECIAL HANDSTAMPS

(1) First Day of Issue – Philatelic Bureau	3		*Royal Mail*
(2) First Day of Issue – Folkestone (map)	3	–	*Royal Mail*
(3) First Day of Issue – Folkestone (Big Ben)	3	–	*Royal Mail*
(4) First Day of Issue – London	4	–	*Royal Mail*
(5) Institution of Civil Engineers, SW1	4	10	*LFDC 123*
(6) British Tunnelling Society, SW1	4	10	*Brad VP No85*
(7) Channel Tunnel (lion and cock), Folkestone	4	10	*Bradbury*
(8) Brush Traction, Loughborough	4	10	*Bradbury*
(9) Le Shuttle, The Channel Tunnel, Folkestone	4	30	*BLCS 94 pair*
(10) Celebrating the Channel Tunnel, Folkestone	4	25	*BLCS 94 pair*
(11) Euro Tunnel Celebration '94, Folkestone	4	25	*B'ham(500)94 pair*
(12) Opening of the Channel Tunnel, Folkestone	4	25	*BLCS 94 pair*
(13) Radio Times, Folkestone	4	15	*Benham*
(14) First through the Tunnel, Laser, Folkestone	4	35	*Benham*
(15) Tarmac Construction Ltd, Wolverhampton	4	–	*n.o.c.*
(16) Design Consultants, Folkestone	4	30	*CoverCraft*
(17) No. 33 Squadron, BF 2421 PS	4	6	*RAF FDC 20*
(18) Woodhead Tunnel, Sheffield Wednesday	4	7	*Dawn*
(19) Busways E.S.O.P., Newcastle	4	7	*Dawn*
(20) Peterborough NVR, Wansford Station	4	10	*Nene V. Rly*

C.D.S. POSTMARKS

(21) Cheriton or Folkestone – tunnel terminal	10		
(22) Ashford – international terminal	8		
(23) King's Cross – proposed new terminal	8		
(24) Waterloo Road, SE1 – existing terminal	8		
(25) Calais or Dover PAQUEBOTS	12		

In addition: Calais Rd., French St., Horn St., Railway Rd., Rising Bridge, Terminal Rd., Terminus Rd., The Link, Trafalgar Square, Undercliff. Prices from £7.

SLOGAN POSTMARKS

(26) Le Shuttle, Folkestone to Calais	10		

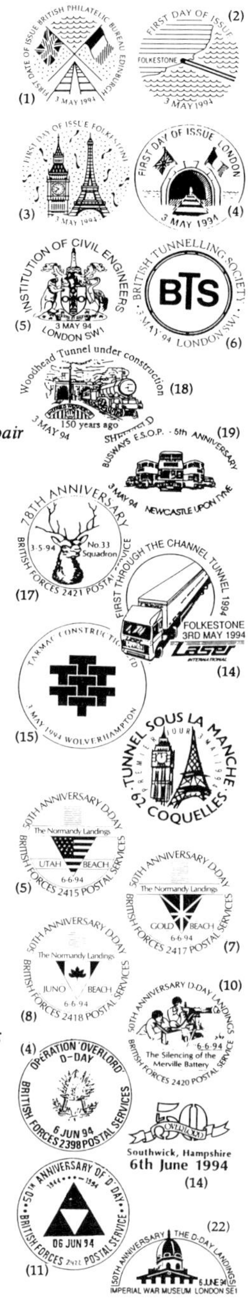

3rd May 1994 – CHANNEL TUNNEL (Double Postmarked Covers)

The Channel Tunnel stamps were a joint Royal Mail/La Poste issue. Arrangements were made for British collectors to obtain the French COQUELLES postmark at the Philatelic Bureau by authority of La Poste, the French postal administration. The Coquelles postmark was applied to the French stamps provided the covers had at least one British Channel Tunnel stamp also affixed. The French Channel Tunnel terminal is located at Coquelles.

	£
(1) Covers with both sets (eight stamps)	20
(2) Any other combination of English & French stamps	10

6th June 1994 – D-DAY

25p Groundcrew reloading RAF Bostons; 25p Coastal bombardment by HMS Warspite;
25p Commandos landing on Gold Beach; 25p Infantry regrouping on Sword Beach;
25p Advancing inland from Ouistreham.

SPECIAL HANDSTAMPS

(1) First Day of Issue – Philatelic Bureau	3	–	*Royal Mail*
(2) First Day of Issue – Portsmouth	3	–	*Royal Mail*
(3) First Day of Issue – London	6	–	*Royal Mail*
(4) Operation 'Overlord' D-Day, BF 2398 PS	6	10	*RAF FDC 21*
(5) Utah Beach, BF 2415 PS	6	3	*Forces(s)*
(6) Sword Beach, BF 2416 PS	6	3	*Forces(s)*
(7) Gold Beach, BF 2417 PS	6	3	*Forces(s)*
(8) Juno Beach, BF 2418 PS	6	3	*Forces(s)*
(9) Taking of Pegasus Bridge, BF 2419 PS	6	3	*Forces(s)*
(10) Silencing of the Merville Battery, BF 2420 PS	6	3	*Forces(s)*
(11) 50th Anniversary of 'D' Day, BF 2422 PS	5	10	*Forces*
(12) HMS Dryad, Portsmouth	5	8	*Royal Mint*
(13) D-Day, 1944-1994, Portsmouth	5	6	*Westminster*
(14) 50 Overlord, Southwick, Hampshire	5	6	*Southwick P.O.*
(15) Operation Taxable, 617 Squadron	5	7	*Cam S.C.*

D-Day (contd.)

	ordinary covers £	official covers £	
(16) City of Portsmouth, D-Day, 50th Anniversary	5	–	*Royal Mail*
(17) D-Day Commemoration, Birmingham	5	5	*Royal Mail*
(18) D-Day + 50 (Eisenhower)	5	10	*LFDC 124*
(19) D-Day, Southampton (square map)	5	10	*Brad VP No86*
(20) Spirit of Britain, London SW1	5	10	*Bradbury*
(21) D-Day Museum, Portsmouth	5	6	*Arlington*
(22) Imperial War Museum, SE1	5	8	*Benham*
(23) National Army Museum, Chelsea, SW3	5	6	*Benham L44*
(24) Radio Times, D-Day Landings, Portsmouth	5	10	*Benham*
(25) FEARLESS, Portsmouth	5	8	*BLCS 95*
(26) D-Day Landings, Portsmouth	5	10	*Benham C.I*
(27) D-Day, Tangmere	5	10	*Benham*
(28) Bletchley Park, Enigma Codebreakers	5	7	*Bletchley Trust*
(29) D-Day Preparations by Rail	5	7	*Dawn*
(30) Invasion of Europe, Portsmouth	5	7	*Cam S.C.*
(31) D-Day, News of the World, London E1	5	7	*CoverCraft*
(32) D-Day The Sun, London E1	5	7	*CoverCraft*
(33) London Taxi Benevolent Assoc'n	5	7	*CoverCraft*
(34) D-Day, 1944-1994, Portsmouth (RAF Wings)	5	12	*CoverCraft*
(35) D-Day Commemoration, Southsea	5	8	*CoverCraft*

C.D.S POSTMARKS

(36) Calais and Dover PAQUEBOTS *pair*	20
(37) Churchill, Bristol or Montgomery, Powys *each*	10
(38) House of Commons, SW1	20
(39) House of Lords, SW1	30
(40) Maritime Mail	12
(41) Normandy, Guildford	15
(42) Portsmouth or Southampton *each*	8
(43) Southwick - SHAEF Headquarters	15

In addition: Battle, The Beach, Boston, Bulford Barracks, Dunkirk, Pathfinder Village, RAF Scampton, Trenchard Lines, Victory Street. Prices from £8.

SLOGAN POSTMARKS

(44) Maritime Mail	12

In addition: Portsmouth 800; European Elections. Prices from £8.

5th July 1994 - GOLF

19p St. Andrews-The Old Course; 25p Muirfield-18th Hole; 30p Carnoustie-Luckyslap; 35p Royal Troon-The Postage Stamp; 41p Turnberry-9th Hole.

SPECIAL HANDSTAMPS

(1) First Day of Issue - Philatelic Bureau	3	–	*Royal Mail*
(2) First Day of Issue - Turnberry	3	–	*Royal Mail*
(3) First Day of Issue - London	4	–	*Royal Mail*
(4) Royal and Ancient Golf Club, St. Andrews	4	12	*LFDC 125*
(5) Golfer's Alphabet, St. Andrews	4	10	*Brad VP No.87*
(6) Gleneagles Hotel, Auchterarder	4	15	*Bradbury*
(7) Tee Time, Philatelic Golf Society	4	10	*Bradbury*
(8) H-C-E-G 250 Years, Muirfield	4	6	*HCEG*
(9) First Open, St. Georges, Sandwich	4	8	*BLCS 96*
(10) The British Open, Greg Norman, Turnberry	4	8	*BLCS 96*
(11) World's Oldest Golf Club, Muirfield	4	3	*Benham(s)*
(12) St. Andrew's, Home of Golf	4	10	*B'ham (500)96*
(13) 250 Years of Golf, Carnoustie	4	3	*Benham(s)*
(14) Mail on Sunday, British Open, Turnberry	4	8	*Benham*
(15) 250 Years of Golf, Royal Troon	4	3	*Benham(s)*
(16) Eighth Hole, Postage Stamp, Royal Troon	4	15	*CoverCraft*
(17) No. 25 Squadron, BE 2429 PS	4	6	*RAF FDC 22*

C.D.S. POSTMARKS

(18) St. Andrews (19p); Gullane (25p); Carnoustie (30p); Troon (35p); or Turnberry (41p) *each*	12
(19) Eagle or Par *each*	10
(20) The Fairway, The Green or The Links *each*	10
(21) Gleneagles Hotel	15
(22) Leith Walk - 1744 home of H.C.E.G.	12

In addition: Ballybogy, Caddy, Golf Road, Hoylake, Lytham St. Annes, Portrush, Prestwick, Sandwich, Wentworth. Prices from £6.

Golf (contd.)

	ordinary covers	official covers	
SLOGAN POSTMARKS	£	£	
(23) New Skoda Women's Scottish Open	25		

TSB Athletics; BUPA; See the Clock/Make a Wish; Any Royal Mail slogans. Prices from £7.

2nd August 1994 - SUMMERTIME

19p Llanelwedd (Royal Welsh Show); 25p Wimbledon; 30p Cowes Week; 35p Lord's; 41p Braemar Highland Gathering

SPECIAL HANDSTAMPS

(1) First Day of Issue - Philatelic Bureau	3	-	*Royal Mail*
(2) First Day of Issue - Wimbledon	3	-	*Royal Mail*
(3) First Day of Issue - London	4	-	*Royal Mail*
(4) Birthplace of Thomas Lord, Thirsk	5	10	*S.P.*
(5) Memorial Cricket Match, NW8	5	10	*S.P.*
(6) Tribute to Lords, Derbyshire CCC	5	10	*S.P.*
(7) Tribute to Lords, Durham CCC	5	10	*S.P.*
(8) Tribute to Lords, Essex CCC	5	10	*S.P.*
(9) Tribute to Lords, Glamorgan CCC	5	10	*S.P.*
(10) Tribute to Lords, Gloucestershire CCC	5	10	*S.P.*
(11) Tribute to Lords, Hampshire CCC	5	10	*S.P.*
(12) Tribute to Lords, Kent CCC	5	10	*S.P.*
(13) Tribute to Lords, Lancashire CCC	5	10	*S.P.*
(14) Tribute to Lords, Leicestershire CCC	5	10	*S.P.*
(15) Tribute to Lords, Middlesex CCC	5	10	*S.P.*
(16) Tribute to Lords, Northamptonshire CCC	5	10	*S.P.*
(17) Tribute to Lords, Nottinghamshire CCC	5	10	*S.P.*
(18) Tribute to Lords, Somerset CCC	5	10	*S.P.*
(19) Tribute to Lords, Surrey CCC	5	10	*S.P.*
(20) Tribute to Lords, Sussex CCC	5	10	*S.P.*
(21) Tribute to Lords, Warwickshire CCC	5	10	*S.P.*
(22) Tribute to Lords, Worcestershire CCC	5	10	*S.P.*
(23) Tribute to Lords, Yorkshire CCC	5	10	*S.P.*
(24) Summertime at Lord's, NW8	5	10	*Brad VP No88*
(25) Outside Edge, Nottingham	5	6	*Benham*
(26) Yatching at Cowes	5	10	*B'ham(500)98*
(27) Braemar Gathering	5	6	*BLCS 98*
(28) Royal Welsh Show, Llanelwedd	5	7	*Benham L45*
(29) Shetland Pony at Braemar	5	7	*Benham L45*
(30) YMCA, 150 Years, Dulverton	5	6	*Arlington*
(31) National Association of Local Councils, WC1	5	10	*LFDC 126*
(32) Summertime Holidays by Train, Manchester	5	6	*Dawn*
(33) Summertime Holidays by Train, Leicester	5	35	*Dawn*
(34) Kirklees Stadium, Huddersfield	5	6	*Dawn*
(35) No.22 Squadron, BF 2431 PS	5	6	*RAF FDC 23*
(36) GSG Technology Centre, Swindon	5	-	*n.o.c.*
(37) Postal Uniforms, National Postal Museum	5	-	*n.o.c.*

C.D.S. POSTMARKS

(38) Builth Wells (19p); Wimbledon (25p) Cowes (30p);
St. John's Wood (35p); Braemar (41p) ....*each* 10

In addition: Bowling, Kennington, Over, Pavilion, Strawberry Hill, Summerhouse, Summerseat, Summertown. Prices from £8.

SLOGAN POSTMARKS

(39) Tropical Places, Exotic Holiday 12

In addition: Biggleswade Festival; Perrier; McMillans; Wilde Weekend in Worthing; Collect British Stamps; Royal Mail slogans. Prices from £7.

27th September 1994 - MEDICAL DISCOVERIES

25p Ultrasonic Imaging; 30p Scanning Electron Microscopy; 35p Magnetic Resonance Imaging; 41p Computed Tomography

SPECIAL HANDSTAMPS

(1) First Day of Issue - Philatelic Bureau	3	-	*Royal Mail*
(2) First Day of Issue - Cambridge	3	-	*Royal Mail*
(3) First Day of Issue - London	4	-	*Royal Mail*
(4) Peak Practice, Whatstandwell	4	10	*BLCS 99*
(5) Peak Practice, Wirksworth	4	10	*BLCS 99*
(6) Peak Practice, Fritchley	4	10	*BLCS 99*
(7) Peak Practice, Crich	4	10	*BLCS 99*
(8) The Lancet, London WC1	4	10	*BLCS 99*
(9) St. Bartholomew's, London EC1	4	10	*B'ham(500)99*

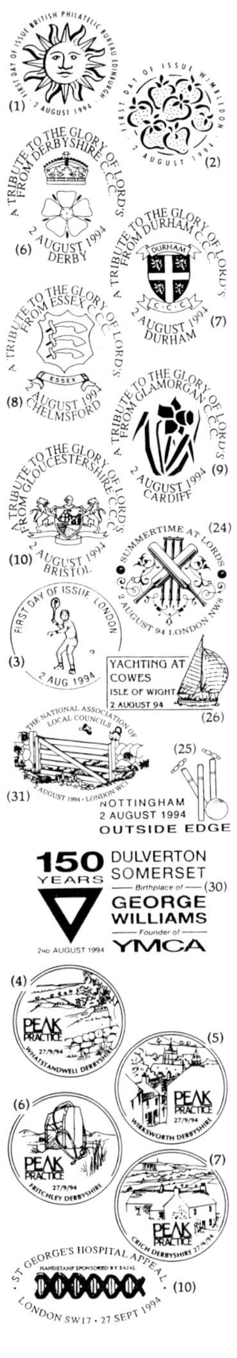

Medical Discoveries (contd.)

	ordinary covers £	official covers £	
(10) St. George's Hospital, London SW17	4	6	*Sajal*
(11) Cystic Fibrosis, Bromley	4	10	*Bradbury*
(12) BMA, Founded 1832, Worcester	4	10	*Bradbury*
(13) BMA, Over 100,000 Members, WC1	4	10	*Bradbury*
(14) Florence Nightingale, SE1	4	10	*Brad VP No89*
(15) Royal College of Surgeons, WC2	4	10	*LFDC 127*
(16) Glasgow Royal Maternity Hospital	4	10	*GRMH*
(17) Blackburn Rovers UEFA Cup	4	6	*Dawn*
(18) No.360 Squadron BF 2432 PS	4	6	*RAF FDC 24*

C.D.S. POSTMARKS

(19) Hospital Post Offices:- Benenden, Milford, Oswestry, Lancaster Moor or Edward VII *each*	8
(20) Glasgow Royal Infirmary	10
(21) Harefield or Papworth – transplants *each*	8
(22) Harborne, Hammersmith or Paddington – Radiology work *each*	8
(23) Headington, Oxford – Electronic Microscope	8

In addition: Brentford, Cambridge, Glasgow, Healing, Pill, New Invention. Prices from £5.

SLOGAN POSTMARKS

(24) Zeneca (pharmaceuticals)	15
(25) Health Education Authority – Fresh Fruit & Veg	15

In addition: Soft Rock; Royal Mail slogans. Prices from £7.

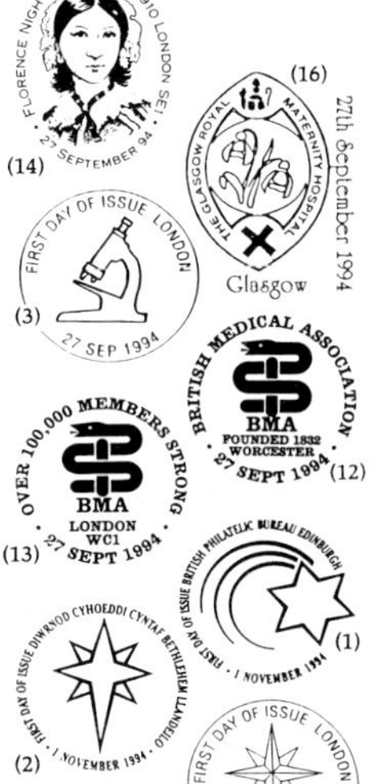

1st November 1994 – CHRISTMAS

19p, 25p, 30p, 35p, 41p Children's Nativity Plays

SPECIAL HANDSTAMPS

	ordinary	official	
(1) First Day of Issue – Philatelic Bureau	3	–	*Royal Mail*
(2) First Day of Issue – Bethlehem	3	–	*Royal Mail*
(3) First Day of Issue – London	3	–	*Royal Mail*
(4) Christmas Common	4	10	*B'ham(500)100*
(5) Hollytrees Museum, Colchester	4	8	*BLCS 100*
(6) The Nativity, Bethlehem	4	7	*BLCS 100*
(7) The Nativity, Nasareth	4	7	*BLCS 100*
(8) Wiseman's Bridge	4	12	*B'ham Gold 100a*
(9) Christchurch Priory 1094-1994	4	12	*LFDC 128*
(10) Bethlehem (angel and trumpet)	4	8	*Brad VP No90*
(11) Santa Claus Distribution Fund, Stoke Newington	4	8	*J. Eldridge*
(12) National Postal Museum, Christmas 94	4	–	*n.o.c.*
(13) Happy Christmas, Royal Mail, EC1	4	–	*n.o.c.*
(14) Christmas Greetings, Lewes	4	6	*FDP Co*
(15) Season's Greetings, Leeds United	4	6	*Dawn*
(16) Aston Villa in Europe, Birmingham	4	6	*Dawn*
(17) Salvation Army, Hackney, E8	4	6	*S.Army*
(18) No.78 Squadron, BF 2436 PS	5	6	*RAF FDC 25*
(19) Peterborough NVR, Wansford Station	5	6	*Nene V. Rly*

C.D.S. POSTMARKS

(20) Nasareth or Holy Island *each*	8
(21) York – most famous Nativity play	8

In addition: Angel Hill, Brentwood Ave., Child's Hill, Christchurch, Jerusalem Street, Narberth, Playing Place, Shepherd's Bush, Shepherd's Well, St. Nicholas, Star, Star Cross. Prices from £6.

SLOGAN POSTMARKS

(22) Walt Disney's Snow White	15

In addition: Collect British Stamps; Control your Dog; Glasgow Concert Hall; Pass on PostCode; Mercurycard Off Peak. Prices from £5.

CHRISTMAS BOOKLETS

£2.50 Covers with pair or block of 4 x 25p stamps	3
Covers with complete pane of ten stamps	6
£3.80 Covers with pair or block of 4 x 19p stamps	3
Covers with complete pane of 20 stamps	9

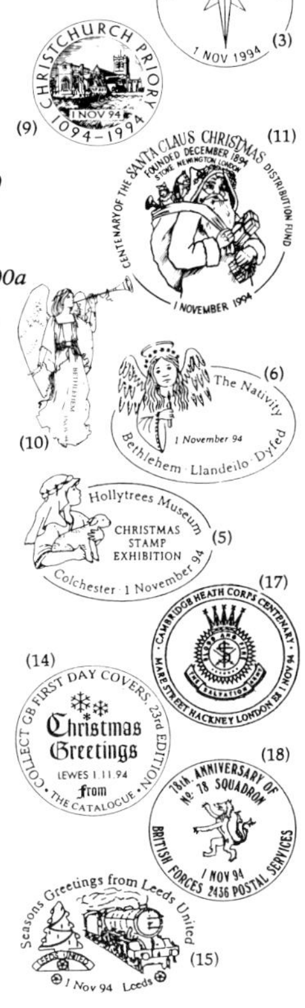

17th January 1995 - CATS

19p black cat; 25p Siamese & tabby; 30p ginger cat; 35p Abyssinian & tortoiseshell; 41p black & white cat

SPECIAL HANDSTAMPS

	ordinary covers £	official covers £	
(1) First Day of Issue - Philatelic Bureau	3	-	*Royal Mail*
(2) First Day of Issue - Kitts Green	3	-	*Royal Mail*
(3) First Day of Issue - London	3	-	*Royal Mail*
(4) Your Cat Magazine, Peterborough	4	8	*Benham*
(5) Cats, Woman & Home, SE1	4	8	*Benham*
(6) RSPCA, Horsham	4	6	*BLCS 101*
(7) Cats Proection League, Horsham	4	8	*Benham*
(8) Cats Proection League, Kirkintilloch	4	8	*Benham*
(9) Cats Proection League, Newtownards	4	8	*Benham*
(10) Cats Proection League, Bridgend	4	8	*Benham*
(11) Cats Proection League, Birmingham	4	8	*BLCS 101*
(12) Catstree, Brignorth	4	10	*B'ham(500)101*
(13) Catfield, Great Yarmouth	4	10	*BLCS 100*
(14) Catsham, Glastonbury	4	10	*BLCS 100*
(15) Catbrook, Chepstow	4	10	*BLCS 100*
(16) Catsash, Newport	4	10	*Benham SG25*
(17) Philatelic Felines, Catsfield	4	10	*Brad VP No91*
(18) Philatelic Felines, Catshill	4	10	*LFDC 129*
(19) Celebrating Cats, Catshill	4	6	*Westminster*
(20) Wood Green Animal Shelters, Royston	4	6	*Wood Green*
(21) Cool Cats Catalogue, Catsfield	4	6	*FDP Co*
(22) Celebrating Cats, City of London	4	10	*Bradbury*
(23) Postal Cats, National Postal Museum	4	-	*n.o.c.*
(24) Tiger Squadron, Flying Pumas, BF 2281 PS	4	6	*RAF FDC 26*

C.D.S. POSTMARKS

(25) Catfield, Catsfield, Catshill, or Cat Cot Road *each*	9	
(26) Earl's Court - Cat Show, Olympia	10	
(27) Horsham - RSPCA & CPL headquarters	10	

In addition: Catbrook, Catcott, Catforth, Catsworth, Lea Village, Mousehole. Prices from £8.

SLOGAN POSTMARKS

Please control your dog; Collect British Stamps Prices from £6.

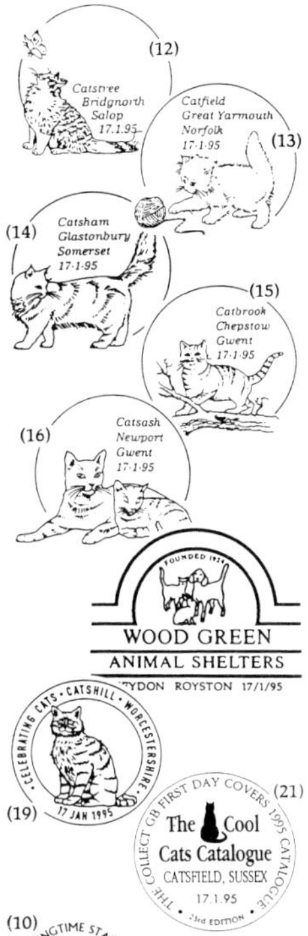

14th March 1995 - SPRINGTIME

19p Dandelions; 25p Sweet Chestnut Leaves; 30p Garlic Leaves; 35p Hazel Leaves; 41p Spring Grass

SPECIAL HANDSTAMPS

(1) First Day of Issue - Philatelic Bureau	3	-	*Royal Mail*
(2) First Day of Issue - Springfield	3	-	*Royal Mail*
(3) First Day of Issue - London	3	-	*Royal Mail*
(4) Springtime, Wingfield	4	10	*BLCS 102*
(5) Springtime, Swallownest	4	6	*BLCS 102*
(6) Springtime, Birdbrook	4	6	*BLCS 102*
(7) Springtime, Ducklington	4	10	*B'ham(500)102*
(8) Springtime, Featherstone	4	6	*BLCS 102*
(9) Rupert, Bearwood	4	8	*BLCS 102*
(10) Springtime Stamps, Springvale	4	10	*LFDC 130*
(11) Springtime Stamps, Royal Botanic Gdns, Kew	4	10	*Brad VP No92*
(12) Springtime, North Norfolk Railway	4	6	*Dawn*
(13) Spring into the new Catalogue, Leaves Green	4	6	*FDP Co*
(14) The 'Saints', BF 2458 PS	4	6	*RAF FDC 27*
(15) Wansford Station, Peterborough	4	6	*NVRly*

C.D.S. POSTMARKS

(16) Chestnut Grove or Hazel Grove *each*	8
(17) Kew Gardens	9
(18) Springbank, Springfield, Spring Grove or Springvale	8
(19) Spring Gardens	9

In addition: Grassmoor, Leaves Green, Spring Corner, Spring Hill, Springside, Swallownest, Wrens Nest. Prices from £6.

SLOGAN POSTMARKS

Tropical Places. Prices from £6.

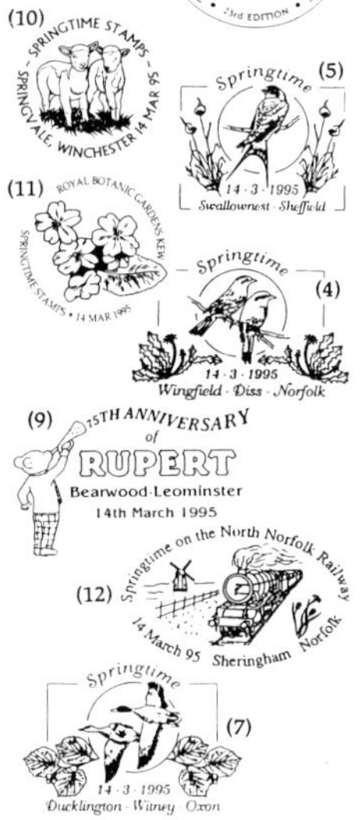

1995

21st March 1995 - GREETINGS.
10x1st Class on the theme of Love & Kisses.

SPECIAL HANDSTAMPS

	ordinary covers £	official covers £	
(1) First Day of Issue – Philatelic Bureau	4	–	*Royal Mail*
(2) First Day of Issue – Lover	4	–	*Royal Mail*
(3) First Day of Issue – London	5	–	*Royal Mail*
(4) Gretna Green	5	12	*Bradbury*
(5) Loversall, Doncaster	5	15	*BLCS 103*
(6) Darlington, Co. Durham	5	20	*BLCS 103*
(7) Lovesgrove, Aberystwyth	5	10	*BLCS 103*
(8) Loveston, Kilgetty	5	10	*BLCS 103*
(9) Honeydon, Bedford	5	10	*BLCS 103*
(10) Lover, Salisbury	5	10	*BLCS 103*
(11) Lovington, Castle Cary	5	10	*BLCS 103*
(12) Darlingscott, Shipston on Stour	5	10	*BLCS 103*
(13) Kislingbury, Northampton	5	12	*B'ham(500)103*
(14) Hugglescote, Leicester	5	10	*Benham D234*
(15) Team Work, Royal Mail, Leeds	5	12	*Royal Mail NE*
(16) Discovery Day, Dundee	5	–	*n.o.c.*

C.D.S. POSTMARKS

(17) Big Top or Playing Place	*each*	12
(18) Greet, Gretna Green or Lover	*each*	12

In addition: Darlington, Kishorn, Portobello Road. Prices from £8.

11th April 1995 – NATIONAL TRUST
19p 100 Years; 25p Protecting Land; 30p Conserving Art; 35p Saving Coast; 41p Repairing Buildings.

SPECIAL HANDSTAMPS

	ordinary covers £	official covers £	
(1) First Day of Issue – Philatelic Bureau	3	–	*Royal Mail*
(2) First Day of Issue – Lover	3	–	*Royal Mail*
(3) First Day of Issue – London	4	–	*Royal Mail*
(4) Queen Anne's Gate SW1 National Headquarters	4	–	*Royal Mail*
(5) Attingham Park, Conserving Art	4	–	*Royal Mail*
(6) St. David's, Saving Coastline	4	–	*Royal Mail*
(7) Congleton, Repairing Buildings	4	–	*Royal Mail*
(8) Crom, Enniskillen, Protecting Land	4	–	*Royal Mail*
(9) Giant's Causeway, Bushmills (oval)	4	–	*Royal Mail*
(10) Blickling Hall, Aylsham, Norfolk	4	–	*Royal Mail*
(11) This England, Oakham, Rutland	4	8	*Brad VP No93*
(12) Country Houses Association, W1	4	8	*LFDC 131*
(13) Steam Yacht Gondola, Coniston	4	6	*BLCS 104*
(14) Brownsea Island, Poole	4	6	*BLCS 104*
(15) Calke Abbey, Ticnall, Derby	4	6	*Benham*
(16) Fountains, Abbey, Ripon	4	10	*B'ham(500)104*
(17) Powis Castle, Welshpool	4	6	*Benham*
(18) Hidcote Manor, Chipping Camden	4	6	*Benham*
(19) Giant's Causeway, Bushmills	4	6	*Benham*
(20) The Old Post Office, Tintagel	4	6	*Benham*
(21) The Clergy House, Alfriston	4	6	*Benham*
(22) Chartwell, Westerham, Kent	4	6	*Benham*
(23) The National Trust, Radio Times, W12	4	6	*Benham*
(24) George Stephenson's Birthplace, Wylam	4	6	*Dawn*
(25) Supertrams, Sheffield	4	6	*Dawn*
(26) The catalogue you can trust, Alfriston	4	6	*FDP Co*
(27) Llangollen Postal Museum	4	8	*Llangollen PM*
(28) No.39 Squadron BF 2459 PS	4	6	*RAF FDC 28*

C.D.S. POSTMARKS

(29) Alfriston – first building acquired by National Trust	8
(30) Atcham or Opton Megna – Attingham Park (19p & 30p).	8
(31) Barmouth – first site acquired by National Trust	8
(32) Haslemere – Home of Robert Hunter (Founder)	8
(33) Lower Shiplake – B/place Canon Rawnsley (Founder)	8
(34) Scholar Green – Little Moreton Hall (41p)	8
(35) St. David's – Featured on 35p	8
(36) Tintagel – Post Office belongs to National Trust	8
(37) Wisbech – B/place Octavia Hill (Founder)	8
(38) Land's End and John O'Groats *pair*	17

In addition: Acorn Street, Bredon, Lacock, Montacute, Oak Tree, Petworth, Shipton-by-Beningbrough Prices from £6.

SLOGAN POSTMARKS

See the Clock etc. Prices from £6.

2nd May 1995 - VE DAY

19p Liberation of Paris; 25p St. Paul's on VE night; 19p Red Cross ; 19p & 25p United Nations.

SPECIAL HANDSTAMPS

	ordinary covers £	official covers £	
(1) First Day of Issue - Philatelic Bureau	3	-	*Royal Mail*
(2) First Day of Issue - Peace & Freedom, SW	3	-	*Royal Mail*
(3) First Day of Issue - London	3	-	*Royal Mail*
(4) First Day of Issue - VE DAY London EC4	3	5	*DailyMirror*
(5) United Nations Association, Whitehall	4	15	*Cover Collection*
(6) United Nations, Peacehaven	4	8	*BLCS 105*
(7) United Nations, London SW1	4	8	*BLCS 105*
(8) Victory in Europe, London	4	12	*B'ham(500)105*
(9) Victory in Europe, Birmingham	4	8	*Benham*
(10) Victory in Europe, Coventry	4	8	*Benham*
(11) Victory in Europe, Edinburgh	4	8	*Benham*
(12) Victory in Europe, Cardiff	4	8	*Benham*
(13) Victory in Europe, Dover	4	8	*BLCS 105*
(14) Daily Express, Hyde Park	4	8	*Benham*
(15) The Mail on Sunday, Kensington	4	8	*Benham*
(16) Victory in Europe, Radio Times, W12	4	8	*Benham*
(17) Victory in Europe, Whitehall (cigar)	4	8	*LFDC 132*
(18) Peace & Freedom, EC4	4	8	*Brad VP No94*
(19) British Medical Association	4	8	*Bradbury*
(20) R J Mitchell Centenary Year, Southampton	4	8	*Bradbury*
(21) BBMF Commemoration, SW1	4	8	*CoverCraft*
(22) Enigma Codebreakers, Bletchley Park	4	8	*Arlington*
(23) St. Dunstan's, London W1	4	8	*Arlington*
(24) Birmingham Evening Mail VE DAY	4	8	*Dawn*
(25) Troops Return, Liverpool	4	8	*Dawn*
(26) British Forces Postal Service 1000	4	8	*Forces*
(27) GB FDC Catalogue, Peacehaven	4	6	*FDP Co*
(28) Llangollen Postal Museum	4	8	*Llangollen PM*
(29) No 8 Squadron, BF 2460 PS	4	6	*RAF FDC 29*
(30) Peterborough Rail 150	4	8	*NVRly*

C.D.S. POSTMARKS

(31) Bladon or Churchill	*each*	9
(32) House of Commons or Lords	*each*	20
(33) London EC - St. Paul's Cathedral (25p)		8
(34) Montgomery		8
(35) Peacehaven		8
(36) Tufton St SW1 - first meeting on UN		8
(37) West Wellow - Florence Nightingale		8

In addition: Biggin Hill, Cranwell, Falls Road, Wonersh, Victory Street. Prices from £6.

6th June 1995 - SCIENCE FICTION

25p The Time Machine; 30p The First Men in the Moon; 35p War of the Worlds; 41p The Shape of Things to Come.

SPECIAL HANDSTAMPS

	ordinary covers £	official covers £	
(1) First Day of Issue - Philatelic Bureau	3	-	*Royal Mail*
(2) First Day of Issue - Wells	3	-	*Royal Mail*
(3) First Day of Issue - London H G Wells SF	3	-	*Royal Mail*
(4) Into the Future, Starboard Way, E14	4	6	*BLCS 106*
(5) Science Fiction, Star Road, W14	4	10	*B'ham(500)107*
(6) War of the Worlds, Worlds End, Newbury	4	6	*BLCS 106*
(7) Time and Space, Star	4	3	*Benham(s)*
(8) Science Fiction, Radio Times, W12	4	6	*Benham*
(9) The First Men in the Moon, Bromley	4	8	*Brad VP No95*
(10) The War of the Worlds, Bromley	4	8	*LFDC 133*
(11) H G Wells 1866-1946, Bromley	4	8	*Cam.S.C.*
(12) Blick, 70 Years Time Recording, Swindon	4	12	*Blick*
(13) Science Fiction Convention, Glasgow	4	12	*Cover Collection*
(14) Message from Mars, Bromley	4	8	*CoverCraft*
(15) Travel Back in Time, Wells	4	6	*FDP Co*
(16) No. IV (AC) Squadron BF 2469 PS	4	6	*RAF FDC 30*

C.D.S. POSTMARKS

(17) Bromley - birthplace of H. G. Wells	8
(18) Sandgate - where he wrote *War of theWorlds*	8
(19) Sevenoaks - where he wrote *The Time Machine*	8
(20) Wells, Somerset	8

In addition: Clockface, Globe Road, Greenwich, New Invention, The Rocket, Worlds End. Prices from £6.

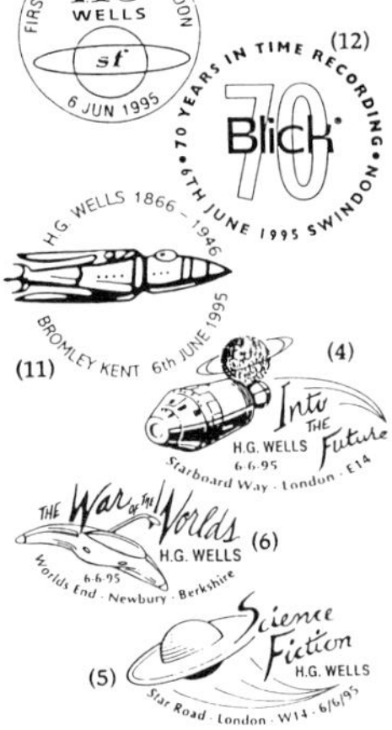

8th August 1995 - SHAKESPEARE'S GLOBE THEATRE

5 x 25p: The Swan Theatre 1595; The Rose Theatre 1587; The Globe Theatre 1599; The Hope Theatre 1613; The Globe Theatre 1614.

SPECIAL HANDSTAMPS	ordinary covers £	official covers £	
(1) First Day of Issue - Philatelic Bureau	3	-	*Royal Mail*
(2) First Day of Issue - Stratford upon Avon	3	-	*Royal Mail*
(3) First Day of Issue - Globe Theatre London	3	-	*Royal Mail*
(4) Henry V, The Barbican EC	4	10	*Benham SG26*
(5) Twelfth Night, The Barbican EC	4	8	*BLCS 108*
(6) A Midsummer Night's Dream, Stratford	4	6	*BLCS 108*
(7) Love's Labours Lost, Stratford	4	10	*B'ham(500)108*
(8) Romeo and Juliet, Stratford	4	6	*Benham*
(9) Stratford Upon Avon (swan)	4	8	*Brad VP No96*
(10) A Midsummer Night's Dream (portrait), Stratford	4	8	*LFDC 134*
(11) A Midsummer Night's Dream (ass), Stratford	4	8	*Cam.S.C.*
(12) Celebrating Shakespeare's New Globe	4	8	*Cover Collection*
(13) Stratford upon Avon (changeable date pmk)	5	-	*Royal Mail*
(14) Shakespeare's Globe, Bankside, SE1	4	10	*Bradbury*
(15) Loughborough Grammar School	4	10	*Bradbury*
(16) Blick Time Systems, Swindon	4	6	*Rlick*
(17) The Hammers, Hamlet, Famous Locos E13	4	6	*Dawn*
(18) The new replica Globe Theatre, South Bank	4	6	*FDP Co*
(19) Covercraft Tenth Anniversary Year	4	6	*CoverCraft*
(20) Port Ellen, Isle of Islay	4	-	*Royal Mail*
(21) No.9 The First Tornado Squadron BF 2470 PS	4	6	*RAF FDC 31*

C.D.S. POSTMARKS	
(22) Globe Road, London	8
(23) London Bridge - nearest PO to the new Globe	8
(24) Old Swan, Rose *each*	8
(25) Stratford upon Avon	8

In addition: Macduff, The Circle. Prices from £6.

5th September 1995 - COMMUNICATIONS

Rowland Hill: 19p Penny Postage; 25p Penny Black; Marconi: 41p Early wireless; 60p Marine safety & navigation.

SPECIAL HANDSTAMPS			
(1) First Day of Issue - Philatelic Bureau	3	-	*Royal Mail*
(2) First Day of Issue - London EC (pillar box)	3	-	*Royal Mail*
(3) First Day of Issue - London (maltese cross)	3	-	*Royal Mail*
(4) Rowland Hill Fund - Philatelic Bureau	3	4	*Royal Mail(s)*
(5) Centenary First Wireless Message, Chelmsford	4	7	*LFDC 135*
(6) Bath	4	8	*Brad VP No97*
(7) Radio Society of Great Britain, Herts	4	10	*LFDC 135*
(8) Alexandra Palace, London N22	4	8	*Cam.S.C.*
(9) Sir Rowland Hill, Kidderminster	4	6	*BLCS 109*
(10) Sir Rowland Hill, Bath	4	9	*B'ham(500)109*
(11) First Radio Message, Chelmsford (square)	4	3	*Benham(s)*
(12) First Radio Message, Flatholm Island	4	6	*BLCS 109*
(13) BT Portishead Radio, Highbridge	4	6	*A. Hyde*
(14) ITN 40 Anniversary, WC2	4	6	*Arlington*
(15) 60th Anniv TV Transmission, Alexandra Palace	4	6	*Dawn*
(16) Royal Navy & British Army Equip Exhib BF 2484 PS	4	6	*Forces*
(17) Blick Time Systems Ltd, Swindon	4	6	*Blick*
(18) Mail by Rail, Sheffield	4	6	*Dawn*
(19) No.32 Communications Squadron BF 2471 PS	4	6	*RAF FDC 32*

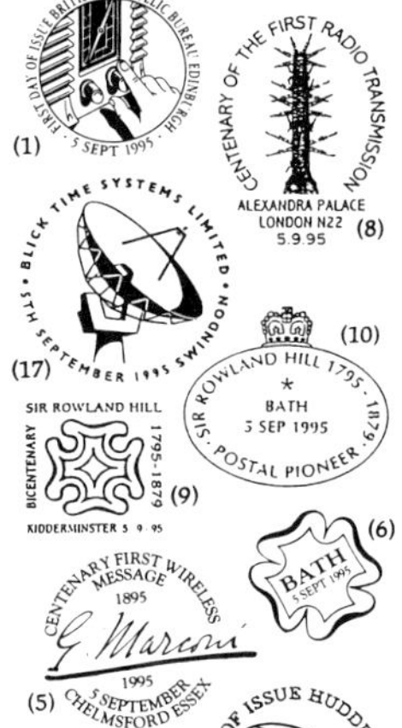

3rd October 1995 - RUGBY LEAGUE

19p Harold Wagstaff; 25p Gus Risman; 30p Jim Sullivan; 35p Billy Batten; 41p Brian Bevan.

SPECIAL HANDSTAMPS			
(1) First Day of Issue - Philatelic Bureau	3	-	*Royal Mail*
(2) First Day of Issue - Huddersfield	3	-	*Royal Mail*
(3) First Day of Issue - London	3	-	*Royal Mail*
(4) Wigan Rugby League Football Club	4	7	*LFDC 136*
(5) Halifax Rugby League Football Club	4	8	*Brad VP No98*
(6) Salford Rugby League Club	4	7	*Dawn*
(7) Centenary of Rugby League, Bradford	4	6	*Benham*
(8) Centenary of Rugby League, Huddersfield (oval)	4	6	*BLCS 110*
(9) Centenary Rugby League, Leeds	4	6	*Benham*
(10) Centenary Rugby League, Wigan	4	6	*BLCS 110*
(11) Centenary of Rugby League, Huddersfield (shield)	4	7	*Cam.S.C.*
(12) Assoc'n of GB FDC Collectors, Kenton	4	7	*AGB FDC*

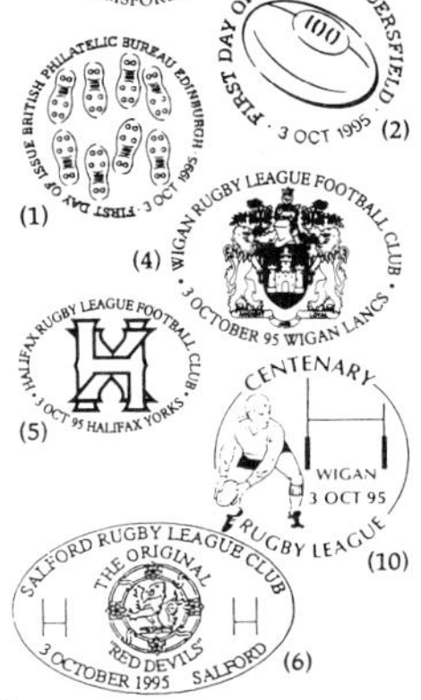

N.B. - More details of the last two issues to follow in next years edition of this catalogue.

DEFINITIVE ISSUES
Including Booklet Panes, Coils, Postage Dues, Framas and Regionals

GENERAL NOTES

Please also read the General Notes at the beginning of this catalogue.

Prices and Condition

1839-1951 Prices vary considerably, according to condition, for all early definitives on first day covers. **The prices quoted are for good covers with clear postmarks.** Superb examples may realise a better price whilst covers in poor condition with fetch less.

1952 to date Prices are for good clean covers with clear postmarks. With the exception of the earlier issues (1950s) covers are usually available unaddressed (or with small printed labels etc.) and the prices reflect this.

Format

This section falls into three broad categories covering the following dates:

1839-1936 Unless otherwise stated prices are for any postmark on plain envelopes.

1936-1970 Prices are given for both plain and illustrated covers, once again with any postmarks. Where known relevant postmarks exist, these have been listed.

1971 - to date All prices are for illustrated covers. The two column price structure now reflects covers with the more sought after Windsor postmarks or for covers with any other type of postmark. Where special handstamps were sponsored for specific issues, these have also been listed.

Scope

DEFINITIVES: Where the first day of issue is known, all new definitive stamps have been listed. With effect from the new *Machin* definitives issued in 1967 the Post Office provided first day of issue facilities for all **new values** and **colour changes**. Varieties in perforations, phosphors, papers etc are also listed where known. However these are not recognised as new stamps by the Royal Mail and are therefore only available with permanent pictorial handstamps or CDS postmarks (see General Notes at beginning of catalogue)

REGIONALS: The first regionals were issued in 1958 - these were for Scotland, Wales, Northern Ireland, Isle of Man, Jersey and Guernsey. By the early 1970s all three small islands were independent stamp producers. Therefore, unless otherwise stated, with effect from the 1974 Regional issue all prices are for sets of three covers with appropriate regional postmarks (Scotland, Wales and Northern Ireland). With effect from 1974 there were pictorial special handstamps provided by the Post Office for new values or colour changes.

BOOKLET PANES: In the main, these are included if their content (whether different se-tenant formats or changes to perfs etc) are different to those previously issued.

PRESTIGE BOOKS: The first Prestige Booklet, *Stamps for Cooks*, was issued in 1969. The issue of these books is now an annual event. Prices quoted are for the full panes on cover - i.e. with the text and pictures.

COIL STRIPS: Prices quoted for single value coils are for covers with at least two stamps adjoining. Covers bearing a single stamp from the coil are worth approximately half the catalogue price.

FIRST DAYS OF NEW SERVICES: Whilst not strictly FDCs, covers marking the first day of new Post Office services, e.g. Recorded Delivery, Speedpost etc. have also been included.

NEW FINDS

The publisher welcomes photocopies or information on any definitive issue not listed in this catalouge.

QUEEN VICTORIA (1837-1901)

All prices from 1839-1936 are for plain (un-illustrated) covers except where stated.

Date of issue		£
5 Dec 1839	Uniform 4d Post	350
10 Jan 1840	First Day of Universal Penny Post	450
6 May 1840	The Mulready 1d Stationery	2,500
6 May 1840	1d Black (imperf.) THE FIRST POSTAGE STAMP	20,000
8 May 1840	2d Blue (imperf.)	25,000
22 Feb 1855	2d Blue (perforated, Plate 4)	2,500
7 Mar 1865	6d Deep Lilac	1,800
1 Oct 1870	½d Rose Red (small format) on Asylum cover	1,000
	½d Rose Red (small Format) printed on postcard	600
12 Apr 1872	6d Deep Chestnut	1,500
1 Sept 1873	1s Green	2,500
1 Jan 1880	1d Venetian Red	1,000
1 Aug 1883	6d First Day of Inland Parcel Service	400
1 Jan 1887	5d Dull Purple & Blue (Jubilee issue)	1,250
	Uniform Penny Postage Jubilee - official envelopes	
16 May 1890	Guildhall handstamp (No. 1)	50
2 Jul 1890	South Kensington handstamp (No. 6)	30
	South Kensington handstamps (Nos. 4 or 5) *each*	70
	South Kensington handstamps (Nos. 2 or 3) *each*	50
	All five South Kensington handstamps on one cover	125
15 Sept 1892	4½d Green & Carmine (Jubilee issue)	3,000
17 Apr 1900	½d Blue-green (Jubilee issue)	900

(1)

(4)

(3)

(5)

(2)

(6)

KING EDWARD VII (1901-1910)

1 Jan 1902	½d Blue-green	75
	1d Red	75
	2½d Blue	250
	6d Purple	350
	The above four values on one cover	800
	-do- with Parliament Street C.D.S.	1,250
1 Nov 1909	4d Brown-orange (on postcard)	600
13 Jul 1911	4d Orange	1,200

KING GEORGE V (1910-1936)

	Imperial Crown Watermark	
22 Jun 1911	½d Green	75
	ditto on Junior Philatelic Society cover	275
	½d Green - printed on postcard	75
	1d Red	50
	The above two values on one cover	150
	Pair of covers with Westminster Abbey C.D.S.	2,500
1 Jan 1912	Redrawn ½d and 1d	1,200
25 Jan 1912	**Wilkinson Meter Mail**	
	First day of new experimental machine	275
	Royal Cypher Watermark	
17 Jan 1913	½d Green	600
8 Oct 1912	1d Red	450
15 Oct 1912	1½d Red-brown.....(International Stamp Exhib. h/s £650)	450
20 Aug 1912	2d Orange	450
18 Oct 1912	2½d Blue.................(International Stamp Exhib. h/s £700)	500
9 Oct 1912	3d Violet	600
15 Jan 1913	4d Grey-green	1,100
30 Jun 1913	5d Brown; 9d Agate - on one cover	2,000
1 Aug 1913	6d Purple	1,600
	7d Olive	1,600
	8d Black-yellow	1,800
	10d Turquoise	2,200
	1s Bistre	2,200
	High values - 'Sea Horses'	
13 Jun 1913	2s 6d Brown	2,400
	Postage Dues	
20 Apr 1914	½d Green (on cover or postcard)	350
	1d Red (on cover or postcard)	400
	2d Black	450
	5d Brown	750

Date of issue	KING GEORGE V (1910-1936) contd.	£
	Photogravure (Block Cypher Watermark)	
19 Nov 1934	½d Green	15
24 Sep 1934	1d Scarlet	15
20 Aug 1934	1½d Red-brown (illustrated cover £50)	15
21 Jan 1935	2d Orange	40
18 Mar 1935	2½d Blue	30
	3d Violet	40
	2½d and 3d values on one cover	75
2 Dec 1935	4d Grey-green	80
	9d Olive-green	100
	4d and 9d values on one cover	250
17 Feb 1936	5d Yellow-brown	550
24 Feb 1936	10d Turquoise-blue	600
26 Feb 1936	1s Bistre-brown	600
	Set of eleven (or nine) plain covers	1,800
	All eleven values on one cover with dates as above	2,500

Queen Victoria Rose Red 1st October 1870
British Asylum for Deaf and Dumb Females cover.

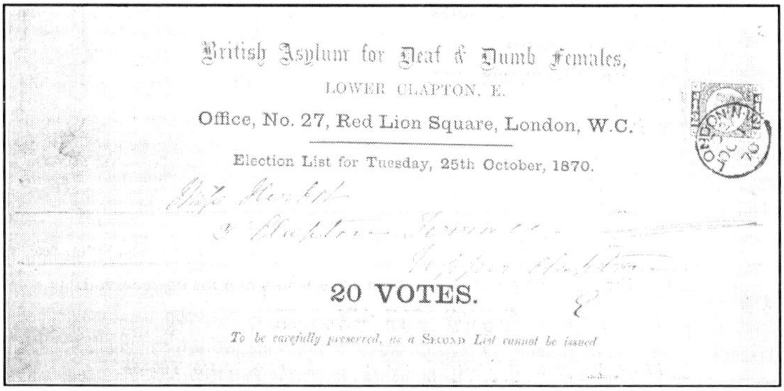

All prices from King Edward VIII reign are for plain and illustrated covers (where known). The abbreviation n.k. indicates not known to exist.

Date of issue	KING EDWARD VIII (1936)	Plain £	Illus. £
1 Sep 1936	½d, 1½d, 2½d	4	125
	ditto King Edward, Banff C.D.S.	125	n.k.
	ditto Windsor C.D.S.	150	n.k.
	ditto Kingstanding, Birmingham C.D.S.	n.k.	150
	ditto Buckingham Gate C.D.S.	100	n.k.
14 Sep 1936	1d	8	150
	ditto King Edward, Banff C.D.S.	120	n.k.

Date of issue	KING GEORGE VI (1936-1952)	Plain £	Illus. £
	Low values - original issue		
10 May 1937	½d Green, 1d Scarlet, 2½d Ultramarine	3	20
	ditto Windsor machine postmark	n.k.	100
30 Jul 1937	1½d Red-brown	3	15
31 Jan 1938	2d Orange	10	35
	3d Violet	10	35
	2d and 3d values on one cover	20	80
21 Nov 1938	4d Grey-green	12	n.k.
	5d Brown	12	n.k.
	4d and 5d values on one over	30	n.k.
30 Jan 1939	6d Purple	30	n.k.
27 Feb 1939	7d Emerald-green	15	n.k.
	8d Carmine	15	n.k.
	7d and 8d values on one cover	40	n.k.
1 May 1939	9d Olive-green	80	n.k.
	10d Turquoise-blue	90	n.k.
	1s Bistre-brown	90	n.k.
	9d, 10d, and 1s values on one cover	275	n.k.
29 Dec 1947	11d Plum	35	100
	Set of fifteen values on eight or more covers	500	n.k.

KING GEORGE VI (1936-1952) contd.

Date of issue		Plain £	Illus. £
	High values - 'Arms' Design		
4 Sep 1939	2s 6d Brown	750	n.k.
9 Mar 1942	2s 6d Yellow-green	950	n.k.
21 Aug 1939	5s Red	350	n.k.
30 Oct 1939	10s Dark blue	1,500	n.k.
30 Nov 1942	10s Ultramarine	1,800	n.k.
1 Oct 1948	£1 Brown	150	n.k.
	Low values - change to pale colours		
1 Sep 1941	½d Pale green	15	n.k.
11 Aug 1941	1d Pale scarlet	15	n.k.
28 Sep 1942	1½d Pale red-brown	40	n.k.
6 Oct 1941	2d Pale orange	30	n.k.
21 Jul 1941	2½d Pale ultramarine	30	25
3 Nov 1941	3d Pale violet	80	n.k.
	Set of six covers	225	n.k.
2 Oct 1950	4d Change of colour - light ultramarine	10	75
3 May 1951	**Low values - colour changes:** ½d, 1d, 1½d, 2d, 2½d	5	30
	ditto Battersea C.D.S. postmark (Festival of Britain)	10	60
	1s Booklet	-	200
	'Festival' High values: 2s 6d, 5s, 10s, £1*	150	650
	ditto Battersea C.D.S. postmark or slogan*	n.k.	900
	* *(on one cover or set of four covers)*		

JERSEY & GUERNSEY WAR TIME DEFINITIVES

Date of issue		Plain £	Illus. £
	Guernsey and Jersey 'ARMS' issues		
7 Apr 1941	Guernsey ½d green	6	40
29 Jan 1942	Jersey ½d green	6	40
18 Feb 1941	Guernsey 1d red	6	40
1 Apr 1941	Jersey 1d red	6	40
12 Apr 1944	Guernsey 2½d blue	20	65
	Jersey 'VIEWS' issues		
1 Jun 1943	½d green	6	20
1 Jun 1943	1d scarlet	6	20
1 Jun 1943	½d green & 1d scarlet on one cover	15	40
8 Jun 1943	1½d brown	15	30
8 Jun 1943	2d orange-yellow	15	30
8 Jun 1943	1½d brown & 2d orange-yellow on one cover	25	50
29 Jun 1943	2½d blue	15	30
29 Jun 1943	3d violet	15	30
29 Jun 1943	2½d blue & 3d violet on one cover	25	50

King George VI 'Festival' High Values
3rd May 1951
One of a set of four covers for this sought after issue - this is a beautiful example.

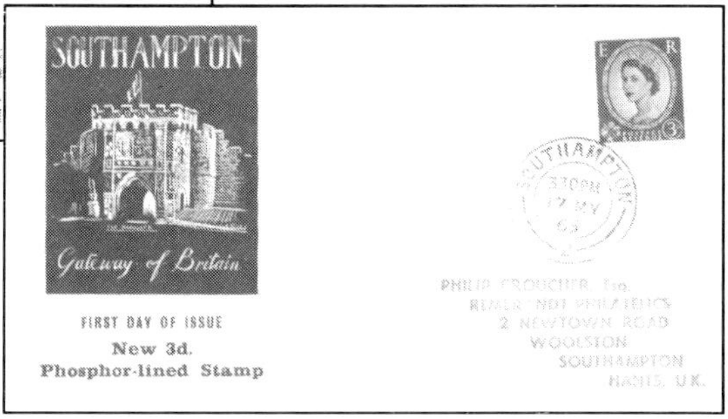

Queen Elizabeth II
3d Deep Lilac Phosphor
17th May 1965

Date of issue	QUEEN ELIZABETH II £.s.d. ISSUES (1952-1970)	Plain £	Illus. £
	LOW VALUE DEFINITIVES		
5 Dec 1952	1½d, 2½d	1	5
6 Jul 1953	5d, 8d, 1s	5	30
31 Aug 1953	½d, 1d, 2d	6	30
2 Nov 1953	4d, 1s 3d, 1s 6d	25	125
18 Jan 1954	3d, 6d, 7d	25	75
8 Feb 1954	9d, 10d, 11d	40	150
	Set of all 17 values on matching covers	150	550
	'CASTLES' HIGH VALUES		
23 Sep 1955	2s 6d, 5s – on one or two covers	75	400
	2s 6d only: Carrickfergus C.D.S. illustrated cover	–	250
1 Sep 1955	10s, £1 – on one or two covers	200	450
	10s, £1 – Edinburgh C.D.S.	–	625
	10s only – Edinburgh C.D.S.	150	–
	£1 only – Windsor Castle C.D.S.	250	–
	Set of 4 values on two or more matching covers	275	1250

Queen Elizabeth
2s Holiday Booklet
1st July 1964
Se-tenant (i.e. stamps of different denominations joined together) booklet pane.
Early definitives of the Queen are sometimes referred to as 'Wildings' because the portrait is based on a photograph by Dorothy Wilding.

Queen Elizabeth
1s Multi-value coil
27th August 1969
This was the first ever se-tenant coil

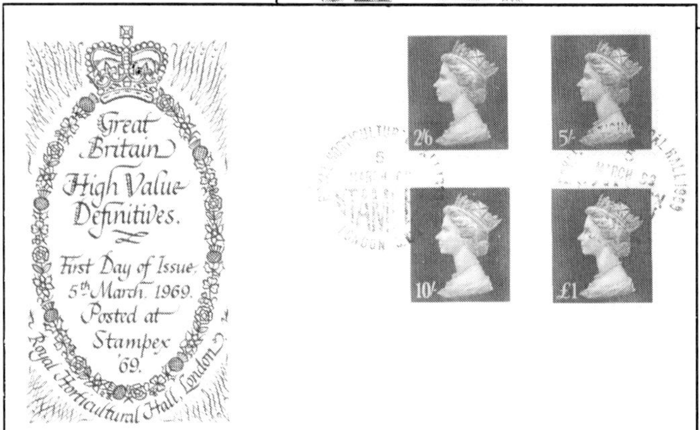

Queen Elizabeth
Machin High Values
5th March 1969
Stampex official cover.
Machin definitives are so called because the Queen's head as appears on all new definitives from 1967 is based on the work of Arnold Machin.

Date of issue		Plain £	Illus. £
17 Jul 1956	**3d ST. EDWARD CROWN WATERMARK**	100	–
	GRAPHITE-LINED ISSUES		
19 Nov 1957	½d, 1d, 1½d, 2d, 2½d, 3d – Southampton postmark	40	80
	Graphite lines were printed under the gum as an experiment in automatic letter sorting at Southampton.		
	FIRST REGIONAL STAMPS		
18 Aug 1958	**3d** with appropriate regional postmarks:		
	Wales or Scotland *each*	3	10
	Northern Ireland or Isle of Man *each*	3	25
	Guernsey or Jersey *each*	3	15
	Set of six covers	20	100
29 Sep 1958	**6d and 1s 3d** with appropriate regional postmarks:		
	Wales or Scotland *each*	3	20
	Northern Ireland	4	30
	Set of three covers	15	90
9 Feb 1959	**4½d NEW VALUE**	15	200
	PHOSPHOR-GRAPHITE ISSUES		
18 Nov 1959	½d, 1d, 1½d, 2d, 2½d, 3d, 4d, 4½d – Southampton pmk	40	100
	Similar to the Nov 1957 issue, but with the addition of phosphor bands on the front.		
27 Jun 1960	**6d PHOSPHOR ISSUE**	–	200
	PHOSPHOR BANDS ISSUE		
6 Jul 1960	½d, 1d, 1½d, 2d, 2½d, 3d, 4d, 6d, 1s3d – Southampton	–	125
	Inauguration of Phosphor Line Sorting Machine.		
1 Feb 1961	**RECORDED DELIVERY:** First Day of new service	60	–
29 Jan 1963	**SCOTLAND: 3d, 6d, 1s 3d (phos)**		
	Scottish postmark	40	100
15 Jul 1963	**ISLE OF MAN 3d CHALKY PAPER:** I.O.M. pmk	60	250
15 July 1963	**2s BOOKLET:** 3 Panes (2 @ 4 x 2½d) + (3 x ½d + 2½d)		
	Se-tenant pane on cover	30	90
	4 x 2½d pane on cover	40	100
	This booklet was issued primarily for holiday resorts.		
6 Sep 1963	**2s BOOKLET:** Reprint of above – both panes	50	85
8 Jun 1964	**2½d REGIONALS:** with regional postmarks		
	Isle of Man	4	25
	Guernsey or Jersey *each*	3	20
1 Jul 1964	**2s BOOKLET:** (4 panes of 2 x 2½d + 2 x ½d)		
	Se-tenant pane with Bournemouth, Ryde, Salisbury, Stratford or Winchester postmark	n.k.	3
	Brighton & Hove (or other holiday) slogan pmks	10	25
1 Jul 1964	**2½d WATERMARK SIDEWAYS:** from 2s booklet	10	30
17 May 1965	**4d DEEP ULTRAMARINE:** – New shade	30	75
	3d DEEP LILAC: – phosphor	30	75
	The issue dates of these stamps were originally planned for 28th April (4d) and 29th April (3d). These were deliberately postponed until 17th May being the official date of issue and the date of the change in the letter rate. Covers are known to exist with earlier dates.		
21 Jun 1965	**6s BOOKLET:** (3 panes of 6 x 4d) – one pane on cover	50	150
16 Aug 1965	**2s BOOKLET:** 2 Panes (2 x 1d + 2 x 3d) + (4 x 4d)		
	– both panes	50	150
	Se-tenant pane only	15	70
6 Dec 1965	**2s CHRISTMAS BOOKLET:** (2 @ 4 x 3d) one pane	50	200

Date of Issue		Plain £	Illus. £
7 Feb 1966	**4d BLUE REGIONALS:** Set of 6 with regional pmks	6	40
	4d Scotland – Phosphor issue	1	8
15 Feb 1967	**7d PHOSPHOR**	200	–
1 Mar 1967	**9d & 1s 6d REGIONALS:** (Wales, Scot., N.I.) Phosphor		
	Set of three covers with regional pmks	–	7
	Wales – 'New Stamp Issue . . .' slogan pmk	5	15
	N.I. – 'New Stamp Issue . . .' slogan pmk	–	15
9 Jun 1967	**5d PHOSPHOR**	100	–
28 Jun 1967	**8d & 1s PHOSPHOR**	150	–
	NEW STYLE (MACHIN HEAD) DEFINITIVES		
5 Jun 1967	**4d, 1s, 1s 9d** (Illus. cover with Windsor F.D.I. £2)	–	1
8 Aug 1967	**3d, 9d, 1s 6d** (Illus. cover with Windsor F.D.I. £2)	–	1
5 Feb 1968	**½d, 1d, 2d, 6d** (Illus. cover with Windsor F.D.I. £2)	–	1
1 Jul 1968	**5d, 7d, 8d, 10d** (Illus. cover with Windsor F.D.I. £2)	–	1
21 Sep 1967	**6s MACHIN BOOKLET:** (3 panes of 6 x 4d) one pane	5	100
25 Mar 1968	**10s 'LIVINGSTON' BOOKLET:**		
	3 panes (6 x 4d; 6 x 3d; 6 x 1d) Stampex pmk	10	100
	'CASTLES' HIGH VALUES: UNWATERMARKED PAPER		
6 Dec 1967	**£1** (London Underground special cover)	–	500
16 Apr 1968	**5s and 10s**	400	n.k.
3 Jul 1968	**2s 6d**	n.k.	300
6 Apr 1968	**2s MACHIN BKLT:** 2 panes (2 x 1d + 2 x 3d)+(4 x 4d)	20	70
4 Jun 1968	**2s 6d CHALKY PAPER**	150	250
10 Jul 1968	**4s 6d CUTTY SARK BKLT:** 3 panes (2 @ 6 x 4d)+(6 x 1d)		
	pair of different panes on cover	20	100
28 Aug 1968	**1s 6d PVA GUM**	–	150
4 Sep 1968	**4d BROWN & 5d BLUE REGIONALS:**		
	Set of six covers with regional postmarks	2	10
	Wales – 'New Stamps . . .' slogan pmk	3	25

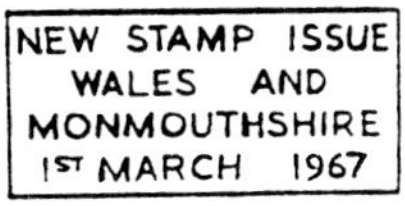

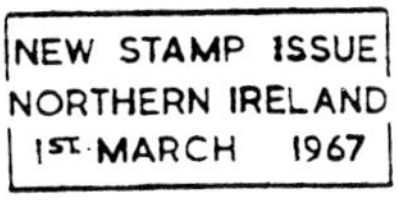

16 SEP 1968: THE BEGINNING OF TWO-TIER POST
1st Class 5d, 2nd Class 4d

Date of Issue		Plain £	Illus. £
16 Sep 1968	**2s, 4s 6d & 10s BOOKLETS:**		
	2s 2 panes (4 x 4d)+(2 x 4d + 2 labels)	5	12
	-do- Windsor postmark	8	30
	4s 6d 3 panes (2 @ 6 x 4d)+(6 x 1d) 2 different panes	10	50
	10s 5 panes (2 @ 6 x 4d)+(2 @ 6 x 5d)+(4 x 1d + 2 x 4d)		
	set of three different panes on cover	15	75
16 Oct 1968	**6s WOODPECKER BKLT:** (3 panes 6 x 4d) one pane	15	90
16 Sep 1968	**4d COIL STRIP:** Pair of stamps on cover	20	150
16 Sep 1968	**4d PHOSPHOR**	10	25
27 Nov 1968	**5s IGHTHAM MOTE BKLT:** (2 @ 6 x 5d) – one pane	15	90
29 Nov 1968	**9d PVA GUM**	–	50
6 Jan 1969	**4d RED & 8d TURQUOISE:** Colour changes	–	1
	Windsor postmark	–	3
8 Jan 1969	**4s 6d BOOKLET:** two panes	15	60
	10s MARY KINGSLEY BOOKLET: three panes	20	75
	(Composition for these two booklets as 16 Sep 1968 but 4d colour change to red). 10s known with 6 January date		
26 Feb 1969	**4d RED REGIONALS:** set of 6 with regional pmks	2	5

Date of issue		Plain £	Illus. £
3 Mar 1969	**2s BOOKLET:** (Composition as 16 Sep 1968 with 4d colour change) – 2 panes	5	50
5 Mar 1969	**MACHIN HIGH VALUES: 2s 6d, 5s, 10s, £1**	2	10
	Windsor F.D.I. postmark	3	15
	Stampex special handstamp	4	25
	ditto Stampex official cover	–	25
27 Aug 1969	**1s MULTI-VALUE COIL STRIP:** (2 x 2d, 3d, 1d, 4d)	1	2
	Windsor postmark	1	4
1 Dec 1969	**STAMPS FOR COOKS £1 BOOKLET**		
	Set of 4 panes – Milk Marketing Board h/s	7	40
	Se-tenant strip from multi-value pane – MMB h/s	2	15
10 Dec 1969	**1s 6d PHOSPHOR:** Southampton postmark	1	5
3 Mar 1970	**5s 'PHILYMPIA' BOOKLET:** (2 panes 6 x 5d) one pane Stampex special handstamp	5	40
28 Sep 1970	**9d SCOTLAND UNWATERMARKED PAPER**	3	20
16 Nov 1970	**1s 9d PVA GUM**	n.k.	80

QUEEN ELIZABETH II DECIMAL ISSUES (1970 to date)

All prices for illustrated covers.

Date of issue		Windsor Postmark £	Other pmks £
17 Jun 1970	**TO PAY LABELS: 10p, 20p, 50p, £1**	–	450
17 Jun 1970	**10p, 20p, & 50p**	4	1
	First Issue of British Decimal Stamps, Windsor h/s	9	–
	15 FEB 1971: 1st Class 3p, 2nd Class 2½p		
15 Feb 1971	**½p, 1p, 1½p, 2p, 2½p, 3p, 3½p, 4p, 5p, 6p, 7½p, & 9p**		
	F.D.I. postmarks with 'Delayed by GPO Strike' cachets	3	2
	Authentic C.D.S. – a few sub offices open during strike	–	12
	F.P.O. (Field Post Offices) pmks – open during strike	–	7
15 Feb 1971	**BOOKLETS:**		
	10p (2 x 2p + 2 x ½p)+(2 x 1p + 2 x 1½p) Vertical format		
	25p (5 x 2½p + label)+(4 x 2½p + 2 labels)+(5 x ½p + label)		
	30p (2 identical panes of 5 x 3p + label)		
	50p (6 x 3p)+(4 x 3p + 2 x 2½p side band)+(5 x 2½p centre band + label)+(5 x ½p + label)		
	Set of 10 panes (with GPO strike cachets)	100	50
	Set of 3 se-tenant panes (with GPO strike cachets)	40	15
15 Feb 1971	**5p MULTI-VALUE COIL STRIP:**		
	(2 x ½p; 2 x 1p; 1 x 2p) with GPO strike cachet	4	2
	Note: these were not officially available until 11 March 1971 - covers sometimes occur with this issue date		
15 Feb 1971	**2½p COIL STRIPS:** Vertical or Horizontal	–	500
	3p COIL STRIPS: Vertical or Horizontal	–	500
15 Feb 1971	**TO PAY LABELS: ½p, 1p, 2p, 3p, 4p, 5p,** New values		
	Authentic C.D.S. postmarks – 15 February 1971	–	350
	Official issue date – 11 March 1971 with C.D.S. pmk	–	125
7 Jul 1971	**REGIONALS: 2½p, 3p, 5p, 7½p** (Wales, Scot., N.I., I.O.M.)		
	Regional special F.D.I. handstamps – set of four covers	–	8
14 Jul 1971	**10p BOOKLET:** (2 x 2p + 2 x ½p)+(2 x 1p + 2 x 1½p) Horizontal format	300	250
23 Jul 1971	**30p BOOKLET:** (2 @ 5 x 3p + label imperf in margin*)		
	One pane on cover	150	100
	**Changes introduced as an aid to the blind – so that they could distinguish the stamps from the labels.*		

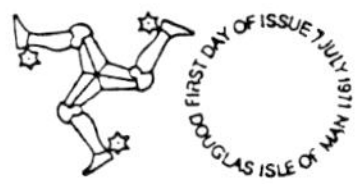

Date of Issue		Windsor Postmark £	Other pmks £
11 Aug 1971	**10p SMALL DESIGN**	2	1
17 Sep 1971	**25p & 50p BOOKLETS:**		
	25p (5 x 2½p + label)+(4 x 2½p + 2 labels)+(5 x ½p + label)		
	Labels imperf in margin* – 3 panes on 2 covers	n.k.	125
	50p 4 panes, only two differ from 17th February issue:		
	(5 x 2½p (centre band) + label)+(5 x ½p + label)		
	Labels imperf in margin* – 2 panes on cover	150	100
	**Imperf so that the blind could distinguish the stamps from the labels.*		
24 Dec 1971	**25p & 50p CHRISTMAS BOOKLETS**		
	25p (5 x ½p + label)+(5 x 2½p + label)+(4 x 2½p + 2 labels)		
	50p (5 x 2½p + label) – different to 25p booklet		
	Four panes on set of covers with Southampton pmk	n.k.	75
	The remaining 50p panes were as previously issued in February or duplicated the above.		
24 May 1972	**WEDGWOOD £1 BOOKLET:** 4 panes		
	Set of 4 panes – Barlaston special h/s	–	90
	Set of 4 panes – Bureau special h/s	–	60
	Se-tenant pane + 2 se-tenant strips – Barlaston h/s	–	20
	Se-tenant pane + 2 se-tenant strips – Bureau h/s	–	10
	N.B. General Note re 'Prestige Booklets' – Prices are for covers bearing the complete pane of stamps + descriptive text. Covers with stamps only are worth considerably less.		
23 Aug 1972	**3p GUM ARABIC**	–	40
13 Sep 1972	**2½p GUM ARABIC**	–	40
22 Sep 1972	**½p GUM ARABIC**	–	40
22 Sep 1972	**2½p (SCOTTISH) GUM ARABIC**	–	40
22 Sep 1972	**2½p (WELSH) GUM ARABIC**	–	40
31 Oct 1972	**4p GUM ARABIC**	–	60
6 Dec 1972	**£1 – REDRAWN '£':** F.D.I. postmarks	7	3
	Larger style Windsor F.D.I. postmark	17	–
14 Dec 1972	**3p (SCOTTISH) GUM ARABIC**	–	40
1 Feb 1973	**50p PHOSPHOR:** Southampton C.D.S. pmk	–	110
	Other C.D.S. postmarks	–	90
	National Postal Museum special handstamp	–	130
2 Apr 1973	**£5 TO PAY LABEL**	–	450
6 Jun 1973	**6p GUM ARABIC**	–	100
6 Jun 1973	**3p (WELSH) GUM ARABIC**	–	40
22 Aug 1973	**3½p PVA/DEXTRIN GUM**	–	40
	10 SEP 1973: 1st Class 3½p, 2nd Class 3p		
10 Sep 1973	**3p PHOSPHOR (Centre Band)**	20	10
10 Sep 1973	**3p GUM ARABIC + 1p, 2p, 3p PVA/DEXTRIN GUM**	50	–
27 Sep 1973	**£1 CONTRACTORS PAPER**	–	500
9 Oct 1973	**½p PVA/DEXTRIN GUM**	–	40
24 Oct 1973	**4½p, 5½p, 8p NEW VALUES**	2	1
30 Oct 1973	**6p PVA/DEXTRIN GUM**	–	125
12 Nov 1973	**4p & 10p PVA/DEXTRIN GUM**	–	125

Date of issue		Windsor Postmark £	Other pmks £
14 Nov 1973	**50p BOOKLET:** Two different panes on cover (2 @ 5 x 3½p + label)+(5 x 3p (centre band) + label)	140	80
30 Nov 1973	**20p CONTRACTORS PAPER**	–	400
23 Jan 1974	**REGIONALS: 3p phos + 3½p, 5½p, 8p new values** (Wales, Scotland, N.I.) – 3 regional special h/s	–	4
10 Feb 1974	**SELF ADHESIVE LABELS:** ½p, 1p, 11½p, (3p + 5p), (½p + 5p)	–	275
20 Feb 1974	**50p CONTRACTORS PAPER**	–	400
22 Mar 1974	**9p PVA/DEXTRIN GUM**	–	125
19 Jun 1974	**SELF ADHESIVE LABELS:** 3p, 3½p	–	50
	24 JUN 1974: 1st Class 4½p, 2nd Class 3½p		
24 Jun 1974	**3½p PHOSPHOR (Centre Band)**	30	6
21 Aug 1974	**7p TO PAY LABEL**	–	40
4 Sep 1974	**6½p PHOSPHOR (Two Bands)**	3	1
9 Oct 1974	**45p BOOKLET:** 2 @ (5 x 4½p + label) one pane	100	60
23 Oct 1974	**35p BOOKLET:** 2 @ (5 x 3½p phos + label) one pane	100	60
6 Nov 1974	**REGIONALS: 3½p phos + 4½p new value** (Wales, Scotland, N.I.) – 3 regional special h/s	–	3
13 Nov 1974	**4½p EXPERIMENTAL PHOSPHOR**	12	3
	Cambridge, Aberdeen, Norwich pmks each	–	20
	(Stamps were distributed to these Post Offices)		
15 Jan 1975	**7p PHOSPHOR (Two Bands)**	2	1
	-do- with phosphor omitted	20	8
	17 MAR 1975: 1st Class 7p, 2nd Class 5½p		
17 Mar 1975	**5½p PHOSPHOR (Centre Band)**	4	1
21 May 1975	**2½p PHOSPHOR (Two Bands)**	10	4
21 May 1975	**5½p PHOSPHOR REGIONALS:** (Wales, Scot., N.I.)		
	Set of 3 regional pmks	–	10
	N.I. only – Ulster Crusade slogan	–	10
18 Jun 1975	**11p TO PAY LABEL**	–	40
24 Sep 1975	**6½p PHOS (Centre Band) & 8½p PHOS (Two Bands)**	2	1
	29 SEP 1975: 1st Class 8½p, 2nd Class 6½p		
24 Nov 1975	**SPEEDPOST:** First Day of new service	–	25
3 Dec 1975	**10p MULTI-VALUE COIL:** (2 x ½p, 1p, 2p, 6p)	4	1
14 Jan 1976	**REGIONALS: 6½p & 8½p** (Wales, Scot., N.I.) Regional special F.D.I. h/s – set of 3 covers	–	3
28 Jan 1976	**6½p & 8½p COIL STRIPS:** vertical format	n.k.	150
25 Feb 1976	**9p, 9½p, 10p, 10½p, 11p & 20p**	5	2
	-do- with Stampex special handstamp	–	7
10 Mar 1976	**10p BOOKLET:** (2 x ½p; 3 x 1p; 1 x 6p)	3	1
	-do- P.O. Telecom Museum h/s on official cover	–	10
24 Mar 1976	**8½p EXPERIMENTAL PHOSPHOR**	2	1

Date of Issue		Windsor Postmark £	Other pmks £
14 Jul 1976	**65p & 85p BKLTS:** (10 x 6½p)+(10 x 8½p) Both panes....	80	30
13 Oct 1976	**6½p & 8½p COIL STRIPS:** horizontal format....................	100	80
20 Oct 1976	**10p & 11p REGIONALS:** (Wales, Scotland, N.I.) Set of 3 regional special handstamps...............	–	3
24 Jan 1977	**SPEEDPOST:** Extension of service......................................	–	125
26 Jan 1977	**50p BOOKLETS:** 2 @ (2 x ½p; 2 x 1p; 2 x 6½p; 4 x 8½p) both panes, right and left format (mirror image)	12	4
26 Jan 1977	**6½p left phos & 6½p right phos** (from above booklets)....	5	1
2 Feb 1977	**50p, £1, £2 & £5**..	20	8
	13 JUN 1977: 1st Class 9p, 2nd Class 7p		
13 Jun 1977	**50p BOOKLETS:** 2 @ (2 x 1p; 3 x 7p; 3 x 9p) both panes, right and left format (mirror image).........	8	4
13 Jun 1977	**7p left phos & 7p right phos** (from above booklets)	5	1
13 Jun 1977	**70p & 90p BKLTS:** (10 x 7p)+(10 x 9p) Both panes.........	20	9
13 Jun 1977	**7p & 9p COIL STRIPS:** vertical format.............................	100	45
13 Jun 1977	**30p & 60p SACHET BOOKLETS**.......................................	150	–
31 Oct 1977	**6p, 7p, 9p & 10p HALLEY PRESS**....................................	225	175
16 Nov 1977	**7p & 9p COIL STRIPS:** horizontal format.........................	100	45
14 Dec 1977	**10p MULTI-VALUE COIL:** (2 x ½p; 2 x 1p; and 7p)........	2	1
14 Dec 1977	**½p & 1p PHOS (Centre Band)** from above coil	2	1
18 Jan 1978	**REGIONALS: 7p, 9p, 10½p** (Wales, Scot., N.I.) Set of 3 regional pmks..	–	5
8 Feb 1978	**10p BOOKLET:** (2 x ½p; 2 x 1p; 1 x 7p + label)	2	1
26 Apr 1978	**10½p COLOUR CHANGE**..	2	1
15 Nov 1978	**£1.60 CHRISTMAS BOOKLET:** (10 x 9p; 10 x 7p)..........	5	2
5 Feb 1979	**70p BOOKLET:** (10 x 7p) Kedleston Hall; **90p BOOKLET:** (10 x 9p) Tramway Museum, Crich. Pair of covers with Derby Postcode slogan pmk......... Pair of covers with appropriate pmk............................. *Issued in conjunction with the opening of Derby Mechanised Letter Office, and to promote the use of postcodes.*	 – –	 120 100
15 Aug 1979	**11½p, 13p & 15p**	2	1
	20 AUG 1979: 1st Class 10p, 2nd Class 8p		
20 Aug 1979	**8p PHOSPHOR (Centre Band)**	2	1
20 Aug 1979	**10p (Phosphor Coated Paper + 2 Bands)**	2	1
28 Aug 1979	**50p BOOKLETS:** (2 x 2p; 2 x 8p; 3 x 10p + label) both panes, right and left format (mirror image)	5	2
28 Aug 1979	**8p left phos & 8p right phos** (from above booklets)	2	1
3 Oct 1979	**80p & £1 BKLTS:** (10 x 8p)+(10 x 10p) Both panes.........	6	3
3 Oct 1979	**10p (Preprinted phosphor paper)** from £1 Booklet..........	2	1
10 Oct 1979	**1p, 2p, 5p & 20p (New phosphor paper)**..........................	2	1
17 Oct 1979	**10p 'London 1980' BOOKLET** (2 x 1p; 1 x 8p + label)... -do- with 'London 1980' slogan postmark	2 –	1 3

Date of issue		Windsor Postmark £	Other pmks £
14 Nov 1979	**£1.80 CHRISTMAS BOOKLET:** (10 x 10p; 10 x 8p)	3	2
14 Nov 1979	**8p & 10p COIL STRIPS:** vertical format	40	10
12 Dec 1979	**1p & 2p phos. coated paper + 8p Enschedé**	2	1
16 Jan 1980	**10p MULTI-VALUE COIL:** (2 x 1p, 8p + two labels)	2	1
30 Jan 1980	**4p, 12p, 13½p, 17p, 17½p & 75p**	3	1
	4 FEB 1980: 1st Class 12p, 2nd Class 10p		
4 Feb 1980	**10p PHOSPHOR (Centre Band)**	2	1
4 Feb 1980	**10p (Phosphor coated paper)**	75	25
4 Feb 1980	**50p BOOKLETS:** 2 @ (3 x 2p; 2 x 10p; 2 x 12p + label) both panes, right and left format (mirror image)	8	3
4 Feb 1980	**10p left phos & 10p right phos** (from above booklets)	2	1
4 Feb 1980	**12p PHOSPHOR (Two Bands)** (from above booklets)	2	1
4 Feb 1980	**£1 & £1.20 BKLTS:** (10 x 10p)+(10 x 12p) Both panes	10	4
16 Apr 1980	**WEDGWOOD £3 BOOKLET:** 4 panes		
	Set of 4 panes – Barlaston special handstamp	–	7
	Set of 4 panes – Bureau special handstamp	–	6
	Se-tenant pane only – Barlaston special handstamp	–	2
	Se-tenant pane only – Bureau special handstamp	–	1
	N.B. prices for complete pane (stamps and illustrations)		
21 May 1980	**2p & 5p Questa, 20p Waddington, 50p non-phos**	2	1
11 Jun 1980	**10p & 12p COIL STRIPS**	50	40
25 Jun 1980	**50p CHAMBON BOOKLETS:** 2 @ (as 4th February) both panes, right and left format (mirror image)	60	40
23 Jul 1980	**REGIONALS: 10p Centre band; 12p, 13½p, 15p** (Wales, Scotland, N.I.) set of 3 regional pmks	–	6
27 Aug 1980	**10p CHAMBON BOOKLET: 'London 1980'**	2	1
27 Aug 1980	**11p (Phosphor coated paper)**	3	2
22 Oct 1980	**3p & 22p**	2	1
22 Oct 1980	**3p PCP1 & PCP2 + 22p PCP1 & PCP2**	10	5
12 Nov 1980	**£2.20 CHRISTMAS BOOKLET:** (10 x 12p; 10 x 10p)	4	3
10 Dec 1980	**½p (Phosphor coated paper)**	2	1
14 Jan 1981	**2½p, 11½p, 14p, 15½p, 18p & 25p**	2	1
	26 JAN 1981: 1st Class 14p, 2nd Class 11½p		
26 Jan 1981	**50p BOOKLETS:** 2 @ (1 x ½p;1 x 1p; 3 x 11½p; 1 x 14p) both panes, right and left format (mirror image)	5	2
26 Jan 1981	**11½p left phos & 11½p right phos** (from above bklts)	2	1
26 Jan 1981	**14p PHOSPHOR (Two Bands)** (from above booklets)	2	1
26 Jan 1981	**£1.15 & £1.40 BKLTS:**(10x11½p)+(10x14p) Both panes	6	3
11 Mar 1981	**11½p &14p COIL STRIPS**	50	35
8 Apr 1981	**REGIONALS: 11½p, 14p, 18p, 22p** (Wales, Scotland, N.I.) Set of 3 regional special handstamps	–	6

Date of Issue			Windsor Postmark £	Other pmks £
6May	1981	**£1.30 NATIONAL STAMP DAY BOOKLET**	3	1
		National Stamp Day – Birmingham special h/s................	–	3
		National Stamp Day – British Library special h/s............	–	3
		National Stamp Day – Cameo Stamp Centre special h/s.	–	3
		National Stamp Day – London EC special h/s.................	–	3
26 Aug	1981	**50p BOOKLETS:** 2 @ (3 x 2½p; 2 x 4p; 3 x 11½p) both panes, right and left format (mirror image)	7	2
26 Aug	1981	**2½p & 4p PHOSPHOR (Two Bands)** from 50p bklt........	2	1
2 Sep	1981	**11½p 'READERS DIGEST' COIL:** (1 x 2½p + 3 x 3p)...... *Note: Although issued in June for a Readers Digest promotion, these were not placed on sale by the P.O. until 2nd September. Covers with June, July and August dates do exist and will command a premium. (June dates from £50)*	2	1
11 Nov	1981	**£2.55 CHRISTMAS BOOKLET:** (10 x 11½p; 10 x 14p)...	7	3
7 Dec	1981	**4p & 20p P.C.P. Waddington printing**	15	5
30 Dec	1981	**12½p 'READERS DIGEST' COIL:** (1 x ½p + 3 x 4p)........	2	1
27 Jan	1982	**5p, 12½p, 16½p, 19½p, 26p & 29p**	4	1
		1 FEB 1982: 1st Class 15½p, 2nd Class 12½p		
1 Feb	1982	**50p BOOKLETS:** 2 @ (1 x ½p; 4 x 3p; 3 x 12½p)) both panes, right and left format (mirror image)	4	1
1 Feb	1982	**£1.25 & £1.55 BOOKLETS:** (10 x 12½p)+(10 x 15½p)......	6	3
1 Feb	1982	**£1.43 BOOKLET:** (4 x 12½p + 6 x 15½p)............................	4	1
1 Feb	1982	**12½p (left & right phos); ½p, 3p & 15½p (two phos)**........ from above booklets	3	1
1 Feb	1982	**12½p & 15½p COIL STRIPS**	40	25
24 Feb	1982	**REGIONALS: 12½p, 15½p, 19½p & 26p** (Wales, Scotland, N.I.)		
		Set of 3 regional special handstamps....................................	–	6
19 May	1982	**STANLEY GIBBONS £4 BOOKLET:** 4 panes		
		Set of 4 panes – London WC special h/s...................(£3)*	–	10
		Set of 4 panes – Plymouth special h/s.........................(£3)*	–	10
		Set of 4 panes – Bureau special h/s ....(£2)*	–	8
		* Se-tenant pane only ***N.B. Prices for complete panes (stamps and text).***		
9 Jun	1982	**1p-£5 TO PAY LABELS:** Stratford handstamp.................	–	300
10 Nov	1982	**£2.50 CHRISTMAS BKLT:** (10 x 12½p; 10 x 15½p).......... *Sold at 30p discount. Star printed on reverse.*	6	3
30 Mar	1983	**3½p, 17p, 16p, 20½p, 23p, 28p & 31p**	5	2
		5 APR 1983: 1st Class 16p, 2nd Class 12½p		
5 Apr	1983	**50p GLOUCESTER 'OLD SPOT' BOOKLET**	2	1
		Cotswold Farm Park h/s............(Benham official cvr £10)	–	5
5 Apr	1983	**£1.60 BOOKLET:** (10 x 16p)	5	3
5 Apr	1983	**£1.46 BOOKLET:** (4 x 12½p; 6 x 16p)	5	3
5 Apr	1983	**1p & 3½p (Centre Band) + 16p (2 bands)** from above....	2	1

1983

Date of issue		Windsor Postmark £	Other pmks £
20 Apr 1983	**16p COIL STRIP**	10	3
27 Apr 1983	**REGIONALS: 16p, 20½p & 28p** set of 3	–	5
3 Aug 1983	**£1.30 PARCEL POST**	7	4
	Philatelic Bureau special handstamp	–	5
	London E16 special handstamp	–	7
	Parcel, Centenary Postcard Salisbury special h/s	–	10
	Hampstead C.D.S.	–	17
	-do- (Pre-released 1st Aug: date of centenary)	–	40
10 Aug 1983	**£1.45 DISCOUNT BOOKLET:** (10 x 16p) *Sold at 15p discount and printed with letter 'D' on reverse.*	7	3
10 Aug 1983	**16p 'D' UNDERPRINT** from above booklet	3	1
14 Sep 1983	**ROYAL MINT £4 BOOKLET:** 4 panes (2 @ 6 x 12½p; 9 x 16p; 6 x 16p + 2 x 3½p + 1 x 3p)		
	Set of 4 panes – Llantrisant special handstamp (£4)*	–	10
	Set of 4 panes – Bureau special handstamp (£2)*	–	8
	*Se-tenant pane only ***N.B. Prices for complete panes (stamps and illustrations).***		
2 Nov 1983	**16p SCOTLAND (Advanced coated paper)**	–	1
9 Nov 1983	**£2.20 CHRISTMAS BOOKLET:** (20 x 12½p) *Sold at a 30p discount with star printed on reverse.*	5	2
9 Nov 1983	**12½p 'STAR' UNDERPRINT** from above booklet	2	1
14 Dec 1983	**10p (Phosphor coated paper)**	2	1
10 Jan 1984	**12½p & 16p WALES (Perforation change)**	–	2
21 Feb 1984	**5p & 75p (Perforation change)**	2	1
28 Feb 1984	**12½p & 16p N.I. (Perforation change)**	–	4
1 May 1984	**'FRAMA' LABELS: ½p-16p** (32 values) on six covers		
	Cambridge special handstamp	–	25
	Philatelic Bureau, Edinburgh, special handstamp	–	20
	London EC special handstamp	–	25
	Southampton special handstamp	–	25
	Windsor special handstamp	20	–
	Set of six covers including above handstamps	–	25
	Set of six covers with related C.D.S. postmarks	–	100
19 Jun 1984	**17p (Advanced coated paper)**	2	1
19 Jun 1984	**26p (Advanced coated paper)**	75	n.k.
10 Jul 1984	**2p (Perforation change)**	2	1
14 Aug 1984	**13p MULTI-VALUE COIL:** (1 x 1p, 3 x 4p)	2	1
28 Aug 1984	**13p, 18p, 22p, 24p & 34p**	3	1
28 Aug 1984	**£1.33 PARCEL POST**	6	3
	Hampstead C.D.S. postmark	–	10
28 Aug 1984	**'FRAMA' LABELS: 16½p & 17p**	2	1

Date of Issue		Windsor Postmark £	Other pmks £
	3 SEP 1984: 1st Class 17p, 2nd Class 13p		
3 Sep 1984	**£1.54 BOOKLETS:** 2 @ (4 x 13p; 6 x 17p) both panes, right and left format (mirror image).....	5	3
3 Sep 1984	**50p BOOKLET:** (3 x 1p; 2 x 4p; 3 x 13p)...........................	3	1
3 Sep 1984	**£1.30 & £1.70 BOOKLETS:** (10 x 13p)+(10 x 17p) pair..	15	6
3 Sep 1984	**13p (left & right phos.) + 17p (two phos)** from above....	2	1
3 Sep 1984	**13p & 17p COIL STRIPS**..	15	3
4 Sep 1984	**CHRISTIAN HERITAGE £4 BOOKLET:** 4 panes		
	Set of 4 panes - St. Mary le Strand special h/s.........(£4)*	-	10
	Set of 4 panes - Canterbury special h/s......................(£3)*	-	8
	Set of 4 panes - Bureau special h/s ....(£2)*	-	7
	Set of 4 panes - Christian Heritage slogan...............(£15)*	-	35
	* Se-tenant pane only		
	N.B. Prices for complete panes (stamps and illustrations).		
23 Oct 1984	**REGIONALS: 13p, 17p, 31p, 22p**..........................set of 3	-	6
8 Jan 1985	**THE TIMES £5 BOOKLET:** 4 panes		
	Set of 4 panes - London WC special h/s...................(£5)*	-	13
	Set of 4 panes - Bureau special h/s ....(£4)*	-	10
	Set of 4 panes - Times 1785-1985 slogan pmk ....(£10)*	-	30
	* Se-tenant pane only		
	N.B. Prices for complete panes (stamps and illustrations).		
8 Jan 1985	**4p (left & right phos) + 34p (two bands)** from above.....	4	2
19 Feb 1985	**75p (Change of paper)**..	75	-
5 Mar 1985	**£1.55 DISCOUNT BOOKLET:** (10 x 17p)........................ *Sold at 15p discount with letter 'D' printed on reverse.*	7	3
5 Mar 1985	**17p 'D' UNDERPRINT** from above booklet......................	2	1
25 Jun 1985	**17p SCOTLAND (PCP/PVA)**..	-	2
16 Jul 1985	**10p (Advanced coated paper)**......................................	2	1
17 Sep 1985	**£1.41 PARCEL POST**..	6	4
	With Parcel Post cancellation	-	10
17 Sep 1985	**31p (Advanced coated paper)**......................................	2	1
29 Oct 1985	**7p & 12p**..	2	1
	Philatelic Bureau h/s and 'ITALIA' cachet	-	4
29 Oct 1985	**12p (Star underprint)**...	2	1
	4 NOV 1985: 1st Class 17p, 2nd Class 12p		
4 Nov 1985	**50p BOOKLET:** (3 x 17p + label)................................ *Sold at 1p discount with Star printed on reverse.*	3	1
12 Nov 1985	**12p COIL STRIP:** vertical format (centre band)...............	8	2
4 Dec 1985	**31p SCOTLAND (Re-drawn lion)**....................................	-	150
7 Jan 1986	**1p (Advanced coated paper)**..	2	1
7 Jan 1986	**REGIONALS: 12p**...set of 3	-	4
14 Jan 1986	**£1.20 BOOKLET:** (10 x 12p Centre Phosphor band)........	6	2
14 Jan 1986	**£1.50 BOOKLET:** (4 x 12p; 6 x 17p)	6	2

Date of issue			Windsor Postmark £	Other pmks £
14 Jan	1986	**12p left phos & 12p right phos** from £1.50 booklet	2	1
25 Feb	1986	**2p & 5p (Advanced Coated Paper)**	2	1
25 Feb	1986	**17p (Wales and N.I.) Advanced Coated Paper** – pair	–	3
18 Mar	1986	**BRITISH RAIL £5 BOOKLET:** 4 panes		
		Set of 4 panes – Crewe special h/s (£5)*	–	15
		Set of 4 panes – Bureau special h/s (£4)*	–	12
		Set of 4 panes – T.P.O. pmks (£8)*	–	25
		Set of 4 panes – Train or Railway slogan pmks. (£10)*	–	30
		*Se-tenant pane only		
		N.B. Prices for complete panes (stamps and illustrations).		
18 Mar	1986	**31p PHOSPHOR (Two bands)** from above booklet	4	2
29 Apr	1986	**17p, 31p & 12p SCOTLAND (perf and paper changes)**	–	2
13 May	1986	**4p & 20p (Advanced Coated Paper - Questa)**	2	1
24 Jun	1986	**26p & 34p (Advanced Coated Paper)**	2	1
11 Jul	1986	**12p (New phosphor ink)**	40	25
29 Jul	1986	**50p BOOKLET:** (2 x 1p; 4 x 12p)	2	1
29 Jul	1986	**£1 BOOKLET:** (6 x 17p) *Sold at 2p discount*	7	3
12 Aug	1986	**50p BOOKLET:** (3 x 17p + label) *Sold at 1p discount*	2	1
		Different to 4 Nov 1985 issue – no Star underprint		
2 Sep	1986	**£1.50 PARCEL POST**	6	4
23 Sep	1986	**12p COIL STRIP:** horizontal format	3	1
7 Oct	1986	**75p New paper & 28p Advanced Coated Paper**	5	2
		20 OCT 1986: 1st Class 18p, 2nd Class 13p		
20 Oct	1986	**50p 'Roman Britain' BOOKLET:** (1p + 13p; 2 x 18p)	2	1
		St. Albans special h/s or Porchester CDS	–	4
		50p 'Pond Life' BOOKLET: (1p + 2 x 5p; 3 x 13p)	2	1
		Pond CDS	–	4
		£1 BOOKLET: (1 x 13p; 5 x 18p) *Sold at 3p discount*	3	2
		£1.30 & £1.80 BKLTS: (10 x 13p)+(10 x 18p) pair	12	5
20 Oct	1986	**5p phos. (centre band) + 18p phos. (two bands)**	3	1
21 Oct	1986	**13p & 18p COIL STRIPS**	20	7
4 Nov	1986	**13p SCOTLAND 'Questa' printing**	–	1
2 Dec	1986	**£1.20 CHRISTMAS BOOKLET:** (10 x 13p)	5	3
		Sold at 10p discount with Star printed on reverse		
		Glastonbury special handstamps (3 different) *each*	–	6
2 Dec	1986	**13p 'STAR' UNDERPRINT** from above booklet	2	1
6 Jan	1987	**18p REGIONALS:** set of 3	–	4
27 Jan	1987	**13p (New phosphor ink)**	2	1
27 Jan	1987	**2 x 50p, £1, £1.30 BOOKLETS:** – set of 4	35	25
		Same format as 20 Oct 1986 but with new phosphor ink.		
27 Jan	1987	**REGIONALS: (Advanced Coated Paper, Questa)**		
		Scotland: 22p, 26p, 28p; Wales 26p, 28p, 31p; N.I. 26p, 28p		
		Regional Philatelic Counter handstamps – set of three	–	6

Date of Issue		Windsor Postmark £	Other pmks £
3 Mar 1987	**P & O £5 BOOKLET:** 4 panes		
	Set of 4 panes – Falmouth special h/s .... (£5)*	–	16
	Set of 4 panes – Bureau special h/s .... (£4)*	–	12
	*Se-tenant pane only		
	N.B. Prices for complete panes (stamps and illustrations).		
3 Mar 1987	**1p (side phos.) + 26p (two phos)** from P&O Booklet	3	2
14 Apr 1987	**REGIONALS: 13p (Scotland, Wales, N.I.) Coated Papers Ltd.**		
	31p (N.I.) Advanced Coated Paper		
	Set of 3 with regional postmarks	–	5
14 Apr 1987	**REGIONAL: 13p (WALES) Dextrim gum**	–	12
14 Apr 1987	**£1.80 BOOKLET:** (10 x 18p) Advanced Coated Paper.....	5	2
5 May 1987	**3p (Advanced Coated Paper)**..	2	1
23 Jun 1987	**1p READERS DIGEST COIL STRIP:**	2	1
	used on 'Readers Digest' envelope	10	–
4 Aug 1987	**'WINDOW' BOOKLETS: 52p** (4 x 13p); **72p** (4 x 18p);		
	£1.04 (4 x 26p); **£1.30** (10 x 13p); **£1.80** (10 x 18p)		
	Set of five panes on cover	30	20
	Each pane is printed with a selvedge around all four sides giving the appearance of small 'sheetlets'. An operational test market to assess customer reaction took place at Bristol, Nottingham, Preston and York.		
	Any of these postmarks – set of five covers.................	–	25
4 Aug 1987	**26p (Redrawn numeral)** from £1.04 Window booklet	20	6
15 Sep 1987	**£1.60 PARCEL POST**..	4	3
29 Sep 1987	**50p Mount Stewart BKLT:** (1 x 1p, 2 x 5p, 3 x 13p)........	2	1
	Belfast pmk. (bkt. features Mount Stewart, N.I.)	–	3
	£1 Holmes BKLT: (1 x 13p; 5 x 18p) *3p discount*............	3	2
	Baker St. C.D.S. (bkt. features Sherlock Holmes)	–	25
	These two booklets were produced with straight edges (i.e. outer long edges had no perforations).		
29 Sep 1987	**1p, 5p, 13p, 2 @ 18p (single straight edges)** from bklts..	3	2
9 Feb 1988	**FINANCIAL TIMES £5 BOOKLET:** 4 panes		
	Set of 4 panes – London EC4 special h/s................... (£5)*	–	15
	Set of 4 panes – Bureau special h/s .... (£4)*	–	12
	Set of 4 panes – Relevant C.D.S. .... (£12)*	–	30
	*Se-tenant pane only		
	N.B. Prices for complete panes (stamps and illustrations).		
9 Feb 1988	**13p phos right, left & centre + 18p, 22p, 34p**..................	5	4
	Questa printings from Financial Times Booklet.		
23 Feb 1988	**2p & 75p (Redrawn numerals)**	2	1
	2p printed on paper supplied by Henry & Leigh Slater.		
18 Mar 1988	**13p MULTI-VALUE COIL:** (1 x 1p; 3 x 4p) ACP	20	10
29 Mar 1988	**REGIONALS: 18p (Scotland & Wales)** pair	–	2
	Henry & Leigh Slater paper		
3 May 1988	**18p COIL STRIP**..	2	1
26 Jul 1988	**2p, 4p, 5p, 75p (Harrison printing)**....................................	2	1
26 Jul 1988	**1p COIL STRIP**	5	2

Date of issue		Windsor Postmark £	Other pmks £
23 Aug 1988	**14p, 19p, 20p, 23p, 27p, 28p, 32p & 35p**	5	3
23 Aug 1988	**'WINDOW' BOOKLETS: 56p** (4 x 14p); **76p** (4 x 19p); **£1.08** (4 x 27p); **£1.40** (10 x 14p); **£1.90** (10 x 19p)		
	Set of five panes on cover	25	15
	Issued on trial at Bristol, Nottingham, Preston and York.		
	Set of five panes with any of these postmarks	-	30
	5 SEP 1988: 1st Class 19p, 2nd Class 14p		
5 Sep 1988	**50p BOOKLET:** (1 x 14p; 2 x 19p + label) *2p discount*	2	1
5 Sep 1988	**£1 BOOKLET:** (2 x 14p; 4 x 19p) *4p discount*	3	2
5 Sep 1988	**£1.40 & £1.90 BOOKLETS:** (10 x 14p)+(10 x 19p)	10	7
5 Sep 1988	**14p & 19p COILS:** 14p vert & horiz. + 19p horizontal	8	3
5 Sep 1988	**14p MULTI-VALUE COIL:** (1 x 2p; 3 x 4p)	3	1
11 Oct 1988	**'WINDOW' BKLTS: 56p, 76p, £1.08, £1.40, £1.90** Set	30	10
	Stamp contents as for 23 Aug issue, but selvedge replaced by straight edges at top and bottom of stamp panes. Printed by Harrisons.		
11 Oct 1988	**'WINDOW' BOOKLETS: £1.40, £1.90** Pair	15	8
	Printed by Questa - no selvedge, stamps fully perforated. These are the first 14p and 19p litho printings.		
11 Oct 1988	**14p & 19p Litho (Questa)**	2	1
11 Oct 1988	**14p, 19p & 27p Straight edges (Harrison)**	5	3
18 Oct 1988	**£1, £1.50, £2 & £5 'CASTLES' HIGH VALUES**		
	First Day of Issue, Bureau special h/s	-	20
	First Day of Issue, Windsor special h/s	25	-
	*Castle High Values, Carrickfergus special h/s	-	30
	*Castle High Values, Caernarfon special h/s	-	30
	*Castle High Values, Edinburgh special h/s	-	30
	*Castle High Values, Windsor special h/s	30	-
	*Special h/s on Benham official cover *each*	60	60
	Set of 4 single stamp covers with appropriate pmks	-	25
	Windsor Castle C.D.S. pmk	200	-
	Carrickfergus C.D.S.	-	250
	Caernarfon, Edinburgh or Windsor C.D.S. pmks	150	150
	Set of 4 single stamp covers with appropriate CDS	-	200
8 Nov 1988	**REGIONALS: 14p, 19p, 23p & 32p** set of 3	-	6
24 Jan 1989	**'WINDOW' BOOKLETS: 56p, 76p**	4	2
	As *23 Aug 1988 but panes have three straight edges.*		
21 Mar 1989	**SCOTS CONNECTION £5 BOOKLET:** 4 panes		
	Set of 4 panes - Inverness special h/s (£5)*	-	15
	Set of 4 panes - Bureau special h/s (£4)*	-	12
	*Se-tenant pane only		
	N.B. Prices for complete panes (stamps and illustrations).		
21 Mar 1989	**14p (side phos.) & 19p, 23p (2 bands)** from above bklt	5	3
25 Apr 1989	**£1 BOOKLET:** (2 x 14p; 4 x 19p) *Sold at 4p discount*	4	2
	ditto Walsall Security Printers special handstamp	-	6
	ditto Walsall C.D.S. pmk	-	30
	printed by Walsall Security Printers with straight edges		
25 Apr 1989	**14p & 19p Straight edges** (Walsall Printers)	2	1
	ditto Walsall Security Printers special handstamp	-	3
25 Apr 1989	**19p SCOTLAND Coated Papers Ltd**	-	2
20 Jun 1989	**19p WALES Coated Papers Ltd.**	-	2

Date of Issue			Windsor Postmark £	Other pmks £
26 Jun	1989	**£1.90 'WINDOW' BKLT:** (10 x 19p) Jumelle Press...........	5	2
10 Jul	1989	**£1.40 'WINDOW' BKLT:** (10 x 14p) Jumelle Press...........	4	2
8 Aug	1989	**50p BKLT:** Chambon Press (Contents as 5 Sept 88).........	2	1
22 Aug	1989	**'WINDOW' BOOKLETS: Non-Value Indicators** **56p** (4 x 2nd) & **76p** (4 x 1st) Walsall **£1.40** (10 x 2nd) **£1.90** (10 x 1st) Harrison ....set of 4	20	15
22 Aug	1989	**NON-VALUE INDICATORS:** 1st, 2nd (Walsall) .... 1st, 2nd (Harrison)	3 3	1 1
19 Sep	1989	**'WINDOW' BOOKLETS: Non-Value Indicators** **£1.40** (10 x 2nd) & **£1.90** (10 x 1st) Questa	10	7
19 Sep	1989	**NON-VALUE INDICATORS:** 1st, 2nd (Questa)..............	3	1
26 Sep	1989	**15p, 20p, 24p, 29p, 30p, 34p & 37p**....................................	5	3

2 OCT 1989: 1st Class 20p, 2nd Class 15p

Date of Issue			Windsor Postmark £	Other pmks £
2 Oct	1989	**50p BOOKLET:** (2 x 15p; 1 x 20p + label).......................... **£1 BOOKLET:** (5 x 20p + label)	2 3	1 2
2 Oct	1989	**£1.16 'WINDOW' BKLT:** (4 x 29p) overseas p/cards.......	3	2
2 Oct	1989	**15p, 2 x 20p & 29p new printings** (from above bklts)	2	1
10 Oct	1989	**15p MULTI-VALUE COIL:** (1 x 3p; 3 x 4p)	2	1
16 Oct	1989	**15p & 20p COIL STRIPS:** horizontal format	3	2
16 Oct	1989	**15p & 20p COIL STRIPS:** vertical format..........................	3	2
28 Nov	1989	**REGIONALS: 15p, 20p, 24p & 34p**.......................set of 3	–	7
28 Nov	1989	**60p WINDOW BOOKLET:** (4 x 2nd) – Harrison.............	15	–
5 Dec	1989	**80p WINDOW BOOKLET:** (4 x 1st) – Harrison.............. *Both panes have three straight edges (top, right and bottom).* *80p Bklt. covers are known with 28 Nov date – value £35.*	15	–

NEW STAMPS FROM BOOKLETS
With effect from 1990 only full panes are listed.
PRESTIGE BOOKLETS
With effect from 1990 prices are for the set of four panes.

Date of Issue			Windsor Postmark £	Other pmks £
10 Jan	1990	**PENNY BLACK ANNIVERSARY** *These stamps have been treated as a commemorative issue.* *The stamps issued in booklet form are listed below.*		
30 Jan	1990	**'WINDOW' BKLTS: Penny Black Anniv.** Set of 4........... **60p** (4 x 15p); **80p** (4 x 20p); **£1.50** (10 x 15p); **£2** (10 x 20p)	20	8
30 Jan	1990	**BOOKLETS: Penny Black Anniversary stamps** **50p** (2 x 15p; 1 x 20p + label) – Harrison Printers **£1** (5 x 20p + 1 label) – Harrison Printers **£1** (5 x 20p + 1 label) – Walsall Printers................set of 3	12	7
13 Mar	1990	**50p Colour variation**..	2	1
20 Mar	1990	**LONDON LIFE £5 BOOKLET:**		
		Set of 4 panes – Tower Hill special h/s	–	15
		Set of 4 panes – Philatelic Bureau special h/s.....................	–	12
		Set of 4 panes – Stamp World special h/s...........................	–	16
		Set of 4 panes – Victorian Heritage special h/s	–	16
		Set of 4 panes – mixed h/s as above......................................	–	15
		Set of 4 panes – relevant CDS or slogans...........................	–	20
		N.B. Prices for complete panes (stamps and illustrations).		

Date of issue		Windsor Postmark £	Other pmks £
17 Apr 1990	**'WINDOW' BOOKLETS: Penny Black Anniversary stamps:**		
	80p (4 x 20p) Harrison (*previously Walsall*) 3 straight edges		
	£1.50 (10 x 15p) Questa (*previously Harrison*) full perfs		
	£2 (10 x 20p) Questa (*previously Harrison*) full perfs		
17 Apr 1990	**'WINDOW' BOOKLET: Standard definitives:**		
	£1.16 (4 x 29p) 3 straight edges ....set of 4	20	12
12 Jun 1990	**'WINDOW' BOOKLETS: Penny Black Anniversary stamps:**		
	£1.50 (10 x 15p) Walsall - 3 straight edges		
	£2 (10 x 20p) Walsall - 3 straight edges ....pair	10	4
7 Aug 1990	**'WINDOW' BOOKLETS: Non-Value Indicators**		
	60p (4 x 2nd); **80p** (4 x 1st); Walsall Printers		
	£1.50 (10 x 2nd); **£2** (10 x 1st) Walsall Printers		
	£1.50 (10 x 2nd); **£2** (10 x 1st) Harrison Printers		
	£1.50 (10 x 2nd); **£2** (10 x 1st) Questa Printers.....set of 8	40	25
4 Sep 1990	**10p, 17p, 22p, 26p, 27p, 31p & 33p**....................................	4	2
4 Sep 1990	**50p BOOKLET:** (3 x 17p) *Sold at 1p discount*	2	1
4 Sep 1990	**£1 BOOKLET:** (2 x 17p; 3 x 22p)	3	1
	17 SEP 1990: 1st Class 22p, 2nd Class 17p		
17 Sep 1990	**17p & 22p COIL STRIPS:** vertical format..........................	5	4
17 Sep 1990	**£1.24 'WINDOW' BOOKLET:** (4 x 31p) Walsall	3	2
27 Nov 1990	**17p MULTI-VALUE COIL:** (1 x 5p; 3 x 4p)	2	1
4 Dec 1990	**REGIONALS: 17p, 22p, 26p & 37p** ....set of 3	–	8
19 Mar 1991	**AGATHA CHRISTIE £6 BOOKLET:** 4 panes		
	Set of 4 panes - Philatelic Bureau h/s	–	12
	Set of 4 panes - Marple, Cheshire h/s	–	12
	Set of 4 panes - Orient Express h/s....................................	–	13
	Set of 4 panes - Sunningdale h/s	–	13
	Set of 4 panes - various CDS pmks.......................................	–	20
	Set of 4 panes - Bite out of Crime slogan	–	25
	N.B. Prices for complete panes (stamps and illustrations).		
14 May 1991	**REGIONALS: 22p, 26p, 37p SCOTLAND &**		
	22p WALES: Coated Papers ....pair	–	5
6 Aug 1991	**'WINDOW' BOOKLETS: Non-Value Indicators**		
	68p (4 x 2nd); **88p** (4 x 1st) Walsall		
	£1.70 (10 x 2nd); **£2.20** (10 x 1st) Walsall		
	£1.70 (10 x 2nd); **£2.20** (10 x 1st) Questa		
	£2.20 (10 x 1st) Harrison ....set of 7	25	12
10 Sep 1991	**6p, 18p, 24p, 28p, 34p, 35p & 39p**.....................................	4	3
	-do- with 'New Postage Rates' slogan pmk	–	6
	16 SEP 1991: 1st Class 24p, 2nd Class 18p		
16 Sep 1991	**BKLTS: 50p** (2 x 24p; 2 x 1p); **£1** (4 x 24p; 2 x 2p)...pair	4	3
	-do- with 'New Postage Rates' slogan pmk	–	6
16 Sep 1991	**'WINDOW' BOOKLETS:**		
	£1.32 (4 x 33p) & **£1.56** (4 x 39p) Walsall Printers.	7	3
	-do- with 'New Postage Rates' slogan pmk.	–	10
16 Sep 1991	**18p & 24p COIL STRIPS:** vertical format...........................	5	4
	-do- with 'New Postage rates' slogan pmk............................	–	9
1 Oct 1991	**18p MULTI-VALUE COIL:** (2 x 5p; 2 x 4p)	2	1
19 Nov 1991	**DEFINITIVE:** 18p Enschedé printing	2	1
3 Dec 1991	**REGIONALS: 18p, 24p, 28p & 39p** ....set of 3	–	8

Date of Issue		Windsor Postmark £	Other pmks £
21 Jan 1992	**3p Redrawn value & 50p Advanced Coated Paper**	2	1
11 Feb 1992	**33p & 39p COIL STRIPS:** vertical format	5	3
25 Feb 1992	**WALES PRESTIGE £6 BOOKLET:** 4 panes		
	Set of 4 panes – Philatelic Bureau h/s	–	12
	Set of 4 panes – Cardiff handstamp	–	12
	Set of 4 panes – Stampex, London SW1 h/s	–	14
	Set of 4 panes – Snowdon Mountain Rly h/s	–	14
	Set of 4 panes – various C.D.S. pmks	–	20
	N.B. Prices for complete panes (stamps and illustrations).		
24 Mar 1992	**SECURITY PRINTING 'CASTLES': £1, £1.50, £2 & £5**		
	First Day of Issue – Philatelic Bureau h/s		14
	First Day of Issue – Windsor h/s	16	–
	*Castle High Values – Carrickfergus special h/s	–	17
	*Castle High Values – Caernarfon special h/s	–	17
	*Castle High Values – Edinburgh special h/s	–	17
	*Castle High Values – Windsor special h/s	17	–
	*Special h/s on Benham 'official' covers *each*	30	35
	'Security Printing' Windsor h/s	18	–
	-do- on Bradbury 'official' cover	35	–
	Windsor C.D.S. or Windsor Great Park C.D.S. *each*	30	–
	Windsor Castle C.D.S.	150	–
	Caernarfon, Carrickfergus or Edinburgh C.D.S. *each*	–	35
	Set of 4 single stamp covers + relevant C.D.S. pmks	–	35
28 Jul 1992	**78p BOOKLET:** (Kelloggs) 2 x 39p	6	3
8 Sep 1992	**£1.32 'WINDOW' BOOKLET:** (4 x 33p) Dextrin Gum ...	4	2
27 Oct 1992	**TOLKIEN PRESTIGE £6 BOOKLET:**		
	Set of 4 panes – Bureau h/s or Oxford h/s	–	13
	Set of 4 panes – Rings End, March h/s	–	15
	Set of 4 panes – Bagendon, Cirencester h/s	–	15
	Set of 4 panes – Meriden, Middle England h/s	–	20
	Set of 4 panes – relevant CDS or slogans	–	20
	N.B. Prices for complete panes (stamps and illustrations).		
9 Feb 1993	**£2.40 'WINDOW' BOOKLET: NVI** (10 x 1st Class)	6	3
	Walsall ACP + PVA with straight edges at the top and bottom.		
9 Feb 1993	**£1 BOOKLET:** (4 x 24p; 2 x 2p)	4	2
	Walsall ACP with straight edges at left and right.		
2 Mar 1993	**£10 BRITANNIA**		
	First Day of Issue – Philatelic Bureau h/s	–	15
	First Day of Issue – Windsor	16	–
	First Day of Issue – London	–	18
	Windsor handstamp (Britannia) (Official cover £40)	20	–
	£10 Britannia, Porth h/s (Official cover £40)	–	20
	£10 Dover h/s (Official cover £40)	–	20
	Britannia Way, SW6 h/s (Official cover £40)	–	20
	Spring Stampex special handstamp	–	20
	Eur-Apex BPT special handstamp	–	20
	Britannia C.D.S. (Bacup or Porth) *each*	–	25
	Windsor C.D.S.	25	–
	Windsor Castle C.D.S.	100	–
	Maritime Mail or Paquebot C.D.S. *each*	–	22
16 Mar 1993	**£1.80 'WINDOW' BOOKLET: NVI** (10 x 2nd Class)	6	3
	Walsall ACP + PVA straight edges at the top and bottom.		
6 Apr 1993	**'WINDOW' BOOKLETS: Non-Value Indicators**		
	96p (4 x 1st); **£2.40** (10 x 1st) Harrison		
	72p (4 x 2nd); **£2.40** (10 x 1st)* Walsall		
	£1.80 (10 x 2nd) Questa set of 5	18	10
	OBA free paper – perfs all round with elliptical perforations.		
	**Walsall £2.40 – two phos. bands (not phosphor coated paper).*		
27 Apr 1993	**6p Enschedé printing**	2	1
8 Jun 1993	**1p, 5p & 10p Enschedé printings**	2	1

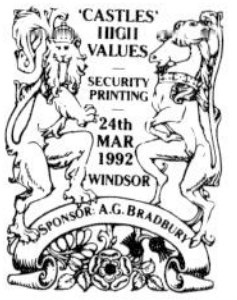

Date of issue		Windsor Postmark £	Other pmks £
27 Jul 1993	**30p Enschedé printing**	2	1
10 Aug 1993	**BEATRIX POTTER £5.64 BOOKLET:** 4 panes		
	Set of 4 panes – Bureau h/s or Keswick h/s	–	20
	Set of 4 panes – London First Day of Issue h/s	–	22
	Set of 4 panes – Near Sawrey h/s	–	35
	Set of 4 panes – Frederick Warne h/s	–	35
	Set of 4 panes – Tom Kitten, Catton h/s	–	35
	Set of 4 panes – The Tailor Gloster h/s	–	35
	Set of 4 panes – relevant C.D.S. postmarks	–	40
	N.B. Prices for complete panes (stamps and illustrations).		
17 Aug 1993	**35p Enschedé printing**	2	1
17 Aug 1993	**96p 'WINDOW' BKLT: NVIs** (4 x 1st) Walsall	4	2
7 Sep 1993	**72p 'WINDOW' BKLT: NVIs** (4 x 2nd) Harrison	4	2
5 Oct 1993	**1st & 2nd Class NVIs in Sheet Format**	2	1
	Windsor – Tudor Rose h/s (official cover £7)	3	–
19 Oct 1993	**SELF ADHESIVE POSTAGE STAMP: 1st Class NVI**		
	First Day of Issue – Bureau h/s or Newcastle h/s	–	2
	First Day of Issue – 1st London	–	2
	Windsor – Britannia (Bradbury official cover £5)	3	–
	Windsor – Coat of Arms (Bradbury official cover £6)	3	–
	Newcastle – Cathedral (Benham official cover £5)	–	3
	Walsall Security Printers h/s (Walsall official cover £5)	–	3
	Lickey End Bromsgrove special handstamp	–	3
	Covers with complete pane of stamps	10	10
26 Oct 1993	**19p, 25p, 29p, 36p, 38p & 41p**	4	2
	-do- with 'New Postage Rates' slogan postmark	–	5
	1 NOV 1993: 1st Class 25p, 2nd Class 19p		
1 Nov 1993	**19p, 25p, 35p & 41p COIL STRIPS:** vertical format	8	4
1 Nov 1993	**BOOKLETS: 50p** (2 x 25p) Harrisons; **£1** (4 x 25p) Walsall; **£2** (8 x 25p) Harrisons set of 3	10	5
1 Nov 1993	**£2.50 'WINDOW' BOOKLETS: NVI** (10 x 1st Class) *Questa with elliptical perfs*	6	3
1 Nov 1993	**'WINDOW' BOOKLETS: Overseas rates** **£1.40** (4 x 35p); **£1.64** (4 x 41p) Walsall pair	8	4
7 Dec 1993	**REGIONALS: 19p, 25p, 30p, 41p** set of 3	–	13
14 Dec 1993	**4p, 20p, 50p Enschedé printings**	3	2
25 Jan 1994	**BKLTS: 50p** (2 x 25p) Harrisons; **£1** (4 x 25p) Walsall pair	5	2
15 Feb 1994	**TO PAY LABELS: 1p, 2p, 5p, 10p, 20p, 25p, £1, £1.20, £5**		
	First Day of Issue – London EC3	–	15
	Tower of London (Benham official covers £20)	–	15
	To Pay Labels, Windsor (Bradbury official cover £25)	18	–
	Authentic Surcharge/C.O.D. postmark	–	125
22 Feb 1994	**WINDOW BOOKLETS: Non-Value Indicators** **£1.90** (10 x 2nd); **£2.50** (10 x 1st + 'Postcard Offer' pane) *Walsall Printers with elliptical perfs*	8	5
26 Apr 1994	**£1 BOOKLET:** (4 x 25p) Harrison	5	3

Date of Issue			Windsor Postmark £	Other pmks £
19 Jul	1994	**19p NEW PVA GUM** Harrison	3	2
26 Jul	1994	**NORTHERN IRELAND £6.04 PRESTIGE BOOKLET**		
		Set of 4 panes – Bureau or Belfast FDI h/s	–	15
		Set of 4 panes – London First Day of Issue h/s	–	18
		Set of 4 panes – Prestige Stamp Book, Belfast h/s	–	20
		Set of 4 panes – Belfast h/s	–	20
		Set of 4 panes – Mountains of Mourne h/s	–	20
		Set of 4 panes – Giant's Causeway h/s	–	20
		Set of 4 panes – relevant C.D.S. postmarks	–	25
		Set of 4 panes – Northern Ireland Booklet slogan	–	25
		N.B. Prices for complete panes (stamps and illustrations).		
27 Jul	1994	**BANK OF ENGLAND COMMEMORATIVE LABEL**	3	2
		Bank of England 1694–1994 300 Yrs (PNC off.cvr. £15)	–	3
		Bank of England (depicts Britannia) (Brad. off.cvr. £15)	–	3
		300 Years Bank of England (Benham off.cvr. £5)	–	3
9 Aug	1994	**60p AIRMAIL RATE**	4	2
		Covers with complete pane of 4 stamps	6	3
		Heathrow Airport special handtamp (complete pane)	–	5
		Heathrow Airport CDS postmark (complete pane)	–	6
17 Aug	1994	**'BOOTS' PROMOTIONAL LABEL**	2	1
		Nottingham 'B' spec h/s (Bradbury official cover £10)	–	3
		Nottingham 'NVI' spec h/s (Benham official cover £8)	–	3
		BUPA or Nottingham Perrier slogan pmks *each*	–	4
20 Dec	1994	**25p (Two Phosphor Bands)** Harrison	2	1
31 Jan	1995	**19p MULTI-VALUE COIL** (1 x 4p; 3 x 5p)	2	1
		Reader's Digest Swindon special handstamp	–	3
11 Apr	1995	**2p Enschedé printing**	2	1
25 Apr	1995	**NATIONAL TRUST £6 PRESTIGE BOOKLET**		
		Set of 4 panes – Bureau or Tintagel FDI h/s	–	15
		Set of 4 panes – London First Day of Issue h/s	–	18
		Set of 4 panes – This England, Oakham h/s	–	20
		Set of 4 panes – Bodiam Castle or Windermere h/s	–	20
		Set of 4 panes – Erddig House or Biddulph Grange h/s	–	20
		Set of 4 panes – relevant C.D.S. postmarks	–	25
		N.B. Prices for complete panes (stamps and illustrations).		
16 May	1995	**SPITFIRE COMMEMORATIVE LABEL (4 x 1st Class)**	3	2
		R J Mitchell Stoke on Trent (PNC off. cvr. £15)	–	3
		Southampton (with signature) (Brad. off. cvr. £13)	–	3
		Southampton Mitchell Spitfire (Benham off. cvr. £6)	–	3
		Stoke Mitchell Aircraft Designer (Benham off. cvr. £6)	–	3
		VE Day BBMF, SW1 (CoverCraft official cover £8)	–	3
		Mitchell Designer of Spitfire BF 2465 PS	–	3
		Biggin Hill, Eastleigh, or Butt Lane, Stoke CDS *each*	–	6
16 May	1995	**£1 BOOKLET (R J MITCHELL) (4 x 25p 2 Phos)**	3	2
		R J Mitchell Stoke on Trent	–	3
		Southampton (with signature) (Brad. off. cvr. £13)	–	3
		Southampton Mitchell Spitfire	–	3
		Stoke Mitchell Aircraft Designer	–	3
		VE Day BBMF, SW1	–	3
		Mitchell Designer of Spitfire BF 2465 PS	–	3
16 May	1995	**25p COIL STRIP:** two phosphor bars	3	2
22 Aug	1995	**£1 & £3 DEFINITIVES**	9	5

The Leading Magazine for Stamp Collectors Since 1890...

Designed to help you gain maximum enjoyment from your hobby. GSM covers all areas of philately including Great Britain, Commonwealth, Foreign, Thematics and Postal History, as well as all the latest news and opinion from around the world. Regular features are devoted to First Day Covers, new issues, varieties, books, machins, fairs and auctions.

- Exceptional value for money.
- 50% more editorial than other magazines.
- Regular features for all collectors from beginners to specialist.
- Authoritatively written by active stamp collectors.
- Includes the unique Stanley Gibbons catalogue supplement to keep you up to date on all new issues.
- Packed with Special Offers and regular Free Gifts.

...Delivered to your Door!

Get Gibbons Stamp Monthly delivered direct to your door each month, Post Free to all UK and BFPO addresses. As a subscriber you'll also get exclusive access to additional special offers on Stanley Gibbons products.

OUT MONTHLY

For a free sample copy and subscription details
Phone GSM subscriptions on
01425 472363

or write to:

Gibbons Stamp Monthly
5 Parkside, Christchurch Road
Ringwood, Hants BH24 3SH, England

Subscription Rates
(Includes postage)

1 year's UK subscription	£24.40
Europe/Overseas (surface)	£34.00
Airmail Zone 1 (Middle East, Americas, India, Africa, SE Asia)	£50.00
Airmail Zone 2 (Australasia, Japan, China)	£53.00

GBFDC7/95

BREDON COVERS

Chapel Lane, Wyre Piddle, Pershore, Worcs.WR10 2JA.
Tel 01386 554393 Fax 01386 561546

THE C.D.S. SPECIALIST for COMMEMS.,BOOKS & DEFINS.

Now incorporating the N.I. business run by 'SAJAL' Philatelics, which incorp. Brian Reeve, S.Muscroft & B.Campling N.I.'s

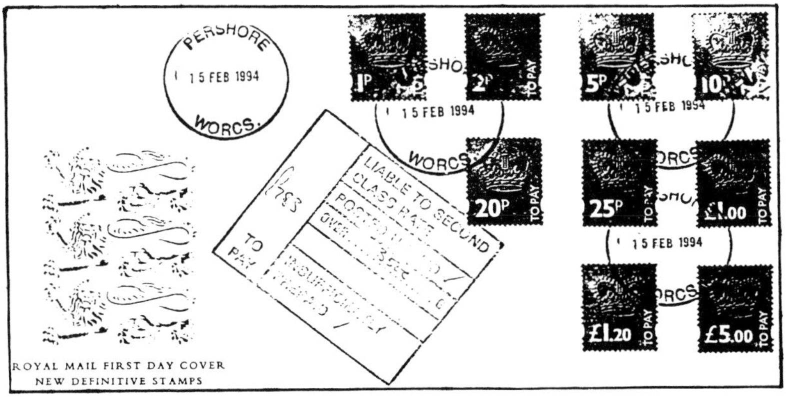

Competitive prices, new issue service, free lists. Slogans, meter marks, 'PHQ' cards and all special handstamps. Send s.a.e. for current lists & N.I. details.

British Postmark Bulletin
The Magazine for Postmark and First Day Cover Collectors

The British Postmark Bulletin is the Royal Mail's magazine for Postmark collectors, providing full information on all forthcoming special handstamps and postmark slogans. Published fortnightly it also contains information on First Day of Issue postmarking arrangements and includes addresses to send your covers for postmarking.

Send for a FREE sample copy from the above address

To receive your Bulletin on a regular basis place your order now with :

British Philatelic Bureau
FREEPOST
20 Brandon Street
EDINBURGH EH3 0HN

Annual subscriptions (post free)	
UK and Europe	£10.00
Rest of World (Air)	£21.75

FOOTBALL LOCOMOTIVE FDCs

The series of 25 Steam Locomotive FDCs, named after Football Clubs is well under way - No.10 is featured opposite. Each cover is produced from a specially commissioned painting and a matching pictorial handstamp is used. Some of the limited edition postcards included, are already increasing in value with postcard collectors! Between 300 and 500 FDCs with full sets produced per issue. Full details on request.

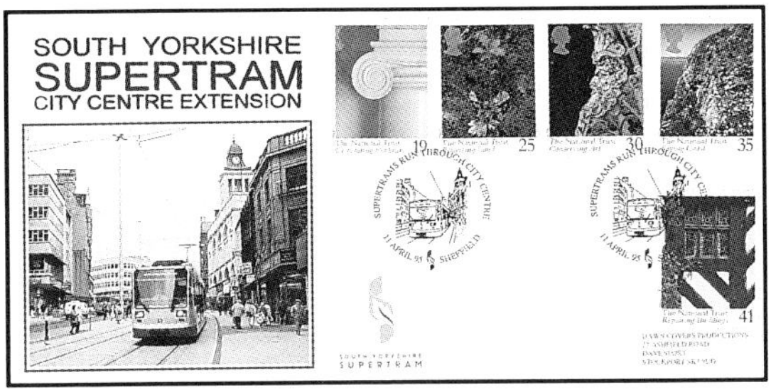

OTHER FIRST DAY COVERS

The Sheffield Supertram FDC in the Transport series is featured opposite, but our stocks are varied. We specialise in Football with match day and FDCs available. Lists sent free on receipt of a SAE to:-

DAWN COVER PRODUCTIONS, 27 ASHFIELD ROAD, DAVENPORT, STOCKPORT, SK3 8UD
Tel or Fax 0161 - 483 - 1297

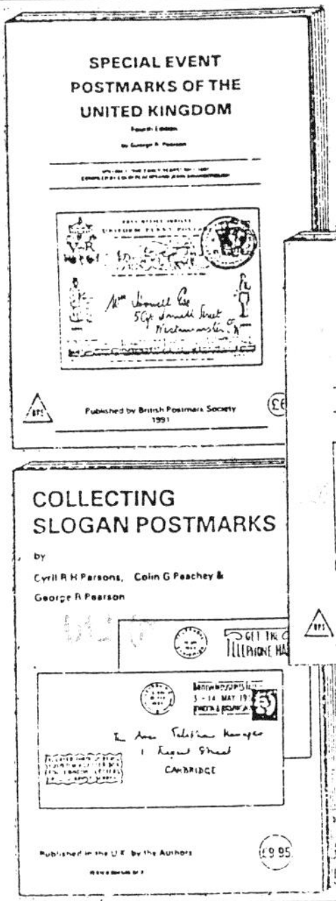

NEW POSTMARK BOOKS

VOLUME III of **SPECIAL EVENT POSTMARKS OF THE UK** is now available! Covers a further ten years, 1984-1993, and includes ALL the special events not just those used on stamp issue days. Channel Islands, Isle of Man, and those semi-permanent "philatelic handstamps' all included. Over 3500 entries in 172 pages. PRICE £9.50 plus £1 postage and packing.

VOLUME I of George Pearson's authoritative work was produced in 1991 (Fourth Edition). Gives valuations of early items from 1851 right up to 1962, with recent discoveries etc. 88 pages, hardback. PRICE £6 plus £1 postage and packing.

. . . but the Third Edition (1984) is not obsolete! With near-6000 entries packed in its 276 pages it covers the years 1963-1983, and becomes **VOLUME II.**
Price £8 plus £1.30 p and p.

COLLECTING SLOGAN POSTMARKS is fun!
This book tells the story of the faltering steps of initial slogan proposals, leading to their usage from 1917. Also the stories of how they have developed, what to look for – early and late uses, inverted, broken slogans etc, etc,and more stories of the"Mole Wrench", "World Refugee Year", of offensive slogans and so on.

Includes *a complete listing* to 1969, including valuations, with Forces, Naval, POSB slogans, complete index, 220 pages. PRICE £9.95 plus £1.30 p and p. Two further volumes available to cover the Seventies (£8.50 plus £1.50) and Eighties (£5.95 plus £1) respectively. **NEW** "NINETIES Part 1: 1990-1994" now ready, price £6.95 plus £1. All these books are available from:

C. G. PEACHEY, 19 Moorland Road, Hemel Hempstead, Herts. HP1 1NH

STAMP MAGAZINE

Britain's Best Selling Stamp Publication EVERY MONTH

Expert articles and authoritative features
All the latest news and discoveries
Stamp fairs and auctions
Postmarks and postcards
Postal Hisory
Contact Column
Beginners features
and our fully detailed, illustrated New Issue Guide with thematic cross-reference
ESTABLISHED FOR OVER 60 YEARS

Subscription details from:
STAMP MAGAZINE
Link House Magazines Ltd
Link House, Dingwall Avenue
CROYDON CR9 2TA 0181 686 2599

ONLY £1.90 EVERY MONTH
FROM YOUR NEWSAGENT

INDEX TO ADVERTISERS